# THE GUITAR AMP HANDBOOK

## UNDERSTANDING TUBE AMPLIFIERS AND GETTING GREAT SOUNDS

# THE GUITAR AMP HANDBOOK

## UNDERSTANDING TUBE AMPLIFIERS AND GETTING GREAT SOUNDS

## Dave Hunter

# THE GUITAR AMP HANDBOOK

## Dave Hunter

*To mom and dad, for the constant encouragement.*

A BACKBEAT BOOK
First edition 2005
Published by Backbeat Books
4501 Forbes Boulevard, Suite 200
Lanham, Maryland 20706
www.rowman.com

Distributed by NATIONAL BOOK NETWORK

Devised and produced for Backbeat Books by
Outline Press Ltd
2A Union Court, 20-22 Union Road,
London SW4 6JP, England
www.jawbonepress.com

ISBN: 978-1-4803-9288-5

EDITOR: John Morrish
DESIGN: Paul Cooper Design

Printed in China

# CONTENTS

# INTRODUCTION

Great players have always understood that their guitars were only half of the instrument that allows them to make music: the other half is found in the amplifier, that noisemaker that links to the guitar we hold in our hands, and which enables it to become the deeply expressive creative tool we know it to be. We might generate our music by picking the guitar strings, but we "play" the amp just as truly—or we should. As a guitarist you will make your best music when you are in tune with the way the amp responds, when working together with it to maximize tone and playing feel according to what your music and your creative muse demands. If you haven't put any thought into the feel, sound, and function of your amp before now, you've only been playing half an instrument. *The Guitar Amp Handbook: Updated And Expanded Edition* is here to make you whole.

Over the past 70 years, tube guitar amplifiers have gone from being the only available choice, the industry standard, to being an endangered species, to once again, in recent years, holding the pre-eminent place on the list of tone tools for guitarists. In some (albeit small) circles there is now more knowledge and understanding of the entire world of tube amplification than ever before; yet many guitar players—the majority perhaps—know little or nothing about how their tube amps do what they do, or even what accounts for a good tube amp in the first place. This includes plenty of professional players, who puzzle and sweat and fret over many aspects of their tone, but lack even the first notion about how what's going on inside their amps affects their precious sound.

That's not a thing to be ashamed of, but it's certainly a situation to rectify if you want to make the most of your sound, and therefore your music. Nobody was born with an innate understanding of tube technology. We all had to learn it somewhere. If you're a guitarist looking to learn more about what makes different amps sound the way

they do, and how to get the most out of your own amps, this book is where you'll find that information.

Making the most of your amp doesn't require a degree in electrical engineering, it just requires a little knowledge of how different components and circuit stages along the signal path interact to affect your sound. And that is exactly what *The Guitar Amp Handbook: Updated And Expanded Edition* will give you—even if you've never looked under the hood of a tube guitar amp before. These chapters will walk you step-by-step through the circuits and parts of dozens of classic and modern guitar amps, and explain, from a player's perspective and in straightforward language, how the variables along the way contribute to differences in sound and performance. The journey will unravel the mysteries behind many sonic wonders: great shimmering clean sounds; where high-gain grind comes from; which tubes and which circuits produce juicy classic-rock distortion; the differences between loose, bluesy tones and tight, spanky twang; the real difference between "class A" and "class AB" amps; what contributes to touch-sensitivity and dynamics; the effect of speakers and cabs; fast tracks to an amp's sonic sweet spot; and much, much more.

These days, many amplifier manufacturers are fighting against this kind of knowledge. They want you to think that you need to buy amp X because it's supposedly "class A," or because it has "real tube tone" thanks to the one lonely tube in its preamp. Maybe they want to sell you a 100-watt amp when you only need a 20-watter, or vice versa. They will tell you that any amp without DSP, four footswitchable channels, digital emulation software, or whatever, is just a dinosaur that ain't worth plugging into. They don't want you to know what really makes a good amp tick—and, just as importantly, what doesn't—because if you can think through the features and options for yourself, you won't buy their second-rate crate of tricks. They don't want you to achieve that great revelation that, hey, great-sounding amps are often very simple, they don't need to carry a lot of features, and they don't necessarily have control panels that look like a NASA command center.

This book will take beginners by the hand and escort them through everything they need to know in order to select the best amp for their own sound, to maximize its potential, and to keep it in top playing condition. It will also introduce experienced amp hounds to plenty of new tips and tricks used by today's top designers and manufacturers, and explode the many myths pervasive in tube amp lore today, which cloud any true understanding of what matters in a guitar amplifier and what doesn't.

Beyond this, in an exclusive interview section, top designers and manufacturers will open the door to their own techniques and secrets. By the end of *The Guitar Amp Handbook* you'll understand what happens to your precious guitar signal from input to speaker, and you'll even be able to build your own small, all-tube recording and practice amp if you so desire. Alternatively, if you're not a hands-on or DIY kind of player, you don't even need to plug in a soldering iron to embrace the knowledge contained in these pages. A good understanding of what goes on inside

that glowing box with the knobs on it will still help you to reach your sonic goals, and save you from wasting a lot of time and money on snake oil and wild goose chases while following your own path to tone heaven.

As the original edition of *The Guitar Amp Handbook*, first published in 2005, approached the end of its first decade on the shelves, the time was ripe for an update and expansion of that publication. This new edition adds several thousand words of new information, new artwork, essential revisions of the existing text, analysis of several added amps in the "Inside The Amps" chapter, the knowledge of five additional designers and manufacturers in the "Meet The Makers" section, and a thorough revision of the Two-Stroke amp project. As such, this updated and expanded edition offers even more to the guitarist who's first venturing inside the world of tube-amp tone, while also bringing in plenty of new material for the enthusiast who already owns the first edition. In short, it offers an even better and more thorough understanding of "the big picture" as regards your guitar tone, and with that comes the power better to craft your own sound. That's a power that will ultimately make you a more expressive player, and help you stand out from the crowd.

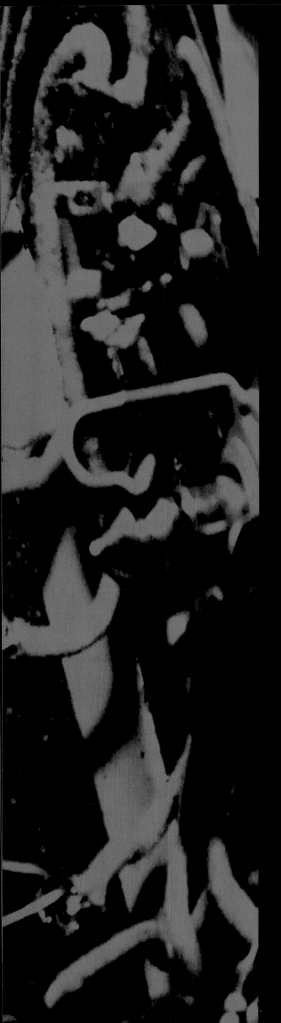

# CHAPTER 1

# The Signal Chain

Ever thought about what happens after you plug your guitar cable into your amp? This chapter follows the basic journey your guitar signal takes, from input to output.

Tube amps aren't rocket science. They're a whole lot more complicated than that. Sure, their circuits might be a lot simpler than NASA-level technology, but they work toward an output that affects both the senses and the emotions. An amp's sound contains a complex blend of objective and subjective elements that's difficult to unravel, even in top laboratory conditions.

On one hand, amplifying a guitar signal is extremely simple stuff compared to, say, designing and manufacturing a CAT scanner. On the other, any effort to quantify the components of sound is going to be fraught with difficulties. But hey, stick with this—you're on the right course. You can crack these tone secrets, and you'll be a better-sounding and more expressive player for it.

In the course of this book I'm going to tell you some things that neither the majority of boutique amp makers nor the mass manufacturers want you to know: the first is that good tube amp tone is a very simple thing. Three knobs, three preamp tubes, a pair of output tubes, two sturdy transformers, half a dozen capacitors and a baker's dozen of resistors is all that's required to make up the finest amp that you or I ever played. Our perceptions might indeed be very subjective, and we might argue over the fine points, but whatever the ingredients, rest assured that the best amps are relatively sparse bags of bones. Sure, you might like—or require—added features and extra channels, whatever tools it takes to get your music made. As for the basics of a great-sounding tube-amp design, well, the purest tone is generally to be had from something … basic.

**Look beyond that jack input.**

The top designers want you to think guitar amplification is tricky, mysterious stuff because they want to justify the "necessity" of spending $3,000 or more to get even a "decent" amp (though don't get me wrong, plenty of great makers today really do earn their fees, and more). In the other camp, the mass manufacturers want to tell you that you need 16 knobs, with pull-boost and voicing and resonance and cut and presence controls, dual masters, four footswitchable channels, switching for "vintage/modern/insane" modes and so on (again, mass-produced amps certainly do have their place, and many can sound damn good). But the truer truth is that if you take out most of the gimmicks, wire together the few essential bits and pieces in a sturdier, more direct way, any of these amps will sound 300 per cent better.

Simplicity reigns in the world of tube guitar amp tone. While quality parts and sound design matter, an uncluttered design with the minimum of components necessary to achieve amplification (but good ones, please) is always going to stomp all over the too-clever, multi-featured Swiss Army Amp for pure tonal considerations. Usually a clever designer and careful manufacturer can add a few knobs and switches to this quota in the name of versatility without sucking too much life out of a great amp's tone, but push it too far and you know something has to be sacrificed. Admittedly, some people definitely need the Swiss Army Amp to get the gig done, and there's nothing at all wrong with that. But you begin to understand the heart of good amp tone by starting with the virtue of simplicity. And when I talk about "simplicity," I don't just mean vintage amps, reissues of such, or the very expensive boutique amps that thrived in the non-master-volume craze of a few years back. Plenty of far less glamorous amplifiers—silverface Fenders, later 1970s and early 1980s Marshalls, others from Traynor, Ampeg, Valco, Gibson, Silvertone, WEM, Selmer—have the simplicity to be made into performers of really high sonic virtue, sometimes with a well-considered tweak or upgrade from a thoughtful tech. But enough of that for now—on with our journey.

## MORE THAN JUST "LOUD"

In order to start understanding your amplifier better, you need to employ a perception shift. Stop viewing it merely as a box with a hole on the front that you jack your guitar into, and some semi-transparent cloth through which the sound emerges, and see it as a series of interdependent parts that all contribute to the final sonic result. Even in the simplest tube amps—I'm thinking 1950s tweed Fender Champ or 1960s Vox AC4—there are a handful of components in the circuit that present enormous variables to the signal chain. Alter one of them, and your final tone changes; alter two, or three, and the tone changes exponentially. Start mixing and matching all the possible values and types of components, and the variables really get out of hand. (The individual components that make up a tube amp circuit are explained in detail in Chapter Two.)

It's nearly impossible for a player without an electronics degree, a lot of experience with tube amplification engineering, and a good laboratory at his/her disposal to quantify, for example, how X type of resistor will change the sound in comparison to Y type of resistor when bypassed by W or Z type of capacitor. And as players, rather than engineers, we shouldn't even really hope or expect to go there. Even so, by understanding that almost any change in the types and values of parts can make a difference, and that there are places in the amp where high-quality (or particular) components might make a major difference and other places where they might not, we can at least begin to take a more active role in shaping that sound we'd like to call "ours." Through the course of experience, too, we do often come to understand what sonic changes such alterations in components will make in our amps, and even to predict them quite accurately.

I've already used the word "science," but this chapter—like this entire book—explores matters firmly from a player's perspective. The intention isn't to learn how to build the perfect guitar amp here; we're just out to investigate what makes a good amp sound the way it does, and what components might make up the kind of amp that's right for us.

There are plenty of myths about tone in the tube-amp world, a lot of which are hard to shake because, once again, sound is an extremely subjective phenomenon (although not entirely so, I would argue). Few people are setting up, or can afford to set up, laboratory-grade A-B-C-D comparative tests to rule out the many variables and

A good guitar amplifier isn't purely about amplification.

prove or disprove so many elements of these myths, so in the case of certain components it is difficult to find an absolute and reliable word on what is real, and what is mere legend. For that reason, we proceed with a pinch of myth, a dash of solid electronics knowledge (even if borrowed), and a lot of trial and error. The aim is really to gain the kind of experience that makes our sonic explorations less of a shot in the dark, and more of an educated guess.

We do also have to take the "grandfather factor" into consideration: the question is, do we like the sounds of classic vintage amps because they universally sounded great, or is it because the music that's now seen as "classic" was played through them, and so by association these sounds have established themselves as the "standards"? Are they really any better than more "modern" sounds, or is it just that they remind us of some "golden age"? If someone built a new amp that could be proved by some laboratory standard to be "officially certified excellent sounding gear," would people necessarily like it?

All of this relates to the fact that a good guitar amplifier isn't purely about amplification of the signal presented to it—in other words, just making it louder. We need the volume in order to be heard, sure, but a good guitar amp is also equal parts distortion generator—even if we are setting it for a "clean" sound, or think we are.

This brings up another truth that you need to get into your head quickly on any quest for an understanding of the ingredients of good sound: the electric guitar on its own is not an instrument. It requires an amplifier—and I would argue not just any amplifier, but a *great and appropriate amplifier*—before it becomes anything close to expressive, emotive, and toneful. Most of us have stuck our guitars into truly clean, cold sounding hi-fi or PA amplifiers at some time or other, and we know the results are not pretty. With a high-fidelity preamp and a big solid-state power amp you can make your guitar sound very loud indeed, but big ain't always beautiful (and sometimes it doesn't even sound "big" in a tonal sense). A guitar amp is an entirely different beast altogether, and it needs to be understood as such.

More players think hard about their guitars than about their amps—they dream of acquiring that Fender Custom Shop Relic Strat, Gibson Custom Shop 1959 Les Paul, Gustavsson Bluesmaster, or D'Pergo T-style guitar, but then they put it through an entirely uninspiring amplifier. I would claim any day that your amp expenditure deserves to be at least equal to that of your guitar expenditure if you're seeking to be a true tone hound ... or, if you're topping out at a few $k on each and have the budget to do so, sure, feel free to spend all you like on that boutique guitar. At the same time, though, I'll swear all day long that you don't need to spend a fortune to get great tube amp sound—more of which later in the book.

Here's a test I've performed many times to help demonstrate the relationship between guitar and amp, and it usually works even if you just do it in your head. Plug an entry-level Indonesian Squier Telecaster into a little budget transistorized Squier combo and play; then plug a top-of-the-range Fender Custom Shop Relic Nocaster into a nice all-tube Dr Z Stang-Ray amp with Z-Best 2x12″ speaker cab and play. Which one sounds better? No contest, right? Now swap the guitars around, and hey—the $2,500 guitar sounds like doo-doo into the $129 amp, but the $169 guitar sounds pretty damn sweet in the $2,250 amp and cab. You can try this all day long with cheap guitar/great amp combinations and the results will nearly always be the same (sure, some of those cheap little tranny amps can make some pretty cool noises for certain funky applications, but you get my drift).

Or try another fail-proof test: I absolutely guarantee you that if you play the same guitar through three very different amps for half-an-hour each, one after the other—say a 1965 Vox AC30 Top Boost set to sparkly clean, a Mesa/Boogie Triple Rectifier set to destroy, and a 1959 tweed Fender Deluxe set semi-filthy—you will find yourself playing quite differently each time. Different guitars will do this to an extent too, but I'd argue that—given a well set-up and easy playing guitar to plug into them—different amps with quite diverse sonic styles will perhaps have an even greater influence on your playing style, as well as on your sound. You'd better believe that amp deserves a lot of consideration.

So the guitar amp as distortion-generator is a crucial part of what we call "the instrument" of the electric guitar player, in some ways maybe the most essential part, but the type and quality of that distortion is critical. Sure, some solid-state amps have been designed to distort in the "right" way and can therefore sound pretty good—and some digital modeling amps too—but they do so by mimicking what we like about tube amps, and they require a lot of extra circuitry and some pretty clever engineering to do what the simplest tube circuits do naturally. Don't misunderstand me, I don't mean to run off course here by dissing transistorized amps; that's not the intention of this book, and many makes and models of solid-state amps serve players' needs very well. The point is to prove what's inherently good about so many tube amplifiers. The smoothness of the distortion that occurs in most good tube guitar amp circuits, and its gradual onset into the overall output blend as you turn the amp up louder, makes the sound not only easy-on-the-ear but ripe with even-order harmonics. It's those harmonics that turn a plucked note from an electric guitar into a fat, rich, shimmering thing, compared to the relatively thin note of the unplugged instrument.

The natural distortion character of a simple solid-state circuit, on the other hand—one without a lot of extra tricks and tidbits added in an attempt to make it sound "tube-like"—is harder, harsher and more sudden. In laboratory terms, I'd describe it more as "electronic noise filth" versus the "smooth, creamy sonic dream" or whatever other adjectives guitarists and amp reviewers have applied to great tube amp distortion over the years.

A lot of this comes down once again to the nostalgia factor. If ultra-clean, powerful, efficient high-fidelity amplifiers with limitless headroom were available to electric guitarists by the early 1950s, they probably would have been playing them. As a result, rock'n'roll might have evolved as a very different beast, perhaps with the gritty old saxophone still front-and-center of the stage. As it was, Danny Cedrone, Cliff Gallup, Eddie Cochran, Chuck Berry, Bo Diddley, Paul Burlison, and others were grinding out this raw, edgy, slightly dirty but oh-so gorgeous guitar sound, packed with drive and emotion and utterly compelling. I'd wager that at least part of the reason we love the sound of a distorted amplified electric guitar is because all of these guys—plus Jimi Hendrix, Eric Clapton, Paul Bloomfield, Jimmy Page, and whoever else—have made stunning, groundbreaking music with that sound. But if the guitar had sounded more dry, sterile and, well, hi-fi during the 50s and 60s, maybe more of the groundbreaking music would have been made on more compelling instruments. Or, who knows, maybe rock'n'roll would have had a lot more trouble evolving into what it is, and hundreds of potentially great players would have given up the instrument early for lack of inspiration. Thank god, then, for the flaws and shortcomings of early tube amplification, because I just can't imagine a world where Gatemouth Brown, Joey Santiago, Zakk Wylde, or Joe Bonamassa would have been strutting his stuff in quite the same way with an old gold-plated Selmer alto sax, or a vintage Yamaha grand piano.

Almost every guitarist seeks a so-called "clean" sound at some point, but look at the basic specifications for distortion in guitar amps, as opposed to hi-fi amps, and you can see that an element of fuzz, fritz and breakup plays a part in even your shiniest rhythm or chicken-pickin' tones. A decent hi-fi amp today might possess a total harmonic distortion (THD) level of something less than 0.05 per cent at a given output level (though never of course at maximum output), while a high-quality tube guitar amp will commonly have 5.00 or even 10.00 per cent THD at a volume level you'd still consider "clean." As guitarists we still want our clean sounds to be springy, dynamic, rich, and sparkling, and at anything close to zero THD, that isn't happening. Harmonic distortion, especially of the type that generates pleasing even-order harmonics, is the salsa on that otherwise bland burrito. It adds body, thickness and multi-dimensionality to that naked "ping" of a plucked wire string. The distortion that a good tube amp produces so naturally and so sweetly has, for going on seven decades

**Every component your guitar signal touches has the potential to alter your sound.**

now, been a big part of what has inspired great guitarists to play. Harken back to that thing about an electric guitar not really being "an instrument" all on its own: you don't sound big and thick and juicy and a little mean, you don't play like some rebel deity unchained. It's that sweet, thick, toneful grind that moves us, baby, and when the amp is giving that to you just right, you want to play and play … and through that, you ascend to the next level, where the playing flows and great music is made.

Distortion. Bless its fuzzy woolen socks.

## THE COMPONENT CHAIN

From the input to the speaker-out, and on down the wire to the speaker itself, every different component that the electrical pulse of your guitar signal touches—and a few that it doesn't—has the potential to alter your sound in some way. In a fairly standard tube guitar amp, when you exclude any onboard effects or gimmicks, there are really only three major stages in the circuit that directly affect the signal: the preamp stage, tone-shaping stages, and output stage; the fourth "side stage," if you will, is the power stage that converts, filters and supplies the voltages to the tubes. Beyond all of this, of course, there's the speaker.

Within each of these few major steps, from input to speaker, there are at least a handful of components that present the many variables I've already mentioned. Even if you're never going to tweak or replace these bits and pieces yourself, understanding where they are in the signal chain and how they can affect your tone greatly increases your overall understanding of a tube amp's function.

To put it simply, a tube guitar amplifier works by letting two different types of voltages pass in two different directions, while not letting the two pass the same way together. In practice the low AC voltage that constitutes our guitar signal, as generated by the guitar's pickups, makes its way from the amp's input toward the speaker output—getting bigger along the way—while the high DC voltage that powers the tubes runs back in the reverse direction, often along some of the same connection points that serve as stage inputs for the AC signal. For this reason, many of the bits and pieces we will encounter while tracing the signal are designed to allow AC to pass through them (or a frequency-selected portion of it at least) while blocking DC from coming back through in the opposite direction, or vice versa. That sounds complicated, but don't get too badly hung up on the details just yet. We're going to examine an extremely simple guitar amp circuit to see what sits where in the signal chain, and what job it performs in doing so.

Let's follow the signal path across the circuit of a 1950s Fender Princeton amplifier (illustrated on p15). As incredible as it might seem, the voltage that represents our guitar signal passes through only three resistors, two coupling capacitors (caps), partially through a further two tone caps, two variable resistors in the form of volume and tone potentiometers, two tubes, and an output transformer before reaching the speaker. That's not a lot, compared to what you see going on inside that $89 VCR you used to have to open up occasionally to un-jam something your toddler mailed through the video slot. Everything else you see in this amp circuit—the capacitors, resistors, and the 5Y3GT tube (none of which amounts to much anyway, it must be said)—deals with governing voltage levels and either blocking part of the signal from escaping, or doing just the reverse, tapping part of it off to ground to divert it out of the signal path. So let's take the journey. (Note: from here on I'll distinguish different paths within the circuit by referring to the sound-carrying path as the "signal" and the power-transferring path emanating from the power transformer and rectifier as the "voltage" or "high voltage." If there are any terms here you're not familiar with, they'll almost certainly be explained in the course of the next couple of chapters, under "Components" or "Circuit Stages", or might be found in the Glossary toward the end of the book.)

## FROM PREAMP TO OUTPUT

The first thing your signal sees is of course the input jack (shown top right of the diagram on the opposite page). Though its job is simply to pass the signal from the guitar cable into the amp, the condition of the socket is critical to good transference. A worn or dirty "hot" contact or a loose grounding connection will harm the signal. Assuming all is well here, the signal passes on down a short length of wire to the first of what we would consider the actual circuit components, a 68k resistor. Although the signal clearly passes through this resistor—it's the only thing standing between the input jack and the first tube—it's not a tone-shaping component in any direct sense. This is the "grid stopper" resistor, and it is present here to suppress oscillation in the amplifier (oscillation in this context is best described as a kind of runaway self-generated noise, akin to a form of feedback). Its value is such that it creates a low-pass filter when teamed with the capacitance between the "grid" at our 12AX7 tube's pin 1 and the "cathode" at pin 3, but this little filter network's frequency range is such that it lets through any signal in the audible range of the guitar, and blocks those that might lead to runaway oscillation.

Also note at this point that the 1M resistor connected across the input jack doesn't do anything to the sound—it's there to prevent open-circuit hum when no guitar is plugged into the amplifier. The way it's wired up to the pair of "switching" jacks (which make the connection to ground via this resistor) means that the one resistor functions on both jacks.

There's a lot of talk in tube-amp circles about the sonic qualities of different types of resistors,

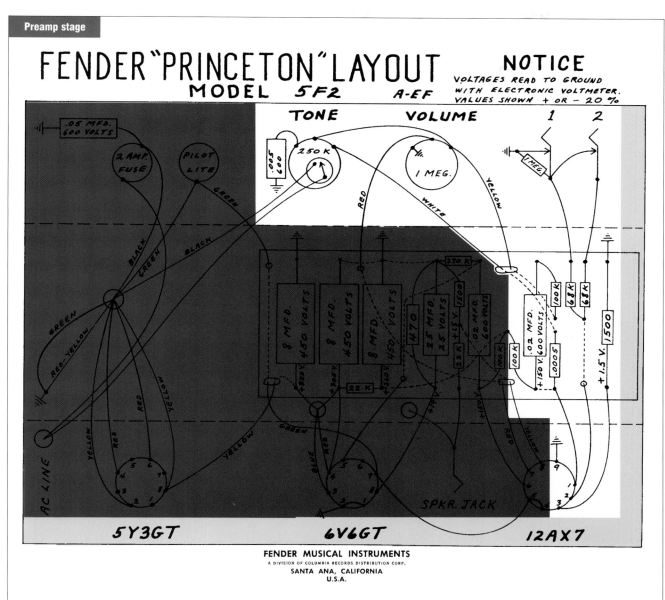

**Preamp stage**

# FENDER "PRINCETON" LAYOUT
## MODEL 5F2 · A-EF

### NOTICE
VOLTAGES READ TO GROUND WITH ELECTRONIC VOLTMETER. VALUES SHOWN + OR − 20%

TONE · VOLUME · 1 · 2

FENDER MUSICAL INSTRUMENTS
A DIVISION OF COLUMBIA RECORDS DISTRIBUTION CORP.
SANTA ANA, CALIFORNIA
U.S.A.

but let's leave this until we've moved on another few steps, and deal with that issue where it becomes a little more significant.

The wire from the far side of the joined 68k resistors, one from each input, runs straight to pin 2 of the preamp tube, which is the input to the first side of the tube in this configuration (or first "triode," since the 12AX7 is a "dual triode," essentially carrying two little tubes in one glass casing). This input is also known as the "grid," and the flow of electrons from the grid to the plate of the tube increases the signal strength, or "gain." The plate is our output from this first gain stage, and is wired to pin 1 on the diagram. This "configuration," as mentioned above, is technically referred to as the "common cathode." Pin 3 connects to the cathode of the first triode, which is the element that determines that part of the tube's operating level. No signal passes

This is one of the simplest popular amplifiers to contain all the three signal stages plus the power stage (the even simpler 1950s Fender Champ had no Tone control at all).

through the 1,500-ohm (or 1.5k-ohm) resistor between pin 3 and ground, but it's there to determine how "hot" the first half of the tube runs, and so helps determine its gain (given the same plate voltage, a higher cathode bias resistor means less gain, a lower one means more gain). Wiring the cathode to ground makes it common (or "in use by') both the grid (input) and plate (output), hence the name. The common cathode is by far the most-used type of preamp gain stage. (Chapter 3 will discuss in detail how changes in value in the components that connect the preamp tube's cathode to ground will alter the signal's frequency content and strength at this juncture, even though the signal doesn't pass through them, by changing the way the tube behaves.)

Onward with the signal path. From pin 1 of the 12AX7 the signal runs simultaneously to the volume and tone controls, and also makes the connection required to supply the operating voltage from the power rail, via a single 100k resistor. This is a slightly awkward tone circuit, which was

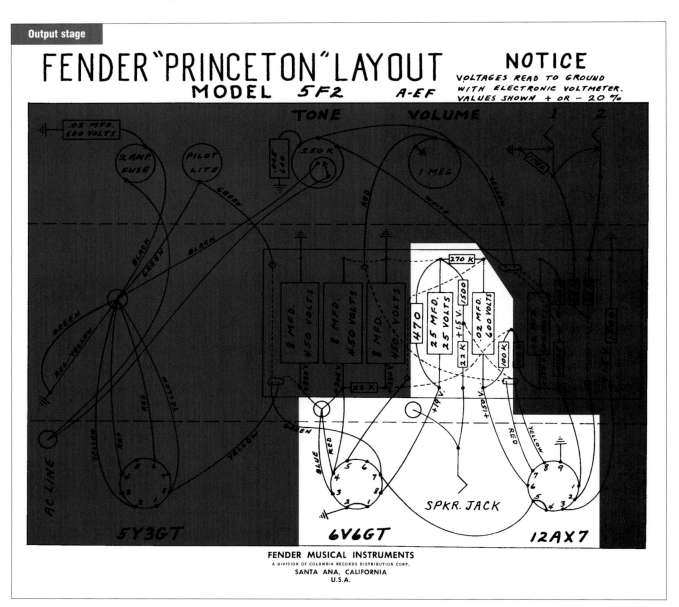

improved upon in the 5F2-A update of the Princeton, but that isn't really a concern here, as it's still an excellent example for following a signal path through its stages. For now, note that this basic tone circuit is designed to affect the high-frequency content of the signal. In this format, the volume and tone controls are pretty interactive, as you might guess from a look at the diagram, which shows you that the signal is going off toward both at the same time. The 0.0005uF (or 500pF) capacitor between pin 1 and the tone potentiometer blocks a large portion of the lower frequencies in the guitar's range from even entering this circuit (thereby leaving these frequencies free to race on toward the volume pot), while the 0.005 cap from the left tag of the tone pot to ground taps off a portion of the high end as the knob is turned down. As such, this is a simple "treble bleed" tone network that passively removes highs from the signal rather than adding anything to it. Once filtered in this way, the signal is passed back to the right tab of the volume control, where it enters this potentiometer for an overall level cut, alongside that portion of the signal that came along a more direct path to this same connection point.

By the way, the round thing on the back of the tone control—with two connection points and an arrow going off askew from one of them—is the power switch for this amp. On smaller amps like the Champ and Princeton, Fender was still saving space in the 1950s by using a volume or tone control with a separate switch mounted on the back, but of course this isn't in our signal path.

The more direct signal to the volume control has come via a 0.02uF coupling capacitor and a 100k resistor, both of which help to shape the voice of this preamp stage. These coupling caps— also called signal caps or blocking caps—are selected to perform two jobs simultaneously: they block DC current from entering the stage before the cap, while also playing a major role in determining the frequency response of our signal. A lower value capacitor here will decrease the signal's low-frequency content, while a higher value cap will increase the bass response. In this case, note that the notion of "higher" and "lower" cap values can be confusing if you don't think carefully about what you're looking at. Since almost all such caps with have a value to the right side of a decimal point, you need to remember that 0.1uF is a *higher* value than 0.047uF, for example, and 0.022uF is a higher value than 0.005uF, and so on. Given the same make and model, the cap of a higher value should be of a larger size, too (provided they are also rated for the same maximum voltage).

Just as the tone controls' fully clockwise position represents the natural state of the signal in terms of frequency, the volume control, when fully clockwise, lets the full signal level pass through. Turning the knob down taps off a portion of that signal level to ground (the arrow symbol running from the left volume tab to the back of the pot represents its ground connection), just as the same action tapped off some of the high frequencies to ground via the tone control's 0.005uF cap.

Whatever is left after the basic frequency filtering and level attenuating functions of the Princeton's simple two-control set-up is passed straight along to the output section via the long wire running from the volume control's middle tab to pin 7 of the 12AX7 tube.

Small amps like this one are a little unusual in that one tube handles both preamp and output duties, thanks to the dual-triode's two-tubes-in-one capabilities and the fact that amps with only one output tube—known as "single-ended"—require no more than a single triode to drive the output stage. In such a circuit, this tube (this half-tube, really, though a complete triode stage) is therefore known as the "driver." In amps with two or more output tubes in a "push-pull" configuration, a triode or two is used differently as a "phase inverter" (PI), to split the signal and send a reverse-phase path to each output tube—more of which later.

In our current scenario, the signal enters the grid at pin 7, which serves as our input for the 12AX7's second triode, and exits at pin 6. The cathode, running from pin 8, is again tied to ground, but separately from the cathode of the first half of the tube. The 1,500-ohm resistor running from the dotted-line portion of the wire from pin 8 to the rail connected to the grounding symbol sets this triode's bias, or operating level, as did the same value of capacitor in the preamp circuit.

There's another little trick in this small amp that appears in some larger amps, and it's called a negative-feedback loop. We'll examine this in detail later, but note for now that the 22k resistor running from the cathode connection to the 1500 resistor to the speaker jack is used for this purpose.

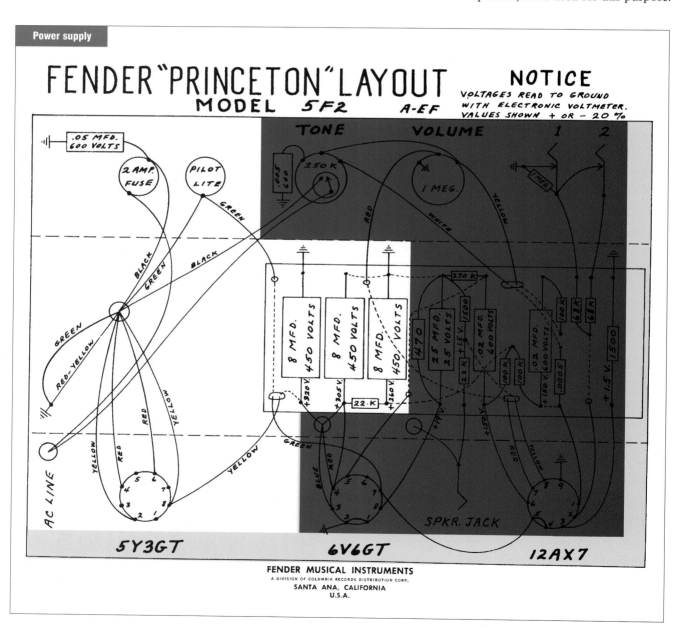

From pin 6 of the driver half of the 12AX7, the signal goes to another junction like that of the first triode: the signal path itself again runs through a 0.02uF coupling capacitor, while another 100k anode resistor joins this path to the power rail, from which is supplied the high voltage on which the tube operates. Our 0.02uF cap again does voicing duties while coupling the driver to the output tube, and sends the signal straight on to the input of the 6V6GT output tube at pin 5. The signal is also regulated at this point by a connection to ground via a 270k resistor.

We've seen a couple of tube stages already, and should be beginning to get the impression that these are a significant portion of what the amp is doing as a whole. The signal goes in one side as it is, and comes out the other side bigger—it's as simple as that. In the case of an output tube, it's even more so. As with our preamp tube, our output tube's input is a connection to its grid, and its output comes from the connection to the plate, at pin 3. From here, the signal runs straight to the output transformer (OT) via the blue wire indicated in the diagram on p16 (we can't see the OT in this diagram because it's mounted on the reverse side of the amplifier chassis).

As with our preamp tube, the output tube's operating level (bias) is determined in this circuit by a resistor tied between the cathode (pin 8) and ground. This 470-ohm resistor decides how "hot" the tube will run in relation to the high-voltage DC supply fed to it. The bias resistor is partially bypassed by a 25uF/25V electrolytic capacitor wired in parallel to it, which further affects the frequency response of this tube, in this case giving it a bigger, deeper sound than it would have with the resistor alone. Note once again that no signal is passing through this capacitor, but that it's helping to voice the output stage by playing a role in determining how the tube operates.

Onward from the 6V6GT's pin 3 to the OT, which converts the tube's high impedance signal to a low impedance signal that can power a speaker, and sends it there via that wire coming up through another hole in the chassis to the speaker jack, as indicated in the diagram. And wham, that's it. The amplifier circuit has done its job, and we have sound in the airwaves again—the same notes as played on the unplugged guitar, except a lot louder, and with a rich spectrum of harmonics, all courtesy of the tube amplification process. But we still have a few more side-chains and connections to examine before tracking back to explore the variables in more detail.

## HEATER SUPPLIES

One of the other visible connections we haven't discussed yet is one that sends the 6.3V AC supply to the tubes' filaments, or heaters (in some amps this is instead a DC supply of approximately 12.6V, which sometimes produces less hum than an AC filament supply). This is the portion of the tube we have to wait to warm up when we first switch on a tube amp, and it's what we see glowing through the glass of the tube. The filaments are called heaters because their job is to heat the cathode to a very high temperature,

A tube's heater needs to be warmed up for a few seconds before it can start to do its job.

which allows it to release electrons that are then collected by the plate—all of which constitutes the amplification process within the tube.

Most relatively recent amps have two wires supplying the heater voltages, carrying half the supply each. Many of the early models, like the Princeton, have just a single supply wire, so the tubes' other filament connections are wired to ground (as are pin 9 of the 12AX7 and pin 2 of the 6V6GT—whose pin 1 actually has no connection to the inside of the tube). You can see that the pilot light sitting beneath that iconic Fender jewel lamp also runs on the same 6.3V AC supply, which is the green wire running from the hole in the top of the power transformer. Because the filament supply voltage is so much lower than anything else used within the amplifier, a tube amp power transformer is made with a separate winding to supply precisely this amount of power.

Amps with tube rectifiers, as virtually all of them were until the early 1960s, also require a second low-voltage supply of 5V AC to warm up the filaments of the rectifier tube, which are different from those of preamp and output tubes. (Note that while both of these filament voltages are low, their current can be extremely high, so thick, stranded wires are usually used for these connections.)

In our Princeton layout diagram (p18) the filament supply arrives at pins 2 and 8 of the 5Y3GT via the yellow wires. The high-voltage AC supply comes in on two separate paths in this type of rectifier, carried to pins 4 and 6 by the red wires. Within a tube rectifier these two AC supplies are combined to a single, higher DC supply, which leaves the tube at pin 8. Yep, the heater and cathode are connected; it may seem pretty confusing that AC is entering here while DC is exiting—and in some ways it is. This isn't a fatal error in design or something you need to worry about; essentially, just know that AC and DC travel in different ways, and can use some of the same pathways and connection points without interfering with each other, if the circuit designer has done his or her job right. This is much the same as the way we had the AC signal passing out of a preamp tube at the same point where its DC supply voltage was passing in. So, unless you're thinking of going into rectifier design or some deeper career in electronics, you don't even need to know how or why that's possible—you can just note the fact, then ignore it and move on. Remember, we're guitar players, not engineers.

A tube amp's power supply needs to be carefully filtered to remove noise-causing "ripple."

## HIGH-VOLTAGE SUPPLIES

The high-voltage DC supply exiting the 5Y3GT at pin 8 will eventually supply our tubes with the power that makes the magic happen, but first it needs to be filtered to remove undesirable noise-causing elements, and stepped down for the slightly lower levels required by different stages in this circuit. The first component in the power rail is an 8uF/450V electrolytic capacitor, known as a "filter" cap because of the job it takes on here. These are polarized caps, unlike the signal caps we encountered in the signal-handling portion of the amp's circuit, and are connected with the "+" to the high-voltage supply and the "–" to ground.

In principle they are capable of doing the same job as signal caps, but have a different composition. This filter cap helps to smooth out the leftover AC ripple present in the DC supply, which would add noise to the circuit if left untreated.

From the first cap's + connection the power trail passes along through a hole in the chassis to the choke. This is an inductor that looks like a small transformer, and it performs more filtering duties before passing the DC further down the line. Another electrolytic capacitor filters the supply again before sending it to the 6V6 output tube, where it makes its connection at pin 4.

We've already seen that this tube's output to the OT comes from pin 3, and the diagram might lead us to believe that alongside the DC supply connection at pin 4 there's a second output to the OT through the chassis hole (via the red wire). In fact this wire is just passing along the same DC voltage that the tube uses to the second connection of the output transformer's "primary." The OT essentially "feeds" off of this DC supply to one side of its primary, while receiving the signal from the output tube at the other side of the primary, and these are transformed within it to the signal that produces acoustic energy at the speaker. An amp with two output tubes in a push-pull configuration would have wires going from pin 3 of each output tube's socket (if it used 6V6s or 6L6s or similar) to two different polar-opposite connections on the OT's primary, with the high-voltage supply going to a third connection between these.

If we backtrack a step, we see that the DC supply carries on via a 22k dropping resistor to yet another 8uF/450V filter capacitor, which gives it a final cleansing before sending it to the preamp tube. The resistor has knocked the voltage level down from a little over 300VDC to 260VDC. A pair of 100k resistors connecting this point to the plates of each side of the dual triode drop it further, to around 150VDC.

And there we have it. It's taken us a few pages to get here but, for all the wonder of amplification, not a whole lot has happened along the way. Just a few stages each for the signal and the DC power supply to pass through as they join to convert that plucked guitar string to a pulsing paper speaker cone. Of course as a player wanting to understand how to get the best out of your tube amp—or how to find the right amp in the first place—you don't need to understand every one of these stages in minute detail. But getting your head around the simple yet enigmatic path that constitutes your signal flow will leave you well equipped to tweak and troubleshoot your tone throughout a career of sonically elevated music making. What I'm saying is, this could all help you sound damn good.

So now we've covered a basic (but great sounding) tube amp circuit, but we need to examine the individual components and stages in more detail to account for some of the variables that help to make every amp sound a little different—or sometimes very different indeed.

# CHAPTER 2

# Components

A closer look at all the multifarious components inside your guitar amplifier—including resistors, capacitors, transformers, and of course tubes themselves, whether preamp, output or rectifiers.

Though they vary in complexity, any tube amp circuit is basically constructed from chains of little stripey resistors, cylindrical (and other-shaped) capacitors, wire-wound transformers, plus a few choice tube "bottles." But what do all these parts do exactly, individually and together, to your guitar signal? Would changing one or another improve your tone? Which are the most important, most universally revered, and most over-hyped?

## RESISTORS

You'll recall that the first thing our signal encountered after squeaking past the input jack was a resistor. These little voltage-blocking cylinders are among the most-seen bits and pieces within any amplifier circuit.

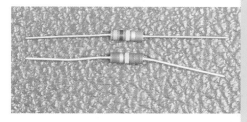

Carbon comp resistors.

Technically, a resistor is any element within the circuit that puts up a resistance to the flow of electric current. In the amplifier circuit this is usually just a partial resistance, which blocks a portion of the current but lets through a precisely determined amount in order to tailor the voicing or gain level or some other parameter of any given stage.

Most of the resistors you will encounter are humble little items, which in vintage amps look much like miniature brown Tootsie Rolls with colored stripes (I'm striving for a polite simile here, you see). These brown resistors in old Fenders, Marshalls, and Voxes—called "carbon comp" resistors—might not look like much more than a thickening of the wire, but are in fact an item of much heated debate in tube amp circles. They are used within the circuit more often as regulators and voltage-governors than as tone-shapers, yet tubeheads continually fail to agree whether or not the makeup of these little cylinders really has any direct effect on an amp's sound.

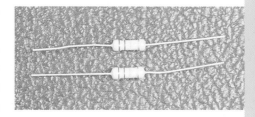

Carbon film resistors.

Resistors of this small, tubular variety put up their resistance thanks to the way in which their critical elements have been "gapped" (or spaced) in the manufacturing process, to put it simply. Aside from the large wire-wound or ceramic resistors that often appear in the high-voltage supply and filtering chain,

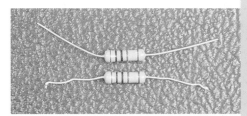

Metal film resistors.

or as output tube cathode-biasing resistors, the most common types are carbon comp, carbon film, and metal film resistors. Carbon comps, the granddaddies of resistors in tube-amp terms, are manufactured by binding together carbon particles in a clay-like substance. The density of this collection of particles determines how much resistance is found between the wire entering the cylinder and the wire exiting it. Carbon film resistors are made by depositing a thin film of carbon in a spiral on a ceramic rod between two contacts, with the tightness or looseness of that spiral determining the resistance. Metal film resistors are made in a similar fashion, replacing the carbon deposit with a thin spiral of, yes, metal film.

Metal film resistors are not only the quietest in audio circuits, they can also be made to the tightest tolerances (meaning to actual values very close to their stated values). Carbon films are a little noisier, and carbon comps are noisier and more inaccurate still. They can be made to provide

**High-powered cement resistor.**

a tolerance of within one per cent of their stated value (inaccurate to one per cent above or below spec), but are usually only within five or ten per cent. They also drift further from spec over time, and carbon comp resistors in a vintage amp can often be a good ten or 15 per cent off their supposed value—and sometimes significantly more—when removed from the circuit and tested with a meter.

Noisy, inaccurate, prone to aging problems ... so why do carbon comps possess this legendary magic vibe? Many amp designers will tell you it's just voodoo, snake oil—that in fact they don't play any magical part in a circuit, for all the reasons described above, but only make it noisier and less accurate (which, for an amp manufacturer, means less consistency from amp to amp). These same technical authorities will also tell you it's purely function and accuracy of performance that matter in a resistor, and they simply don't affect an amp's sound in any way, other than perhaps making it less reliable. In a sense, they are dead right. But guess what—carbon comp resistors do distort slightly when operating at high voltages and hit with signal peaks. This distortion seems to be minimal, but it might just be enough in some circumstances to have an audible affect on the signal, depending on where such resistors are used. We already know that so much of what we love about guitar amps has to do with distortion, to the extent that, for most players, "no distortion" means "no tone" (even when we desire, or think we desire, a clean sound).

A number of authorities have written about this phenomenon, and I think R.G. Keen states it in a way that makes most sense to guitarists: "Carbon comps have excess noise, high drift, high pulse power, and high variability. They also have a high voltage coefficient of resistance. That means the resistance actually varies with the voltage across the resistor ... We have resistor distortion ... That's what carbon comp resistor mojo really is—the resistors are distorting, but in a way our ears like." (From *Using The Carbon Comp Resistor For Magic Mojo*, by R.G. Keen, 2002, published online at www.geofex.com.)

So, carbon comp resistors are flawed, but as with so many elements of tube guitar amp technology, it's highly possible that the flaws actually contribute to the tone, by adding thickening, harmonically-rich distortion. I'm not going to make any final pronouncement on the great carbon comp debate, but there certainly seems to be enough evidence afloat to indicate that maybe all resistors are not created equal. The wisest approach would perhaps be to use carbon comps where they are likely to distort in a tone-enhancing manner, and use quieter carbon film or quieter-still metal film in all other positions in the signal path.

Keen suggests that when used as plate resistors, and especially in the stage just before the driver or phase inverter—where high signal voltages are present—carbon comp resistors might yield their most audible effect. In most other positions, and especially at some of the early preamp stages where the signal level running to the tubes' inputs is very low (before it has had a chance to be amplified by the preamp tube itself), Keen suggests they simply aren't going to make an audible difference, other than introducing noise into your sound.

In most amps all the resistors are the same type, other than a few in the power supply—makers don't generally pick and choose resistors to suit particular positions. Open up an unmolested Fender amp made any time between the late 1940s and the late 1970s and you will find carbon comps throughout, and many builders today making reproductions of classic tweed Fender designs use the same types of resistors to precisely replicate what these vintage amps were doing.

Many modern manufacturers, on the other hand, eschew any supposed "mojo" from carbon comps and use metal film resistors throughout their circuits for their quietness and relatively higher tolerances. Michael Zaite of Dr Z, for one, finds carbon film resistors a good halfway house between the noisy, inaccurate carbon comps and the arguably "sterile" metal film variety. Plenty of other makers—some of them interviewed toward the end of this book—have made pronouncements on the issue.

The late Ken Fisher told me, "I've never heard an amp with metal film resistors that didn't sound harsh. A lot of guys will say, 'But they make the lowest noise.' Oh, absolutely, they're far lower noise. Carbon film is lower noise than carbon comp, but metal film is way lower noise than either one of those two. Yeah, you can get less noise, but you won't get as good a guitar tone." Similarly, Victoria's Mark Baier declares, "Sure, [carbon comp resistors] are a little noisier. So what? The noise floor disappears the minute you strum the first chord. Occasionally one of them will get sputtery, but you just have to fix it."

Victor Mason of Mojave Ampworks, on the other hand, has made many of his amps with metal-film resistors throughout, and they are *great* sounding amps.

Despite all of this supposed (or apparent) resistor distortion, noise, reliability and so forth, you, as a guitarist, probably don't need to have a thorough understanding of the workings of the humble resistor. But knowing a little about how they do or do not affect a circuit (or about how they might, if we admit the jury is still out) can help you define what you are looking for in an amp, or possibly help you avoid being taken in by some manufacturer making extraordinary claims for a product.

## SIGNAL CAPACITORS

If voodoo and magical mojo are talked up in the world of resistors, they certainly hang thick in the air in capsville, believe me. In the Princeton diagram we used as an example in Chapter One, our signal only passes through two signal capacitors all the time, and partially through another two in the tone circuit, in a proportion determined by the setting of the tone potentiometer. The two main 0.02uF signal caps (also listed as "MFD" on many older schematics) that are always in circuit are used in positions where they are also referred to as "coupling caps," because they couple together different stages of the amplifier. In this particular case they couple the preamp to the driver—via the tone and volume network—and the driver to the output tubes. Other common capacitor values in these positions range from as little as 0.001uF to as high as 0.1uF, with some extremes beyond these in rarer cases—numbers like 0.047uf, 0.022uF, and 0.01uF are among those you'll probably see most.

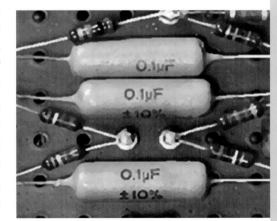

**Mustard caps in a vintage Marshall JTM45.**

Even in larger amps there usually aren't very many more coupling caps than this in each signal chain (or channel) because these three basic stages are common to many different types of amp - though you might see more in the circuit diagrams to account for the stages of different channels, or for added gain or gain make-up stages in amps with more complex tone circuits. Also, modern high-gain amps with complex preamps will naturally have more coupling caps in that part of their circuit, and of course push-pull amps with two output tubes will have a pair of caps running from the sides of the phase inverter to the output tubes.

With only two such capacitors in our Princeton and, once again, every drop of your tone passing through them at all times, you can bet that they play an important part in shaping the sound of the amp. We've already discussed how their value determines the voice of the amp, by which I mean the frequency response, and this is the most significant way in which they influence the tone. Again, by increasing the value of one of these caps, you increase the bass response; by lowering it, you decrease it. But while increased bass response might generally seem like a good thing (if you're from the "more is always better" school), it can also lead to boominess or woofiness at a certain point. Looked at another way, too much bass response might shape the signal's frequency range in a way that other components or configurations further down the signal chain have trouble handling—a little like trying to force too much water into too small a balloon too fast. Decreasing bass response might even "open up" the sound of some amps, helping to voice them right in the sweet spot, but going too far can run the risk of thinning out the sound.

Also be aware that the 0.02uF cap that gives a certain voice in a tweed Princeton won't necessarily create a similar frequency response when added to a Fender Twin Reverb in place of a particular coupling cap of a different value. The voicing of any stage within the amp is always a combination of how these caps are filtering the frequency passing through them and the frequency response of the tube stage prior to the cap, as determined by its plate and cathode resistors and so on; beyond that, it will also be differently shaped by the ways in which it is handled by the signal stages that follow. Most thoughtful amp designers will voice each stage with all of these variables in mind. Which isn't to say that tweaking cap values might not unveil a magical sweet spot in an amp that previously sounded flat or constipated. For example, years ago I built an amp based roughly on Fender's 5E3 tweed Deluxe schematic, but one that I was tweaking for more headroom and a bolder tone. In addition to other changes—higher plate voltages, a bigger OT, a choke for more filtering, and some altered resistor values here and there—the amp only really came into its own when I swapped out the 5E3-spec 0.1uF coupling caps for some 0.022uF caps. The change sent less low end down the chain, but the entire amp sounded bigger and punchier as a result. Just right, in fact.

Along with the value (or "size') of a signal cap, its makeup also plays a part in its sound. In other words, not only will our tweed Princeton sound a little different if you change either of its 0.02uF coupling caps for, say, a 0.047uF coupling cap (not even taking into consideration the fact that the original might have failed after 50-plus years in service), but it can also sound different if we substitute a considerably different 0.02uF capacitor.

Now, many analysts with a lot of good science and education behind them will poo-poo this notion and tell you, "caps is caps, it's the value that matters." But plenty of tinkerer-guitarists like myself, with just enough knowledge under their belts to be dangerous, know from experience that signal capacitors of different compositions do sound different. Plenty of other designers and makers who know their stuff will agree, too. Very often you really can hear the difference when you replace just a single coupling cap with another of the same value, but of a different make or composition. And sure, sometimes you can't—but the "can" occurs enough to make it a valid consideration by my own, admittedly unscientific, standards. It's subtle, but it's there.

I've tested this myself on many occasions, and it's a fascinating exercise in the variability of one little thimble-sized part. I have, for example, gathered four different makes of 0.022uF cap for a circuit that requires that value in a particular coupling position, rigged them to a four-way selector switch, and noted with great interest that each does make the amp sound slightly different. The change is usually pretty subtle, I admit—sometimes extremely subtle, sometimes virtually imperceptible—but often it's enough to evoke some ultimate preference of cap type in some cases, according to differences in transparency, graininess, warmth, openness, note definition, or whatever other factors might come up. You can even record the results, if you like, for later comparison in a more immediately side-by-side situation.

The sonic changes don't lie. In their interviews toward the back of this book, both Brian Gerhard of TopHat and Mark Bartel of Tone King, as well as others, will attest to the very real ways in which different makes of capacitor can influence different tones in certain circuits. The trick is knowing how they'll do that, and that's not an easy one to crack, since capacitors of different compositions will influence different circuits and stages in different ways, depending upon all else that's going on around them. The skill, for the thoughtful amp maker, is to learn from experience what any type of cap is likely to do where, and to select the cab that best enhances his sonic goals.

Yellow Astron cap.

Blue tube Mallory "Molded" cap.

I probably need to apologize to some of you at this stage. Maybe you didn't pick up this book with any intention of being dragged into a debate on the differing sounds of polyester caps vs polypropylene. Stick with me—it all goes to the greater good. Once again, I'm not even suggesting you go swapping caps in whatever amp you presently own. The point is purely to reinforce the fact that small components can and do make a difference, and can lead to a network of infinite variables.

Capacitors are made up of a pair of plates with a lead going into each, and a form of insulation separating them, known as the "dielectric." In most caps used in the signal chain, these leads have no polarity, so the caps can be connected in either direction—this isn't the case with electrolytic capacitors, which we'll look at in a moment. In the old days the dielectric was often waxed paper formed in rolls between the foil of the plates, or sometimes oil or paper in oil (the latter remains popular with high-end hi-fi enthusiasts and even some boutique tube guitar amp makers). Modern caps are more often made

Orange Drop cap.  Paper/oil cap.

from a range of plastics or ceramics, like mica, polypropylene, polystyrene, or polyester (although the last type is mostly an older breed). Technically, the signal doesn't pass "through" this dielectric, the substance merely insulates the plates.

Even so, some different types of dielectrics do appear to contribute to different-sounding caps. I won't pretend to be able to tell you why, and I don't think I've encountered anyone yet—whatever his or her training—who can do so completely satisfactorily. It largely comes down to the fact that this insulating material affects the way the conducting material behaves, while different materials also absorb some of the signal to greater or lesser degrees, and these factors in turn affect the character

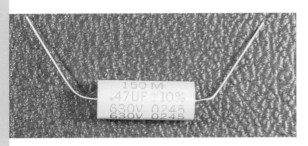

Mallory cap.

of the sound to which different types of caps contribute. Just be aware that the difference exists as a phenomenon. That information might not end up meaning much to you, or it might prove significant.

Plenty of tube amp gurus talk about the "warmth" of the cap types found in vintage amps, which often contain waxed or oiled paper or mylar dielectric with or without an exterior of some molded plastic. But as with so many other components of vintage amps, the sonic perceptions can often be attributed partly to the fact that these parts have aged severely, and might even be failing.

If you are a hobbyist or modder or tinkerer yourself and you can acquire some old-style caps without paying an arm and a leg for them, and also get them tested for both tolerance and leakage, they are worth trying. Some certainly sound great: most of the old yellow Astron caps from 1950s Fenders, or the tubular blue Mallory caps labeled "Molded" that are found in brown and blackface 1960s amps (not the waxy-blue "candy drops'), sound extremely full and smooth. But sometimes they haven't aged well and are really useless. Unlike "new old stock" (NOS) tubes—which in theory can sit on the shelf forever and be as good as new when finally plugged into an amp—vintage caps, used or not, can sometimes age in a deteriorating fashion, even when just resting in their original supply box, so the NOS concept often doesn't apply to them.

Even more of a risky buy than these are used vintage signal caps put on the market by repairmen who have pulled them from old amps, usually to replace them with functional new Xicons or Orange Drops. In such cases you can guarantee someone is getting ripped off: either the old blue tubular caps were perfectly good and the tech replaced them unnecessarily with new caps that are arguably sonically inferior, at a hefty bench charge, meanwhile devaluing a vintage amp in the process; or, they needed to be replaced and he is now trying to sell you faulty goods.

Plenty of new caps do capture some of the lauded qualities of vintage types, ageing factors aside, and are almost universally better than the dirt-cheap consumer-electronics-grade components that many mass manufacturers are using in amplifiers today. Polystyrene Sprague or SBE Orange Drops have a certain body and edge that can be really appealing in many amps. Some builders find their upper-frequency response just a little harsh, but I often find this is a matter of circuit and application. If anything, they often offer a certain slurring of the lows and mids that can sometimes work nicely in vintage-type circuits. In some applications—both vintage and modern designs—Mallory caps, and others like them, will prove smoother and more open, with a little more sparkle too.

Paper-in-oil types, with either aluminum foil or copper foil plates, like those made by Jensen in Denmark (also sold with the Audio Note or Angela brand stamped on them), have been raved about in audiophile circles for years, and some high-end guitar amp makers are starting to use them too. They can be very expensive—from $5 to $100 or more per cap depending on value, compared to about a buck for an Orange Drop 716P (which in itself can be considered expensive by mass-manufacturing standards).

There are a few new caps on the block that have recently been getting a lot of attention for their efforts to replicate the performance of vintage makes. Sozo's original yellow caps and the Mojotone Dijon (geddit?) are both supposedly made to the same specs as the famed "mustard caps" used in some early Marshall and Vox amps, and seem to be pretty good products. Sozo also makes a

BlueMolded to replace the, well, blue "Molded" caps in 60s Fenders, while Jupiter makes Vintage Yellows and Red Astrons, intended to replicate the sounds of different caps in tweed-era American

amps. Many hi-fi nuts, uh, enthusiasts have been raving about products like AuriCaps, V-Caps, MusiCaps and others, although it's worth remaining aware that what's great for linear hi-fi sound reproduction isn't always great for gritty rock'n'roll tube amps. If you're curious, and plan to mess with some cap alternatives anyway, some aren't so prohibitively expensive and might be fun to try out.

MojoTone's "Dijon" signal cap, a reproduction of the famed British "mustard cap."

For a manufacturer, though, they would be an exorbitant part to use; for my own part, if anything, I've sometimes found such high-end hi-fi caps a little sterile and even harsh. When considering "deluxe" cap options, or those of any new component that promises to be the missing link to true vintage tone, you need to keep a level head and shake a pinch of salt on any grand claims that come your way—and maybe occasionally remind yourself of how Leo, Dick, and Jim did it.

Parts prices like those charged for many of the new paper-in-oils were unheard of in the old days, when "a good cap" was as much as any high-end builder hoped for. When some hi-fi and guitar amp builders started using the Jensen aluminum foil paper-in-oil caps years ago, they were touted

as the epitome of the breed—miles above anything that previously dared to call itself a capacitor. Then Jensen came out with their copper foil upgrade and, wow, suddenly that was considered so much smoother, warmer, and more articulate... at around $15 to $20 per cap for values used in most guitar amps, and a lot more from some distributors. Keep in mind that the capacitors used in the vintage Fender, Marshall, and Vox amps that we all rave most about were good caps, yes, but bought by the manufacturer in bulk for pennies per unit. They weren't excessively analyzed or over-engineered, but were made to do a job, and did it.

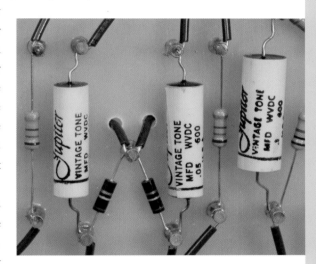

New Jupiter caps in a Dr. Z Therapy amp head.

If your amp sounds good to you, don't spend all your waking hours wondering if it could sound even better. Just get out and play. I have fallen prey to that bug myself at times, and believe me, it's debilitating. Tone-tweaking can be fun and rewarding, and sure, that's largely what this book is about. But something new and better will always come along, and if your amp is constantly on the workbench, you're not going to get a lot of playing out of it.

Be aware, too, that what passes for "warmth" in a lot of tube-amp chat regarding components is often in fact really down to low fidelity, some attenuation of highs, and perhaps a muddying of lows or mids—together or separately—all of which can give an impression of a darker, mellower tone. Finding caps, tubes, resistors (or whatever) that offer a genuine, complex, fully dimensional warmth as part of a linear frequency response with no major humps or notches across the spectrum, is another trick entirely.

The supposed "warmth" that's typically perceived in vintage gear is very often simply a result of aged and softened speakers, burned-in tubes, slightly leaky coupling caps, drifted resistors, or what have you. That said, plenty of the signal caps used in amps built 40 and 50 years ago were indeed really great-sounding items and sometimes offer some special "mojo," and if you stumble across functional ones they are worth trying or passing along to an appreciative tonehound friend. Quality modern caps, on the other hand, are almost always made to higher tolerances, are generally more reliable, and offer a more consistently full-frequenced response. Sample, explore, test, and see what you discover for yourself.

If you do install some upgraded new or NOS signal caps, bear in mind that these often take some time to "burn in," just as tubes and speakers do, and might not sound their best the first time you fire up the amp. Given 15, 20, or maybe 30 hours to burn in, new caps that sound a little dull and flabby at first will often become warm, deep, rich and open.

I'm not trying to suggest that you need to shop for your next amplifier according to what signal caps it contains—you'd most likely end up pretty frustrated if you did. But it all goes toward topping up the information pool; the more you know and understand about these things, the less you are going to be deceived—either by yourself, or by someone else trying to sell you a trumped-up bill of goods. Swapping and testing different signal caps can certainly be fun and interesting (get a good tech to do it with you if you aren't trained in safe practices yourself), and can help you put that dusty pawn shop find into top shape.

## ELECTROLYTIC CAPACITORS

These are the large can-like capacitors found in the power supply, which are often unseen under that "cap can" on the back of a 1960s and 1970s Fender amp chassis, or in upright cans on the top of a vintage Marshall chassis. They also appear as some smaller pieces further up in the circuit for other filtering or cathode-bypass duties. As power filters, no signal passes through them, but they do affect an amp's sound according to how well or poorly they perform their job of "cleaning up"

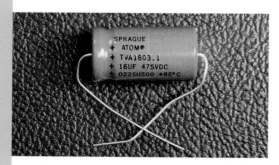

Sprague Atom cap.

Astron Minimite cap.

the power supply. Unlike signal capacitors, electrolytics are polarized and will be connected with their positive side toward the voltage supply and negative side toward ground.

Put simply, electrolytic capacitors are used to remove AC ripple that's left in the DC power supply after it has undergone the rectifier's AC-to-DC conversion. Left untreated, this ripple can cause a number of problems generally associated with unwanted noise: these can take the form of a pulsating current, a dirty hum, a flabby and distorted low-frequency response, or even ghost notes, which sound something like a dissonant harmonic following along beneath the actual note played. None of these are desirable, and it's the filter capacitor's job to eliminate them.

Any guitar amp will have a number of filter caps in the power supply chain, with other smaller versions in other sections of the circuit. I don't know of any popular (or playable) designs that carry fewer than three filter caps in the power supply—usually linked at their positive ends by resistors that drop the DC levels down to whatever is required by each subsequent stage being filtered and supplied.

Our sample tweed Princeton carries an unusually small filter cap in the first position with a value of 8uF. This was upped to 16uF in the revised

Princeton that followed, and that's about the lowest-value filter cap you will find in the first position of most guitar amplifiers. In addition to merely helping remove potential noise artefacts from the power supply, the size and placement of the selected filter caps helps determine the "sharpness" of an amp's sound, and the firmness of its bass response in particular. Even though no signal passes through these cans, their quality and accuracy can influence your tone for better or worse.

A good designer will consider a number of factors when selecting cap values—it isn't simply a matter of "bigger is better." For one thing, tube rectifiers are only happy with so much filtering in the first position. A solid-state rectifier and large-value filter caps work hand-in-hand to help powerful amplifiers offer a tight overall response and firm, bold lows (which of course also defines the criteria for any bass amp). On the other hand, over-filtering can sometimes choke and tighten up an amp that might sound more dynamic and open with lower-value caps in the power supply.

The pure quality of this component also matters greatly, as we're finding it does with most every component in the circuit. Audiophiles can get extremely hung up on the virtue of electrolytic caps in their tube hi-fi amps, and the respected types can easily cost more than $100 a unit; with a few of such pieces required in most amps this can become pricey stuff. Quality counts in filter caps for guitar amps too, but fortunately this doesn't stretch to such extremes. Better-respected electrolytics for guitar amps come from makers like Sprague Atom,

Ilinois Capacitor filter caps in a Dr. Z Therapy.

Illinois, Samwha, and LCR, while JJ Electronic, CE Manufacturing, and F&T make a good range of multi-section can caps for amps that use such configurations. Size isn't *necessarily* any ultimate denotation of quality—and even some of the reputable brands might hide a little airspace within that can to puff up their images, rather than being packed to the gills with electrolytic goodness—but the better makes usually aren't the most petite options on the shelf. A chunky 22uF/450V Sprague or Samwha might cost upwards of $3 per piece, however, compared to the less than $0.50 cost of smaller, generic bulk-buy electrolytics, so cost-cutting keeps them out of all but the better amps. Having your local tech stick three to five of these in your precious vintage amp—or potentially cool-sounding budget tubester—to replace the dried-out originals can be a well-spent $15, and your tone will thank you.

Some power supplies include a choke in the DC rail between filter caps instead of one of the large voltage-dropping resistors, so this is a good time to deal with these little transformer-like inductors. Even though this choke appears to replace a large resistor in its position between filter capacitors, in designs that are otherwise similar, it is performing a very different job. Rather than dropping the voltage down like the resistor does, the choke is further smoothing the residual AC ripple from the DC voltage. It's a common component of amps seeking a tight, bold delivery (or almost all amps of 30 to 40 watts or more), or of some small amps in which AC noise is of particular concern.

A multi-section "can" cap from JJ, with one 40uF cap and three 20uF caps, all at 500V.

Some players and designers feel that a choke can indeed "choke" the sound of certain small amps a little, and that these sound hotter and more open with the component omitted. Of course some small amps were and are built without chokes because it's simply cheaper to do so. Either way, it's another variable that isn't always a matter of better or worse: amps without chokes are not necessarily inferior, it depends what the designer was trying to achieve—although larger amps will almost certainly want and need a choke to sound their best.

## TUBES

Yes, these are the babies that so many players keep raving about. Any discussion of tube type, or tone, the quality of new versus old, and so forth, can be a real can of worms. So get out your can openers…

No matter what else is going on in an amp's circuit, a change of tube brand or type can often make the most dramatic tonal alteration that can be achieved from a single item swap—other than, in many circumstances, a speaker change. While the pedant can argue that any particular make or type of type doesn't "have a sound" in and of itself, different tubes clearly contribute to different sounds coming from the circuits in which they are used, and this is something you can hear even when swapping between different compatible tube types in the same amplifier.

All amplification tubes carry at least four elements within their vacuum-sealed glass bottles: a cathode, grid, plate (also called "anode"), and filament (or "heater"). The most basic tubes are called "triodes," named for the first three critical elements (the filament is always there, so it's ignored in the naming process). Pentode tubes, which account for most output tubes and a few preamp tubes, carry two further grids, a screen grid and a suppressor grid, which essentially help to overcome capacitance between the control grid and the plate. In simple terms, a tube's job is to make a small voltage into a big one, and the basic elements of the triode or pentode work together to do so.

Many guitarists never think about it this way, but each time you pluck a string you are sending a small surge of voltage to the input of your amplifier, created by the steel string's vibration within the guitar pickup's magnetic field. This signal voltage is applied to the grid, which we've already seen as the tube's input in Chapter One, and as it increases with the plucked note, it causes electrons to boil off of the cathode and onto the plate at a correspondingly increased rate. This is how the sound gets bigger. Amazing, isn't it? So much of the magic of a tube guitar amp's sound is created in that process—and while of course there is a whole lot of science that governs precisely how this happens, it's a pretty crude reaction and interaction in many senses. And as you can imagine, it's open to plenty of variables too, with different makes and types of tube offering discernibly different sounds. One of the greatest variables among tubes involves the manner in which they distort, whether in slight amounts during normal duty, or in greater amounts when pushed near their limits.

In Chapter One I talked about the role distortion plays in creating the multidimensional sonic picture that we think of as a great amp sound. This is more relevant to tubes than to any other component. Groove Tubes founder Aspen Pittman is fond of saying that he doesn't think of tubes as amplification devices, he thinks of them as distortion generators, and there's a lot to be said for that. Certainly tubes are responsible for amplification—in simple terms, the signal goes into one side of the tube at X voltage, and comes out the other side much bigger than X—but there are other ways of amplifying a signal. The beauty of tubes as amplification devices is that they don't just make a sound bigger, they make a sound bigger with style.

A circuit as simple as our tweed Fender Princeton example certainly amplifies a guitar signal, but if you wind the dial up anywhere past the early numbers you can tell pretty quickly that it adds plenty of distortion—and very sweet distortion, too. Construct a simple transistorized amplification circuit with similarly few components involved, and it will also clearly make your signal louder, but any distortion added—and there will be plenty when you crank it up—will be of a pretty nasty, jagged breed.

I've already discussed the virtue of simple tube amp circuits against more complex circuits in terms of pure tonal integrity, but this is where tube amplification really shines. Put the simple tube circuit up against a simple transistor circuit, and you soon realize that any tranny amp designer is going to need to put in a whole lot of extra sound-shaping just to make the "simple" featureless circuit sound remotely pleasing for guitar amplification. They can do so, for sure, and plenty of solid-state amps today can sound pretty damn good. But they're not simple affairs by any means— which continually leads me to ask myself the question: why labor over something that requires 50 parts and intensive design efforts just to make it sound almost as good as the thing made with 14 parts wired up according to a 50-year-old diagram? Of course the answer usually comes down to cost. The "simple" 14-part tube amp will often be time-consumingly hand-made, and will generally use much more expensive, brand-name components, all of which makes it a less cost-effective exercise nowadays than production-line mass-market solid-state circuits. Even well-executed high-gain tube amps that maintain a lot of sonic integrity are relatively simple circuits compared to other types of consumer electronics. Often, they just have a little more of the same things going on as the simpler circuits.

But it's the way tubes distort that makes us love them. We know the sound of a maxed Deluxe Reverb or JTM50 Plexi or Vox AC30, and we lust in our sleep over the addictive thrill of what is clearly a very heavy dose of distortion in that gorgeous tone. But at virtually any audible amp level, tubes are introducing an element of distortion that's very largely responsible for livening up even what we think of as a clean sound. Lower levels of distortion in tube amps set to "clean" are producing mainly second-order harmonics, which don't come across as a dirty, crunchy or fuzzy sound like extreme distortion, but as a richer and more multi-dimensional tone than what we'd be hearing if the sound was truly clean. Essentially we have two types of distortion produced by tube guitar amps: the obvious, intentional distortion that's part of the classic rock lead sound, and the subtler distortion that's always with us, making clean sounds a little warmer and shinier.

You've probably all read elsewhere about the nature of tube distortion versus transistor distortion, and how tubes ease gradually and smoothly into breakup as more signal is applied, while trannies will for the most part clip off their output harshly when finally pushed too far. If you haven't read this before, well, there it is. Such explanations are usually accompanied by two diagrams: the smooth if slightly off-balance sine wave of a clipping signal through tubes (usually with some shading toward the tops of the waves to indicate distortion), and the angular square wave of a signal clipping through transistors.

Short of going into some deep science (which, as a humble writer and guitarist, I can't pretend to fully understand), that's all you probably want to know about the comparative functions of tube/transistor distortion; more importantly, you probably already know the difference in sound. As mentioned already, tube distortion sounds so good because of the types of harmonics generated. The addition of harmonics relative to the fundamental note is what makes any instrument—acoustic guitar, piano, oboe—sound like more than just the thin tuning-fork tone of a pure pitch. These

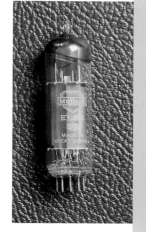

EL84

6V6

12AT7

harmonics are present even when you pluck the string of an unplugged electric guitar; but plug it in, and these are amplified, and others added by the distortion of the amp itself. The louder the amp gets, the greater the balance of these distortion-generated harmonics compared to the pure fundamental of the note/pitch, and the thicker our sound—up to the point of heavy clipping, when the tube's ability to keep amplifying starts to shut down and we just get mush rather than volume when notes are hit hard.

We've already encountered the term "harmonic distortion," and this is what tubes do so well, and why they make our guitar amps shine. At this point it's worth introducing the notion that different tubes produce distortion differently, and they definitely have their own tonal characters— voices from which you can pick and choose to tailor your own sound.

The tubes we encounter in guitar amps always come in at least two types, and sometimes three: preamp tubes, output (or power) tubes, and occasionally rectifier tubes. As with other amp components, but even more so, tubes present another multi-dimensional variable. Different types of tube clearly account for different sounding amps—an EL84 versus a 6V6GT, for example—but different makes of the same tube type can also have characteristics that differ to an extent that is sometimes surprising.

(In order to offer a more detailed look at specific types of tubes and some of their characteristics without breaking the flow of this chapter, I've put a comprehensive guide to tube types in an Appendix toward the back of the book. There you can investigate the most popular types in use now and in the past, along with their gain factors and distinguishing features, plus some of the notable different makes of the major types, and a little philosophy on substitutions, new makes versus NOS, and so on.)

Now let's move on to consider the major differences between preamp and output tubes. Preamp tubes are easily identified as the smaller bottles that usually correspond in position to your amp's inputs and early gain and tone stages (be aware that they are sometimes covered by metal shields, which are easily removed with a twist and a pull). Since the mid 1950s these have mostly been of the smaller nine-pin variety, with the 12AX7 being by far the most common type (also known by the European designation ECC83, or the high-grade US alternative 7025). Others that occasionally make an appearance are the 12AY7 that was original equipment in many tweed Fender and Gibson preamps of the "tweed" era, the 12AT7 that sometimes appears as a reverb driver or phase inverter, and the lesser-seen 12AU7. All of these are "dual triodes," which, as already mentioned, means they have two independent tubes in a single bottle. The only pentode preamp tube seen with any

regularity in guitar amps today is the EF86 (or 6267), which appeared in a few early Vox amps, and more recently in models from Matchless, Dr Z, and a few others. The EF86 fits into the same nine-pin bottle, but operates with entirely different circuit requirements. Another somewhat similar pentode preamp tube, the 5879, was the voice behind many Gibson amps of the mid 50s to early 60s, and has more recently appeared in some models from Divided by 13 and in Victoria's re-creation of the Gibson GA-40 Les Paul Amp. Many amps of the early 1950s and before also used larger eight-pin ("octal") preamp tubes, such as the 6SC7 and 6SL7 dual triodes that appeared in early Fender and Gibson amps, and the lesser-seen 6SJ7 pentode, and several boutique makers have revived these tubes in contemporary designs.

All of these small tubes can be driven into distortion, just as their big siblings in the output stage can, and any amp's overall distortion content is usually a combination of distortions from both of these stages, and sometimes the driver/phase inverter too. But the character, or quality, of preamp tube distortion is quite different from that of output tube distortion, and that's something we will explore a number of times in the course of this book.

Makers of effects or "hybrid" amps that carry a single 12AX7 tube in the preamp (and usually a lot of added diode clipping and other solid-state tone and distortion-enhancing stages to help create that "real tube sound") are fond of praising these little bottles for the "warmth and smooth distortion" they add to such products. If truth be told, when a 12AX7 is driven into distortion, the resulting sound is frequently bright, edgy, and a little harsh—which can be a great thing in some circumstances, but shouldn't be confused with "warmth." Certainly cascading one triode gain stage after another from a series of 12AX7s run into each other does work to create the classic high-gain preamp sound that works so well with a lot of modern rock, and has become the signature tone of countless shredders, grungers, metalheads, and other wailers. But that's a sound in itself—a great one at times, to be sure, but not the instant ticket to "real tube warmth and classic rock tone" that so many marketing departments would have you think it is. Be aware from the start that the character and quality of any form of natural tube distortion that is generated by a particular amp, whether it's preamp or output-tube generated, comes down to the quality and integrity of the design, and what the designer was hoping to achieve. You can get smooth, thick and creamy from both types; and raw, jagged and nasty from both types; while the majority might lie somewhere in between. It all depends on what you're after.

KT66

EL34

What these preamp tubes really excel at is amplifying a signal up to the point just short of truly audible preamp distortion, and passing it on to a subsequent gain stage that will help produce a more contemporary high-gain distortion, or to an output section that can be driven into the kind of juicy, fat breakup that's responsible for most of the classic rock tones we all lust after. Once again, both categories of tubes can be responsible for distortion created within the amp, but the distortion produced by preamp tubes is by no means just a smaller version of that produced by output tubes.

In most amps the output tubes will appear as the larger pair or quartet of identical-looking bottles placed furthest from the input section. A few, mainly EL84s in current-production amps, are roughly the same diameter as preamp tubes and fit in the same nine-pin sockets, but are clearly longer and therefore are still easy to identify. The other popular types—mainly 6V6GT, 6L6GC, 5881, EL34, and 6550, and occasionally the odd KT66, KT77, or KT88—all fit in larger eight-pin sockets. While they might appear interchangeable in terms of socket size, most have different circuit, voltage and bias requirements, and they cannot simply be substituted one for the other in most amps. One exception to this is our DIY dual-single-ended amp project toward the end of the book, and this is another variable I have specifically designed it to test. It will run on a pair of 6V6s, or just one of them, or a single 6L6, EL34 or KT66 without modification, and therefore makes for a great hands-on lesson in the differences between these tube types. As a matter of fact, it's also a great test bench for a range of 12AX7 types, since just one preamp tube swap takes care of those

GZ34

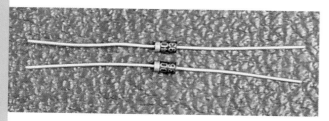

**Rectifier diodes.**

duties for the entire amp, both first gain stage and output driver. The maker THD has also specialized to some extent in making amps with swappable output tubes—such as the UniValve and BiValve—while this kind of fun can likewise be had with Victoria's Regal II, and the Groove Tubes Soul-o-Single will also run on a range of tube types.

The different characters of these output tube types will be discussed in more detail in following chapters, when the circuits of some of the classic amps that contain them are analyzed. But as the final amplification unit before our signal is converted by the OT back into a form of voltage that can drive a speaker, you have to believe that the output tube/tubes have a major influence on an amp's overall sound. That said, plenty of amps with precisely the same output tubes sound nothing alike, so it's got a lot to do with the output stage shaping and amplifying whatever signal is presented from the preceding stages.

As mentioned at the start of the book, an amp's signature sound is always going to rely on the sum total of a large number of variables that sit along the signal path, and whatever the signature sound of a 6L6 or an EL34, a change in preamp biasing levels or coupling caps from one amp to another will significantly alter what those tubes present to us. For that reason, you can't base your tone quest on tube type alone when surveying a broad range of different designs, because other elements in the circuit might radically shape or alter the way that these tubes behave, resulting in something nowhere close to the signature "Fender sound" or "Marshall sound" you were expecting to find.

The third tube we occasionally find in a guitar amp is the rectifier tube, although many designs—and larger amps in particular—substitute solid-state diodes in this role. In fact, tube rectifiers are diodes too; they contain two critical elements, plus heater. A rectifier tube has a job that is completely different from that of amplifying a signal. By passing along the positive part of the AC signal and blocking the negative (or vice versa, in some instances) it converts AC from the amp's power transformer to the DC that the tubes use for amplification duties. Again, no signal passes through this tube, but the efficiency with which it performs this task—or the lack thereof—will influence the feel and response of an amp, and to some extent its sound.

The same tubes running at different voltage levels will have different sounds and different touch-sensitivity characteristics, so a rectifier that does a very efficient job of AC-to-DC conversion will make an amp sound different to one that does a very inefficient job of it. Solid-state diodes, for what it's worth, are extremely efficient. On top of this, and assuming a correctly functioning rectifier tube supplying the voltages required by the amplifier design, this stage is also responsible for a lot of what guitarists call the squash, sag, or compression in a tube amp. With the amp turned up high and the tubes hit quickly with a heavy load from a hard-whacked power chord, for example, the demand on the rectifier can be more than it can handle. Its power output can drop momentarily while it catches up with the job, creating a sag-and-swell effect akin to that of a compressor. This sag is more prominent in smaller rectifiers like the 5Y3 found in compact American amps, or the EZ81 in a Marshall 18-watter, less prominent in the larger 5AR4/GZ34 types that the big Fender tweed amps, early Marshall JTM45 and Vox AC30 had in common—although even these will give up a little squash when slammed hard in a cranked amp. Compared to all of these, solid-state diodes exhibit the least sag.

The sag effect gives a softened edge to a player's pick attack, coupled with a swelling rise in volume following the initial drop of the note—both of which can be really appealing for many playing styles. On the whole it's more a "feel" than a "sound" thing, making these amps feel more dynamic and interactive, though it's certainly a phenomenon you can hear to some extent too. For many types of music—from fast-pickin' country to hard-riffin' metal—this sag-and-swell is really undesirable, and the efficient performance of solid-state diodes will be preferable.

One other facet of the tube rectifier's function, and one that really has nothing at all to do with sound this time, is the slow warm-up that many types provide. During the seconds it takes for the rectifier's own heaters to warm up, they refuse to complete their AC/DC conversion duties and don't pass along any high voltages, which in turn lets the preamp and output tubes warm up gradually before being slammed with the high-voltage assault. This characteristic allows many amps with tube rectifiers to be made without a standby switch, as the tubes receive a slow, safe warm-up from the rectifier itself when switched on.

## OUTPUT TRANSFORMERS

These hunks of iron, wire and paper are given little consideration by many players, but they play a crucial role in the final sound that passes out of any tube amp, and therefore in shaping its tone. As mentioned when we traced the signal path through our little tweed Princeton, the output transformer—OT for short—converts the tube or tubes' high-voltage low-current output to a low-voltage high-current signal, which makes the tubes' high-impedance output into a low-impedance signal that can drive a speaker. The OT's input, known as the primary, will see something in the range of 2,000 to 10,000 ohms and have a certain wattage potential, depending on the type and number of tubes used, and convert this to a signal of a certain strength which the speaker sees as a low impedance in the range of 2 to 16 ohms, depending upon requirements. This all sounds pretty matter-of-fact, perhaps, and more of a mechanical function than a sound-shaping stage, but as with so much else within the amp, the way different makes and designs of OTs perform this job—again, their efficiency or lack thereof in particular—plays a huge role in determining any amp's overall sound.

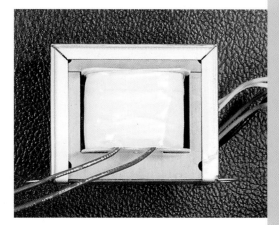

Victoria 35210 OT.

Our Princeton carries a very small OT, though one a little larger than that of its little brother, the Fender Champ of the same era. This and the presence of a tone control are the only significant differences between the two amps—their circuits are virtually identical otherwise (the 5F2 Princeton carried a choke while its successor the 5F2A did not; the 5F1 Champ had no choke). The Princeton's slightly larger OT gives it just a little more volume—a half to 1 watt more at most—but makes itself most known in a fuller low-end response. Both amps were running through 8″ speakers by the late 1950s, but if you get the chance to try originals in good condition side-by-side, you'll hear a meatier performance from the Princeton.

Any output tube has what you could call a maximum wattage potential, which can be reached depending upon plate voltages, bias levels, and the way that bias is achieved (whether an amp is cathode-biased or fixed-bias, which will be explored in depth later). But this output potential still can't be fully realized without an adequate OT. Examine a blackface Fender Bandmaster and Super Reverb, for example. They carry similar tubes and run at similar voltages, but the latter puts out around 10W more power and has a noticeably bolder sound, with a firmer low end in particular. If you look under the chassis of the two, you'll find a much sturdier OT in the Super Reverb. The same applies for plenty of other amps carrying output tubes that could potentially give them similar wattage ratings, all else being equal, but output transformers that render them very different performers.

The rule of thumb for output transformers goes: "More iron = more volume and better bass response." In other words the sturdier an OT appears relative to the requirements of its output tubes, the better it will likely be able to translate their potential into realized volume—and, in particular, the better it will be able to handle the low end of the frequency spectrum. Of course plenty of other factors go into building a good transformer; interleaving and winding techniques, accuracy of primary and secondary impedances, the way in which taps are achieved, the quality of the iron used, and so forth, will all contribute to an OT's quality, or lack of it. But we can't even hope to go in-depth into magnetics and the principles of transformer design in the space we have here—and attempting to do so would probably sidetrack us perilously. The main thing to be aware of is that while you can certainly find large OTs that are well built and large OTs that are poorly built, the heavy, sturdy examples are usually the sign of a manufacturer who is willing to spend money on adequate components, while those cutting corners will fit slightly smaller, flimsier OTs every time. This is likely to be one of the two or three single most expensive parts in any tube amp, along with the power transformer (and perhaps speakers), so the quality of an output transformer is usually some indication of the maker's overall approach to the amp.

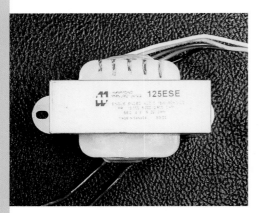

Hammond 125ESE OT.

Mercury Magnetics OT in a Mojave Coyote amp.

That's not to say Fender, Marshall, and the other great original makers were spending top dollar (or pound) on their OTs, by any means. They were the mass manufacturers of their day—and of course still are—and costing out this large part correctly always played a major role in determining their profit margin. But back in the 50s and 60s there was only so low you could go and still put out an adequate product, and these makers were definitely aiming to make adequate products. Fortunately for anyone who owned a Fender or Marshall or Vox back in the day, or is lucky enough to own a vintage one now, off-the-shelf OTs available to tube amp makers in the 50s and 60s (at anything above the real bottom level) were of a pretty good quality, thanks largely to the higher quality of the iron going into them. These makers could certainly have done it more cheaply: compare a Fender Bassman OT to a Silvertone 1484 OT for example, or a Marshall JTM50 OT to a WEM Dominator 50 OT, and you'll see that cheaper examples were available for the given tube.

Better OTs were available as well. Compare all of the above to a high-end tube hi-fi amplifier of the same era and you'll usually see a much beefier OT on the audio gear. I have a pair of British-made Leak TL12+ monoblock tube hi-fi power amps from the early 1960s, each of which uses a pair of EL84 output tubes to produce a rated 12 watts. These weren't even top-end units for their day, but the OTs on them are considerably larger than on any quality vintage or boutique 15-watt to 20-watt 2 x EL84 guitar amp I have ever seen, and about as big as those on plenty of good 50-watt amps. The bigger, better OTs on decent audio amps is a factor in the linear performance and full-frequency response of these units, and a result of the designers' efforts to achieve low levels of THD. But guitar amps don't even need to be linear or full-frequencied (a quality hi-fi OT will achieve a frequency response of 30Hz to 50KHz, a guitar amp typically 100Hz to 15KHz or so), and they were never trying to be especially low in distortion, in hi-fi terms at least. If you ever feel you've been stung by the $125 price tag of a replacement OT for, say, your Vox AC30 (and it won't be a period-perfect OT at that price either), be glad you didn't blow the transformer on a high-end audio amp—which could easily cost you $300 to $500 or more.

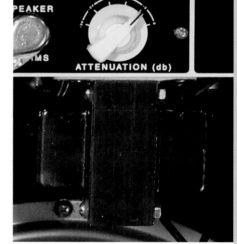

The output transformer in a Tone King Imperial combo.

What I'm getting to here is that you could certainly put a much better-engineered OT in most guitar amps, but most players probably wouldn't like—or need—the result. Even in the case of what we consider a very good OT for a guitar amp, like you'd find in anything from a Bogner to a Matchless to a Carr to a Mojave, its attenuated frequency response can help to keep out noises that are above and below the guitar's frequency range anyway, and its lack of linearity often lends a good midrange grunt that's right at the heart of the guitar's muscle. Taken even further, a designer can consciously employ an OT's limitations to intentionally attenuate bass response that might stress or even blow a particular speaker type being used—as, for example, with Leo Fender's use of a compromised OT in the 2 x 10″ tweed Super Amp. In a more powerful amp with the same two 6L6s but a sturdier speaker complement (like a pair of 12s), this OT's soft low end might be seen as a failing. But driving a pair of vintage 10s from the 1950s, which lacked the ability to give you a firm, powerful low E-string in the first place, the OT and speakers are working together to roll off frequencies that would only cause problems.

The fact is, though, that OT quality is more often than not a reflection of price than of any intensive thought or extensive R&D, except in the case of a handful of very high-end boutique makers who are willing and able to consider such details (Mark Sampson of Matchless and Star and Brian Gerhard of TopHat, among others, discuss some of their thoughts regarding transformer selection in their interviews toward the back of the book). Assuming a maker is using a unit that is at least rated for the correct primary impedance to match the output tubes and the correct secondary impedance to match the speakers, the weightier OT is usually going to give you a better general performance. In contemporary small-run tube amps, OTs by the likes of Hammond, Heyboer, Mercury Magnetics, Triad, or Cin-Tran are usually a good indication of a quality product overall.

From left to right, the choke, output transformer, and power transformer in a Komet 60.

After the output transformer makes its run to the speaker

jack, there is of course one final and very major component in our signal chain: the speaker. I'm going to devote an entire chapter to speakers and cabinets a little later in the book, because they certainly deserve it, and rarely get the attention.

## POWER TRANSFORMERS

Much of what applies to an output transformer regarding quality, sturdiness and pure function also applies to the power transformer (PT)—although of course this chunk of iron isn't processing any signal, so size has no immediate equation to frequency response. A good PT not only needs to supply the correct voltage, as required by the amp design, but to supply enough of it, as demanded

by the number of tubes in the amp. Ideally it will be somewhat over-spec'd for the job, so it can stand up to the required current draw, and then some, without overheating if excessive demands are put upon it for one reason or another over a period of time.

That said, bigger isn't necessarily better, because you certainly don't want higher voltages than your circuit requires... not that size equates to voltage, but you see where I'm going. Many tube-type and circuit combinations will run on higher supply voltages than specified, but they will sound different than intended (as we'll explore in upcoming chapters). An amp may operate "just fine" with, say, 390VDC on the plates of the output tubes, as opposed the 350VDC intended by a particular design, but the excess will throw off bias points and other

**Power transformer.**

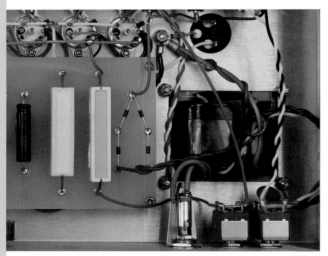

**The power transformer's internal connections to the heaters, the diode rectifiers, and the entire powers supply.**

parameters laid out by the designer and manufacturer, and will sound different than its designer intended, too. For these reasons, a PT's quality is really defined by its ability to do the specified job, and to keep doing it without complaint over the long haul. If a high-end manufacturer is willing to lay out a little more cash for one make of PT over another, assuming each meets required specs, it'll probably be in the hope of greater reliability rather than any sonic variables the upgraded part might present. That said, a better, bigger OT with greater current capacity (but one putting out the same voltage levels as the relatively smaller one) can be a primary factor in a tight, punchy amp with a broad frequency range and a fast response, characteristics which can also enhance harmonic content and depth and dimension of tone, when coupled with other factors.

As we have already seen, a PT's job has a number of facets. It converts the mains voltage of approximately 120V AC (or 230V to 240V in Europe) that you get from the wall outlet into a somewhat higher AC voltage that the rectifier will convert to an even higher DC voltage. At the same time, it provides a lower 6.3V AC voltage at a high current for the tubes' heaters to feed off. In amps with tube rectifiers, the PT will also provide a high-current 5V AC filament supply to heat those. If a PT can hit these specifications accurately, and do so for many hours at a time without getting hot enough to fry an egg on, it's a job well done.

## MISCELLANEOUS PARTS

Other components used in an amp's construction, and the different ways in which the parts can be assembled into a whole, can also affect its sound and performance, but some of them are not always easy to discern.

I'm thinking of things like the chassis and the type of metal it's made from, the type of wire used to assemble the circuit and harness the components together, the material the circuit board is made from and the way it's laid out, the way in which the grounding points have been achieved, whether the amp maker has done a good job of shielding the AC signal path from the DC voltage supply path, and so on. For now, be aware that as well as the many different parts available to the amp-maker there are many different ways to do all of these things too.

For example, the waxed-cloth-covered solid core wire that Fender used from the 1950s to the early 1970s has different properties and performance characteristics than either the high-end stranded wire that boutique makers might use today, or cheaper, thinner wire that many modern mass manufacturers might use. Other differences include whether or not components are wired together literally point-to-point—which accurately means directly from component to component, not just hand-wired on an eyelet card or between terminal strips—or on a printed circuit board (PCB), on epoxy tag strips, on turret boards, on phenolic boards, or on pressed paper eyelet boards. The last method, for instance—as used by Fender in the old days—carries its own capacitance and can sometimes allow small amounts of stray signal to travel across it, and therefore will arguably have its own effect on the sound of an amp, compared to the exact same design constructed on a phenolic board. Hold tight, we'll dig into more of these oddities when we look at individual amps that contain them in Chapter Four, where you can check out the insides of designs by Marshall, Vox, Fender, Dr Z, Soldano, and others to see how they differ.

# CHAPTER 3

# Circuit Stages

This chapter splits the amplifier into four basic stages: the preamp stage, for gain-boosting and tone-shaping; the effects circuits (vibrato, reverb, effects loops, etc); the output stage, with phase inverter, output tubes, and output transformer; and the power-delivery stage, with power transformer, rectifier, choke, and larger filter caps.

We've now traced a complete signal chain and examined individual components in detail, so it's time to explore more closely some of the variations at different stages within the amp. The 1950s Fender Princeton we used as an example in Chapter One is a very simple design, but even so it presents plenty of variables along the signal path. Amplifiers with more complex stages for preamp, tone shaping, output, and power supply offer even more variables, and there are many, many different possible topologies (the way the components are positioned and connected) in such stages too.

## PREAMPS

By now you should have an understanding of a very basic, single-triode gain-stage preamp, but many other types of preamps exist. However complicated they get, though, they do have this factor in common with our ultra-basic tweed Princeton: they increase the gain of our guitar signal to a certain level, and pass it on to the output stage for final amplification. So far I've usually spoken separately about preamps and tone stages, but the one is usually contained within the other, particularly in designs that include a first gain stage, followed by a tone-shaping stage, followed by further gain or gain makeup stages—which accounts for a lot of amplifiers. For ease of discussion, let's deal with gain stages here under "preamps," and accept that a tone stage (often known as a "tone stack" because of its stacked appearance on a lot of schematic diagrams) is an entity existing between these, which we'll check out below as a further part of the same preamp section.

We'll want to move along to look at some more complex preamps than the single gain stage of our Princeton, but there are more issues to address here than mere numbers of gain stages and how many 12AX7s an amp designer has strung together. The way that the gain of the individual triode stages is set, their biasing configurations, and other factors throw up a myriad of variables even within the single-gain-stage preamp. Looking back, you can see that the first triode of the 12AX7 in our Princeton is biased with just a 1,500-ohm resistor straight to ground. We discussed early on in Chapter One how a higher resistor here would mean less gain from the triode, and a lower resistor would mean more gain. But other factors can help to tailor both the gain and voice of this stage.

Check the same stage in many other amps—anything from a Fender Deluxe to a Peavey Classic 30 to a WEM Dominator 50, and countless others—and you will find a capacitor bypassing that resistor from the tube's cathode to ground. This cap creates a frequency-dependent gain boost in the tube, in effect raising the level of a specific frequency range passing through this part of the preamp (remember, no signal is passing through this bypass capacitor; this "tuning" is all achieved by altering the way in which the frequency-handling portion of the triode functions). The most common value of capacitor used here, which is a large-value but low-voltage 25uF/25V (or 50V) cap, provides a low-frequency roll-off that's below the range of the guitar, so it doesn't create any odd emphasis or de-emphasis of a portion of your signal. In effect, it boosts all of it, although the result is more often a low and low-mid emphasis, or "fat boost" as many makers label it, which thickens up the sound without overshadowing the highs.

Other cap values offer different frequency emphases—the 0.68uF cathode bypass cap of the

Marshall "plexi," for example—and they work in conjunction with the overall voice of the amplifier to create the desired effect. Bypassing the biasing resistor to create a low or high-frequency emphasis, or something with a roll-off in-between, doesn't mean the amp as a whole is going to reflect an excess of that frequency range. The Marshalls with 0.68uF bypass caps are, as it happens, pretty thick, ballsy sounding amps to start with, so that merely helps to give their highs more bite (part of what makes them great lead amps). To use a different example, our little tweed Princeton doesn't need a boost from a bypass cap because little single-ended tube amps like this are already pretty gainy as they are, and "fat" enough all on their own. Adding a 25uF bypass cap to this simple circuit might create a useful "fat boost" in some instances, but in others it will overwhelm further stages of the amp, creating a muddy, woofy tone.

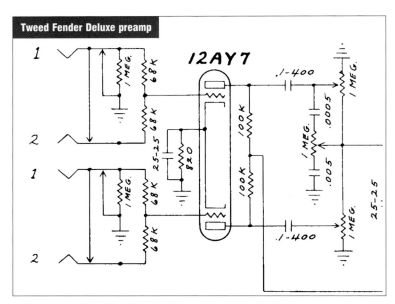

**Tweed Fender Deluxe preamp**

**Preamp stage in a tweed Fender Deluxe. The 820-ohm bias resistor in the first gain stage isn't increasing the tube's gain from that of a Princeton, because the 12AY7's two cathodes are biased together here, which requires halving the resistor value.**

Some contemporary makers—TopHat, for one—provide different bypass cap values on a switch to offer selectable voicings (which that maker generally uses on the 12AX7 in a cathode-follower EQ stage). A three-way on/off/on switch with the cathode resistor always to ground and 25uF/none/0.68uF cap selections bypassing it to ground would give fat boost, no boost, high boost, in that order. (It's an extremely simple but versatile voicing switch which we can easily try in our DIY amp project in Chapter Nine.)

The DC voltage on the plates of the individual gain stages will also affect both the sound and feel of the stage, and of the amp as a whole. Amps of a more "vintage" design usually have around 150VDC on the plates of the first gain stages, as does our Princeton and all other tweed Fenders (give or take 10 volts), classic Marshalls, Vox AC30s, early Gibsons, Valcos, and so on, and a lot of newer amps that emulate these designs. Given a fixed cathode resistor, higher voltages yield higher gain from the triode stage, but of course it's easy for any designer to alter that resistor to get about the same gain levels at any practical plate voltage. Plate voltages are crucial, though, in helping to determine the "feel" of the amp. Lower voltages in this range are often a contributing factor to the designs of amps described as being more touch-sensitive, tactile, and dynamic—amps that are a little "softer" in feel—meaning the player has a great amount of control over the amp's response just by manipulating the strength of his or her pick attack.

With many great amp designs, you can set the volume at a point just on the edge of breakup, and achieve a range of textures through pick attack alone: pick gently for sparkling, liquid clean sounds; dig in a little harder for crunchy rhythm work; or really attack the strings for overdriven lead sounds or meaty power chords. If you've never experienced dynamics like this, it's a real surprise when you discover such versatility in a good tube amp. It instantly makes a mockery of the derogatory "one-sound amp" tag that so many traditional designs got labeled with during the channel-switching amp boom era.

Blackface Fender amps of 1963-67 (and the silverfaces after them) commonly have from 210VDC to 230VDC on the plates of the first preamp gain stage, and some players find them less touch-sensitive at this point, partly for that reason. The change works toward other goals, though, and it's really a matter of horses for courses—different amps suit different players and styles. Higher first preamp-stage plate voltages are also found on a wide range of amps, including models like the Vox AC50 and a number of larger Traynor and Sunn amps, all of which have the goal of achieving a tight response with high headroom. Don't get me wrong, good versions of these models can still be very dynamic and pretty touch-sensitive, but parameters have shifted with these types, and the preamp plate voltages do make a difference.

The evolution from simple to more complex preamps isn't necessarily a chronological thing— which is to say it isn't truly an "evolution" at all. Ever since the main designs established themselves in the late 1950s and early 1960s, makers have simultaneously offered small amps with very simple preamps and larger amps with more complex circuits. Many versions of each type continue to be made today to much the same designs. Other than the multi-staged preamps of high-gain amps that have proliferated since the 1980s, the thing that will most often complicate a preamp beyond a single gain stage is the necessity of a gain makeup stage to bring signal levels back up after a tone stage has depleted them.

There's a quick lesson to be learned in this: for the most part, the more components you put into an amp in general, the more the signal level will suffer as it passes through all the potentiometers and other parts, meaning you have to put in even more in the form of extra tubes to re-amplify the signal and boost it for its journey to the output stage. The most obvious example of this is the gain makeup stage that follows the tone controls on the Normal channel of a larger blackface Fender, such as a Super Reverb, Pro Reverb, Twin Reverb, and so forth; and plenty of other makes follow the same topology—the Silvertone 1484 and 1485, Selmer Treble'n'Bass, and countless larger amps from a range of contemporary makers. Sometimes these added gain stages can add to an amp's sonic virtue, and sometimes they might detract from it. It all depends on how well the design and build are rendered, and what you are seeking to hear in an amp.

You can see from the diagram of a Silvertone 1485's preamp section on p46 that the first gain stage (involving half of a dual-triode tube) looks much like that of our Princeton's one and only gain stage, but following the Bass, Treble and Volume controls the signal is boosted by another triode before being sent on to the phase inverter (PI).

The Vibrato channel of the larger silverface Fender amps is a little more complicated still. These amps have Treble, Bass, Middle and Volume controls between the same two gain stages, but they put the signal through a third gain stage after the post-tone-stack gain makeup stage. It's interesting to note that the two channels—usually labeled Normal and Vibrato—bear an out-of-phase relationship to each other in these blackface and silverface Fenders: the signal reverses phase each time it passes through a triode stage, so the differing numbers of such stages here account for this factor. It doesn't mean much when the channels are used independently, but players trying to jumper them together to achieve a fatter sound, as they might do with earlier tweed amps, quickly discover that this can't be done satisfactorily (a "jumpered" connection is achieved by plugging your

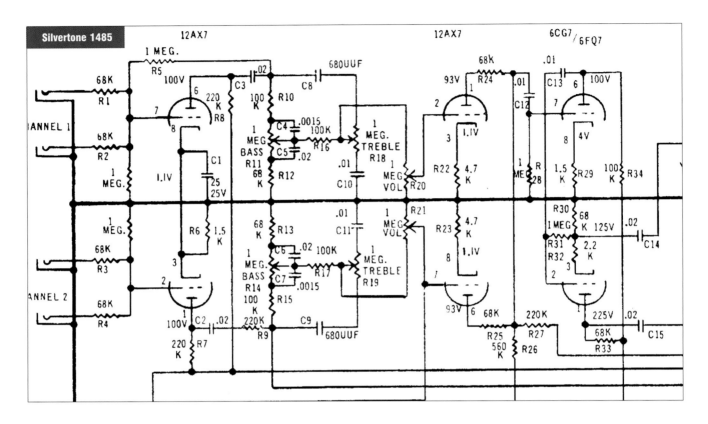

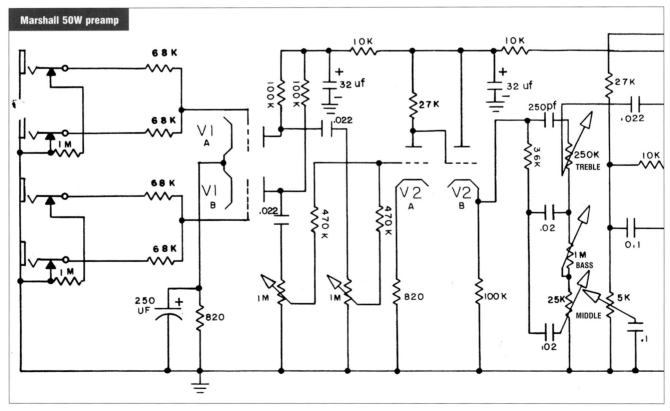

instrument into Input 1 of one channel and running a short lead from Input 2 of that channel to Input 1 of the other channel). In fact, with both volume controls set close to the same positions, the two channels' signals will partially cancel out each other.

These preamp designs were happening at Fender by late 1960, and at some other makers around that time or soon after, but in the tweed years an equally stage-heavy preamp circuit had already been in use. Larger narrow-panel tweed Fender amps like the Bassman, Pro, Super and Twin, and subsequently the Marshalls that closely copied them, had their gain makeup stages *before* the tone controls, so they weren't really makeup stages at all, but boosted the levels even higher after the first gain stage to help it survive its trip through the two or three-knob tone section that followed. (See Marshall 50W preamp diagram on p46.)

Again, the first gain stage looks much like that of our Princeton: the signal exits the first triode at the plate and heads for a volume pot via a 0.02uF cap. After that, though, both sides of a dual-triode tube are used to amplify it further. The classic Hiwatt preamp similarly boosts the signal prior to the tone stage, rather than adding a stage afterward to make it up again, but does it with a single triode and a slightly different configuration overall.

Other makers were certainly using some different designs at that time, but nothing of much importance varied widely from these topologies until the Mesa/Boogie format was established in the early 1970s. In rhythm mode, the Mesa/Boogie MkI goes through a first gain stage, then the tone stack and volume control, then a gain makeup stage, then a further gain stage before heading on toward the output—not unlike the three-triode gain stages of a blackface Fender's Vibrato channel. But when it's plugged into the lead input, the guitar signal journeys through an extra first gain stage, with related volume control, before joining the rhythm channel's path. In this mode the signal level can be governed by the player in three different places: at volume controls following each of the first two gain stages and again at a master volume placed right before the signal exits the preamp for the output stage.

This type of preamp (the schematic for which is seen at the top of p48) is called a cascading gain circuit, because the gain levels of four triode stages in series are configured to spill over one into the other. By cranking up the first volume control, the following gain stage can be driven into overdrive, regardless of how much signal is ultimately sent on to the output tubes via the master volume. This is where that sizzling, ultra-saturated preamp distortion sound was born; it became a hot item in the late 1970s and the 1980s, and has been with us ever since.

The Mesa/Boogie MkII series added a fifth gain stage to the preamp in lead mode (now footswitchable), and configured them slightly differently, with a total of four volume controls in the signal path—including a lead master and output master—to govern how much gain cascaded over from one stage to the next. With all of this preamp-tube distortion going on, the Mesa/Boogie's output stage is usually not driven into distortion itself, but is designed to provide a fairly accurate amplification of the high-gain signal coming into it. Run like an "old-fashioned" non-master-volume amp—with the rhythm channel selected, the master volume maxed and the clean volume cranked up enough to introduce some power tube breakup—it can behave a little like an amp with fewer preamp gain stages, but it really isn't configured to sound its best in this mode. That said, plenty such amps have great sounding clean channels, too, depending what you're looking for.

The success of Randall Smith's ultra-hot Mesa/Boogie preamp designs sent other major

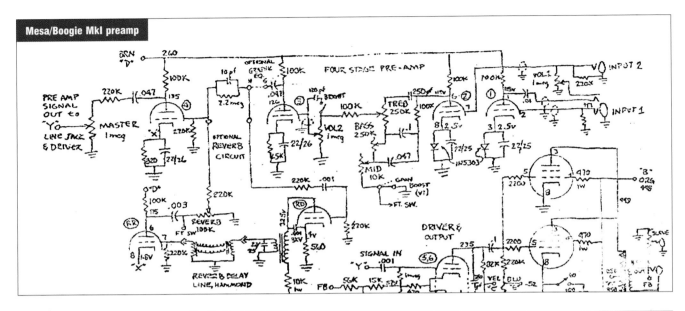

Mesa/Boogie MkI preamp

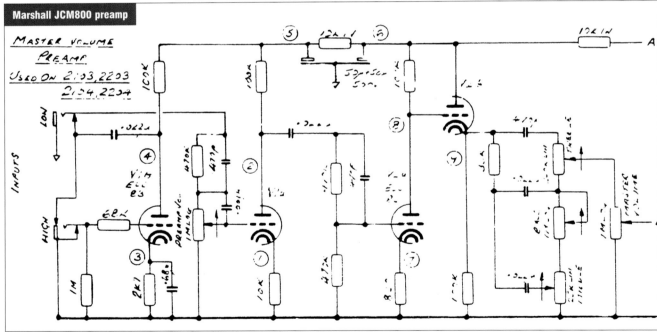

Marshall JCM800 preamp

manufacturers scrambling to emulate the sound. By the mid 1970s Marshall, Fender and most other makers carried master volumes on their amps, and often added gain or "boost" stages besides. Marshall's new flagship model of the 1980s, the JCM800, was one such amp that made a name for itself in the waning of what we could call "the vintage years" of that maker.

The JCM800, introduced in 1981, had a preamp circuit that was considerably different even from Marshall's Master Volume models that had preceded it. Almost any amp with a master volume control allows you to max out the first gain stage for preamp distortion, while reining in the output for lower volume levels, and this is the way Fender, Marshall, Traynor, Peavey, and others were doing it through much of the 1970s. But the JCM800 (left) added a hotter preamp on top of the master volume configuration, which in some ways was like the first couple of stages of the Mesa/Boogie MkI. The new Marshall design had four gain stages in lead mode, but placed and configured its tone stack differently—basically in a more traditionally Marshall fashion (or tweed Bassman, if you prefer).

In lead mode (with guitar plugged into the High input), a fourth triode is added to the signal chain to provide an extra gain stage at the front of the preamp, giving a considerable boost to the signal. Plugging into the Low input bypasses that first gain stage to follow a path that's not terribly unlike that of the classic Model 1987 plexi models, although it now has a volume control placed slightly awkwardly in front of its first gain stage. In any case, the lead mode is what most players sought out these new Marshalls for, and that extra half a triode made for one hot rock amp.

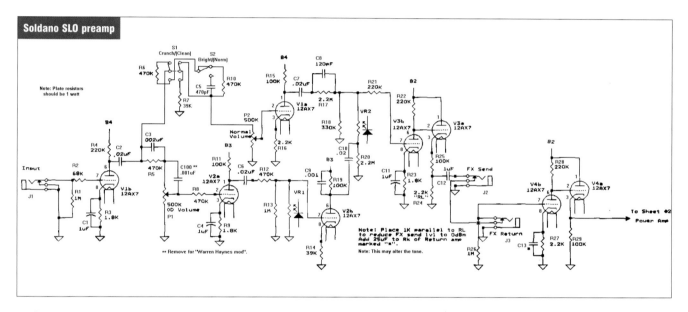

**Soldano SLO preamp**

Other makers appeared who specialized purely in the high-gain market, though they often included some pretty sultry vintage-voiced clean channels as well. Rivera and Soldano arrived in the mid 1980s, and pretty quickly made big names for themselves in the rock and blues-rock arenas. Soldano's SLO (Super Lead Overdrive) was a high-gain beast aimed at the rock lead player. In overdrive mode, this amp's preamp (above) adds an extra two triode gain stages in parallel to the signal chain that the clean channel runs through. This makes for two gain stages in clean or crunch mode, and three in overdrive, running parallel up to the point of the FX loop driver, which is shared by both channels.

The clean channel remains on even when overdrive (OD) is switched in, but its sound is swamped by the OD's much higher gain. Interestingly, though, the clean and overdrive channels are out of phase with each other (as mentioned in context of the old black/silverface Fenders, the signal reverses phase each time it passes through a triode stage), so some players feel that having even low levels of the clean channel in circuit can deplete from the OD's frequency response. Most don't notice it, amid the buzzsaw of this amp's grind and wail. In any case, it's a clever preamp that can appear complicated from one perspective, but really quite simple from another.

Other modern preamp designs can be equally or more complicated; Peavey's 5150 has as many as six triode stages in the circuit before the signal even reaches the tone stage, with plenty of other complex switching and voicing networks running alongside the signal chain. The OD channel of Bogner's high-gain Ecstasy amp runs five triode stages before the tone stack, with quite a few clever little voicing networks running off the signal path along the way, but nothing like the switching complexity of the 5150.

We've now looked at a handful of quite different preamp configurations, and hopefully have come to some understanding of how few or many gain stages can work together to create clean, crunch, or extreme overdrive sounds—all still preamp-generated at this point. But more than just stacking up tube gain stages, clever designers also clearly use various voicing and gain-governing techniques, comprising different bias points on preamp tubes, little high-pass and/or low-pass networks strung along the signal chain, and other techniques in order to tailor the overall tone and gain of their preamp designs.

We've come a long way from the pure and uncluttered single gain stage of our tweed Princeton. So let's now plug a range of tone stages into the equation.

## TONE STACKS

Our Princeton's tone circuit is an extremely simple one, and somewhat limited too, but other configurations of tone stages can be an effective part of an amp's sound-shaping capabilities. Many tone stages, or "tone stacks," do more than merely shape the frequency range that's passed along the signal chain, and in fact can provide a further means of boosting or cutting the gain of the signal that passes through them. Many experienced players know how to use even the simplest one, two and three-knob tone sections to really shape the sound and feel of an amp, rather than merely to cut highs, mids or lows.

The tone stacks in most guitar amps are passive networks, which is to say they don't provide any boost of the frequency range they govern, but merely tap off different portions of it to ground, enabling you to voice your signal through what remains. Even so, such passive networks can often be extremely interactive, and some simple bass and treble circuits behave a little differently than you might at first guess.

Even if our 5F2 Princeton's single tone control isn't especially clever, many other single-knob tone stages can be surprisingly versatile. The version on the 5F2A that followed was pretty effective, and didn't impinge on the volume control's function as much. The single tone control on the classic 5E3 tweed Deluxe (left) works similarly, using two caps—a 500pF and 0.005uF—for frequency filtering, but is connected to the volume controls somewhat in the reverse fashion. Even so, it's a pretty effective knob: keep it down in the 4 to 6 range (out of 12 on the tweed scale) and the amp is warm and mellow; wind it up to 7 or 8 and

Fender 5E3 Deluxe tone section

beyond, and it not only brightens up the signal, but adds a little more crunch to the brew as well.

The way in which the signal path splits off toward both the tone and volume control might remind us of the Princeton, but the reverse wiring of the Deluxe's volume pot seems to enable the tone control to function a little more as desired. Again, though, this control doesn't add highs to the signal, it merely cuts them as you wind it down, while also letting through a little less gain as the sound mellows.

The sole tone control on a Vox AC15's normal channel is a little simpler still, tapping part of the signal to ground via a single 0.022 cap; and the one on the little AC4 works in the same way. Some very straightforward boutique amps don't use a whole lot more than any of the above. The Matchless Spitfire, for example, employs a very slightly modified and improved version of the 5E3 tweed Fender Deluxe tone-pot arrangement, with a more logical layout and different capacitor values. Again, all of the above are just filters, much like the tone controls on your Stratocaster, Les Paul, or ES-175. They channel some of the high frequencies away from the signal chain, but don't add anything to it. As such, "full up" actually represents the signal's natural state, but few ears can take the onslaught of treble that this usually induces.

The really legendary step up from these one-knob wonders—both chronologically and technologically—is the three-pot tone stack shared by the larger tweed Fenders of the late 50s, the classic Marshall JTM45 and JTM50 plexi and many later models, and the Vox AC30 Top Boost circuit (as a two-knob tone stack in this case). On Fender's larger new narrow-panel tweed amps of 1955, the single tone pot was upped to a pair to give separate control over treble and bass. A presence control was also included, although this functioned in the "negative feedback loop" between the speaker output and the cathode of the PI, and not in the tone stack itself.

The actual tone controls were configured in a "cathode-follower" stage, between the cathode of a second gain stage made up of two triodes (one 12AX7) and the input to the PI. This positioning has become legendary among many guitarists for yielding great dynamics and player sensitivity— often just referred to as "touch'—and for helping to make the amps that carry such circuits especially sensitive instruments in themselves.

This tone stack reached its zenith on the "F" series Bassman and Twin circuits of around 1958, where a middle control was added for the first time, to give a three-knob tone section plus presence control (see Bassman detail in diagram on p52).

Fender only stuck with its cathode-follower tone stack for around five years—and its climactic three-knob version for about three—before changing it completely in the brownface amps of 1960 and the blackface amps that followed, in the quest for a cleaner preamp signal and more headroom. But because Marshall lifted its circuit wholly from a 5F6A Bassman in 1962, this tone stage was passed on to the British legend, and it resided across the pond a lot longer than it had stayed with Fender, remaining a mainstay of many Marshall circuits to this day.

While players talk of great differences between Marshall's classic original JTM45 and the following JTM50 plexi (either of which is fantastic, depending upon what you're looking for), the circuit under the hood remained much the same, and in fact that Bassman-inspired, cathode-follower tone stack plus presence control can still be identified in vintage Marshalls up into the 1970s, and even in more modern designs well beyond this. The changes between the JTM45 and plexi had more to do with rectifiers, voltages and transformers—all of which were enough to alter

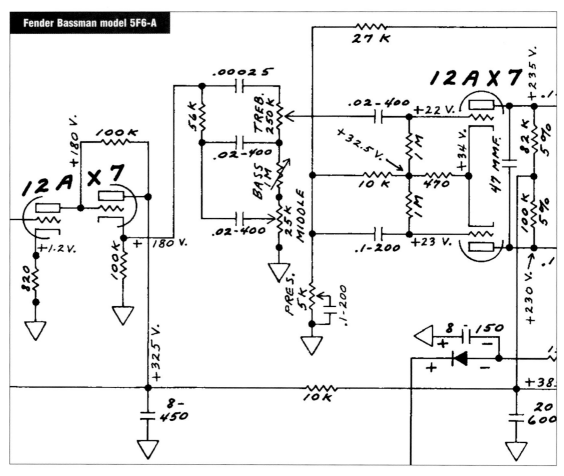

Fender Bassman model 5F6-A

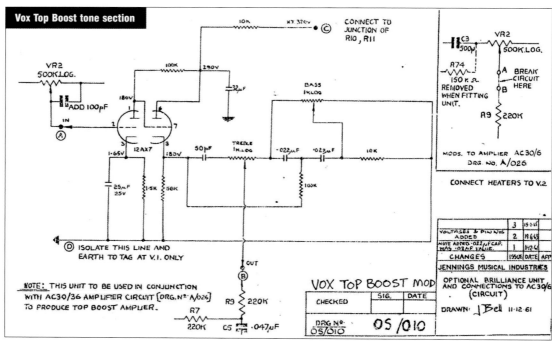

Vox Top Boost tone section

the sound noticeably, even with the signal running through much the same preamp and tone-stack circuits.

A look at the schematics of a few other very different makers shows two- and three-knob cathode-follower tone stacks popping up in some more surprising places. Not many players associate the sound of a Vox AC30 with that of either a tweed Super or a Marshall stack, but trace the basic circuit of the famous Top Boost tone stage on (p52) and you soon see that's what you're looking at. Legend has it that the Top Boost circuit was actually lifted from a tweed-era Gibson amp, the GA-70, but other than an odd grounding of the far side of the bass pot this EQ network is very similar to that used on the mid-sized Fenders of the era.

Top Boost arrived in 1961 as a back-to-factory retrofit on the AC30, and became a standard upgrade option in 1964. The "cut" control that these amps also carried might seem to act like a reverse presence control, damping high frequencies as it's turned up, but in fact it is placed in a very different part of the circuit, between the PI and the output tubes, rather than between the amp's output and the front of the PI, as a presence control would be.

Variables in other parts of the Vox circuit mean that the Top Boost tone stack functions somewhat differently in these amps than it does in Fenders, Gibsons and Marshalls. On the AC30, the bass and treble controls feel even more active and interactive, and extreme settings of one without consideration of the other can produce some slightly odd voices. Used wisely, though, they make another very effective tone stack, and boutique makers from Matchless to 65amps to Top Hat have employed variations of the circuit in their amps in recent years. With the 12AX7 preamp tubes run at higher voltages, as they often are in these designs, and other factors working toward an extremely bright, crisp signal—which the EL84 output tubes only accentuate—this tone stack can sound spikey and icepick-sharp if used in anger. Many players find themselves winding the treble control down well below the halfway mark, which would be unusual on most other amps. But the extent to which all these amps have proved themselves legendary speaks for itself: obviously the cathode-follower tone stack is helping to work some magic in there too.

Some Traynor amps used the cathode-follower tone stack in a more Marshallesque fashion, notably the YGA-1 and the YBA-1 Bass Master, and the latter even carried 6CA7 output tubes, the North American equivalent of the British EL34. Other Traynors used a range of both simpler and more complex tone stages—such as the complex treble and bass expander networks on the YBA-3 Custom Special.

When Fender moved away from this configuration, it did so with a broad stroke. The sonic goal throughout most of Fender's earlier years—as it was for most amp companies at the time—was to achieve the maximum volume with the minimum of distortion. Beginning with the Vibrosonic Amp introduced at the summer NAMM show of 1959, and carrying on through the entire new Tolex-covered line-up of amps in 1960 (in other words, the brownface amps that preceded the blackface era), Fender totally redesigned its tone stack in order to offer independent controls on each of two different channels.

The new circuit did away with the shared cathode-follower stage that followed the first triode gain stage in each channel, and put the tone stack between the two triodes of a single tube. This offered what, with hindsight, probably looks like a more conventional topology than what had preceded it: a first gain stage, followed by a tone stage and a volume control, followed by another

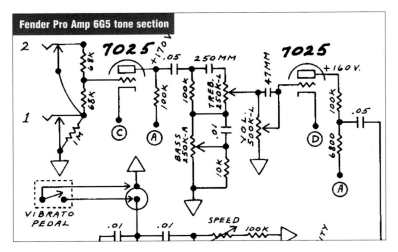

Fender Pro Amp 6G5 tone section

triode stage for gain makeup. (See Pro Amp schematic detail, left, for an example of Fender brownface/blackface tone section.)

The result was successful in terms of passing along a cleaner signal to the PI, and therefore squeezing a little more headroom out of the amplifier overall. Many players feel, though, that these amps sacrificed some of the dynamics and touch sensitivity of the tweed designs, so there was certainly a trade-off, even if Fender and others using this circuit didn't see it as such. It's undeniable that many of the good brown, black, and silverface Fender amps using this tone stack still have bags of touch sensitivity and dynamics, so I don't mean to imply that the change choked them off entirely. Marshall, of course, stuck with the cathode-follower tone stack, and it's interesting to see how many blues-rock and trad-rock players fall into two different camps today: the tweed Fender and/or Marshall players, and the blackface Fender players. The former tend to enjoy a little grit and sizzle in their tone, while the latter seek definition and articulation. The new tone stack also lost the Middle control that the biggest Fenders had for a few years, and they didn't regain it until the Twin Reverb and Super Reverb of 1963.

Hiwatt amps were always seeking to achieve more clean power and undistorted punch than their British rivals Marshall, and they carried a tone stack that suited this goal. They might have looked, externally, much like a restyled Marshall, but under the hood they were put together with very different objectives in mind. Following two fairly straightforward triode gain stages per channel, with a volume control between each, Hiwatt placed a three-pot tone stack that was a little more complex than either the Fender/Marshall cathode-follower or the blackface topology that followed. A further two triodes followed these controls for gain makeup. In all, the design helped to make Hiwatts into bold, powerful amplifiers.

Tone stages in the majority of tube amps made today follow either the Fender tweed (aka Marshall) cathode-follower, Fender blackface, or Vox Top Boost topologies, but a few more original designs do exist. Dr Z uses a fairly simple but clever and unusual tone stage in his Route 66 and Z28 amps, partly enabled by the high-gain EF86 in the preamp, which doesn't require a gain makeup stage. The bass and treble controls in these amps are both highly effective at frequency sculpting, and also play a large part in passing higher gain levels along to the output stage, via the single volume control that follows them. Makers like Garnet, Orange, Magnatone, Traynor, Ampeg and a few others have occasionally used a tone stack derived from the hi-fi world that's known as the "Baxandall" tone circuit. This offers broader control over frequency attenuation than the traditional cathode-follower tone stack used by Fender, Marshall and Vox, but doesn't seem to be sonically flattering in all amps.

From the simple to the complex, there is usually more going on behind a tone, bass, treble or middle control knob than the label on the front panel might suggest. Not only do most of these stages help to shape the voice of the amp, but they can often play a big part in determining gain and headroom, and overall playing feel too. As we've seen, the same tone stage can also behave differently depending on the preamp stages that precede it, and the output stages that follow it.

## EFFECTS AND LOOPS

There are too many variations on the effects circuits that appear in guitar amps to get to all of them here, but I'll dig into a few to give you an idea of where they're placed, and how they might affect your tone—both when switched in, and switched out. The main effects of interest to us here are tremolo, reverb, and effects loops (the latter more the potential for further effects than an effect in itself). In traditional tube amp circuits, including those built today to trad-inspired designs (as so many still are), the simple answer is to say that most onboard effects are placed after the assorted preamp gain stages and the tone stack but before the PI, but often it isn't as straightforward as that. In many cases, your signal doesn't actually pass through an onboard effects circuit, or not entirely at least. These are usually run as side chains that are blended back in with the dry signal further down the line, at a proportion determined by your setting of the depth, mix, or intensity knob.

## Tremolo

The oldest of onboard amp effects, tremolo has come throbbing back with a vengeance in recent years. As simple as it is, this relatively simple effect is perhaps better appreciated now than ever before for the texture and atmosphere it can give to your tone. Properly speaking, tremolo is the modulation of a signal's strength (volume), while vibrato is the modulation of frequency (pitch). Fender, one of the big names in tremolo-equipped amps, muddied the waters early in the game by referring to the effect as "vibrato" on many of its amps' control panels and accompanying literature, when the circuit within actually created a tremolo sound—other than in a handful of more complex early 60s brownface amps that approach something akin to subtle pitch-modulating vibrato. Several of Magnatone's larger amps have also produced true vibrato, as have a few others, but by and large you will find this effect as tremolo 95 per cent of the time.

As simple as it sounds, tremolo can be created in a vast number of ways. Essentially, any circuit that interrupts the steady signal at a desired rate determined by a speed knob will do the trick. While, on paper, you'd think any circuit that successfully produced tremolo at a useful range of depths and speeds would sound about the same, different types do have their fans, and will indeed display nuanced differences of tone when compared closely.

Many of the earliest tremolo-equipped amps used bias-modulating (oscillating) circuits, which didn't carry the signal at all, but instead acted upon a tube further down the line—most commonly in the output stage—to modulate its bias, switching it on and off at the desired rate, to produce the effect. Such circuits can modulate the bias voltage applied to the grids of

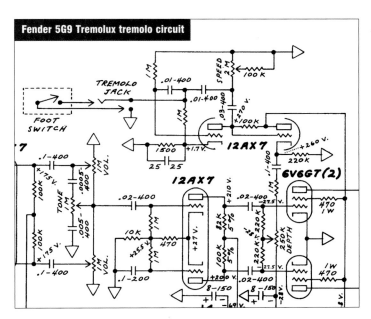

Fender 5G9 Tremolux tremolo circuit

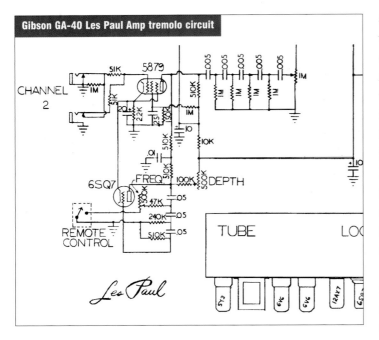

Gibson GA-40 Les Paul Amp tremolo circuit

an amp's output tubes, or it can do its thing by wiggling the bias of the PI tube or even a signal-carrying preamp tube. Many early Gibson, Valco and Ampeg models carried bias-modulated tremolo, and this was the type of tremolo that arrived on Fender's first trem-equipped amp, the 1955 Tremolux (p55). Early iterations of the tweed Tremolux, which was first issued in a cathode-biased amp as the 5E9, used 12AX7-powered bias-modulating circuits attached to the PI. In 1957 Fender changed the amp to a more efficient fixed-bias output stage for the 5G9 model, and produced the tremolo by modulating the bias on the output tubes.

Fans of bias-modulating tremolo talk about its warmth and richness, and the infectious swampiness of its pulse. To be fair, these adjectives might apply to any great amp-generated tremolo (and several good pedal-generated renditions too, perhaps), but the best renditions of these early circuits do seem to have such qualities in abundance. Another bonus of the bias-modulating tremolo is that, in most cases, it works on both channels of a two-channel amp, since it does its thing post-preamp.

Signal-modulating tremolo circuits certainly have their fans, too, and plenty of them sound outstanding. One of the favorite early renditions is possibly that found in Gibson's GA-40 Les Paul Amp of the mid 50s to early 60s (above). A fairly complex circuit, it uses an octal-based 6SQ7 tube in a network that oscillates the signal as it leaves the 5879 pentode preamp tube in the amp's second channel.

Signal-modulating tremolo often affects just one channel, since it works directly on an individual

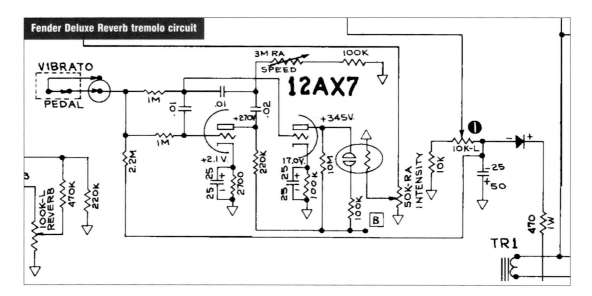

Fender Deluxe Reverb tremolo circuit

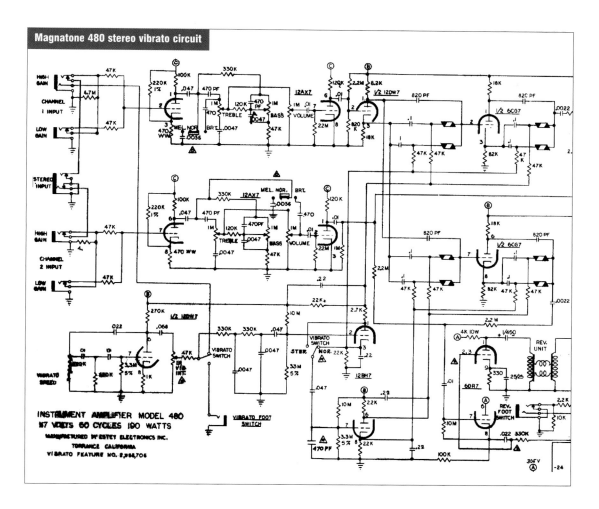

Magnatone 480 stereo vibrato circuit

preamp circuit's signal path. The most common rendition of this effect is that found in the blackface and silverface Fender amps, which to many players represent the standard for reverb-and-tremolo-equipped guitar amplifiers. When these amps were introduced in 1963, Fender also introduced its new tremolo effect (opposite page), which acted upon the amp's second channel by way of a 12AX7-powered circuit employing an opto-cell to oscillate the signal on its way to the phase inverter. It's interesting to note that, contrary to most "effects logic," the tremolo happens after the reverb in Fender amps that carry these effects. Also, a simple modification can apply the effect to both channels on blackface and silverface amps (available as performed by Brinsley Schwartz in Aspen Pittman's *The Tube Amp Book: Deluxe Revised Edition*, as well as from other sources).

Fender fans rave about the "true vibrato" in the larger brownface amps of 1960-63, which is really just barely an approximation of pitch-shifting vibrato (while sounding glorious regardless). The king of vibrato, however, is arguably found in several Magnatone models of the 50s and 60s, some of which—like the 480 (above)—even produced a true stereo vibrato that can be otherworldly. The Magnatone vibrato is backed by a whopper of a circuit, powered by several more obscure preamp tube types, and you'd hate to foot the bill for any major repairs to a failed vintage example, but wow, what a sound.

As impressive as the Fender brownface and Magnatone vibrato effects can sound, they can also

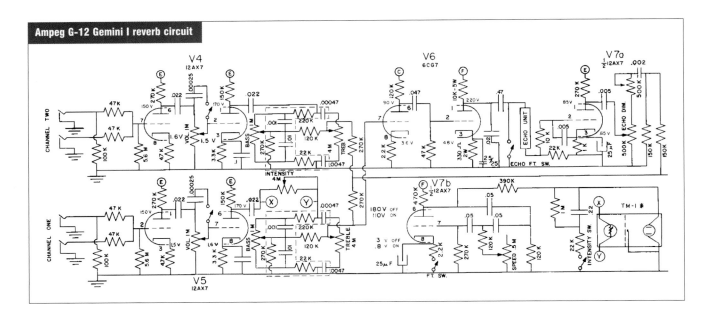

Ampeg G-12 Gemini I reverb circuit

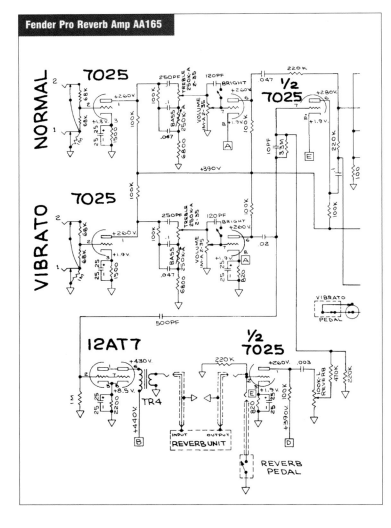

Fender Pro Reverb Amp AA165

be too much of an "effect" for some situations, if you see what I mean. After a few tunes—for some styles of playing, at least—that pitch-warbling wobble can often sound a bit of a novelty item, and a little wearing on the ear, where standard old tremolo, when done well, rarely becomes tiring. Still, it can be an amazing sound, and one you should experience firsthand at some point in your playing career.

## Reverb

Reverb effects generally follow more of a route you'd expect from any signal tampering: the signal chain is tapped off into the reverb circuit, amplified through the reverb springs, and blended back into the dry signal that passes around it. You might guess that the signal is sent off to the reverb circuit in a proportion determined by the control labeled "reverb" or "depth" or "echo" or whatever, but in fact it's almost always configured as fully tapped into this circuit, and only blended back proportionally by the control setting.

Ampeg is considered, by many, to have produced the lushest and sweetest reverb of the vintage crowd, but these amps did so much in the same way most others have done: using a side-chain effect with a driver tube pushing a signal into a reverb tank, and a recovery tube following, with a blender pot (labeled "Echo" on many vintage Ampegs) to mix the wet signal back into the dry as it enters the PI (schematic top left).

Once again, however, the Fender blackface and silverface amps—which almost every guitarist will have at least played through at some time, if not owned—very much set the standard for reverb, which is not to say they are the very best, but a very good reverb on a line of amps that is otherwise extremely versatile and popular, too. Somewhat like the Ampeg circuit—although different in many details—the standard Fender blackface reverb (bottom left) uses one preamp tube to drive the reverb signal (this time it's a 12AT7, and wired in parallel to act as a single gain stage), with another half of a 7025 (or 12AX7) to recover the signal from the reverb spring pan, and the second half of that tube to further boost it before sending it onward. It's interesting to note that these reverb circuits are really little amplifier circuits in and of themselves: think of the springs as the speaker, the 12AT7 in front of it as a low-wattage output stage, and the 7025 after it as a preamp to recover the signal from the transducer at the output end of the springs. In the archetypal Fender reverb amp the effect, like the tremolo, functions only on the second channel (often labeled Vibrato), but mods are available to make it work on both channels.

## Effects Loops

The effects placement that's most relevant to modern amps, when we're talking about inter-circuit effects rather than pedals placed before the input, usually happens in an effects loop. This "loop" can be seen as a pair of jacks that break the circuit, one at the output of the preamp, a second at the input of the power amp.

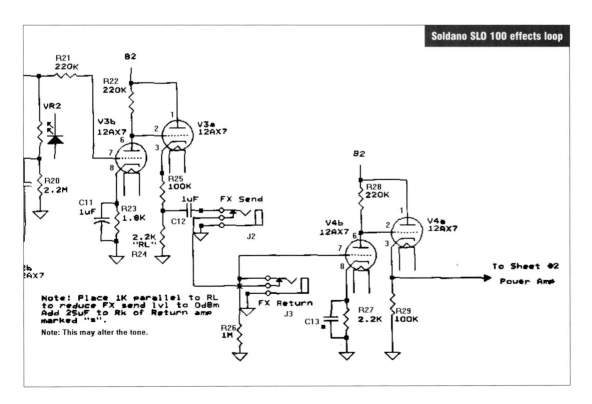

Effects loops come in two flavors—series and parallel. The series loop takes the entire signal through whatever effects are inserted in the chain, which can be a long and seriously tone-depleting detour in some cases. The parallel loop does exactly what it says, and runs parallel to the signal chain, with a control labeled "blend," "mix," or "level" to tap off a desired signal blend into the effects network. Both can be "buffered" or "unbuffered." A buffered effects loop has its own driver and recovery stages (provided either by tube triodes or transistors) to help drive and reamplify levels as necessary. Unbuffered loops are entirely passive and have no related circuitry other than a straightforward break in the signal path afforded by two jacks. Effects loops of the latter type tend to use a pair of switching jacks wired up so that the signal is passed directly from one to the other when nothing is plugged into the "send," otherwise a jumper cable would need to be inserted between them to complete the path. Even some high-end amps are surprising homes to the unbuffered, straight-out, straight-in series effects loop—the Matchless DC30 for one—and it's by far the simplest means of sticking certain effects between your amp's own tube preamp and tube output stages.

All effects loops can cough up tone-loss trouble spots if not designed well or used correctly, and this is one place to look if you feel your multi-effected sound has lost a lot of its guts or clarity in "dry" mode. Series loops inevitably connect long cable lengths in the signal path, as well as roping in all the switching and wiring runs within the effects themselves, so a lot of capacitance can be added to the signal (otherwise know as "tone sucking'). This saps some of the clarity, punch and dynamics from your sound, and generally weakens it slightly. If your sound involves a lot of effects, then a little of this really isn't something to worry about. The effects will mask the minimal losses, and your end result should be entirely satisfactory. As ever, it's the end result that matters. If, on the other hand, you only use the effects occasionally or for a little spice on the side and rely mainly on the virtue of your dry tone, you might want to find other ways of getting these effects into your sound chain, rather than loading up a potentially tone-sucking loop.

Avoiding tone-sucking is one of the main jobs of a well-designed effects loop. A quality buffer, tube or solid-state, should help to get your signal through all the outboard wire and effects and back again without too much depletion of its original character and dynamics. But if you don't need the types of outboard effect that are used within effects loops, you might find more satisfaction playing an amp that doesn't have one, because you might be paying for the added feature—in both cash and tone loss. Then again, if the amp that nails "your sound" just happens to have an effects loop in the circuit that you don't need, simply ignore it. With nothing plugged into it, a good loop should behave as if it isn't there.

Effects most commonly used within the loop include those that sound best after the preamp and overdrive processing—things like reverb, delay, and sometimes chorus and other modulation effects. Some players like to place their vintage analog chorus and phaser pedals in front of overdrive pedals or preamp stages, and in such cases you just have to play around with pedal orders to decide what's right for you.

As a rule of thumb, most rack effects work best in a loop, although those with overdrive or distortion facilities should be placed before the amp's input. In some cases, more sophisticated multi-FX units offer a split of functions, letting you tap the OD section into your amp's front end, and run from the amp's loop send back into the FX unit for the delay functions, and back to the amp loop return again. The majority of pedals, especially older ones, will sound best plugged into the front of the amp. Distortions, overdrives, compressors and wah-wahs fit this category. Others might be optional as far as front-end versus loop placement goes. Do check, though, that any effect used within a loop is able to withstand the output levels it will see from the amp's effects loop send. Comparing specs from both the amplifier and the effects unit in question should give you the answer to this.

## OUTPUT STAGES

The output stage, properly speaking, consists of the driver or phase inverter (PI), the output tubes, the output transformer, and all circuitry related to their function. You will find all of these elements in any separate tube power amp, a hi-fi amp for example, and although people often group the PI in with the preamp in discussing guitar amps—because it employs the same tube type—it really lives in the output stage. We examined output tubes and output transformers in some depth in Chapter Two, but there is a lot more to investigate regarding this stage. Phase inverter topologies can vary greatly in sound and performance, and other factors like biasing techniques, class of operation (whether class A or class AB), the presence or lack of a negative feedback loop and so forth can greatly influence the sound of any given output stage, and therefore of the amp as a whole.

### Phase Inverters

The driver or phase inverter is the gateway to the output stage. In amps that carry just one output tube, such as our Princeton, only a single triode is needed here to produce the current required to drive the bigger tube. A few single-ended amps even carry preamp tubes that are powerful enough to drive the output tubes on their own—the Vox AC4 for one, with an EF86 driving an EL84 all on its own (the amp's 12AX7 is used entirely for tremolo)—but these are rare indeed. In amps with two or more tubes in push-pull, an entire dual triode is used for driver/phase inversion duties. The job here is to take the AC signal from the preamp and split it into two different AC signals of equal strength (current) but in opposite phase to each other. And while this is more of a functional operation than a tone-shaping one, the way different phase-inverter designs perform their duties has a major impact on an amp's overall sound, and its distortion content and character in particular.

The king of all phase inverters is the "long-tailed pair"—so-called because of the "tail" of the two-into-one resistors coming from the linked cathodes as it appears on most schematic diagrams—which was in use by Fender by around 1958, and by others like Vox and Gibson soon after, and of course Marshall by 1962, having been inspired by Fender. The vast majority of quality medium-to-large amps have used this design

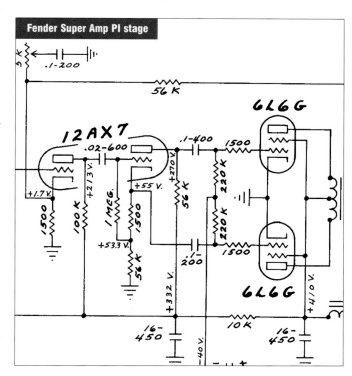

**Fender Super Amp PI stage**

since that time, and they can thank it for passing a clean, true signal from preamp to output stage. But it was not always thus. Many guitar amps of the late 1940s and early 1950s were using a perfectly functional but far less linear phase inverter derived from the paraphase or self-balancing paraphase topology. These split and inverted the signal just fine, but were incapable of delivering a clean, linear load to the output tubes, and in fact distorted at levels well short of what larger tubes like 6L6s would otherwise have been capable of achieving. Many players relish these amps for their great blues and vintage rock'n'roll sounds, characterized by a smooth, early distortion with lots of compression and attenuation of both highs and lows. If you're looking for any power, punch, twang or clean bite—or even the genuine sound of large output tubes being pushed to distortion—a different PI is required.

By the mid 1950s a lot of amps, including Fender's "E" series, carried the more efficient split-load PI, also called the "cathodyne" or concertina inverter (best known in the 5E3 tweed Deluxe, but also seen in some larger amps like the Pro and Super, which still had it in the "F" series). This design uses one triode of a 12AX7 to ramp up the necessary current, and the second half to split the signal, sending one leg off from the plate and one from the cathode. The split-load PI is capable of producing a sharper signal with a little better fidelity than the earlier paraphase PI, but when pushed hard it still offers up some of its own distortion, and therefore is still unable to push the output tubes to their own maximum potential before—and during—distortion. Its distortion is a little sweeter and richer than the paraphrase and is a big part of the mid-sized tweed Fender sound, but it still doesn't give us full output-tube crunch and roar (see p61 for Super PI stage).

Enter the long-tailed pair, which, as with most everything else in the early days of the field, came to the world of guitar amps from the realm of high-quality tube audio amplifiers. Although many of us relish the distortion in our amps, plenty of players want it to come either from the output

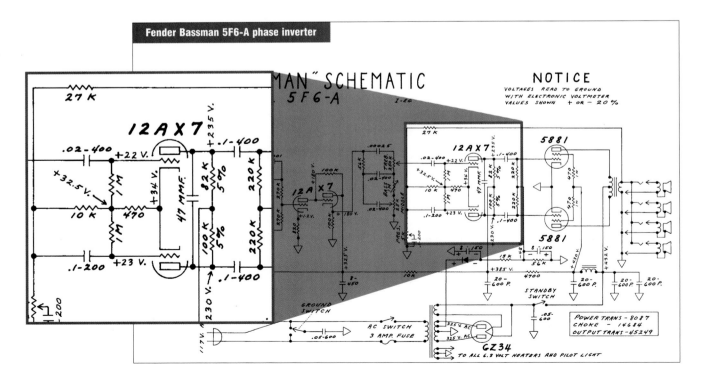

**Fender Bassman 5F6-A phase inverter**

## Marshall 50W amp phase inverter

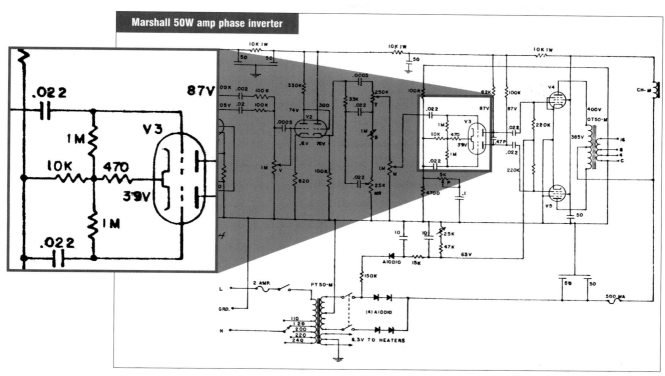

## Mesa/Boogie MkIIB phase inverter

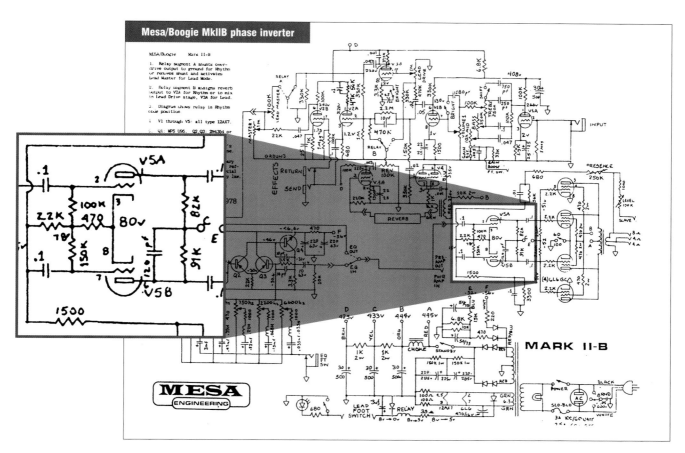

tubes or from the preamp tubes in a high-gain circuit that passes it on to the output stage without further muddying via the PI. The long-tailed pair does this with great efficiency. It's seen in its most refined form in the larger "F" series Fender amps of the late 1950s, such as the Bassman and Twin (and, surprisingly, the final version of the medium-sized 5E9 tweed Tremolux), and in an often slightly-less-complex form in the designs of other good makers then and after (p62-3).

Considering all of the other circuit variations from maker to maker over the past 45 years, the presence of the long-tailed pair probably links quality amp designs more than any other element in the field. That said, plenty of makers and players seeking an earlier breakup and a somewhat gnarlier distortion overall are still delighted with the split-load PI, while plummy, heavily-compressed blues licks might still sound their best on the paraphase PI in a scruffy old 5C5 tweed Pro Amp.

Whatever sound you seek, the considerable variables offered by different PI topologies are definitely worth keeping in mind. This is the kind of thing that isn't talked about a whole lot (it's not often you see advertising copy for a new amp model boasting, "Genuine split-load phase inverter!"), but it has a major impact on an amp's performance. If you're trying to get a firm, powerful low-end with serious power-tube grunt when pushed hard, you're not going to achieve it to total satisfaction with a cathodyne PI, or at all with a paraphase. Or if you want that juicy, sweet overdrive and easy compression that a mid-sized tweed amp provides at lower-to-medium volume levels, a long-tail pair PI might have trouble delivering. This isn't the sort of element you correct with modifications or add-ons, either; if your dream sound is the spongy, soft overdrive at low output levels, trade in that amp with the long-tail PI for a Fender 5E3 Deluxe or one of its many clones. Start with the amp that best characterizes the heart of the sound you're after, and build the tweaks, effects and nuances from there.

## Output Tubes

We've already seen that there are two main breeds of output tube configuration: push-pull (PP) and single-ended. With PP, two, four, six and occasionally more tubes divided into two equal teams share the load of driving different cycles of the signal, which of course takes the visual form of an alternating waveform of "hills and valleys," if you like. The two-tube format is easiest to visualize: one tube "pushes the hills" while the other "pulls the valleys," then they swap. Since AC (alternating current) carries constantly alternating hills and valleys even through a single signal line, each tube of the PP setup receives a steady stream of each. With more tubes, always in equal numbers, the teams are simply wired together in parallel. Thanks to the clarity of early Fender schematic diagrams (which is why I'm tending to use them here) it's easy to discern the two opposite-phase signal paths running from PI to output tubes. In the diagram of the 5F6A Bassman PI (p62), these follow the connections from the two halves of the 12AX7 via the 0.1-400 (watt) coupling caps into the grids of the 5881s.

In many guitar amps—the majority in fact—each side of the PP setup actually shuts down briefly during some part of the cycle, when the other side is at its peak of current flow. "Hang on," you might be thinking, "one tube shuts down while the other amplifies?" That's right, and then they swap. Looks crazy on paper, but of course it all happens so fast that there's no audible gap in the performance. Because the 360-degree waveforms being amplified by each side of the PP setup are out of phase with each other, there's no volume loss as one side dips and the other rises. And you should know—you've heard it time and time again, because the majority of the world's guitar amps function in this way, including classics like all the big Marshalls, Fender Bassmans and Twins, Peaveys, Mesa/Boogies and so on.

And this takes us into another main factor of output stages: operating class. Amps that perform as I've just described are class AB amplifiers. By definition, one side of the PP tube pair of a class AB amplifier rests for at least some portion of the cycle (when measured at maximum volume before clipping). In simple terms, that's really all there is to the definition of class AB—or at least all you need to worry about.

An output section operating in true class A has the tubes working the entire cycle of the waveform (again, when measured at maximum volume before distortion). This is true even of push-pull amplifiers where both tubes are sending the signal along to the OT together at all times, not alternately resting as with class AB. As such, class A output stages are somewhat less efficient than class AB stages, which can be driven to higher output levels. Players and amp-makers often talk of sweeter distortion in class A amps, but true class A operation actually has less distortion content at a given output level, albeit a smoother onset of distortion when it comes, and one that's usually heard as being harmonically richer.

But the fact that definitions of operating class are measured at maximum output before distortion should tell you something: a lot of voodoo is talked about class A, particularly by amp-makers' marketing departments eager to sell you a particular new model. The sound of true class A, operating within the realm of its definition, is actually something different than the advertising slogan "real class A tube amp" means to imply. As I'll go into in a moment, and in later parts of the book, relatively few of the amps sold as "class A" really fit the definition. Not that this is anything to worry about at this juncture. The characteristic sound of different classic tube guitar amps is determined by far more than their class definition, and remember again that many of the world's most desirable amps—the tweed Fender Bassman or Deluxe Reverb, the Dumble Overdrive Special, the Marshall

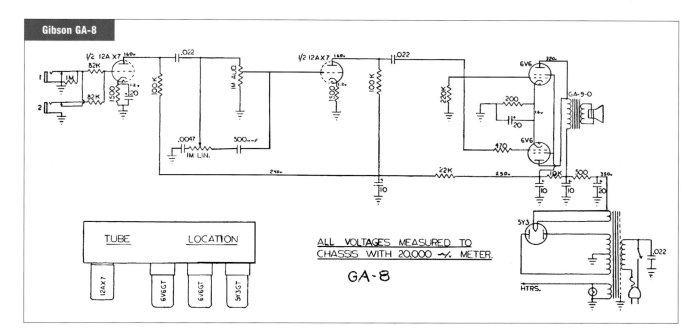

**Gibson GA-8**

JTM50 or little plexi 18-watter—are all class AB amps. They all sound pretty damn good when driven into distortion, too.

A few paragraphs ago I mentioned "two main breeds" of output stage, and the second and lesser-seen is also the type that always guarantees class A operation: the single-ended amplifier. These are almost always small amps of the Fender Champ, Vox AC4, Gibson GA-5 variety, and by definition carry a single output tube. As you might guess pretty quickly, this single output tube can't rest for any portion of the waveform, not in a functioning guitar amp circuit anyway, so it instantly fits the definition of class A. These amps are always pretty inefficient, but often sound hot, sweet and harmonically rich along with it. They make some of the greatest recording amps available, partly because of this genuine class A operation through both clean and overdriven operation, and partly of course because they can be driven hard at fairly low, studio-friendly volumes.

In the form of guitar amps, single-ended tube output stages only ever stray into the medium-sized amp at best, and the lower end of the category at that, in the form of dual-single-ended amps (also called parallel single-ended). These amps use a pair of output tubes working in parallel to increase the potential output. Rather than working in turns like the push-pull pair, these are really pretending they are a single tube for operational purposes, both pushing the same signal the entire time. Production examples of these are extremely rare (which is partly why I have included a project to build one of my own design at the end of this book). The only two that spring readily to mind are Gibson's GA-8 (see schematic on p65) from the vintage camp, and THD's BiValve from the modern era. The GA-8 uses a single 12AX7 as both preamp gain stage and driver, much like our Fender Princeton in Chapter One, but a pair of paralleled 6V6 output tubes rather than just the one.

Such amps are still very inefficient compared to PP amps using the same tube complement. A design like the GA-8 probably only puts out about 8-10W, compared to the 18W rating of the PP Gibson GA-20 or Fender Deluxe. Still, it's one way of getting a little more power out of a true class A design than the measly 4W a Champ can drum up.

Larger dual-single-ended amps are a rare thing, partly because of the demands put on the output transformers in such designs. OTs designed specifically for single-ended use are made with air gaps to help protect them from voltage spikes that can occur because of the offset DC current in the primary, and end up being much larger than push-pull OTs wound to reflect the same primary impedance and output potential. A single-ended OT designed to put out 40-50 watts in a guitar amp would be an enormous beast... and I guess most makers just don't want to bother with them. Also, single-ended amps are prone to be noisier by nature, thanks in part to their lack of the "humbucker-like" noise canceling properties of two tubes working on opposite-phased signals. They require larger and more carefully designed filtering stages. More trouble, more expense.

While single-ended amps are always class A because they have no choice, designers seeking true class A performance in PP amps achieve it by the manipulation of two factors we've already touched upon elsewhere: the voltage on the output tubes' plates, and their bias setting. The tubes are forced into this state of constant operation by carefully setting their bias point, which is a very complex matter, and one that we'll leave to the professional tech (and again a thing which in actuality doesn't occur all that much in guitar amps). But this does bring us to the discussion of bias, and the role that different bias techniques can play in determining both an amp's efficiency and its inherent sound.

We already visited a cathode-biased output stage in our single-ended Princeton, where the tube's bias voltage was generated across a 470-ohm resistor connected between the cathode and ground (hence the name). Cathode biasing was used almost exclusively in the earlier tube amps, up until the early 1950s when better makers began to use fixed biasing to squeeze more wattage out of their larger amps. Many smaller amps remained cathode-biased, and still are today.

That little tweed Princeton makes an interesting case in point for us because, as a single-ended design, it is both true class A and cathode-biased. A confusion of the sound and function of these two very different points of amplifier definition is behind much of the "class A" hype of today. Many makers who make loud claims for class A performance are really talking about amps that are cathode-biased, for one thing, which induces a lot of the sonic characteristics we have come to label as "class A." An output stage in cathode bias is less efficient than one of the same tube complement set as fixed bias, but has a softer, somewhat more harmonics-rich onset of distortion, with a little more compression from the output tubes too. This all occurs regardless of whether true operational class is A or AB—but these characteristics are all frequently assigned to the former.

The lack of a negative feedback loop in many cathode-biased designs, which also makes an amp a little gainier, looser, and more saturated sounding, further supports the misrepresentation of the "class A" label. More of that later, but notice for now that our Princeton, all Champs, and most other single-ended amps that are true class A and cathode-biased do in fact possess negative feedback loops around their output sections, rather than excluding them. These amps are inherently hot, gainy, sparkly, and rich, and need a little reining in, if anything, hence the loop. The fact that

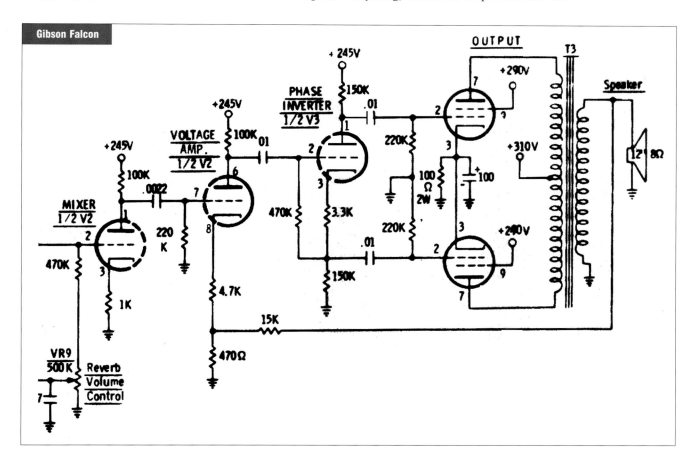

these single-ended designs—which are among the only amps out there we can undisputedly call class A—carry a number of circuit elements that go against the rule for "class A sound," as defined by many modern models, makes them interesting cases for consideration.

One of the larger cathode-biased amps is the Vox AC30, which was the original source of so much of the class A legend in the first place (it also happens to lack a negative feedback loop). If you dig through a stack of vintage catalogs and magazine ads, you won't find Vox touting the AC30 in bold letters as a class A amp. That wasn't a buzzword in the early 1960s, but in later years players and techs analyzing a few great examples and deciding they must be running in class A have helped to create much of the hype. If there's something to it, fine, but it's important to understand that the main defining factors of "that sound" we think we're seeking in a class A amp have more to do with cathode biasing and a lack of negative feedback.

Our second flavor of biasing is fixed-bias, which is a misleading name. Any cathode-biased guitar amps you might occasionally peep inside will have a resistor permanently soldered from the cathode to ground—'fixed," you might be tempted to say. But fixed-bias amps are those that have their bias level determined by a DC voltage applied to the grid that's negative with respect to the cathode (which itself is usually tied directly to ground in this scenario). In the early days, this was in fact often "fixed'—by which I mean non-adjustable—by means of a selenium rectifier employed in a small biasing circuit. These days, most fixed-bias amps have some form of adjustment of bias level, which is required when a new set of output tubes is installed. By the way, fixed-bias amps can be set to run class A, theoretically at least, because the bias level plays the critical part of a tube's operation point, and thereby class. So which do you think would sound "more class A" to us, or to a hype-proliferating marketing manager: a fixed-bias amp with global negative feedback around the output stage set up to run in true class A, or a cathode-biased amp with no negative feedback set up to run class AB? Let's not even go there...

As we discussed in regard to preamp tubes, the voltage applied to the plates of the output tubes also greatly affects their feel and response. Output tubes can operate at a pretty broad range of voltages and still do their job, provided the voltage level and bias setting work hand-in-hand to maximize their efficiency at any given level. But relatively higher or lower voltages do yield different characteristics from the tubes. To put it simply, the harder you push the tubes with respect to plate voltage (assuming a bias point adjusted accordingly) the closer you get to achieving that tube type's maximum wattage capability, and a high level of clean headroom.

Depending upon other factors, tubes run at maximum plate voltage can sometimes sound a little cold or sterile—if loud—if other elements of the circuit don't combine to warm them up a bit. Output tubes running at lower plate voltages tend to distort more quickly, while perhaps offering a thicker or grittier tone even at "clean" settings (thanks to what is actually a higher distortion content, among other things), and they can have a more dynamic feel overall.

I'm oversimplifying grossly, but this offers a rule-of-thumb that points us in the right direction at least. Most amp designers will seek a midpoint that combines good usage of the tube's output potential and a touch-sensitive playing feel. Some of the all-time classics achieve their tone partly by leaning either high or low of this compromise: for instance the sweet, dirty tweed Fender Deluxe that runs its 6V6s a little on the low side, or the heavy-metal assault of the 1970s metal-panel Marshalls that are pushing their EL34s pretty hard. The blackface/ silverface Fender Deluxe Reverb and the Matchless Lightning both run their output tubes—6V6s and EL84s respectively—at much higher voltages than the maximum specified by the tube types, but this contributes to the punchy, well-defined sounds of these amps. Despite the high voltages, these are also both very dynamic, touch-sensitive amplifiers.

A negative feedback loop taps a portion of the signal at a particular stage's output and sends it back to the input. In the case of the output stage, the output would be the speaker-out's positive terminal, and the input usually a connection point to the cathode of the phase inverter tube. The effect is a slight—or sometimes considerable—dampening of the amp's response, and an overall firming-up of the sound, heard usually as a tighter low-end and crisper note definition overall. Negative feedback loops help some amps run at higher volume levels without the output-dampening squash of excessive distortion. Done correctly they make for bold, punchy amplifiers; used to extremes, they can choke and constipate a sound.

The negative feedback loop is a real sleeper that many players don't even consider in the wakeful hours late at night when they toss and tumble and fret over their tone. This component of design will be part of a maker's overall objectives for any particular model—notably a contribution to the objective of a slightly tighter, more in-focus sound with firm lows and a controllable feel, as mentioned—and isn't really intended to be monkeyed around with in isolation. But I'll tell you this, simply adding or removing a negative feedback loop, which often comprises just one resistor and two lengths of wire, can make an instant change in the sound and feel of many amplifiers. Some don't handle its removal well, sliding into runaway oscillation and a generally uncontrollable feel. For others, cutting the loop or changing to a higher resistor (meaning less feedback returned from the output of the stage to its input) can really open up the amp and breathe new life into it. Among others, I have disconnected the loops in vintage brownface Fender Pro and Super Amps, blackface Bassman and Super Reverbs, and a silverface Champ, and found that it really made them sound a lot more open, dynamic and sizzling in each case—not that you'd want the loop out of circuit for all playing styles. Other amps with the loop cut just felt too raw and freaked-out. But in all of these (which ended up with mini toggle switches to keep the amp normal or loop-less), the sound was a lot more dynamic and lively, with a little more breakup at lower levels. If that's not desired, though, the loop should definitely stay.

(Note that I'm not advocating modifications to vintage amps as a general rule—but this is an extremely minor, totally reversible mod, and the switch can even be positioned in an existing spare hole on the chassis underside, which sometimes only needs to be widened slightly.)

Adding a loop to some amps that lack it can help to bring an over-sensitive, grainy, slightly farty amp into better focus and tighter control in some cases, while in others it might make no noticeable improvement. The best way to try something like this for yourself is to have a reputable technician carefully de-solder one end of the feedback loop in an amp you are interested in modifying as described. If you like the change, you can have a small switch installed to bring the loop in and out as desired, and it can usually be tucked away out of sight under the back edge of the chassis.

## Output transformer

In discussing negative feedback loops we skipped around one very significant component of our output stage, the output transformer. That's because we discussed this individual part in some depth in Chapter Two, when we broke down the amp component-by-component, and there isn't a whole lot more to say here about its function. Like so much else within a guitar amp, the OT and the output tubes are extremely interdependent: the OT can only transform what is handed to it by the tubes, and the tubes can't live up to their maximum wattage potential without a sufficient OT. For maximum potential all around in terms of undistorted output levels (or even maximum distorted output when you really crank things), the PI, output tubes and OT all work together, aided by other ingredients like the biasing technique selected and the presence or lack of a negative feedback loop.

It's simple, really: if the PI passes a compromised or dirtied signal to the output tubes, they will in turn pass an amplified corrupted signal on to the OT. Of course a signal corrupted or tonally depleted earlier in the chain—at the preamp, tone stack, a gain makeup stage, or effects loop—is similarly going to mean amplification of a dirtied signal by even the most impressively designed and constructed output stage. As the saying goes: crap in, crap out. With guitar amps, of course, sometimes maybe crap is what we are looking for.

The output transformer, then, is the last link not only in the chain of the output stage, but in the entire signal chain within the amp. It converts—or transforms, as the name suggests—the high-voltage low-current signal from the tubes into a low-voltage high-current signal that can drive a speaker. It's a mistake not to think of the speaker itself as part of the amplifier's circuit; a lesson proved by the fact that you can severely damage that circuitry in many cases if you unplug the speaker from it. But it's best to deal with speakers elsewhere in the book (see Chapter Eight), as this truly final link takes us out of the realm of the purely electronic and into the electro-mechanical, and finally once again the acoustic.

Top, the massive power transformer in a vintage Vox AC50. Below, its smaller counterpart in a vintage Traynore Bassmate.

## POWER SUPPLY

The power supply includes everything involved in converting your AC domestic current into the DC that the tubes run on, filtering it, and delivering it cleanly throughout the amp. This includes the power transformer (PT), rectifier, choke, and filter capacitors. Even though your signal never touches this stage, it plays an important part in how your amp functions, and can even greatly affect how your amp "feels', which itself translates into an important element of your tone *et al.* For some reason—who knows what it was—I didn't cover the power supply in the original edition of this book, but felt it was important to probe it here. Build the exact same amp but with a dramatically different power supply topology, and I guarantee you will find, when playing the two side by side, that they respond and even sound different. The type and design of an amp's power supply helps to shape crucial performance factors such as its response speed when you pick a note, the tightness or looseness of its playing feel, its headroom and harmonic content, and the character of its transients—all of which can present desirable characteristics at either end of the spectrum, depending on what you're looking for.

Power transformers were discussed in some detail toward the end of both Chapter One and Chapter Two; the main thing about them is that they should be spec'd right for the job, and any clever, conscientious amp designer should be selecting a PT according to how well it will do what he or she needs it to do, not according to price alone. Given equivalent specifications regarding voltage and current conversion and delivery, a larger PT is often an indication of a superior product, but there's also no point going overkill for the job at hand. In relative terms, an increased current capacity can work toward speed, clarity, and fidelity in the amp's overall performance, but there's not point going big for big's sake, since it will also mean added weight, heat dissipation, and power consumption. There's no scope in this book for trying to teach you to spec out power transformers: if you need a replacement, you should rely on a qualified tech or quality transformer manufacturer to supply one equivalent to the original in your amp. Understanding just a little about these size/current factors can help you identify what some amps are trying to achieve, though, and make you a better-informed guitarist.

**The GZ34 rectifier tube in a Komet 60 amp head.**

Going in the other direction, a smaller, lower-current PT might also be a crucial part of the playing feel of a vintage or vintage-style amp, contributing to desirable characteristics in that design. Changing it for something more robust and efficient might entirely derail the soft, cushy blues tone you had previously enjoyed.

Rectifiers come in two main flavors: tube and solid state. Either converts the transformer's ramped-up AC voltage to an even higher DC voltage that lets the tubes do their thing. Different types of tube rectifiers do different jobs of this effort, from producing a minor increase in voltage at a not-entirely-efficient rate, to producing an impressive increase at an extremely efficient rate. Solid-state rectifiers, made from silicon diodes, are at the hyper-efficient end of the scale in both regards.

The amount of DC any tube rectifier produces from the AC delivered by the transformer's secondary will be particular to the specific amp design, and the tube selected to deliver that voltage to within fairly tight tolerances. This is really something of a "black and white" performance, with little gray area, and the only major variable being in a tube rectifier that is under performing. Where you do feel the performance of different types of tube rectifiers is, well, in the way they contribute to your amp's playing feel. Less powerful tube rectifiers (ie those producing less DC out of the AC they're given) also tend to do their work somewhat more slowly, that is, they take a little longer to ramp up to full performance when hit by a hard surge. The result is a certain softness and swell in the attack of the note, something usually referred to as compression, and this can either work toward or against your playing style. Softer tube rectifiers like the 5Y3 in a tweed Deluxe or the EZ81 in a Vox AC15 will exhibit considerable compression when the amp is cranked up and you're playing hard. Firmer types like the GZ34 in a Vox AC30 or the 5AR4 in a tweed Bassman will work more efficiently, but their response won't be quite instantaneous, so they will still contribute to a tactile playing feel.

Other elements within the amp, such as the PI and output tubes in particular, will also sag and

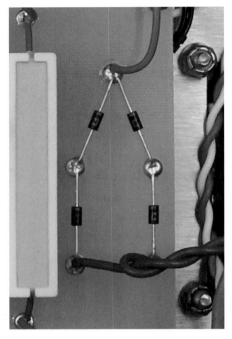

Four silicon diodes used in a bridge rectifier inside a Komet Aero 33 amp head.

compress when played hard—to degrees determined by the amp's overall design—so we can't attribute all compression characteristics to tube rectifiers. For this reason, even amps with solid-state rectifiers will exhibit some sag when cranked up high and played with a vengeance. But those equipped with silicon diode rectifiers are also more likely to present a bold, tight, cutting performance, so these can be your friends for everything from snappy country to thumping metal—although, not always: Komet's K60 and Aero 33, several Trainwrecks, some renditions of TopHat's Club Royale, and plenty of other extremely touch-sensitive amps have also been made with solid-state rectification, so you can't always jump to conclusions about a rectifier's intentions.

After it leaves the rectifier, the DC supply is cleaned up by a handful of electrolytic (aka "filter") capacitors, sometimes in conjunction with a transformer-like component called a choke. Then it is passed along to various stages of the amp via large dropping resistors that reduce it to the levels required by different tubes at different points in the circuit. As covered to some extent in the High-Voltage Supplies and Electrolytic Capacitors sections of Chapter One and Chapter Two respectively, the choke and filter caps help to smooth out any leftover AC ripple that remains in the DC supply, which would otherwise be detrimental to the tubes' performance, and your tone.

Properly spec'd filtering is one of several elements contributing to a low-noise amp, but the degree and amount of filtering also affects the sound and feel of the amp. More lightly filtered amps tend toward a relatively softer playing feel and a raw tone (all else being equal—and often we're

Filter capacitors in a tweed Deluxe.

Filter capacitors in a Matchless Spitfire.

talking just slight shades of difference here), while more heavily filtered amps can be bolder, punchier, and clearer. You will hear the affects of heavy filtering in the low end in particular, which should be fuller and firmer as a result of relatively high-value electrolytic caps.

Compare, for example, how the filtering used in two relatively simple 15-watt amps differs, and the tone and feel that results from these variables. Fender's tweed 5E3 Deluxe has no choke and just three 16uF filter caps supplying all tube stages within the amp, which includes two preamp tubes and two output tubes, with a simple front end of two channels with a single gain stage each and a shared tone control. The Matchless Spitfire, by comparison, also has two preamp tubes and two output tubes (EL84s this time), although its first 12AX7 is wired in parallel and used for just one channel, with a single tone control much like that of the 5E3. Its filtering, though, includes a choke plus four filter caps, each of a higher value—two 33uF, and two 22uF. As a result, while you might expect a small, simple 2xEL84 amp like the Spitfire to be creamy and squishy, it actually has a fairly tight performance with decent headroom for its size (factors to which its GZ34 rectifier tube also contribute, especially when compared with the Deluxe's looser 5Y3).

Ultimately you're not likely to choose your amp based on a look at its power supply—plug in, play, and tone and feel should rule the day every time—but this brief look at how this otherwise enigmatic, seemingly non-tone-shaping stage might affect your amp's performance should lead you to a better understanding of the holistic nature of amp design and construction.

# CHAPTER 4

# Inside
# the Amps

The best way to see how different amps are put
together is just to look inside a few. This chapter
explores the innards of some classic tube amplifiers,
both vintage and modern—more than 50 years of
amp expertise is on show here.

Now that you have a grounding in a range of the components and stage topologies that can exist inside a guitar amplifier, it's time to lift the lid on some specific examples.

The entirety of Chapter Four is devoted to examining the circuits and stages of 18 tube guitar amps, each of which is either a vintage classic, a modern classic, or simply a good example of the breed to examine. I'll take you inside these chassis with the use of large color photos, accompanied by annotated "key photos" with numbered guides to help us identify different stages' points of interest. This seems like a friendlier way of doing things, without stamping numbers and arrows and diagrams all over the full-size color pics (the insides of some of these amps are works of art in themselves). It also avoids blocking out any components we might be trying to view, or those that you are just curious to examine for yourself. We've positioned the pictures on their sides simply in order to squeeze in as much detail as possible—just turn the page 90 degrees clockwise to get the "real" view.

Yes, this chapter is heavy on Fender amps, but Leo Fender's company laid much of the groundwork—early on in particular—that many other makers have followed to this day, so the extra attention is deserved. More amps continue to follow what you could call a "Fender-ish" format than any other long-established style, so a lot of what you learn from early Fenders will echo down through the years in other makes and models.

This chapter is also vintage-heavy but that's mainly because many great early designs set the templates that others have followed. You'll also notice that most of the amps here contain circuits that are hand-wired using discrete components, rather than printed circuit boards (PCBs) with components that are, in many cases, loaded and soldered by machines. This is for two reasons: the first is simply that hand-wired amps are by and large much simpler to trace visually; the second is that maintenance, modification, and tone-tweaking are much easier on hand-wired amps (in most cases, anyway), so it's more straightforward to comment on these in this regard. In this *Updated And Expanded Edition*, however, I have added a few new "modern classics," as well as a couple of vintage or semi-vintage amps that deserve to be discussed and a few examples of different types of build style than were included in the original selection of 12 amps.

Even devoting this much attention to 18 individual amplifiers, there isn't room to discuss every single element within each metal box. But we will get a good look at the major stages and components that make different tube amp designs tick, paying particular attention to the things that give each make and model its distinctive character. You will begin to see common ground between amps that you might previously have believed were different in every respect; likewise, you'll detect some points of originality where you might not have expected them. It would be fascinating to devote an entire book to this kind of examination, but after probing the 18 different circuits here you'll have gleaned enough to take away and apply to a broad range of amps not covered. Most guitar players don't take the trouble—or aren't given the opportunity—to see inside this many different amplifiers in a lifetime, and what you will find there is sometimes surprising, and even exciting.

Note: the internal circuits should be viewed by turning the page 90 degrees clockwise.

# Fender 5E1 Champ (1956)

The tweed Fender Champ (model 5E1 shown here) is about as simple as it gets. The amp has one preamp tube, one output tube, one rectifier tube, and just a single Volume control with the power switch mounted on the back of the pot (potentiometer). It doesn't even have a Tone control like the Princeton we examined in Chapter One. Despite this simplicity—or more likely because of it— the Champ is a renowned little tone machine and a classic recording amp that has been used by many pros down the years to achieve hot, raunchy overdrive sounds at levels that any microphone could handle. Eric Clapton's 'Layla'-era recordings are a great example of this sound, and plenty of others have committed the Champ to record too.

## Input And Preamp

**1a** Each of the Champ's two input jacks is connected to pin 2 of the single 12AX7 preamp tube (in other words, the input of the first triode) via a 68k grid resistor. These resistors are seen mounted on the top-right corner of the circuit board—two brown carbon comp resistors, each with the color code blue-gray-orange-silver—joined in a "V" shape at their lower end. From here, a wire runs under the board to the preamp tube, mounted almost directly below them on the bottom edge of the photograph (seen covered in its familiar metal shield).

**1b** The large tan-colored canister mounted below and to the right of these resistors is the 25uF/25V bypass cap tied to pin 3 of the 12AX7, the cathode. The resistor that sets the bias for the first triode is hidden on the right side of this large Astron cap. The next evolution of the Champ, the 5F1, did away with this bypass cap to tighten up its sound a little; but it also dropped the choke that this model carries, a change that would loosen up the sound in other ways. The changes were a form of trade-off, and saved Fender some money by dropping two components.

**1c** From pin 1 of the 12AX7, the signal runs through the large, yellow 0.02uF Astron coupling cap to the volume control, and from the volume control straight back to…

## PI And Output

**2a** The second triode of this lone 12AX7 acts as the driver for the output stage. The signal enters at pin 7, and departs at pin 6. Pin 8 of the second side of the tube is connected to its cathode, which is wired to the 1.5k resistor (brown-green-red-silver) on the upper part of the board, between the second yellow signal cap and the tan filter cap.

**2b** From pin 6, the signal flows through another yellow 0.02uF Astron cap straight to pin 5 of the single 6V6GT output tube. There are only two signal caps in this entire amp; the third yellow Astron cap, seen top-left connected to the fuse holder, has an entirely non-signal-carrying function.

**2c** The 6V6GT (whose pin connections can be seen protruding from the bottom edge of the chassis toward the large filter caps) is cathode-biased, with pin 8 connected to the large 470-ohm resistor (yellow-violet-brown-silver) and the 25uF/25V capacitor, which helps to fatten up the sound.

**2d** Negative feedback is used around the Champ's output stage, to tighten up the tone a little and help

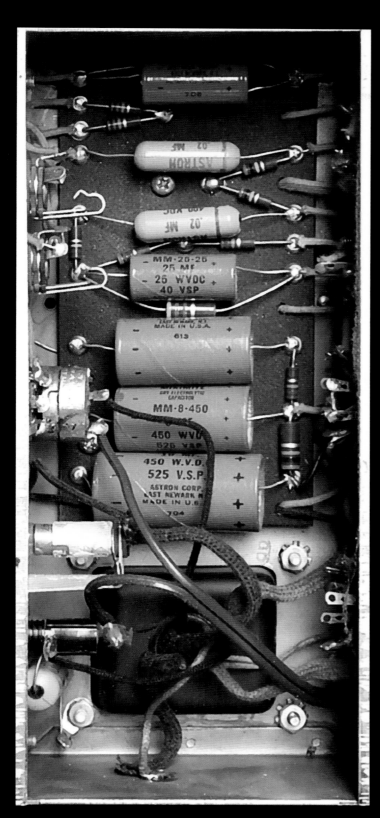

1a   68k input resistors
1b   25uF/25V bypass capacitor
1c   .02uF coupling capacitor
2a   pins of 12AX7 tube
2b   .02uF signal capacitor
2c   470-ohm resistor & 25uF/25V capacitor
2d   22k resistor
3a   16uF electrolytic capacitor
3b   10k dropping resistor
     (see text for more details)

prevent runaway oscillation. The 22k resistor (red-red-orange-silver) to the lower-left of the second yellow signal cap is connected to the driver triode's cathode at one end, and the speaker-out at the other.

## Power Supply

**3a** Despite its small size and the simplicity of its preamp circuitry, the Champ carries a power supply and filtering stage that's not a whole lot smaller than that on the larger Deluxe amp. Schematics for the 5E1 specify three large 8uF/450V electrolytic caps, but this all-original example carries a larger 16uF cap in the first position, as on the 5F1 that followed. Often Fender circuits didn't change abruptly but rather evolve gradually, so perhaps this is a transitional model.

**3b** The 5E1 Champ is also supposed to carry a choke in its filtering chain, but this one instead has the 10k dropping resistor of the 5F1 (seen between the lower leads of the first two filter caps)—further evidence of a transitional model.

# Fender 'TV-front' Deluxe (1951)

The Fender Deluxe was introduced in the original Fender "Woodie" line of 1946, moved to the "TV-front" cab design in 1948, and took the form you see on page 79 about a year later, with the diagonal tweed and brown linen grille cloth. The example shown here is from around 1951.

Through a range of incarnations, the Deluxe remained a perennial Fender favorite, and one of the most popular small-to-mid-sized amps of all time. Although circuits and details changed over the years, the 2 x 6V6 output stage and 1x12″ speaker remained at the core of its format until 1986.

Like most amps of the late 1940s and early 1950s, the TV-front tweed Deluxe was relatively low-powered by today's standards, and provided a characteristically smooth, rich, mid-heavy tone when driven hard, with lots of sag and compression to soften the notes. It's a classic blues amp, heard

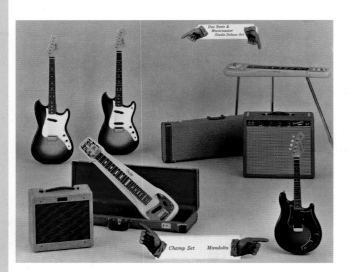

behind plenty of early blues and rock'n'roll recordings. The "wide panel" and "narrow-panel" versions of the mid and late 1950s refined the sound somewhat, although the smooth overdrive and easy breakup remained definitive characteristics of the tweed Deluxe sound throughout the 1950s. Neil Young used a slightly later wide-panel tweed Deluxe to coin the grunge sound (as perhaps heard to greatest effect on the albums *Rust Never Sleeps* and *Ragged Glory*). The later narrow-panel 5E3 of 1953-60 has become a highly desirable recording and small-gig amp.

The brownface Deluxes of 1961 gained a long-tailed-pair PI, fixed bias, tremolo, and a little more output power and headroom. In 1963, the blackface model also gained reverb. Output was now rated at 22 watts, thanks to the high voltages at which the 6V6GTs were run (beyond their maximum specs,

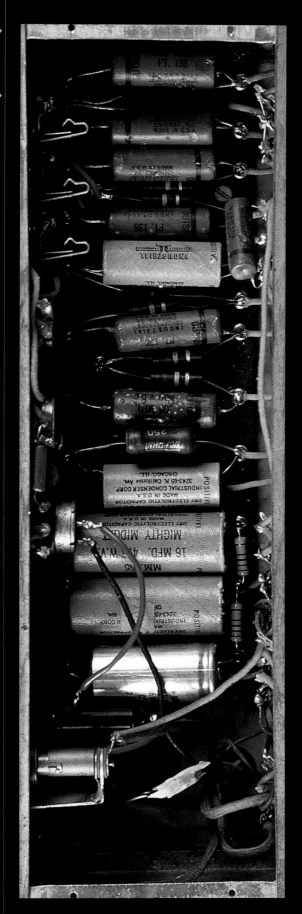

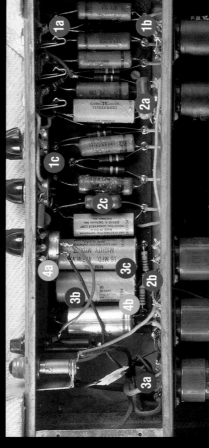

| | |
|---|---|
| 1a | three inputs |
| 1b | pins for 6SC7 octal tube |
| 1c | .05uF coupling cap |
| 2a | second 6SC7 tube |
| 2b | pair of 6V6 output tubes |
| 2c | 250-ohm resistor & 25uF/25VDC bypass cap |
| 3a | 5Y3 tube rectifier |
| 3b | four 20uF/450VDC electrolytic capacitors |
| 3c | 10k (metal film) dropping resistors |
| 4a | power switch on back of tone control |
| 4b | see text |
| (see text for more details) | |

in fact). These Deluxe Reverbs became classics in their own right; they were another club-gig favorite, and still had a juicy overdrive sound when driven hard, but their sound was characterized by a crisper, more defined tone with a slightly broader frequency range. They had more headroom, too, but could still be driven into breakup pretty easily. The blackface version remains a definitive studio amp for the country player, and is great for anything from jazz to rock'n'roll besides.

As for our TV-front Deluxe here, the combination of the octal 6SC7 preamp tubes, the paraphase inverter, lower voltages on the 6V6s, and a small paper-bobbin OT all make for a warm, chocolatey sound that flatters the traditional electric blues soloist like few other amps out there.

### Input And Preamp

**1a** The "TV-front" Fender Deluxe has three inputs, one for "Mic" and two for "Inst'. Each grouping shares a triode (half of the preamp tube) and has its own volume control. Note that, in a configuration that looks extremely unusual compared with more modern schematics, the signal passes through a 0.05uF coupling cap on its way to each side of the tube.

**1b** Early Fender preamps used octal tubes, until 12AY7 and 12AX7 nine-pin types replaced them around 1954. This 1951 Deluxe carries two 6SC7 octals, one for the preamp and one for the PI. These are still dual-triode tubes, but require somewhat different circuits than the nine-pins that would become popular. Rather than the cathode-bias technique used for later tweed amps, these tubes were still biased with 5-megohm resistors tied to the grids (something not much seen today, if at all). The 6SC7s also ran at much lower voltages than would become the norm, about 92VDC in this case.

**1c** This signal passes from each half of the preamp tube to the respective volume controls via another 0.05uF coupling cap. From here, it is joined through the common tone control before moving on to the PI. This early Deluxe's simple tone circuit is much like the one that would be used on models throughout the 1950s. It employs a 500pF (0.0005uF) cap between the volume and tone, and a 0.01uF cap (rather than the later 0.005uF) from the left tag of the tone pot to ground.

From the volume and tone network, the signal runs directly to the PI without passing through a coupling cap.

### PI And Output

**2a** The second 6SC7 tube is used in a paraphase inverter circuit to drive the output tubes. Its first triode is a driver stage—with a cathode bias resistor and bypass cap, as seen on later designs—while its second triode takes phase-inversion duties. This is an outdated PI topology that is prone to distortion in guitar amp circuits, and yields a spongy, compressed, mids-heavy sound.

**2b** A pair of 6V6 output tubes is used in push-pull, both driven at around 350VDC on the plates to generate around 12 watts at best. More efficient circuits would later get a lot more output from these tube types, but this is pretty good going for 1951.

**2c** The output tubes are cathode-biased with a large 250-ohm resistor and a 25uF/25VDC bypass cap—the same pair that would be found in tweed Deluxes throughout the 1950s. (Note that back when even lower-value filter caps were still a lot larger than big resistors, this configuration appears more like a cap with a "bypass resistor" running around it, but of course it functions as a bias resistor with bypass cap, whichever is the bigger.) This model of Deluxe also has no negative feedback loop. A slightly later model would add the loop briefly, then drop it again. The wide-panel and highly desirable narrow-panel tweed Deluxes (which offered a punchier, more versatile sound) would never carry a negative feedback loop either, although it became standard on the brownface and blackface models.

## Power Supply

**3a** Tube rectification comes from a 5Y3. This provides both the gradual warm-up that permits the lack of a standby switch here, and lots of compression-like squash when the amp is cranked up and played hard.
**3b** Power filtering is done by four 20uF/450VDC electrolytic capacitors. As you can see from the photo, one of this amp's three original Astron filter caps has been replaced. In truth, given its age, all three should probably be replaced by now.
**3c** The two original carbon comp 10k dropping resistors between the caps have also been replaced with sturdier metal film resistors (the blue resistors between the lower legs of these caps, seen in the large color photo). These resistors come under a lot of strain over the years, and frequently need to be replaced in vintage amps.

## Other Features

**4a** The power (on/off) switch is mounted on the back of the tone control, as is more commonly seen on later tweed Princetons.
**4b** Other than the first 20uF filter cap and the two dropping resistors, everything else appears to be original in this 64-year-old amplifier..

# Fender 5F6A Bassman (1959)

The "narrow-panel" tweed Fender Bassman, particularly the final 5F6A model as shown here, is one of the greatest rock'n'roll, blues, R&B—you name it—guitar amps of all time. As you might guess from the name, the amplifier was designed for bass reproduction, and from the circuit to the speakers was intended to offer a full, firm amplification of the relatively new electric four-string Fender bass guitar, with as little distortion as possible. Like any amp of its day, though, when you turned it up far enough it distorted like a demon, and sounded fantastic for six-string guitar. At lower levels, guitarists also loved its clean-with-bite tones and full, rich voice, and it became a staple of many six-string slingers when their four-string-playing colleagues moved on to larger and more powerful amps.

The Bassman used such a long, narrow chassis that squeezing in the entire thing would require reducing the visible dimensions considerably, and all that's really been lost is a view of the top end of the power transformer (as can still be seen in the "key" photo here).

The amp photographed here is in excellent original condition internally, and doesn't appear to have been tampered with in the least (three of the amp's four speakers have been replaced, and a modified wiring harness has been fitted, but only the chassis-end of the latter can be seen here—it's a brown wire in the gap between the preamp tubes and output tubes). The yellow Astron caps and carbon comp resistors clearly on display are the stuff of any vintage tone-hound's dreams. On the whole—other than the slight fading of the brown cardboard covers on the Astron Minimite electrolytic caps—this chassis looks nearly as fresh as it did the day it left the Fullerton factory.

The tweed Bassman has become known as the archetypal blues amp, but there's even more to it than that. While a good one can certainly grind out the smooth, rich tube distortion that blues lead players love, the amp's circuit design, transformer complement, cabinet format, and speaker configuration all lend themselves beautifully to a broad range of guitar styles. Plenty of great jazz and country players played through Bassman amps in days gone by, and they have seen duty doing anything from Bruce Springsteen's epic rock, to Teenage Fanclub's indie jangle, to Pearl Jam's grunge.

The round, open voicing of the preamp circuit combines with the lower-gain 12AY7 tube in the first gain stage to keep the signal from getting too filthy early on in the chain. A cathode-follower second gain stage and tone stack certainly fatten things up, yielding a lot of touch-sensitivity to the amp's playing feel besides, and the long-tail-pair PI passes a clear, full-frequencied signal onto the output stage. With the volume down in the lower third of its range, the amp offers firm lows, plummy mids, and ringing, well-defined highs; up a notch or two from here, a tactile edge of breakup starts to crackle in; cranked past about one or two o'clock, it really starts to wail, with rich output tube distortion. Of course that's if you're using a single-coil Fender-type guitar. Show it a Les Paul, SG, ES-335, PRS, or something with P-90s, and the breakup and distortion come on a lot quicker. If there's an amp for all occasions, this might be it—compromised only, perhaps, by the serious speaker distortion from those Jensens at high output levels … although these speakers, when original, are another big part of the Bassman's charm.

## Input And Preamp

**1a** The 68k input grid resistors on the larger tweed Fender amps are found in pairs on the circuit board (one for each input jack), rather than soldered directly to the input jacks themselves, as on the later Fender amps.

**1b** From the 68k resistors, the signal passes under the circuit board and directly to pin 2 of the first preamp tube, a 12AY7. These are direct replacements for the 12AX7s more commonly used today, but they provided a lower gain. The tube helped to yield a smooth sound with decent headroom in these large tweed amps, which could otherwise get dirty fast. From pin 1 of the 12AY7 (the plate of the first triode) the signal passes through a large, yellow 0.02uF Astron coupling cap to the volume control for the first (Normal) channel. The 0.02uF signal caps of the Bassman are among the main ingredients that contribute to its signature tone. Note that the circuitry of each of the amp's two channels is exactly the same, except for the small 100pF "bright cap" (not easily seen in these photos) placed across the first and second tabs (input and wiper) of the Bright channel's volume control.

**1c** The edge of the tube's 820-ohm cathode-bias resistor can just barely be seen behind the large, archaic-looking bypass capacitor to the far-right of the circuit board. Rather than the more commonly seen 25uF/25V bypass cap, the 5F6A Bassman used a 250uF/6V cap, for a deep, full sound.

**1d** The third "V" of resistors in the preamp circuit is made up of a pair of 270k resistors that blend the amp's two channels. There is only one signal path through the rest of the amp from here; from this point it enters the second preamp tube, a 12AX7, which constitutes the cathode-follower gain stage prior to the three-pot tone stack. Thanks to the fact that the two channels are mixed early on in the circuit, and go through exactly the same number of tube triode stages, the Bassman's two channels can be blended with a jumper cord (running, for example, from Ch1 input 2 to Ch2 input 1, with a guitar plugged into

# Fender 5F6A Bassman (1959)

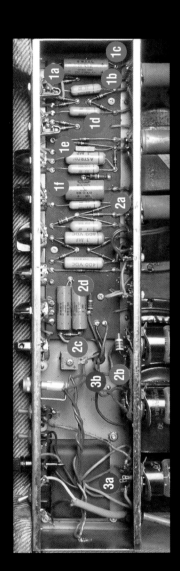

| | |
|---|---|
| 1a | 68k input grid resistors |
| 1b | pins of 12AY7 & .02uF coupling cap |
| 1c | 250uF/6V bypass capacitor & 820-ohm cathode-bias resistor |
| 1d | pair of 270k resistors |
| 1e | signal capacitors |
| 1f | .02uF capacitor |
| 2a | three-into-one resistor alignment |
| 2b | pair of 5881 output tubes & 470-ohm grid resistors |
| 2c | selenium rectifier |
| 2d | 27k resistor |
| 3a | GZ34 (5AR4) tube rectifier |
| 3b | see text |

*(see text for more details)*

Ch1 input 1). This gives the benefit of a fuller voice and slightly higher gain, using both triodes of the first preamp tube in parallel. Later blackface and silverface Fenders can't do this without experiencing out-of-phase relationships at points on the volume controls, unless the preamp circuits are modified.

**1e** These signal capacitors make up the frequency-shaping network behind the Treble, Bass, and Middle controls in the Bassman's shared EQ section.

**1f** A cathode-follower tone stack plays a big part in setting the gain of the preamp (that is, how hot a signal is passed along to the output stage), and the Bassman's treble control is the boss here. While the bass and middle controls help shape the frequency content, the treble control passes the signal on to the PI, via another 0.02uF cap.

## PI And Output

**2a** This configuration can be found in many many other large amplifiers from this period onward—the three-into-one resistor alignment that frequently tips off the long-tail-pair phase inverter.

**2b** A pair of 5881 tubes take output duties here. In the late 1950s and 1960s these were actually heavy-duty 6L6s, although in later years the only difference between the two (especially when they were Russian or Chinese-made) was in the name. You can clearly see the large 470-ohm grid resistors mounted directly on the tube socket terminals. What you don't see—because they were removed in the 5F6A's evolution from the 5F6 circuit—are the 1,500-ohm "swamper resistors," intended to help stabilize the amp. Many players feel these can also make it sound a little tight for guitar, so the later "A" Bassman has become the preferred variant of this vintage classic.

**2c** This class AB output section is fixed bias, which in the early Bassman's case really was fixed (as in preset). Rather than the adjustable bias pot of later fixed-bias Fender amps, the tweed Bassman has a small network made up of resistors, capacitors and, crucially, a selenium rectifier (the blue-green cube with the "+" sign seen bolted directly to the chassis here) that together create the correct negative DC voltage at the output tubes' grids in relation to the cathodes.

**2d** The Bassman (and all large Fenders at that time, and after) carried a negative feedback loop around its output stage, to help stabilize and smooth out the sound, particularly at higher volumes. The 27k resistor here is connected between the speaker outs and the cathode of the PI tube. The amp's "Presence" control taps into this loop and filters its high-end content, which makes it function somewhat like a "bright" control operating within the output stage. Although there is nothing on the control panel to tell you otherwise, and its performance might make a player think it's part of the tone stack along with the treble, bass and middle controls, the presence control works on an entirely different part of the amp's circuit.

## Power Supply

**3a** The 5F6A Bassman carries a GZ34 (5AR4) tube rectifier, which many players consider to be another part of its magic.

**3b** Other elements of the Bassman's power supply are impossible to see here, because the choke and large electrolytic capacitors that perform filtering duties are all mounted on the reverse of the chassis. The DC supply wires disappear and return through this rubber grommet in the chassis.

# Marshall JTM45 (1962)

The Marshall JTM45, seen here in a rare and very early "offset front" example, is responsible for ushering in the era of the big rock amp, but sounded somewhat different from the plexi and metal-panel models that would follow by the end of the 1960s. Seeking a powerful amp to make available to British musicians, Jim Marshall, Ken Bran and Dudley Craven essentially copied the circuit and overall electronic design of the 5F6A tweed Fender Bassman—a very expensive line of imported amps in Britain at that time. Different from the later Marshalls (which we'll examine in due course), these early JTM45s used a tube rectifier and American 5881 output tube types at first, followed by the compatible but European-made KT66s. More than that, they followed the Bassman circuit almost to the letter.

But a vintage JTM45 doesn't sound exactly like a tweed Bassman, and there are a number of reasons for that. First of all, imagine a skilled hobby builder today deciding to make an exact copy of an original late-1950s Fender Bassman by examining the circuit, drawing his/her own schematic diagram from it, and building the amp from parts available off-the-shelf in the 21st century. The results would probably look, spec, and sound about as different from the original Fender as did Marshall's JTM45, made with British parts and transformers that were largely of the same value but different makes and compositions than the US supplies. Now imagine this builder connects their "copy" to a closed-back 4x12″ cabinet carrying Celestions rather than an open-back 4x10″ carrying Jensens … Ah, the differences are now further compounded, in a major way.

The JTM45 is a little softer, smoother and warmer than the later Marshalls with solid-state rectification and EL34 or 6550 output tubes, and it also yields a little more sag when pushed. It's a fantastic blues and classic-rock amp, but not as crackly-crunchy as the "plexi" that followed, and therefore not the classic heavy rock sound a lot of players seek, despite the Marshall name on the front. Connect it to an open-back 4x10″ carrying Jensens and, yep, it sounds a hell of a lot more like a tweed Fender than many people might ever suspect.

■ A Fender schematic on the Marshall page (page 87)? No, it's not a misprint. For the reasons explained already, the Marshall JTM45 is so similar to Fender's 5F6A Bassman that to trace its circuit entirely here would mostly just mean a repeat of what's on the preceding pages. A look at an original Fender layout diagram beside the inside of this early JTM45 shows how very similar the amps are, down to the positioning of individual components on the circuit board, and so forth. Of course the top-mounted tweed-era Fender chassis had the tubes mounted at a 90-degree angle from the board, rather than in the upright position of the Marshall (the photo shows the view of the circuit board from the underside of the chassis, from which the tubes protrude on the other side)—but the view on this "flattened" diagram even accounts for that change.

## Input And Preamp

**1a** Although the component values used to govern them are the same (for example, 68k grid stopper resistors, 820-ohm cathode-bias resistors, 25uF/25V bypass caps, 100k plate resistors and so on), Marshall used the higher-gain ECC83 (aka 12AX7) preamp tube in the first stage rather than the 12AY7 of the Bassman.
**1b** Often the "differences between the similarities," if you will, are interesting to note here, too. The JTM45 uses the same 0.022uF coupling cap values, but you can see that the size and composition of these are different from those in the Bassman. These are the beloved foil and polyester film "mustard caps," manufactured in Britain by either Mullard or Philips.

**1c** This JTM45 carries its 470pF cap in series with the mixing resistor carrying the signal from the second channel's volume control to the second gain stage (pre-tone stack), something not seen on the Bassman.

### PI And Output

**2a** The tell-tale three-into-one resistor set-up of the long-tailed-pair PI.

**2b** While later Marshalls are known for the sound of EL34 output tubes, these early JTM45s carried 5881s (a military-grade 6L6 equivalent) just like the Bassman. These were soon changed for fat-sounding European KT66s, also a direct substitute for the 6L6.

### Power Supply

**3a** GZ34 tube rectifier

**3b** The varying values, type, and positioning of the filter caps are among the main noticeable differences between the Fender Bassman and Marshall JTM45. Marshall made more use of good European multi-cap cans.

**3c** This Marshall uses a 16uF filter cap for the preamp supply following the large 10k dropping resistor, rather than the 8uF of the Bassman.

### Other Features

**4a** Note how the circuit board was made up from a generic supply, mounted with turrets in positions that almost directly mimic the eyelets on Fender's tailor-made eyelet boards of the day.

# Vox AC15 (1962)

The Vox AC15, in its original form, is one of the most highly-prized of smaller vintage amps. In either its 2x10", 1x12" or 2x12" combo format (the latter two often with gorgeous Celestion-made Vox "Blue Bulldog" alnico speakers), it is an amp that excels in the studio, yet is loud enough for most club gigs—or anywhere, when miked through a good PA. Its big brother the AC30 might be somewhat better known, but the AC15 easily rivals it in terms of price on the vintage market, thanks largely to the fact that you can crank it up to that sweet spot at volumes that don't get the sound engineer or the audience shouting, "Turn it down!" Players who have had the pleasure will tell you this is one of the sweetest-sounding distortion generators on the planet when turned up past one o'clock or so on the Brilliant channel.

The AC15 was designed around 1956 by Dick Denney as the flagship of Tom Jennings' new Vox guitar amplifier line. It's often credited as being the first tube amp designed specifically with the guitar in mind, which is really to say that it was taken less directly from the Western Electric and RCA tube applications notes and manuals from which so many other "guitar amps" directly flowed. The AC15's preamp circuitry was designed specifically to emphasize the midrange frequencies in which the guitar dwells. When in good condition this amplifier runs the gamut of growling to chimey tones, with a dynamic, open voice and great definition and edge throughout.

This is the archetypal "class A amp," meaning more precisely that it has a cathode-biased output stage with no negative feedback. The AC15 develops a little more than 15 watts from a pair of nine-

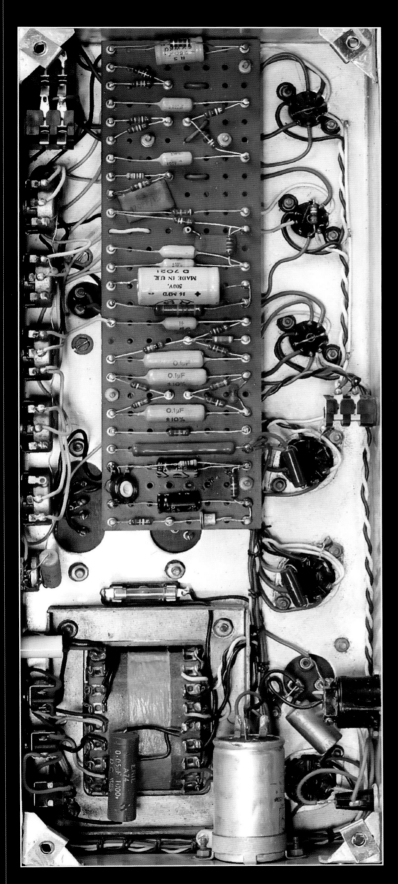

FENDER "BASSMAN" LAYOUT
MODEL 5F6-A

NOTICE

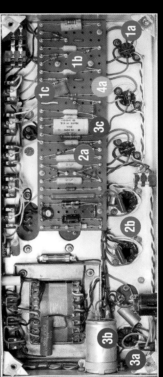

1a   pins of ECC83 (12AX7) preamp tube

1b   .022uF foil/polyester film 'mustard'
      coupling caps

1c   470pF capacitor

2a   long-tailed-pair phase inverter

2b   5881 output tubes

3a   GZ34 tube rectifier

3b   filter capacitors

3c   16uF filter cap for preamp supply

4a   circuit board

(see text for more details)

pin EL84 tubes, and their characteristically shimmering top, easy compression, and midrange grind when pushed are a big part of this Vox's tone. Most 2 x EL84-based amps that followed owe at least a little something to the AC15—especially many boutique models of the recent era—but few others have used the EF86 preamp tube employed in the vintage AC15's Normal channel (sometimes also referred to as the Brilliant channel). These can be noisy if the tube or amp are not in prime condition, and the quality of newer makes of the type has often been disappointing.

When Dick Denney needed a larger amp for British bands like The Shadows, who were playing in bigger and bigger venues, he used the AC15's preamp as a template and doubled the output section to 4 x EL84s and, voila, the AC30. But after a year or two of production Vox dropped the EF86 from the larger amp, where it was particularly problematic in a roaring, rattling, heavily-vibrating 2x12″ combo at top-whack.

■ Disgruntled amp techs have given vintage Vox amps the reputation of having real spaghetti-junction circuits underneath their upper back panels, but there is a certain logic to the things nonetheless. The relationships of the dual circuit boards means the amp doesn't have the logical flow of the Fender and Marshall amps we've already looked at—or certainly the newer Dr Z and Mojave "boutique" amps examined later in the chapter—and it can be tricky to follow the signal across a two-dimensional representation of this circuit.

It will still be useful to us to probe some of the main elements of the circuit and construction, and to glean at least a little of what's going on where inside these great Vox amps. The way the Vox manufacturers positioned the preamp circuitry and tubes and the output circuitry and tubes on, literally, different planes, means that these amps don't flow from input to output in the same way as most others. But let's dig in and identify some major components and stages nonetheless.

## Input And Preamp

**1a** The inputs follow the rule for the majority of classic vintage and contemporary amps. A 68k grid resistor is tied to the hot terminal of each input jack, and from there the signal flows directly to the input grid of the tube that forms the first gain stage of the relevant channel: a 12AX7 (ECC83) in the Vib/Trem channel, and a high-gain EF86 in the Normal channel.

**1b** The first three tubes here are all used in the Vib/Trem channel's preamp and effects circuits (the bases of the preamp tube sockets can be seen in a row along the middle of this portion of the chassis, between the circuit boards). The first ECC83 functions as the input gain stage for the channel, the second is the modulator tube for Vib/Trem, and the third—an ECC82 (12AU7)—is the oscillator tube for the effect.

**1c** Vox was among the few manufacturers to use EF86 preamp tubes (in the AC15, AC10, AC4, and very early versions of the AC30), but didn't stick with it for all that long. These nine-pin pentodes can sound fantastic in the right preamp, with a fat, full-frequencied voice and a lot more gain than a 12AX7, but they are prone to "microphony" (which is the amplification of mechanical or vibrational noise through a tube and into the electronic circuit) and can make major issues of noise and stability. The tube was revived in the early years of the "boutique era" by Matchless and Dr Z amps.

The use of this high-gain tube here means that no further gain stages are needed in this channel. The signal flows straight from the EF86 via a coupling cap, a "Brilliant" (bright) switch, the volume control, and another coupling cap, straight into the PI.

**1d** Due to the complex, switchable vibrato/tremolo effect on these amps, the Vib/Trem channel is a much more involved affair. In addition to using a full three tubes for gain and effects stages, it occupies a large portion of this lower circuit board.

# Vox AC15 (1962)

| 1a | 68k input resistors |
|----|---------------------|
| 1b | pins of ECC83/ECC82 (12AU7) tubes |
| 1c | pins of EF86 preamp tube |
| 1d/1e | Vib/Trem channel components |
| 1f | 'cut' pot |
| 2a | long-tail-pair PI |
| 4a | Wima signal capacitors |
| | (see text for more details) |

**1e** The Vib/Trem channel carries switches for vibrato/tremolo selection and a three-way speed selector, as well as a trim pot —placed inside the amp on the circuit board—for presetting the depth of the effect.

**1f** A Cut pot positioned here controls a filtering network positioned between the PI and the output tubes. As such, the control works on both channels, to fine-tune the amp's high-end content.

## PI And Output

**2a** Dick Denney knew his onions when it came to design, and employed a version of the sturdy long-tail-pair PI in this relatively small amp, when Fender's 15-watters were still mostly using the slightly cruder split-load PI. The "long-tail" is more difficult to identify here, though, due to the circuit layout.

The remainder of the output stage (tubes and some of the related circuitry) is mounted on the horizontal plane on the other side of this vertical portion of the chassis. The amp uses a pair of EL84 output tubes in cathode-bias, with no negative feedback around the output stage—what's normally referred to as a class A output.

## Power Supply

**3a** Nope, can't see much of that here either. The EZ81 tube rectifier is mounted on the second, horizontal chassis along with the output tubes, as are most of the larger filter caps used in the amp.

## Other Features

**4a** Note the proliferation of great-sounding Wima signal capacitors throughout this circuit. These are the light-gold-colored caps with red print seen here and in many other positions, not to be confused with the gold caps with black print seen in a few positions, which are lower-voltage electrolytic caps used mainly as cathode bypass caps and so forth. These older style Wimas are smooth, clear and rich, and are highly prized by tonehounds.

# Fender Super Reverb (1965)

The Fender Super Reverb is a classic of the blackface era (1963-67). One of the all-time great blues amps, it's also excellent for jazz, country, and rock'n'roll. The amp generates approximately 45 watts from a pair of 6L6GC output tubes, with six dual triodes for preamp, PI, and effects duties. The open-backed cab carries 4x10″ speakers wired parallel for a 2-ohm load. This, its tube rectifier, and the Middle control in the Vibrato channel often lead it to be named as the heir to the tweed Bassman, but other elements of the Super Reverb's design and construction are considerably different.

Rather than using the cathode-follower tone stack of the Bassman and other big tweeds—which places the tone circuit and pots after the second gain stage, and is credited with a lot of the great touch-sensitivity of those amps—the blackface amps sandwich their tone stacks between two more traditional grid-input/plate-output gain stages. The tone controls are placed before the volume, too, rather than after. These, and numerous other (less obvious) changes in the output stage, all aim to achieve more headroom for a louder, cleaner performance.

The same goal is attained here by using a 12AT7 rather than 12AX7 in the PI, which doesn't drive the output tubes into breakup as quickly or easily as the PI in the big tweed amps, even those

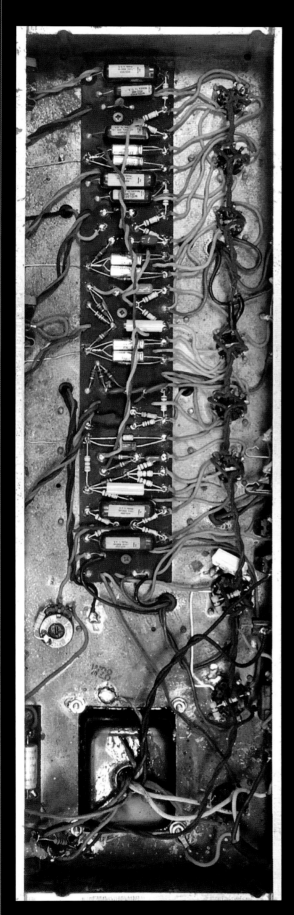

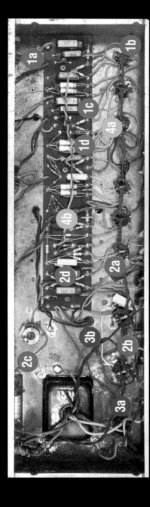

1a   68k grid resistors

1b   pins for preamp tube

1c   signal capacitors (.1uF, .022uF, 250pF, .047uF & .02uF 'chocolate drop')

1d   biasing resistors

2a   pins of 12AT7 PI tube

2b   pair of 6L6GC output tubes

2c   biasing network

2d   820-ohm resistor for negative feedback loop

3a   5U4GB tube rectifier

3b   grommet for power supply to reach other side of chassis

4a   12AT7 & 7025 reverb/vibrato driver tubes

4b   optocoupler for tremolo effect

*(see text for more details)*

with the same long-tailed-pair PI circuit. That's a lot of changes, as you can see—yet it's still a titan of tone that's nearly on par with the legendary Bassman.

Good Super Reverbs offer a big, bold low-end and shimmering highs, with a more recessed midrange than the tweed amps of the 1950s, all of which gives them an open, airy, and yet firm tonality. They do remain clean up to a reasonable volume level, about 4 on the dial—with single-coil pickups especially—but they certainly know how to break up, too, when cranked high enough. Once pushed into overdrive, a Super has a powerful, gnarly growl that's characteristic of the 6L6; this makes a stunning crunch sound for rock rhythm, and forms the core of one of the most compelling blues lead tones known to man. Add the lush reverb and deep, haunting vibrato, and you've got an extremely versatile amplifier.

## Input And Preamp

**1a** In the tradition of Fender amps post-1960, the Super Reverb's 68k grid resistors are not located on the circuit board, but mounted to the positive tab of each input jack, and soldered together at their adjoining ends. From this point, the signal runs under the board to pin 2 of the first preamp tube.

**1b** Unlike the bigger tweed Fender amps, which shared preamp tubes for first gain stages and following stages, the blackface amps use both triodes of an individual tube for the first stage and gain makeup stage (following the tone controls) of each channel, plus a further third triode stage in the Vibrato channel. So the placement of the inputs for each channel next to their respective volume and tone controls mirrors the layout of the circuit inside.

**1c** Notice how the three signal capacitors in this position—a 0.1uF, a 0.022uF, and a 250pF (the small, brown ceramic disc cap)—mirror the first three on the board. These form the filter network for the Vibrato channel's tone stack, while the previous three belong to the Normal channel. In each, the signal runs from the first gain stage to the tone caps and pots, then the volume pot, and into the second gain makeup stage. Although the Vibrato channel carries a Middle control that the Normal channel lacks, they still use the same capacitors to shape the frequency response. The network is just configured slightly differently in each.

From this point onward, these channels differ considerably. The signal from the Normal channel heads toward the PI in a long wire run under the board via a 0.047uF cap (the third big blue cap in from the right). The Vibrato channel's signal, on the other hand, enters the reverb circuit via a smaller, brown 0.02uF "chocolate drop" cap.

Note that most of this amp's prized original blue tubular polyester Mallory caps are still present; these are often called "Molded" caps because that's what's printed on them. A couple have been replaced with newer yellow Mallory caps, and many of the original carbon comp resistors have been replaced with newer carbon film types. A few blue metal film resistors are also present on the output tubes and in the power supply.

**1d** While the first triode of each of the first two preamp tubes is biased individually with a 1.5k resistor and 25uF/25V bypass cap (these pairs laid out together between the signal caps of the first and second channel), the second triodes of these tubes have their cathodes linked (pin 8) and are biased together here on the board. This is a somewhat unusual arrangement, but works fine nonetheless. It does mean, though, that substituting a "nearly compatible" 12AT7 tube in the first channel's socket, in an attempt to obtain a cleaner tone, renders the second channel's 12AX7 inoperative (and vice versa), because it robs it of the required bias voltage. A 12AY7 or 5751 causes no problems.

## PI And Output

**2a** Blackface Fenders use a 12AT7 in the PI for a gentler, smoother drive than a 12AX7—all part of Fender's continued quest for more headroom. Right above this tube, the last in a row of six preamp tubes, is the three-into-one resistor configuration of the long-tail-pair phase inverter. From the PI, the signal runs via two more large, blue 0.1uF coupling caps to …

**2b** A pair of 6L6GC output tubes in a fixed-bias, push-pull configuration, which generates about 45 watts of power.

**2c** The biasing network is located on its own small board (partially obscured by the chassis fold), with an adjustment pot located to the right of it.

**2d** A negative feedback loop—seen here as a simple 820-ohm resistor connected between the PI and the speaker jacks—helps to raise the headroom further in blackface amps. This is a very low value of negative feedback resistor; the lower the value, the more negative signal is fed back to the PI.

## Power Supply

**3a** The Super Reverb carries a 5U4GB tube rectifier.

**3b** From the rectifier, the power supply runs through a grommet to the other side of the chassis, where two large 70uF electrolytic caps and three slightly smaller 20uF/450V caps are mounted in their own "cap can." This is another significant design advancement of Fender amps post-1960 (and a few larger ones before)—the protective can helps to keep a blowing cap from messing up other parts of the circuit. It also allows these crowded tremolo-plus-reverb circuit boards to be feasible at all. In addition, the Super's power supply also carries a choke.

## Other Features

**4a** The Super Reverb has two onboard effects, reverb and tremolo (which Fender persistently labeled "vibrato," except on the Tremolux). The three preamp tubes between those for channel gain and makeup and the PI are associated with these effects. This 12AT7 is the reverb driver; half of the 7025 following it (a 12AX7 equivalent) takes up the reverb signal after the spring pan (mounted in a bag at the bottom of the cabinet), while its second half is used as a third gain stage for the Vibrato channel. As you might guess, this design makes channel 2 a little more powerful than channel 1.

**4b** The 12AX7 before the PI takes tremolo duties. This black "bug" on the circuit board is the optocoupler (LDR) that produces the pulse of the tremolo effect.

# Marshall JMP50 (1971)

The Marshall JMP50 Model "1987" is an all-time classic rock amp. (By the way, Marshall amp model numbers have nothing to do with the year from which an amp originates, although they might look that way. Marshall's earliest 50-watt "Lead" amps, for example, all carried the Model 1987 designation, which stayed with them from the JTM45 to the JMP50 amps.) There is very little difference sonically or electronically between the "plexi" models of 1967-69 (so-called because they had a gold-painted plexiglass control panel) and these metal-panel models, although the latter are certainly a little more affordable on the vintage market. Many guitar stars of the late 1960s and early 1970s used the 100-watt models to pump out the necessary volume for their big stadium tours, but the 50-watt heads are generally more desirable today. They are a little easier to push into that gorgeously crunchy sweet spot—though make no mistake, still loud as hell—and can be used in a wider range of venues than a fierce 100-watt stack.

In a range of variations, this is essentially the sound of Jimmy Page, Paul Kossoff, George Lynch, early Eddie Van Halen, classic Jimi Hendrix, Cream-era Eric Clapton, and so many others I could keep listing them into tomorrow. Unlike a lot of guitars and amps, where the first incarnations of the brand are usually considered "archetypal," when guitarists think of "Marshall" it's most often the JMP50 (or JTM50 plexi) that comes to mind.

The evolution of the model's bright channel (called the "High Treble" channel by Marshall) is a significant change, but the move to EL34 output tubes played an even bigger part in the sonic evolution from JTM45 to plexi/metal 50-watter. These can actually be driven to higher voltages than the 6L6/5881/KT66 types used previously—in the wake of the Fender Bassman that provided the template for the company's first amp—and helped to provide the louder amplifier that rock players were demanding, even in its "smaller" 50-watt version. They also provided the tonality that quickly helped to define the genre. Despite the higher power, EL34s also compressed and broke up a little more quickly, and some would say more sweetly, than 6L6 types in a similar circuit. That gritty, chewy, slightly crispy sounding EL34 grind is a standard of the heavy rock sound that was clearly established by Marshall, and has been emulated by countless manufacturers ever since.

In the mid 1970s, the arrival of the printed circuit board and—shortly after—the master volume control ended the "vintage years" of Marshall production as far as many players and collectors are concerned. But the company continued to make some storming amps that really excel at the big rock sound.

■ We've already seen two circuits nearly identical to this one. Although an early 1970s Marshall looks very different to a late 1950s tweed Fender while bolted into its fierce black cabinet, poke your nose inside the chassis from the same angle—figuratively, please—and the layout is still virtually identical, aside from the mounting positions for the tubes. Even 11 years down the road, the circuit and format of Fender's 5F6A Bassman casts a heavy shadow over metal-panel Marshall amps like this one. As we saw a few pages earlier in this chapter, the imprint was even stronger on the early JTM45, but the top-ology survived through the plexiglass Marshalls that preceded this one, and remains here with few changes.

This is a beautiful example of the breed, which appears to be all-original internally, aside from a replaced power switch and fuse socket and perhaps a new green metal film resistor on the second preamp tube. There has possibly also been an alteration to one of the bypass caps tied to one of the first preamp tube's cathodes, but it's difficult to tell if this was a factory alteration or not.

1a .68uF bypass capacitor

1b .022uF 'mustard' coupling caps

1c .022uF caps

2a pins of preamp/PI tube (with 'long tail' resistors above)

2b EL34 output tubes

2c negative feedback loop, with 47k resistor

2d AB fixed-bias output stage & trim pot

3a solid-state rectificier

3b bases/mounting pins of 50uF/50uF multi-section filter
    capacitors

*(see text for more details)*

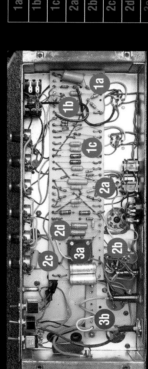

## Input And Preamp

**1a** Unlike the tweed Bassman and JTM45, the two triodes of the first preamp tube are now individually biased. The change allows Marshall to use a different bypass cap around the cathode-bias resistor of one side to create its notoriously crunchy bright channel (a 0.68uF cap). The spec bypass cap for the other channel is a 320uF, for a fuller, warmer sound, but that does not appear to be present here.

**1b** The signal runs from the first gain stage in each channel to the volume controls via a pair of 0.022uF coupling caps—in this case these are the highly prized "mustard caps" that Marshall was still using. Fender had already moved away from this voicing more than ten years before, but these cap values contribute to the full, open sound that many players prize in Marshall amps.

**1c** These 0.022uF caps and the tube below them function in the famed cathode-follower tone stack that this Marshall model retains.

**1d** The second channel also carries a bright cap across the input and wiper of the volume pot itself; this is a bright, bright channel—rightly dubbed a High Treble channel.

## PI And Output

**2a** The third "preamp" tube here takes care of PI duties, and is utilized in the now-familiar long-tail-pair configuration (its "long tail" of resistors is clearly visible on the board above it).

**2b** As significant as any of the small changes within the circuit, the plexi and then metal-panel Marshalls changed from 5881s or KT66s to British EL34 output tubes. These are powerful tubes that provide a little more output level when driven at higher voltages, and produce a crispy, compressed, mids-heavy crunch when pushed hard. It's thanks largely to this tube change that these are the amps most players think of when they think Marshall.

**2c** A negative feedback loop runs around the amp's output stage to provide a smoother sound and a little more stability at higher levels. The amp's presence circuit taps this loop with a 5k potentiometer and a 0.1uF capacitor to ground to provide some control over the amp's brightness content at the output stage. The blue resistor on the board, just left of the final yellow 0.022uF coupling cap, is the 47k resistor between the PI and the speaker jacks that sets the level of negative signal fed back into the front of the output stage.

**2d** The JMP50's class AB output stage is in fixed-bias. This small network creates a negative DC voltage at the tube's grid, and carries a small trim pot (seen side-on) for adjusting the bias level.

## Power Supply

**3a** Rather than the tube rectifier of the JTM45, these later Marshalls had solid-state rectification (a change made in the plexi amps a few years before).

**3b** Not a lot can be seen of this amp's power supply, because the large filter capacitors are comprised of multi-section can types mounted on the reverse side of the chassis, alongside the tubes and transformers. You can just make out the bases and mounting pins of a pair of 50uF/50uF multi-section caps here.

**3c** Something you can't even see a trace of here is the fact that Marshall is now running these output tubes at higher voltages, which—along with the change to EL34s—added up to a lot more output level. Although these amps are commonly referred to as "50-watters" they can often put out closer to 60 watts. The higher DC voltages, replacement of tube rectification with solid-state, and heavy filtering (which included a hefty choke in the filtering chain) also added up to a sound that was tighter and punchier than the JTM45 could ever deliver.

# Traynor YBA-1 Bass Master (early 1970s)

Like a Marshall plexi amp, the Traynor YBA-1 has four inputs, six knobs, three 12AX7/ECC83 preamp tubes, two EL34 (6CA7) output tubes, diode rectification, a cathode-follower tone stack … the similarities go on. But there are differences too, which are thoroughly outlined in the stage-by-stage analysis below. The YBA-1 really is designed to be a bass amp (well, so was the Bassman, but the distinction was less, eh, distinct back in the 1950s) and benefits with hindsight from the tweed Fender's failings in this department, with circuit and speaker updates more suited to the four-string. That said, it is so close to Marshall plexi specifications that it would make a great candidate for conversion for a guitarist. The result would be a hand-wired, vintage-era amp with very similar characteristics at a small fraction of the cost.

These amps, manufactured in Canada by Pete Traynor and Jack Long under the umbrella of their Yorkville Sound Inc, were extremely well built, carried quality components and good transformers, and were popular items north of the US border (and often in the States too) throughout the late 1960s and 1970s. Traynor amps never had the romantic image of vintage Fender, Marshall, or Vox models, but appear to have been just as well made, and are again gaining respect among guitarists today who stumble on them as a "hidden secret" on the used market.

Traynors built specifically for guitar range all the way from the more powerful 100-watt YGL half-stacks down to the smaller, 20-watt YGM series with EL84s—both with a terrific, deep reverb that this bass amp lacks.

The YGA-1 (and other Traynor heads) are built with durability and hassle-free maintenance in mind. A repair technician can easily access the inside of the chassis of this amp, and thus the circuit, by unbolting four bolts from the top of the cab and simply removing the top panel—a lot simpler than pulling out the whole chassis. And once you're in there, there's plenty of elbow room too.

■ This book doesn't cover bass amps as such, so the literary detectives among you will notice a thematic link in the inclusion of this Traynor Bass Master. Many elements of its design have evolved from another bass amp that fared better as a guitar amp, the tweed Fender Bassman, although the YBA-1 Bass Master takes its cues from the first famous "homage" to that design, produced by Marshall.

Unlike the majority of Marshalls, though, the YBA-1 adapts the format for use with bass once again, but it's just a few minor changes away from being a classic rock guitar amp. So I'm including it here as a nod to one of the many "hidden bargains" out there. You can usually pick these up for even less than a silverface Fender Bassman, and they are only a few steps away from being a great Marshall plexi-a-like.

## Input And Preamp
**1a** The YBA-1's two channels share the first preamp tube. This 12AX7's cathodes are biased individually rather than together, by the familiar 1.5k resistor and a lesser-seen 125uF/16V bypass cap. Change one of these to a 0.68uF bypass cap, and you are on your way to creating a Marshall-style High Treble channel.
**1b** Just like the Bassman/JTM45/plexi, the signal in this amp runs from each triode of the first preamp tube to the channel's respective volume controls via a 0.02uF cap. The difference—something you can't see—is that the Traynor runs its first gain stage at 225VDC on the plates rather than the 150VDC of these other amps.

The higher voltage gives it a tighter voicing with more headroom, qualities that most players would seek in a bass amp.

**1c** Following the volume pots, the two channels are joined and sent through the shared second gain stage, then the cathode-follower EQ stage. The grid resistors mixing the two signals are 100k rather than the 270k of the Fender and Marshall amps, and again this 12AX7 has higher voltages on its plates: 215VDC and 350VDC, as opposed to around 180VDC and 325VDC.

**1d** While the positioning of the YBA-1's tone stack is similar to those classic amps, its precise configuration and the values of the caps used for frequency filtering are somewhat different. Whereas the Fenders and Marshalls have oddly-ordered Treble, Bass, Middle controls, the YBA-1 carries Treble, Bass, and Low Range Expander. In place of the other amps' Presence control, it has what is labeled a High Range Expander. (These "Expanders" are really just tone filters using different cap values from the Fender/Marshall standards. The Bass Master manual said that they "change the tonal coloring of the amplifier.") Again, the voicing here is intended for bass amplification, but a few quick changes and a couple of replacement caps could render an exact copy of the Fender/Marshall cathode-follower tone stack.

Note also that most of the signal caps on the board are of a similar appearance and composition to the legendary "mustard caps" used in vintage Marshall amps, as seen on preceding pages.

## PI And Output

**2a** 2a The familiar three-into-one resistor configuration of the long-tailed-pair PI. Traynor uses different values here, but the underlying design of the PI is the same.

**2b** A pair of 6CA7 output tubes (the North American equivalent to European EL34s) generate around 50 to 60 watts.

**2c** The YBA-1's output tubes are wired in fixed-bias, with (in this case) a non-adjustable network to generate a negative voltage on the grids in relation to the plates. You can see the green diode that is central to this circuit tucked between a large resistor and a filter cap.

**2d** The amp's negative feedback loop uses a much higher resistor than many others, a 100k; this delivers less of the negative signal back to the input of the PI, lowering the dampening effect of the loop.

## Power Supply

**3a** 3a Four silicon diodes are used as a full-wave bridge rectifier. This differs from the tube rectifier of the Fender 5F6A Bassman and Marshall JTM45, but echoes the solid-state rectification of the plexi Marshall JTM50 Model 1987 amp.

**3b** A pair of multi-section "can caps" carry two 40uF/450V electrolytic capacitors each. The YBA-1 lacks the choke of the Fender and Marshall, but has pretty firm filtering from these components.

Other than the changes to some resistors and signal caps to make a plexi-conversion from this Traynor, the dropping resistors in the power supply would need to be increased in order to lower the voltages to the plates of the first two gain stages. Otherwise, the Bass Master is already 80 per cent there.

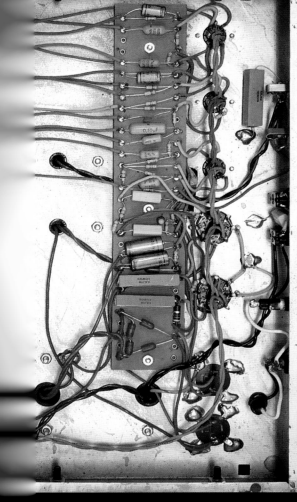

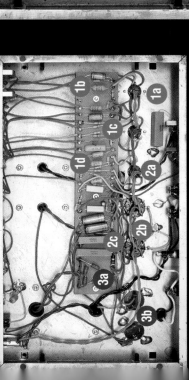

1a  pins of 12AX7 preamp tube
1b  .02uF capacitor
1c  100k grid resistors
1d  signal/filter caps
2a  long-tailed-pair PI
2b  pins of two 6CA7 output tubes
2c  diode to generate negative  voltage on grids
2d  100k resistor for negative feedback loop
3a  silicon diodes as full-wave bridge rectifier
3b  pair of multi-section 'can caps' with two 40uF/450V
     electrolytic caps each

*(see text for more details)*

# Peavey Prowler (late 1990s)

The Peavey Prowler is an affordable tube amp that offers players a good, versatile range of sounds in a compact package, and for not a whole lot of cash. This channel-switching 1x12″ amp carries three 12AX7s in the preamp and PI, and two 6L6GCs in the output stage, to deliver a declared power level of 45 watts. Front-panel controls include: Volume, Low, Mid and High controls for the Clean channel, with Bright button and Channel Select; Gain, Volume (master), Bottom, Body, and Edge for the Lead channel, with Gain Boost and Volume Boost pushbuttons; Reverb, and effects Send & Return jacks. A further pushbutton on the back panel selects Loose/Tight speaker dynamics.

Even a cursory look reveals that resistors, capacitors and other parts used here are of a smaller type and more generic, consumer-electronics grade than those used in vintage or high-end modern amps. But the Prowler retailed for around the $450 mark when it was still available, and this amp—and others like it—provided many players with usable, versatile tube amp tones at levels within their limited budgets, so it and its kind deserve some respect nevertheless.

The Peavey company was founded in Meridian, Mississippi, by Hartley Peavey in 1965, and primarily manufactured guitar amps and PA systems up until the late 1970s, when its first guitars were introduced. Since that time, the company has branched out into all realms of musical instruments and amplification electronics. Currently, Peavey guitar amps cover a broad range of formats and intended users—from small solid-state practice amps to big multi-channel tube stacks. The most famous of the latter is certainly the 5150 Edward Van Halen signature amp, now discontinued in the wake of the guitar star's departure as an endorsee. The Joe Satriani JSX series looks poised to take its place. In between these price brackets, low-to-moderately priced Peavey tube amps such as the Classic series, and the Prowler examined here, have remained perennial favorites with players of limited resources—a category that has included most of us at one time or another.

■ This recent Peavey Prowler takes us into new territory: that of the affordable, printed-circuit-board-based tube amp of the modern age. Like other mass-manufactured PCB amps, the signal flow of this Prowler can be difficult to follow across a two-dimensional photograph because many of the electronic connections – or 'traces' – run along the underside of the board, which is also where most PCB-mounted components are soldered. But we can still examine many of the amp's major stages, and probe the componentry in general.

## Input And Preamp

**1a** High-gain and low-gain inputs offer two gain structures; the second would normally be used to avoid overloading the first gain stage when using high-output humbucking pickups.

**1b** The Clean and Lead channels share the two gain stages offered by the first 12AX7 (its PCB-mounted socket is seen here). Following the first gain stage, in Clean mode, electronic switching routes the signal through the channel's EQ and Volume controls then on to the second, or gain makeup, stage; in Lead, the signal flows from one triode to the Gain control, then to the second gain stage, and on to …

**1c** Further gain stages that are provided by the second 12AX7, creating the typical 'cascading gain' high-gain topology, as originated by Mesa/Boogie back in the early 1970s. The Prowler's Lead channel's EQ section – labelled Bottom, Body and Edge (bass, middle, treble) – follows this, and is in turn followed by the channel's master Volume control.

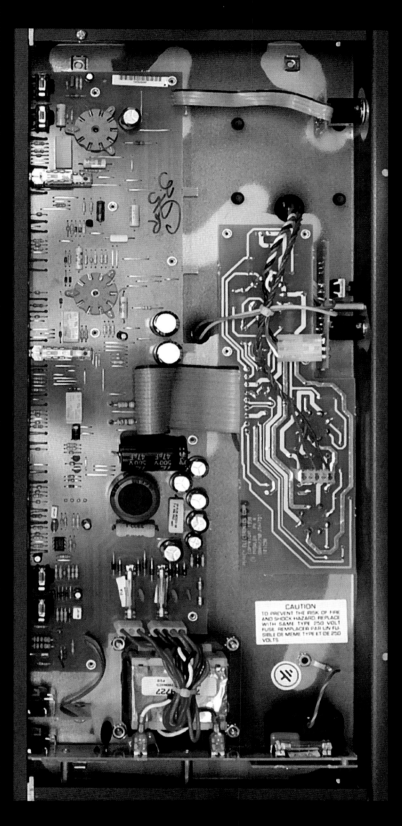

1a    inputs

1b    12AX7 socket

1c    second 12AX7

1d    silicon diodes (for 'signal clamping')

2a    separate PCB for PI & output tubes

2b    wires carrying signal & DC supply to/from 6L6 output tubes

3a    silicon diodes (rectifiers)

3b    power-filtering caps (inc 47uF/500V axial cap & multi-section radial cap)

4a    op-amp reverb circuit

*(see text for more details)*

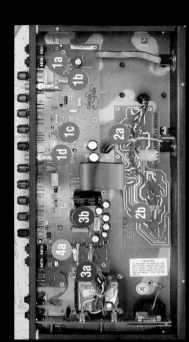

**1d** Although the layout of this PCB board makes it difficult to determine their exact roles without a schematic, silicon diodes like these (the small, black, tubular, resistor-like components seen here behind channel 2's control section) are often used for 'signal clamping' to provide further clipping of the signal, and thus extra distortion in addition to that provided by the tube stages alone.

### PI And Output

**2a** This amp's PI and output tubes are located on a separate PCB, which makes repair a little easier than it would be for the tech who had to pull one large board to service everything. The nature of the board's layout, though, makes it impossible to analyze the topology of the PI used here without access to a schematic.
**2b** The Prowler carries a pair of 6L6 output tubes in class AB, fixed-bias. The brown and blue wires here carry the signal from the plates of the 6L6s to the push-pull sides of the OT's primary, while the red wire carries the high-voltage DC supply to its center tap. The white, green, and black wires running back through the rubber grommet in the chassis take the signal from the OT's secondary to the speaker outs. The Prowler's output is rated at 45 watts, although the amp carries a rather small OT for that level of power.

### Power Supply

**3a** The silicon diodes here perform rectification duties.
**3b** There's a considerable amount of power filtering in the Prowler, seen here in the form of a large 47uF/500V axial cap, another large multi-section radial cap, and a number of smaller-value caps.

### Other Features

**4a** There are no further tube stages in this amp. The driver and signal pickup functions of the Prowler's reverb are, therefore, performed by op-amps (chips). Such a circuit provides the effect at a much lower cost than that of the traditional Fender-style two-tubes-plus-transformer reverb circuit.

# Fender Blues Junior (early 2000s)

Fender introduced the Blues Junior in 1995 as an upgrade of the more basic Pro Junior that debuted the year before. An extension of the new and very successful Tweed Series of 1993, which brought contemporary features to the looks and, to some extent, the sounds of Fender's seminal amps of the 50s, the 15-watt, 1x10" Blues Junior combo was a relatively affordable "club" sized combo that packed a lot of proven Fender tone and features, and which became a huge success as a result—remaining one of the most popular sub-20-watt tube amps in circulation today.

Although their circuits were different in several regards, we can think of the Blues Junior as a contemporary Princeton Reverb, without the tremolo but with the addition of a Fat boost switch. And with one other notable difference: instead of two 6V6s, the amp uses a pair of EL84s (aka 6BQ5s), an output tube not seen in Fender amps since the short-lived 1961 blonde Tremolux. The EL84s give the Blues Junior a little more of the crispy midrange crunch when cranked and a sweet chime in the highs, although the overall impression is still one of handy, portable, and versatile smaller club-sized combo.

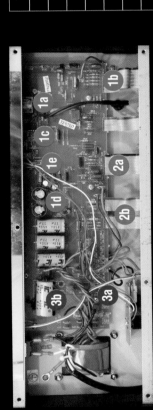

| | |
|---|---|
| 1a | inputs |
| 1b | ribbon leads to first 12AX7 |
| 1c | Volume control |
| 1d | Treble, Bass, and Middle controls |
| 1e | push-button switch for Fat boost function |
| 2a | PI, powered by another 12AX7 |
| 2b | ribbon leads to the two EL84s |
| 3a | Diode rectifier bridge |
| 3b | 47uF/450V filter cap |

Outwardly, the Blues Junior follows the late-50s Fender pattern, with an upper-rear mounted control panel and a narrow-panel style cab with floating baffle (this version is covered in black Tolex, although special editions have been offered in tweed and other coverings). Unlike either the tweed or the blackface/silverface Fenders, the circuit's signal flow puts a volume control after the first gain stage provided by the first triode of a 12AX7, with a second gain stage provided by the second triode of that tube after the pot, followed by the three-knob tone stack and a third gain stage. This sandwiching of the Treble, Bass and Middle controls between two gain stages is a lot more like what we've seen in blackface and silverface circuits, but that first triode will already have ramped up the gain further than that achieved in any of those 60s and 70s designs. After that third triode in the preamp the signal hits a Master control, then rolls on to a long-tailed-pair PI populated by a third 12AX7. The reverb is driven by a solid-state network, and sounds perfectly fine for it. The Fat boost is a simple but effective network to take the cathode bypass cap on the first gain stage in and out of ground, accessible via a push-button switch on the control panel or a footswitch plugged into the underside of the chassis.

All of this leaves us, interestingly enough, with one unused triode, the second half of V2, which some hot-rodders have made good use of in their modified Blues Juniors. Whether you create yet another gain stage, or a cathode-follower buffer to make the tone stack more tweed-like, this presents interesting possibilities. The output tubes are configured in non-adjustable fixed bias, and there's a negative feedback loop around the output stage (from speaker out to the input of the PI) to tighten up the response. Another popular Blues Junior mod is to add a bias-adjust pot, which enables the player to more precisely set the amp's idle to match different EL84s, yielding an optimal tone and improved tube life.

The Fender Blues Junior exhibits the kind of construction you'd expect to see in an amp that's manufactured in great numbers and sold at a relatively affordable price, but this observation doesn't cast any aspersions on its quality, or its success as a design. This has been one of the most popular club amps of the past couple decades, and thousands of Blues Juniors have delivered tens of thousands of gigs with good tone and no complaints.

As with other PCB amps, the signal flow of this can be difficult to follow across a two-dimensional photograph because many of the electronic connections are out of view. The flying "ribbon" connections between the board and the chassis-mounted tube sockets aren't easy to follow from point to point without a three-dimensional, "in person" look either. That said, this mostly follows a somewhat familiar Fender topology, if one that has evolved from its predecessors of 50-plus years before.

## Input And Preamp

**1a** The single input takes the signal straight to the first triode of the 12AX7 via a 10k grid-stopper resistor, an unusual value in contemporary amp design.
**1b** This "ribbon" lead takes all signal- and voltage-carrying and biasing duties to and from the first preamp tube (and similarly for all tubes, for that matter). From here, the signal goes on to…
**1c** The Volume control, then back to V1b for the second gain stage, before …
**1d** The tone stack, comprising Treble, Bass, and Middle controls sandwiched between the second and third gain stages.
**1e** The push-button switch for the Fat boost is found here. Note the wires that run from this position to the lower-left corner of the chassis, where the Fat boost footswitch jack is mounted on the bottom panel.

## PI And Output

**2a** The phase inverter carries the amp's third 12AX7 in a long-tailed-pair circuit, not easy to discern on this printed circuit board without close-up inspection.

**2b** Two further "ribbon" leads take signal and power supplies to the EL84 output tubes.

## Power Supply

**3a** The silicon diodes here perform rectification duties.

**3b** The Blues Junior has pretty firm power filtering for an amp its size, seen here in the form of a large 47uF/450V axial electrolytic cap, plus three 22uF/450V caps to the right of it.

# Soldano Decatone (2000)

The Soldano Decatone is a powerful rock amp that takes this famous California high-gain designer into even more versatile territory. One of its most appealing factors is of course its Overdrive channel, which offers a good version of the famous lead sound first heard in their renowned Super Lead Overdrive. But its Clean channel is generally considered to be a little sweeter than that of the SLO, and it also carries an excellent Crunch channel. Of course all of this requires some pretty complex circuitry—especially when you seek to achieve it with all the tonal integrity of a Soldano—and this is a real spaghetti-junction of a board to fathom. Such involved designs make the use of PCBs almost inevitable, but Soldano's are extra thick and double-sided, with wide, carefully laid-out trace runs and hand-wired leads between the board and all chassis-mounted components.

Michael J. Soldano entered the amp business in 1987 with the release of his SLO, and the Decatone was introduced around 1997, to celebrate the company's first decade in business. Plenty of major players have taken up the Soldano banner at one time or another, including George Lynch, Gary Moore, Eric Clapton, Mark Knopfler, Joe Satriani, Steve Vai, and others.

Four 5881s generate the Decatone's 100-watt output, while five 12AX7s perform preamp, FX loop and PI duties. The amp is available as a head or 2x12" combo. Front-panel controls include individual Preamp (gain) knobs for the Clean, Crunch, and Overdrive channels, each with its own Bright switch and pushbutton selector; shared Bass, Middle and Treble; and an independent master Volume control for each channel. There are also shared Presence, Depth (low-end emphasis) and overall Master Volume controls. The back carries the FX loop's send & return jacks, FX Level control, and an impedance selector for the dual parallel speaker-outs.

Soldano's bigger amps are neither overtly souped-up Marshall nor hot-rodded Fender, but carry elements of both, along with plenty of original touches. They mostly use the Fender-ish 5881 and 6L6GC output tubes, but carry the cathode-follower tone stack that has become a Marshall trademark (although it originated with tweed Fender amps, and Soldano's follows after an FX loop, besides). Overall, they are very much their own amps.

■ Thanks to their use of double-sided printed circuit boards—boards with conductive tracks etched into both sides, often carrying signal voltages one side and high-voltage supplies the other—amps of this design are difficult to trace visually from photographs, without a three-dimensional, hands-on probe inside the chassis. A look at a Decatone schematic diagram would reveal everything a repairman could ever need to know, but for our purposes here there is still a lot to be pointed out under the hood of the Soldano.

## Input And Preamp

One of the first things you'll notice on examining these photos of the Soldano is that its circuitboard flows from left to right (preamp to output and power supply), the reverse of the other amplifiers examined in this chapter. This allows the chassis to be mounted tubes-up in a head, with the input at the left end of the control panel, à la Fender, which some players feel is a more logical arrangement.

**1a** After entering the Decatone's single input, the signal reaches the first tube gain stage, which is common to all three channels of the amp. Preamp sockets are a little more difficult to identify visually when PCB-mounted as they are here, but you can just make out the solder tabs arranged in a circle through the board. Trace from left to right from this first preamp tube, adjacent to our "1a" label above, and you will locate the solder tabs of the five 12AX7s used in the Decatone's preamp and PI.

**1b** The first three potentiometers here are the individual gain controls for the Clean, Crunch, and Overdrive channels. Each has, mounted beside it, a mini toggle switch for Bright and an illuminating pushbutton for channel select. Like most modern high-gain amps, the Decatone generates its overdrive sound by cascading further gain stages following the initial single triode used as the first gain stage for all channels.

**1c** Amid the crowded signal routing of this complex three-channel amp, you can identify the opto-isolators used for the electronic switching.

**1d** The blue resistors seen throughout the circuit are metal film types. The brownish-orange signal capacitors, while they appear somewhat like the Orange Drops we've discussed elsewhere, are actually a slightly smaller, less expensive, but nevertheless good quality make of capacitor.

## PI And Output

**2a** Four 5881 output tubes (a sturdy 6L6GT equivalent) produce an output of approximately 100 watts. The octal tube sockets for these are mounted on a separate board located to the rear (bottom in this photo) of the chassis.

**2b** The Decatone's output stage is fixed-bias, with a small network of capacitors, resistors and a single diode to provide a negative DC voltage to the grid in relation to the cathode.

**2c** A rotary impedance selector sends the required tap from the OT to the amp's dual parallel speaker output jacks.

## Power Supply

**3a** Four silicon diodes form the full-wave bridge rectifier that converts the PT's AC output to a DC supply. Larger amps run their output tubes at high voltages (often in the upper 400s) to provide a firm, punchy amplification of the preamp-generated overdrive and crunch tones.

**3b** Four big radial electrolytic capacitors offer plenty of filtering to the power supply, aided by …

**3c** A chunky choke, internally mounted here rather than positioned on the outside of the chassis.

## Other Features

**4a** The Decatone carries a series/parallel effects loop. The send and return jacks are mounted on a small board positioned vertically here on the back panel, beside the dual-ganged blend control (FX level).

**4b** Flying leads run from the send & return jacks to the point on the main PCB that forms the junction between the preamp and power amp, and from the blend control to its tube-powered driver/buffer circuit at an earlier point in the preamp (labeled 4c).

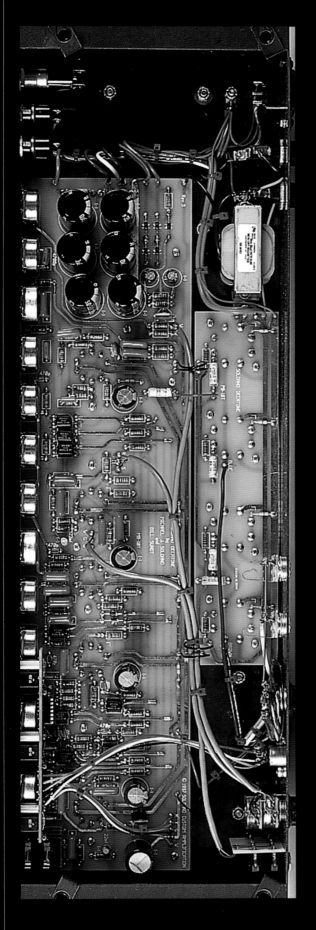

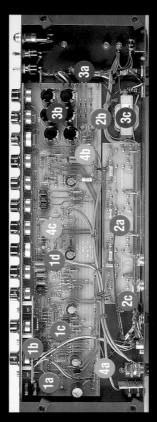

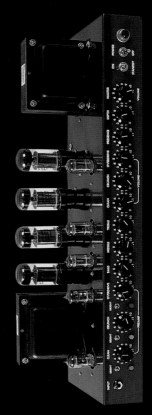

| | |
|---|---|
| 1a | solder tabs for 12AX7 preamp tubes |
| 1b | potentiometers, with mini toggle switch & pushbutton |
| 1c | opto-isolators for electronic switching |
| 1d | blue metal film resistors & brownish-orange signal capacitors |
| 2a | separate PCB with octal sockets for four 5881 output tubes |
| 2b | output stage, with caps, resistors & diode |
| 2c | rotary impedance selector |
| 3a | four silicon diodes as full-wave bridge rectifier |
| 3b | four radial electrolytic filter capacitors |
| 3c | choke |
| 4a/4b/4c | effects loop & connected circuitry |
| | *(see text for more details)* |

# Dr Z Z-28 (2004)

The Dr Z Z-28 was released in around 2000, and is available as a head and as 1x12", 2x10" (seen here) and 4x10" combos. It generates 22 watts from a push-pull 2 x 6V6GT class AB output stage in fixed-bias, with a single EF86 pentode in the preamp and a 5751 phase inverter. Like all Dr Z amps, it is totally hand-wired on a phenolic turret board (sort of a rugged modern version of Fender's eyelet card or Vox's "tag-strip" circuit board), with tube sockets, pots, and switches all mounted directly to the high-grade aluminum chassis. The transformers are sturdy units from Cin-Tran.

Controls are limited to just Volume, Bass and Treble. It's a minimalist, "low feature" amp that aims to prove how much great tone can exist in simple but intelligent designs. Originality and simplicity are both characteristics of Dr Z designs, and this amp is typical of the company's work. Despite the spartan three-control format, it can take some playing around with to get the most out of it (which is to say, to get the hang of it … it's all in there waiting for you). The tone stack in particular is deceptive. Despite its two-knob simplicity, its design is one that's not seen in other guitar amps I know of (other than Dr Z's own Route 66), and offers an extremely interactive stage that governs the amp's gain structure as well as its EQ. With Bass and Treble kept at around 12 o'clock there's a lot of clean headroom available for an amp of this size, with taut mids, full lows, and snappy highs. Wind up the tone controls and a lot more grind comes in, even with the volume still down around the nine or ten o'clock range. Take levels up from here, and the amp segues through some great crunch tones to full-on lead mode up near the top of the dial.

The EF86 preamp yields a thick, full-frequencied voice that also stands up to front-end pedal effects very well. This tube doesn't overdrive as easily as a 12AX7 in many circuits (though it certainly helps to overdrive those 6V6s), so booster and overdrive pedals really kick the whole game up a notch, rather than inducing that tizzy fuzz they bring to some amps. Dr Z's preamp design also makes the EF86 far less microphonic than it is in many other amps. Instead it provides a firm, rich, punchy front-end in the Z-28.

## Input And Preamp

**1a** The Z-28 uses a single input with the traditional 68k grid resistor and a 1M resistor to ground, the configuration used for most amplifiers' "high" or "number one" inputs.

**1b** A single EF86 (6267) pentode takes preamp duties here. This is a nine-pin tube, but with different wiring requirements than more common dual-triodes such as the 12AX7. Even so, the bias resistor and bypass cap seen above it on the board are similar to those found in this stage in many other circuits—a 1.5k resistor and 25uF/25V cap. But its plate resistor, the red/red/yellow resistor at an angle above it and to the left, is of a much higher value than a 12AX7 would normally use, a 220k in this case.

**1c** From here, the signal actually goes entirely to the tone pots (via the orange 0.022uF coupling cap, then split in two directions across a resistor and a film cap) before reaching the volume, which is a somewhat lesser-seen approach to the tone stack. The high-gain EF86 allows this circuit to work without too much signal loss through the tone controls, and the combination of this preamp tube and an unusual tone circuit helps give the Z-28 its unique voice.

The large orange caps inside this amp are made by the SBE company, the heirs to the Sprague "Orange Drop" designs, although these versions are polyester caps specified by Dr Z rather than the more common polystyrene P715 and P716 Orange Drops. Other than a few large, blue metal film resistors used in the power supply, the Dr Z amp uses carbon film resistors throughout the circuit.

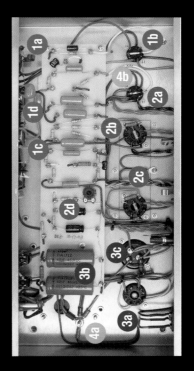

1a single input/68k grid resistor/1M resistor to ground

1b pins for EF86 (6267) preamp tube, with 1.5k bias resistor, 25uF/25V bypass cap & 220k plate resistor above

1c .022uF coupling cap

1d volume pot bridged with .0047uF cap

2a pins of 5751 PI tube

2b long-tail-pair PI resistors

2c pair of 6V6GT output tubes

2d voltage trim-pot (& caps, resistors and diode)

3a 5AR4/GZ34 tube rectifier

3b pair of 40uF/450VDC Sprague Atom filter caps

3c multi-section 'can cap' with pair of 20uF filter capacitors

4a 'star grounding' point

4b secret message ('Hi Art')

*(see text for more details)*

**1d** The volume pot is bridged with a 0.0047uF "bright cap" (a larger value than normally used for this job). This amp carries no onboard effects or effects loop, so from here the signal heads straight for the PI and output stage via a 0.047uF coupling cap.

## PI And Output

**2a** The Z-28 uses a 5751 tube for phase inverter duties. This is a dual-triode that can be used as a direct substitute for the 12AX7, but it has a lower gain factor and offers a smoother sound in some applications.

**2b** The amp uses the traditional long-tail-pair PI, seen in most larger, quality guitar amps since the late 1950s. The three resistors joined together at their far ends with a fourth resistor heading to ground usually tip us off to this format, and you see the same quartet appearing in classic circuits from Fender, Marshall and others (though with occasional variations in resistor values).

**2c** A pair of 6V6GTs in push-pull generate approximately 22 watts of power, which is just a little short of the maximum output available from these tubes (a Fender Deluxe Reverb, for example, produces about the same from its 6V6GTs, while a tweed Deluxe only generates around 15 to 18 watts from the same tubes). The Z-28 runs its 6V6GTs at around 375VDC, which is higher than the specs sometimes call for, but still quite a bit lower than the blackface and silverface Deluxe Reverbs pushed their tubes.

**2d** This is a fixed-bias amp, with a small network of caps and resistors and a single diode to generate a negative DC voltage on the tubes' grids in relation to their cathodes. This voltage can be adjusted using the small trim-pot mounted on the circuit board just below and left of the final orange coupling cap in the circuit.

## Power Supply

**3a** Tube rectifier (a 5AR4/GZ34). Although the Z-28 uses a tube rectifier, it's actually quite a fast, tight amp in many respects (in the good sense), with an articulate response and excellent note definition. This is due to a number of other factors, one of which is …

**3b** For an amp of its size, the Z-28 uses pretty heavy filtering—about as much as a tube rectifier likes to let a circuit get away with (you can see here a pair of 40uF/450VDC Sprague Atoms in the first two positions). Another element that you don't see here is the amp's large choke, which is positioned on the reverse (the top side) of the chassis. Together, these components will partly help to account for the amp's big, firm bottom end, and the articulate response described above. A degree of squash comes into play when the amp is cranked, but this clever power supply helps to keep it from becoming excessive.

**3c** Further filtering is provided by a multi-section "can cap" housing a pair of 20uF capacitors with a common ground connection.

## Other Features

**4a** The Z-28 employs a degree of "star grounding," with many critical ground connections made at a single point on the chassis (it gets its name from the star-like appearance of the ground wires emanating from this connection). This configuration can help to minimize noise.

**4b** "Hi Art"—before coming to the author for examination (and other forms of fun), this Z-28 was sent to *Guitar Player* magazine for review. The hidden greeting carried on this wire to the PI's cathodes is intended for Art Thompson, a reviewer and senior editor at the magazine. The review was done by Darrin Fox, but Art—an invariable poker-around in the circuit of any great gear at hand—says he got the message even so.

# Mojave Coyote (2004)

The Mojave Coyote is a hand-made, low-output, minimum-feature amplifier designed to produce creamy, British-flavored lead tones at studio and small-club volumes. The model was first introduced in 2001 as a head (seen here) and 1x12″ and 2x12″ combos. Like Dr Z on the preceding pages, Mojave takes simplicity to new heights with this model, achieving lush, playable sounds through the directness of its design and the quality of its components and manufacturing.

By "simplicity," though, I don't mean to imply a lack of creativity or originality. The single-channel Coyote carries no single volume control in the traditional sense, but offers level controls for two internally-linked, independently-voiced channels that cover the bass and treble portions of the frequency range (with some overlap), plus a shared tone control. Together they yield a surprisingly broad spectrum of tonal options.

The amp is rated at a mere 12 watts, provided by a pair of EL84s in cathode-bias with no negative feedback for a nominal class A output stage. But it sounds far louder than this power rating, thanks to the dimension and depth offered by its harmonic content. Mojave is sacrificing some of the potential efficiency of the EL84s in the name of a richer, more textured tone. Nominally "class A" amps like the Vox AC15 or Matchless Lightning usually get around 15 watts from two EL84s; class AB designs that used these tubes, like the Marshalls, squeeze out closer to 18 or 20 watts.

To the surprise of many players who plug in one of these little amps, the Coyote nails an excellent "cranked vintage Marshall" sound; not so much that of the small 18-watt Marshall, but a smaller version of the big 50-watt plexi. A big sound, just a little less of it—if you see what I mean. That said, its design and build are actually very different from that of any Marshall.

Despite its solid-state rectification, it also offers a very dynamic, responsive playing feel, thanks to the combination of a sizzling class A output stage and a very tactile, full-frequencied preamp circuit. It's an amp that sounds rich and shimmery at lower-to-medium volumes, and really roars when you crank it up.

## Input And Preamp

**1a** A pair of inputs, one high-sensitivity and one low, lead to the Coyote's first gain stage. Although this is not a channel-switching amp, the use of an external A/B footswitch into these inputs provides switching for two different gain levels.

**1b** The 12AX7 tubes in the dual first gain stages have both of their triodes wired in parallel. Rather than increasing the gain as with triodes in series, this wiring yields a higher frequency-to-noise ratio, setting the stage for a full-frequencied yet low-noise performance from the preamp.

**1c** The signal goes from these parallel-wired 12AX7s to the Treble, Volume, and Bass Volume pots via different coupling capacitors that help to determine the individual voices of these two internally-linked channels. This circuit provides a wide blend of "fat" and "bright" voices, offering different player-governable degrees of breakup in the different frequency ranges. The design is almost as if you were taking the two channels of a tweed Fender Deluxe and voicing them differently, then linking them—although there is somewhat more going on here. Like the Deluxe (and many simple but great-sounding designs) the Coyote has a single tone control, which works on both of these "channels."

Mojave uses custom-ordered film and foil polypropylene signal capacitors (and silver mica for the small-value caps), and metal film resistors. The latter are considered by some amp makers to be "cold" or "harsh," but they are a much more precise, low-noise component than carbon comp resistors, and the Mojave amps are designed to yield warm, rich sonics from the circuits containing these parts.

**1d** A Mid Cut/Emphasis switch affecting the Treble channel only retains or removes the natural emphasis on midrange frequencies.

## PI And Output

**2a** The Coyote's third 12AX7 is used as a long-tailed-pair PI. The resistor layout for this stage looks different on this circuit board than on most other amps because of Mojave's fluid, linear method of circuit design.

**2b** A pair of nine-pin EL84 tubes wired in push-pull cover output duties for the Coyote. Note that the finish has been shaved away from an area around the left tube socket to provide a better ground connection to the aluminum chassis.

**2c** The EL84s are cathode-biased with a high-wattage 125-ohm resistor and Sprague bypass cap to fatten the sound. Mojave's linear style of circuitboard layout places these components at some distance from the tubes themselves.

## Power Supply

**3a** Whereas many other low-output amps use tube rectifiers, the Coyote uses a full-wave bridge made of silicon diodes for AC-to-DC conversion. This provides a consistent, reliable power supply, but the combination of the amp's "brown" output stage and high-resistance elements within the DC chain still offer lots of tactile squash and sag when the Coyote is pushed hard.

**3b** The early-position 22uF/400V Mallory electrolytic caps providing power filtering are placed in the traditional position at the left end of the board …

**3c** But note how those filtering the preamp are located nearer to their respective stages. Another unseen element of the filtering stage is a large, high-quality choke mounted on the outside of the chassis with the transformers.

## Other Features

**4a** It might be difficult to determine from a photograph, but Mojave makes its amp chassis from high-grade, non-magnetic aluminum which, among other things, offers a quieter performance due to its lack of interaction with magnetic transformers mounted on it. Some other makers using aluminum chassis include Dr Z, Trainwreck, and of course the very early Marshall JTM45s. Many other makers use steel instead of aluminum.

**4b** Equally difficult to deduce from the pictures, Mojave uses Teflon-coated silver wire for all hookup jobs within the circuit and between components. Silver provides excellent conductance, and Teflon yields excellent resistance to melting during both soldering and general operation at high voltages.

Downright impossible to see—because they're mounted on the reverse side of the chassis—the Coyote carries a power transformer, output transformer and choke made by Mercury Magnetics, one of the most respected suppliers of transformers for guitar amps today.

**4c** As already mentioned, Mojave uses an extremely neat, linear method of circuitboard layout for these hand-wired amps, which is impressive even alongside the best of the breed of great hand-wired, high-end "boutique" amps available today.

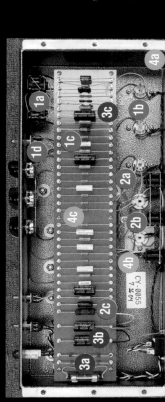

1a  inputs, high and low-sensitivity

1b  12AX7 preamp tubes

1c  coupling capacitors (film and foil polypropylene) & metal film resistors

1d  mid cut/emphasis switch

2a  third 12AX7, used as long-tailed-pair PI

2b  pins for pair of EL84 output tubes

2c  125-ohm resistor and Sprague bypass capacitor

3a  silicon diode rectifiers

3b  22uF/400V electrolytic filter caps

3c  preamp filter caps

4a  aluminum chassis

4b  Teflon-coated silver wire for hooking up components

4c  linear circuitboard layout

(see text for more details)

# Mesa/Boogie Mark IIC+ (1984)

Randall C. Smith's Boogie amps were a sensation right from the introduction of the Mark I in the early 70s, and had even been making a splash on the California scene of the late 60s in the form of his hot-rodded Fender Princetons. The Boogie introduced the notion of cascading gain to the world, and many, many other makers' designs that followed owe a debt of gratitude to Smith. As future iterations appeared, Boogies gained more stages, and gained more gain, but many aficionados of the Mesa/Boogie agree that the format achieved its zenith in the mid-90s at the end of the Mark II range, with the Mark IIC+, often named as one of the sweetest-sounding lead amps ever created.

The Mark series amps received their designations as each evolution succeeded the previous. The Mark I was only so-named after the Mark II came out, and there were several further gradations within that run. The Mark IIA (again, only given its name in hindsight), IIB, IIC, and IIC+, each of which was just a tweak or several away from what the previous had offered. After the Mark IIC+ the three-channel Mark III arrived, and at the time of writing the Mark V is still going strong after several years on the market ... but back to the IIs, and the glory that is the IIC+.

Given that this wasn't an *entirely* new amp but just a tilting forward of what had come before, what was the big deal about that Mark IIC+ circuit? Depending upon how you look at it, the answer can be "a lot," or "just a little." Technically speaking, the Mark IIC and IIC+ used a slight modification of the same circuit board found in the Mark IIB. Mesa Engineering never officially distinguished the "+" in the literature at the time, either; it was simply the latest iteration of the "C" line. Externally, the Mark IIC+ is recognized by the "+" sign added by hand in black marker above the power cord entry point on the back of the chassis, and by a slight change in the front control panel, which says "Pull Deep" above the Master 1 control, rather than "Gain Boost". Much of what was different about the Mark IIC+, therefore, was begun with the Mark IIC, itself an upgrade that cured the Mark IIB's noisy reverb circuit (on the amps that had reverb at all, of course) and "popping" lead/rhythm channel switching. What inspired the good folks at Mesa Engineering to tweak things a little further, though, and to add that hand-inked "+" to the chassis, seems to have been a staff member's own quest for the ultimate shred tone.

While Smith was the brainchild of the original Boogie, and still the head honcho at Mesa Engineering to this day, staffers Doug West and Mike Bendinelli put in most of the elbow grease behind the "+" revisions. According to information compiled by Edward P. Morgan through direct chats with West and Bendinelli (much of which has been published in his informative entries on the Boogie Board forum, where he posts as "Boogiebabies"), the pair dug their hands into the Mark IIC lead circuit in late winter of 1983 while Smith was away at the Musicmesse trade show in Frankfurt, Germany. Engineer Bendinelli pushed the gain further and further, also voicing it for West's request to make it brighter, adding another gain stage to the already toothsome cascading-gain lead circuit for which Boogies have long been famous. Smith approved the revisions when he returned, and the Mark IIC+ went into production in February of 1984. The run, however, was short, and the "+" went out of production surprisingly quickly, as the new Mark III—with added crunch channel—was brought in around March of 1985.

# Mesa/Boogie Mark IIC+ (1984)

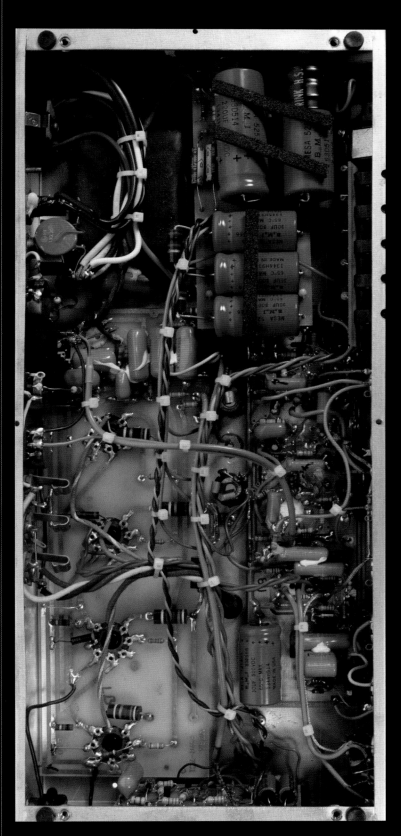

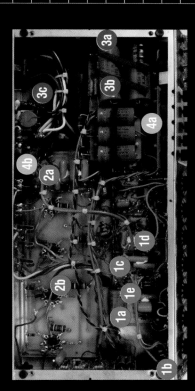

1a  heavy duty printed circuit board
1b  input, with footswitch jack beneath
1c  preamp tube socket
1d  push-pull switch for "Pull Deep" boost function
1e  Sprague 715P "Orange Drop" signal cap
2a  PI, mounted on separate output board
2b  Output tube socket
3a  Diode rectifier bridge
3b  High-value filter caps
3c  Large power transformer
4a  Graphic EQ
4b  Effects loop send and return

Like the Mark amps before and after them, Mark IIC+ Boogies were available with a wide range of options. To the base 60-watt head or combo you could add reverb, graphic EQ, 100 watt output stage with SimulClass (a simultaneous use of Class A and Class A/B tube pairings, or one or the other independently), an export power transformer, an upgraded Electro-Voice or Altec speaker, and an exotic hardwood cabinet with wicker grille. This one, courtesy of owner Todd Duane, has it all.

## Input And Preamp

**1a** Regarding the general layout, note that the Boogie has a lot going on inside a very compact chassis, and this fully loaded Mark IIC+ has more than many of them. Smith used quality printed circuit boards laid out to carry the components in each part of the amp, but the individual parts are hand-wired throughout the chassis.

**1b** The amp has a single input with a traditional 68k grid resistor. The jack beneath the input is for the channel footswitch.

**1c** The circuit layout places the preamp tubes close to the controls that govern their functions, helping to make the most of the limited space within the chassis and keeping signal runs relatively short as gain ramps up from tube to tube.

**1d** This Boogie makes the most of its switching potential by using push-pull pots on six of its seven front-panel controls. This one's for the "Deep" function, mounted on the Master 1 pot.

**1e** Note the use of Sprague 715P "Orange Drop" signal caps throughout.

## PI And Output

**2a** It's difficult to see under the components here, but the PI tube is mounted at the end of the output-stage board, and follows the long-tailed-pair configuration we first saw in the 5F6A Bassman.

**2b** Output tubes—two 6L6s in fixed bias and two EL34s in cathode bias, delivering the Mark IIC+'s SimulClass options.

## Power Supply

**3a** The diode rectifier bridge is tucked in at the far end of the power-supply board.

**3b** Heavy filtering helps to keep the output stage tight and the lows firm, all part of the high-gain goals.

**3c** The amp carries a hefty power transformer, which is part of what makes it so heavy for its compact size.

## Other Features

**4a** The five-band graphic EQ, a feature of the fully loaded Boogie.

**4b** The effects loop (send and return mounted vertically here) is considered one of the improvements on the IIC+.

# Hiwatt Custom DR103 (1969)

While other major English makers such as Vox, Marshall, and Selmer were bigging-up their designs through the mid-60s amid the Brit-rock quest for more volume, Hiwatt was *born* loud. Hiwatt founder Dave Reeves was working at Arbiter's Sound City ampworks in the mid 1960s when he developed the notion of building a better amplifier. He began prototyping the Hiwatt designs in 1967, and Pete Townshend, before moving on to actual Hiwatt products, played Sound City amps in 1967 and 1968 that were highly modified by Reeves himself.

To achieve his goal, Reeves designed new amplifier circuits from the ground up, with punch, girth, and cutting power in mind every step of the way. To get it all done right, he commissioned military-specification chassis wiring from Harry Joyce, who did other high-end contract electronics work, including wiring jobs for the Royal Navy. Military-grade components were used wherever possible, alongside rugged Partridge transformers, massive hunks of iron that also played a big part in rendering the Hiwatt sound with such enormity.

Outwardly, the big Hiwatt heads might have looked like quality Marshall clones, but despite the big black cabs and block logos, Reeves took few—if any—cues from the popular Marshall amps. In place of the crunch and grind that's injected into a JMP100's signal at every step in the chain, the DR103 is engineered to pass along a bold, full-frequencied signal from the preamp to the output stage, where it can be amplified to ear-pummeling levels. Oh yeah, there's plenty of gain in the circuit—with more gain stages than the classic tweed-Bassman/Marshall-plexi topology—but the amp handles it elegantly at every turn, achieving impressive efficiency and maximum power from the entire design. Although the Bass, Treble, and Middle controls on the front panel imply a descendant of the Fender/Marshall tone stack, the Hiwatt's EQ functions occur in an entirely different part of the circuit. After each channel's first gain stage the signal hits a volume control, then Ch1 and Ch2 are joined running into a second gain stage, with the three-knob tone network configured between the plate (anode) of this triode and the input of yet *another* ECC83 (12AX7) following it, which constitutes a further two gain stages to condition the signal before passing it along to the phase inverter (PI). This is very different from the cathode-follower tone stack of Marshall and the big tweed Fenders, and a little more like the tone network of the blackface Fender amps if anything, but still something unto itself.

Also, like larger post-1963 Fenders, Hiwatts used a 12AT7 (an ECC81 in Euro-speak) in the PI, a tube that has less gain than a 12AX7 and is therefore likely to distort the signal less as it passes it along to the output tubes. But the DR103's PI involves far more than tube choice. According to Victor Mason of Mojave Ampworks and Plexi Palace, who has handled more vintage Hiwatts than most, "the magic part of the Hiwatt, and [the reason] it will produce such a powerfully clean sound, is its phase inverter. It has a bias on the grid. That bias prevents the phase inverter from shifting upwards or downwards as does a typical Fender or Marshall, which gives rise to early distortion." This so-called 100-watter runs its four EL34s *hard*, and likely achieves 120 watts RMS or more at full throttle. Notice, though, the master volume that Reeves very thoughtfully included in the design—an early example of this control, which would proliferate through the following decade. This was a professional amp, for the big stage, but at least you could rein it in a little when desired.

As if all this stuff weren't special enough, the 1969 DR103 I'm honored to feature here (courtesy of current owner Jack Wright) was originally owned by Ronnie Wood of The Faces. It was built for the band by Reeves himself in 1969, in the small garage of his house in New Malden, Surrey, when

Hiwatt was still a one-man operation. If immaculate solder work and right-angle wiring turn you on (and let's assume they do) you'll need a dribble bib after a peak inside this chassis. This is classic Dave Reeves overbuilt wiring work, a standard he insisted on maintaining even after expanding the company and jobbing out the assembly to Harry Joyce. And while these early Hiwatts were all "Custom" to some extent, the big-artist examples were often more custom than most: for one, this one has Reeves's option for a half-power switch on the back, enabling easier low-volume grind … though you've got to believe the thing was *still* loud regardless.

### Input And Preamp

**1a** An ECC83 (12AX7 equivalent) supplies the first gain stage for each channel.

**1b** A 0.022uF "mustard cap" couples each channel's first gain stage to its respective volume control.

**1c** A 220pF bright cap across the input and wiper of the Brilliant channel's volume pot is the only thing that really differentiates the channels.

**1d** This tube socket is the second and third of several gain stages in the DR103's preamp.

**1e** Master volume control; an unusual feature in an amp of this early a vintage.

### PI And Output

**2a** The PI socket, which holds an ECC81 (a 12AT7 equivalent) isn't fourth in the row of preamp tubes, where you might expect to find it.

**2b** One of four sockets housing the EL34 output tubes.

**2c** Half-power switch, another unusual feature in an early amp.

### Power Supply

**3a** These diodes constitute the amp's solid-state rectifier.

**3b** One of several large chassis-mounted can caps that provide the DR103's firm filtering.

# Supro Model 24/1624 (1965)

For many years relegated to the B-list vintage amp bin, the Supro Model 24 (aka 1624T) has more recently become legendary for its supposed associations with Jimmy Page. There has been plenty of debate over which Supro Page used to record his classic tones on *Led Zeppelin I* and *II*, and several pundits will point elsewhere. But if the scant evidence leads us anywhere, it is here—given JP's difficult-to-trace yet widely accepted past statements that it was a "small, blue Supro" and a "1x12" combo." Ultimately it matters little. Even if no name artist ever played through a sweet little mid-60s Supro Model 24 like this one (even though he did), it's still one of the hippest looking and coolest sounding 45-year-old tube combos on the planet.

During all those years when Fender was dominating the American amp market, with Gibson and a few others occasionally nipping at its heels, Valco designed and manufactured a broad range of amps for re-branders such as Supro, Oahu, Gretsch, and Airline that totally disregarded the Fender standard. They all did their own thing, and did it very well. Components were mostly of a slightly lesser standard, and cabinetry (which varied from brand to brand) was occasionally thinner and lighter weight than that used by Fender and Gibson, but the circuit designs themselves are difficult to fault,

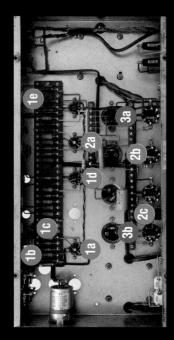

1a  ECC83—first gain stage for
    each channel

1b  0.022uF "mustard cap"
    coupling V1 and Ch1's volume pot

1c  220pF bright cap on Brilliant
    channel's volume pot

1d  ECC83—second and third gain
    stages

1e  master volume control

2a  PI socket, holding an ECC81
    (12AT7)

2b  EL34 socket

2c  half-power switch

3a  diode rectifier bridge

3b  high-value filter caps cans

and often took some clever, original twists that have been rediscovered for their sonic goodness.

Compared to the chassis of some other leading amps of its vintage, the inside the Model 24 at first looks like a rat's nest of wiring strung out along a series of terminal strips. Look a little closer, though, and you'll see fairly tidy workmanship, and a neat logic to the design. Valco managed to fit a simple yet extremely effective circuit into a confined space, and to string together a series of stages out of the tube design handbooks of the day that really work together to pump out some exemplary guitar tones. One of the surprises in here is the extensive use of ceramic disk coupling caps where you'd normally expect to see larger, more robust axial (tubular) coupling caps. The relatively low voltages found in several stages of the amp, however, allow such caps to thrive, while also giving the amp's tone a thick, chocolatey, and slightly gritty character that you don't hear elsewhere. At lower volumes this adds some body to the stew, and cranked up to crunch it gives the Supro's voice a meaty bite.

A big part of this amp's voice lies in its pair of 6973 output tubes. This tube's nine-pin layout and narrow bottle leads plenty of people to make the assumption that it "sounds like an EL84", but that's a long way from accurate. Even on paper—physical appearances aside—the 6973 is a very different tube, with maximum plate voltage ratings of around 440 volts DC compared to the EL84's 350 VDC, a different pin-out, and different bias requirements. The robustness of this tube implies you can get a little more juice out of it if you try, and you can. These tubes were favored by jukebox manufacturers of the 50s and 60s for their firm, bold response, although few (if any) guitar amps tapped them for their full potential. In our Supro, they put out about 18 watts from well under 350 volts at the plates, and sound round, chunky and, if slightly dark, crisply and pleasantly so. The Supro Model 24 is capable of pumping out a surprising amount of volume for its size; anyone with a recently acquired original example that seems wimpy or anemic in that department should look to the tubes, filter caps, and/or speaker, and expect the amp, in good condition, to have a bolder voice than the average tweed Deluxe, for example. Its thin 5/8″ pine cab makes it extremely lively and resonant along with it. Add in a superb tremolo with a wide range of settings, from gentle pulse to swampy throb, and the Model 24 is a major tone machine, and surprisingly versatile too.

## Input And Preamp

**1a** Channel 1 inputs. Each channel has inputs labeled Bass and Treble: plug into one in Ch1 and patch to the other in Ch2 to blend an extremely gutsy tone.

**1b** Typical ceramic-disc cap—this one on Ch1's tone pot—of the type found throughout the amp.

**1c** Socket for the first 12AX7 in the preamp.

**1d** Jack to connect tremolo footswitch, with speed and intensity controls either side.

**1e** Wiring might look chaotic, but a Supro in good condition isn't usually any noisier than other vintage amps of the era.

## PI And Output

**2a** Socket for the 12AX7 in the phase-inverter position. The amp uses a paraphase inverter circuit similar to that found in earlier TV-front and wide-panel tweed Fender amps.

**2b** One of two sockets housing the 6973 output tubes.

**2c** Large 250-ohm cathode-bias resistor on the 6973s (incidentally, the same value resistor used to bias many 6V6-equipped amps of a similar power rating).

**2d** Output transformer, mounted to the underside of the chassis.

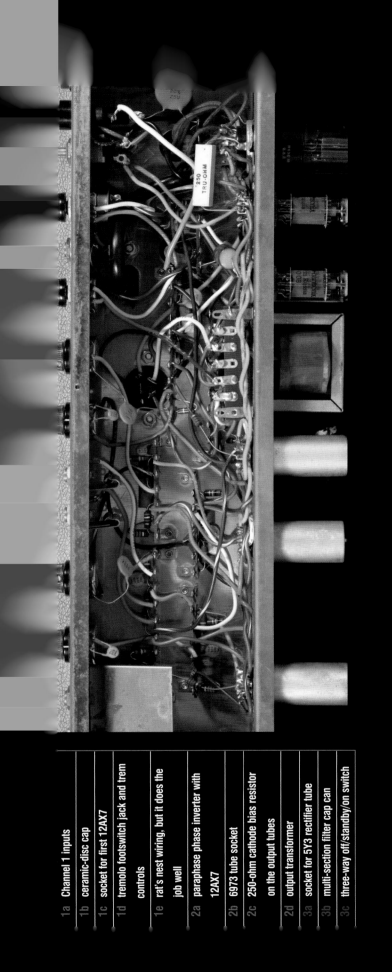

1a   Channel 1 inputs

1b   ceramic-disc cap

1c   socket for first 12AX7

1d   tremolo footswitch jack and trem controls

1e   rat's nest wiring, but it does the job well

2a   paraphase phase inverter with 12AX7

2b   6973 tube socket

2c   250-ohm cathode bias resistor on the output tubes

2d   output transformer

3a   socket for 5Y3 rectifier tube

3b   multi-section filter cap can

3c   three-way off/standby/on switch

## Power Supply

**3a** Socket for 5Y3 rectifier.

**3b** The amp's larger filter caps are in the multi-section can mounted horizontally here.

**3c** This nifty (though difficult to replace) three-way switch performs off/standby/on duties all in one.

# Matchless DC-30 (1996)

The Matchless name has long been synonymous with several facets of high-quality modern amplifier design and manufacturing. It has been at the forefront of the "boutique" crowd virtually since it was founded in California in 1989; it remains the best-known manufacturer using true point-to-point wiring; and it is still, arguably, the premier name in "Class-A tone" (however much we might like to add "nominally" to the front of that, in the name of strict accuracy). The DC-30 combo featured here has been the company's flagship model from the very beginning. As such, it embodies the desire of designer Mark Sampson (who co-founded Matchless with Rick Perrotta, and is interviewed later in this book) to build a better and more robust AC30 for the touring professional, and remains an undisputed "modern classic" to this day.

Players who have heard of the Matchless mystique but have little or no first-hand experience with their performance will often grumble at the prices that these amps sell for new (which, it has to be said, aren't at all out of line with other top-of-their field brands), but a probe inside this DC-30 chassis pretty quickly tells you where the expense comes from. In addition to using top-quality components throughout the build—from over-spec resistors to custom-made transformers—Matchless puts a phenomenal amount of hand labor into each amp it builds. In addition, its amps carry a great many features that set them apart from most anything else in the field (or did until so many makers that came after tapped into aspects of what made Sampson's amps sound and perform the way they do).

The DC-30, for example, is much more than "just a sturdier AC30." Its two channels pair up the iconic Vox Top Boost preamp from the AC30 and the fat, juicy EF86 pentode preamp of the AC15, modified and made more versatile with a six-way tone switch that routes the signal through six different coupling caps to voice the channel as desired. The amp has a bypass-able Master that lets you rein in the output levels when desired (I always feel they sound their best with this bypassed though, wailing full steam ahead), and a nifty half-power switch around back that cuts two of the four EL84s to reduce the amp to around 18 watts. This doesn't cut the volume in half, by any means, but drops the headroom somewhat, and brings on that juicy output-tube grind a little more quickly. Another cool but surprisingly useful feature is the provision of two rectifier tube sockets: the amp comes supplied with a single GZ34, which provides a fairly firm, fast, robust feel, but you can substitute two softer 5V4 rectifier tubes for a little more compression and a more forgiving attack. There's also a useful Speaker Phase switch on the back panel to flip the speaker-out's phase in order to help the amp play better with other amps in a multi-amped rig.

On top of all the "features," the way the amp is laid out and built is just damn cool. Preamp tube sockets are positioned close to the knobs or related components that control their functions, so the signal flows a shorter distance than in many amps, straight across the leads of a coupling cap soldered right between a volume pot and the tube socket, for example. And if all that's not enough

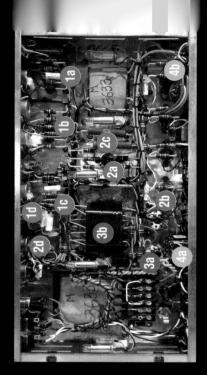

1a  first channel's 12AX7 socket, concealed beneath components

1b  12AX7 for the Top Boost tone stack

1c  socket for the EF86 pentode preamp tube

1d  six-position tone switch

2a  socket for the 12AX7 in the long-tailed-pair PI

2b  EL84 socket

2c  cathode-bias resistors

2d  Cut control

3a  rectifier tube socket

3b  filter caps

4a  Speaker Phase switch

4b  TRS jacks for individual effects loops

for you, hey, the control panel lights up! Mark Sampson and Rick Perrotta departed Matchless in 1999 after a confluence of economic circumstances affected a temporary halt in production, but production manager Phil Jamison stayed on to head up the company, and continues to turn out the DC-30 and other models, old and new, to the same exacting standards as ever.

While the DC-30's circuit might look intimidating to the uninitiated, it's fascinating for being a very direct and linear analogue of its "on-paper" design. Look closely, and you can see how the signal runs from point to point via the components that do their thing along the way, having to jump very few longer distances on connecting "hook-up" wires. Everything is right there in front of you, and from the tone perspective, the evidence seems to show that this makes for a very fast, responsive amplifier.

## Input And Preamp

**1a** The first 12AX7 in the Top Boost channel lurks here. Note how all of the capacitors and resistors related to it are connected directly to the pins of the tube socket.

**1b** Here's the 12AX7 for the cathode-follower Top Boost tone stack, right behind the controls for Treble and Bass. All related components in the EQ stage are connected directly to either the tube socket or to the pots.

**1c** The socket for the EF86 in the second channel.

**1d** This six-position Tone switch—achieved with a pretty tight and complex bit of wiring—lets the player select different coupling caps to differently voice this inherently fat, juicy pentode-preamp channel.

## PI And Output

**2a** The socket for the 12AX7 in the long-tailed-pair phase inverter is positioned—again, very logically—part way between the preamp stages and the output tubes.

**2b** The left-most of four sockets carrying the EL84 output tubes.

**2c** The two big cathode-bias resistors for the EL84s. Just one is employed in full-power model, while flipping the switch (on the rear panel just below this position) to half-power adds another in series to approximately double the resistance, as required by two EL84s.

**2d** This "Cut" control acts within the output stage to tame highs as desired.

## Power Supply

**3a** The left-most of two available rectifier-tube sockets.

**3b** The power supply's larger filter caps are all stacked together here, shielded by lashings of electrical tape.

## Other Features

**4a** Speaker Phase switch, allowing you to reverse the phase of the connected speaker to match other amps in your rig.

**4b** Dual passive series effects loops, one for each channel.

# Tone King Sky King (2013)

The Sky King from Tone King was something of a departure for this Baltimore-based amp company when released in 2013, though very much in its wheelhouse in other ways, too. Tone King has been a reputable member of the so-called "boutique" clan since the release of the original Imperial model back in 1993 (see interview with main man Mark Bartel in the *Meet The Makers* section), but has always done things somewhat differently from most high-end makers. Until this release, Tone Kings used high-quality printed circuit boards for reliability and consistency of layout, while the majority of the (mostly two-channel) tones they've generated have aimed at modified blackface clean to crunch on one side, and mid-level tweed to Marshall grind on the other.

The Sky King has a similar footswitchable two-channel, ostensibly rhythm-lead architecture to its predecessors, the Meteor and the Metropolitan; but it was designed around an ultralinear output stage, which configures the cathode-biased 6L6s and the output transformer differently for a warmer, rounder, more syrupy tone that might be thought of as leaning toward Valco/Supro or Magnatone. For Tone King traditionalists, the output mode is switchable to standard pentode wiring, which yields a brighter, snappier, more scooped tonality and increased volume, without actually changing the output wattage.

You can also seriously reduce your output volume—again without changing the wattage—by engaging either of the two built-in Ironman attenuators, each independently switchable and tied to each channel, to take the Sky King's full 35 watts down to sub-bedroom practice levels. This configuration allows you to select different output levels for each channel (to drive lead harder, for example, while keeping rhythm sparkly clean, both at comparable volume levels), and the settings are automatically engaged when the channel is selected.

Construction-wise, the Sky King departs from Tone King tradition in its hand-wired circuit, which is extremely original in and of itself: note the individual "circuit blocks" constructed of components wired between triangular circuit cards, each independently devoted to each stage of the signal chain and mounted right atop the tube socket that powers that stage. I can't say I've seen this type of construction anywhere else, other than within Tone King's hand-wired 20th Anniversary Imperial model. It's a clean and efficient way of getting the job done, and packs a lot of signal treatment into the space allowed—a task aided by Tone King's nifty deep chassis with top-mounted, fold-out control panel.

The Sky King also benefits from two great old-school onboard effects. Its bias-modulated tremolo is rich and warm, with a broad range of parameters from the rate and depth controls. The tube-powered spring reverb is lush and shimmery, and doesn't get in the way of your core tone until you really crank it up to beyond-surf mix levels. All in all, the Sky King is a superbly versatile "grab'n'go" combo that is likely to prove a great gig companion to many guitarists.

## Input And Preamp

**1a** The single input is routed to the clean or lead channel depending on your footswitch selection (or the position of the control panel switch).

**1b** Triangular circuit block devoted to the lead channel. These make it tricky to see the actual coupling caps and resistors used at each stage, which are all mounted on a vertical orientation between lower and upper circuit cards. See the inset of the angled view inside the chassis, which makes it a little easier how these blocks are wired up.

**1c** Triangular circuit block devoted to the rhythm channel (and so on, throughout the preamp).

**1d** Note that the preamp tube sockets aren't readily visible from this angle; they are hidden beneath each circuit block, with their pins connected directly to the bottom circuit card.

## PI And Output

**2a** A similar block hides (and configures) the PI socket.

**2b** Two sockets housing the 6L6 output tubes.

**2c** Switch to select ultralinear or pentode output mode.

## Power Supply

**3a** Socket for the 5U4G rectifier tube.

**3b** Circuit block dedicated to the power supply filtering and dropping resistors. These larger components are somewhat easier to see than those in the blocks of the preamp stages.

## Other Features

**4a** Ironman output attenuator. Note the several components used in this complex attenuator, which is widely regarded as one of the better units available.

**4b** Dual attenuator switches, one for each channel, so your attenuator setting is automatically engaged with channel changes.

# Komet Aero 33 (2014)

The Komet Aero 33 is a smoking rock'n'roll machine, pure and simple. In some ways, Komet can be seen as a torchbearer for the late Ken Fischer, and its amps do stick pretty close to the Trainwreck ethos. (There's a new interview with Komet's Holger Notzel in the *Meet The Makers* section of this edition, along with the original interview with Fischer himself.) This amp maker, based in Baton Rouge, Louisiana, was launched in 1999 on the Komet 60 model, designed from the ground up by Fischer to be a powerful and extremely touch-sensitive lead guitarist's gigging machine; each of the few subsequent Komet models has stuck to the touchstones of superb dynamics, extreme sensitivity, and superbly rich tone.

The Aero 33 is the latest Komet offering as of the time of writing, and one of Komet's original designs. That said, there's plenty of Fischer DNA here, and a few tricks lifted right from the original 60 model, so it's a kissing cousin of some Trainwreck amps at the very least. Outwardly a Marshall-meets-Vox mashup, the Aero 33 is based around four EL84 tubes in a cathode-biased output stage with some negative feedback around it, and an extremely interactive front end that nails the "wired to your fingertips" touch sensitivity that Komet strives for in each of its amps.

The straightforward yet versatile control layout carries no master volume (a Komet no-no), and these amps are meant to be *cranked* to do their thing. The Aero 33 (and each of its brethren that I've tried) sounds extremely good wound down to clean volume levels, with a full, shimmering, harmonically resplendent tone that makes any great guitar really shine. Get the volume up to two o'clock or beyond, though, and you discover what this thing was really born to do: in short, this amp gushes with one of the juiciest, most infectious rock tones I've ever experienced—the kind of inspiring voice that makes you just want to play and play.

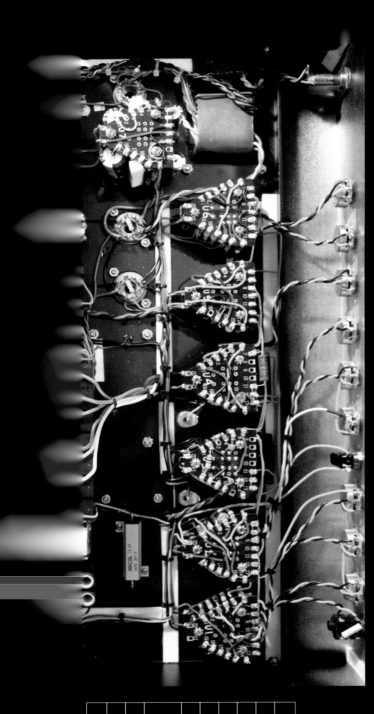

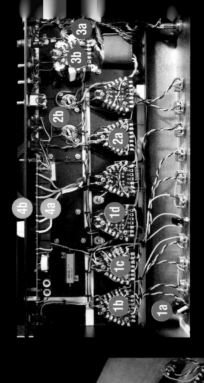

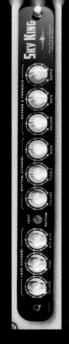

1a  single input for both channels
1b  circuit block for lead channel
1c  circuit block for rhythm channel
1d  preamp tube socket (left of this
    marker, unseen beneath circuit block)
2a  PI socket and circuit block
2b  6L6 sockets
3a  socket for 5U4G rectifier tube
3b  power supply circuit block
4a  Ironman output attenuator
4b  dual controls for Ironman settings

Among the real keys to the Aero 33's sonic virtue are a design that emphasizes tone and touch-sensitivity at every turn, a straightforward and uncluttered signal path amid the cleverness, top-quality components (military-spec, in many places, all inside a laser-cut aircraft-grade aluminum chassis), and outstanding workmanship. A lone volume control governs multiple gain stages fueled by two of the amp's three 12AX7 preamp tubes, in a contemporary re-think of an old-school "high gain" design, intended to be controlled with playing dynamics and your guitar's volume control. The EQ might outwardly appear just a somewhat modified Brit-inspired tone stack, but nothing within the circuit is directly lifted from anything that has gone before … other than a little past Komet and some Trainwreck here and there. The back panel holds what is arguably the most powerful control in the Komet arsenal—a "Touch Response" switch with "Fast" and "Gradual" settings that dramatically alters the playing feel of the amp, as well as the gain and the degree to which playing dynamics induce breakup. A descendent of Ken Fischer's design for the K60, this switch is a re-think of an option occasionally found on older tube hi-fi units. The switch taps into a split-load circuit in the preamp. In "Fast" you get the first gain stage as designed, with fairly hot biasing on the first tube; switching to "Gradual" splits the plate resistance between two resistors in the preamp, lowering the gain and altering the touch sensitivity response. Simple, but the result is two dramatically different feels from one amp. The amp sounds great either way—more "classic rock" in "Gradual", more hot-rodded lead monster in "Fast"—with Komet's signature sweet, hovering harmonic feedback even more readily achieved in the latter.

### Input And Preamp

**1a** The amp's single input. The grid-stopper resistor is shrink-tubed to the shielded signal wire at the tube socket end.

**1b** The first 12AX7 provides two gain stages, with a further stage from the second tube.

**1c** Volume control, with three-way bright switch (bright/off/brighter) tied across its input and wiper tabs.

**1d** The Fast/Gradual switch; note how it taps between two load resistors on the board.

**1e** Note how components throughout the signal chain are shrink-tubed to conceal their makes and values.

### PI And Output

**2a** Typical long-tailed-pair phase inverter, fuelled by another 12AX7.

**2b** One of four sockets housing the EL84 output tubes.

**2c** Presence control, which taps a negative feedback loop in the output stage (somewhat unusual for this type of amp design) to add an extra something to the highs. Next to it, a Hi-Cut control to tame the highs at the output, as necessary.

**2e** Cathode-bias resistor for the EL84s, oriented markings-down to conceal its value.

### Power Supply

**3a** Diode (solid-state) rectifier.

**3b** Large dual-section can cap for robust filtering, in addition to …

**3c** Three 22uF filter caps on the power-supply board.

# Komet Aero 33 (2014)

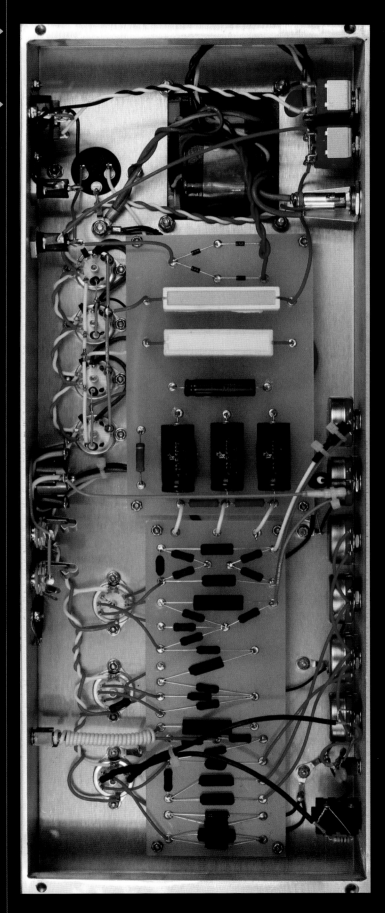

| 1a | single input |
|----|----|
| 1b | first 12AX7, with two gain stages |
| 1c | volume pot and three-way bright switch |
| 1d | Fast/Gradual "Touch Response" switch |
| 1e | shrink tubing on components |
| 2a | long-tailed-pair PI with 12AX7 |
| 2b | EL84 socket |
| 2c | Presence control |
| 3a | diode rectifier bridge |
| 3b | dual-section filter cap |
| 3c | 33uF caps |

# CHAPTER 5

# Choosing Your Amp

Price and physical size will obviously play a part in your amplifier selection, but from a musical perspective the amp world is your oyster. With so many variables involved, what should you look (and listen) for when trying a tube amp? And crucially, how do you know it will be right for you?

Everything so far in the book has been about giving guitar players a good grounding in what really makes tube amps tick. I've paid a lot of attention to what matters and what doesn't; what affects your sound, and how; what is purely functional (does its job but doesn't affect the sound a whole lot); and what is often just hype. Short of doing a diploma course in electrical engineering and putting a lot of time into studying how tubes perform in guitar amps (while having a lot less time to play your guitar), you should now have a reasonable understanding of the major components and circuit stages. So what good is any of this to you? That's simple: by extrapolating from what you have digested here, you should be a lot better equipped to select the right guitar amp for your own playing, and hopefully know when to quit flogging a model that's all wrong for your sonic desires.

Countless guitarists waste a lot of money and precious playing time whacking away at amps that aren't ever going to deliver what they hope to achieve, and weren't designed to do so. They get into this bind for a number of reasons: some bought the only amp they could afford and have been trying to make the best of it; some were convinced by a salesman or an ad campaign to buy an amp that was never right for them; some were chasing the sound of their guitar hero, but it turns out that doesn't suit their own style, or maybe they've just moved on; some bought the best amp they could, but were taken in by price and features rather than by appropriateness of sound—and so on. Whichever of these might apply to you, the guts of this chapter's advice is simple: sell the dead horse, do your research, find the one that will fly with you, and go for that. Our real goal is to take in the essential knowledge here, apply it, then spend as much time as possible playing our guitars through great, expressive amps rather than messing around and modifying amps that aren't going to cut it for us.

I'm not necessarily saying you need to take out a second mortgage to buy the hottest new boutique amplifier out there (and we'll look at price and affordability issues a little later here). In fact the hottest new boutique amp might be the one that's all wrong for you, the one you need to get rid of. The key is to identify the amp that's tailored to your playing, and since you now know the basic types and topologies, that should be a lot easier to do. A number of factors come into play, and you've already had a glimpse at all of them. If you're shopping for a new or used amp, it's even worth making a list of which characteristics are best for "your sound." It might seem pedantic, anal-retentive even, but it could help prevent you going too far down the road of buying the wrong amp, seduced by extraneous features or a salesperson's pitch. I would argue that three main elements combine to define the character of any amp: breakup point in relation to volume, distortion character, and the joint effects of speed and tightness.

## BREAKUP POINT

This is where it all begins. The early or late onset of distortion in an amplifier is one of the main selection criteria for most players—or it certainly should be. In non-channel-switching amps this is critical, but even in two and three-channel models with high-gain preamps in one or two of the channels, this is a factor you assess to some extent as well. In the lead channel you will of course be looking for high saturation, what you hear as total distortion (although "total" would be total mush); but in the clean and crunch channels, the onset of distortion is as critical as it is in any vintage-style amp.

In either case, the player needs to assess how much clean headroom he needs in order to get the job done, and at what point he wants to be able to really lay into the guitar—or step on a booster pedal or something—to ease into either crunch or total overdrive. If you don't have any need for either mildly or seriously distorted sounds from the amp, or if you intend to get them entirely from pedals (just because you like the sound of your distortion pedals, I guess, which is totally valid), you will want an amp that runs to your total volume requirement, and a little beyond, without breaking up to any great extent. But as I've mentioned a number of times already, a little bit of tube distortion is still going to add to the texture and richness of that "clean" sound of yours, so any player other than those desiring ultra-pristine clean will want to determine that point at which the amp's tone is still undistorted—sharp, tightly-focused, fairly full-frequencied, and with good note definition—but is, in reality, benefiting from just a little of the thickening, multi-dimensionality and harmonic richness of some tube distortion. Find an amp that does all these things at just the point you want them to occur, and I'll bet you you're 80 per cent of the way toward finding an amp you'll be very happy with.

I was fascinated to follow the progress of the DIY and kit-building craze that involved a lot of guys building tweed Deluxe-style amps in the late 1990s, something that's still popular today. A great amp, to be sure. But a sizeable proportion of the DIY builders were writing letters and posting on the web looking for ways to get a little more headroom out of the thing. Solutions included raising voltages a little from around 350VDC to 375VDC, adding a choke, sometimes adding a little negative feedback, and so forth. All of which can also make for a great-sounding amp, with a little more clean bite and what you might call "twang". But it's a different amp. There's nothing wrong with wanting more of these characteristics in an amp, and there's also nothing wrong with loving a 5E3 tweed Deluxe for being exactly what it is—a gritty, juicy, hot and easily-compressed little overdrive machine. All of this just helps to emphasize how a few subtle changes in components, voltages, and specs can make for a significant change in the voice of an amp.

## DISTORTION CHARACTER

This is an obvious consideration with regards to high-gain amps used by soloists, or vintage-style amps that will likewise be cranked for lead playing. But once again it applies to degrees of clean playing as well. Listen to your favorite distortion sounds on a wide range of recordings, and while you're at it check out some that turn you off, too. Try to define what it is about these sounds that you like or dislike, and prepare to assess it in different amps as you play them yourself.

As well as the point at which distortion occurs in an amp, its gradual or sudden segue into that distortion is also a very important factor. Players who want to use the onset of distortion as a dynamic element of their playing—by bringing it on with a turn of the guitar's volume control, or even a firmer pick attack or slashed power chord—will most often be looking for a smooth, somewhat gradual onset of distortion. You might think you'd prefer a sudden onset for dramatic impact, but for the playing I'm talking about you can always get that from a pedal. With a smoother onset, you've got the option of textured clean playing with a soft touch, a little crackling around the edges of notes with a little more attack, and a crunchy breakup when you really dig in. Believe it or not, a lot of good amps of this type can give you all three characters without flicking a single knob or switch.

As for a late-but-sudden onset of distortion, this might well be the character of an amp that's ideal for loud, clean playing, not intended to be pushed hard—so it's a matter of finding the breakup point and staying just below it. (Or, if you like the character of that distortion once it finally occurs, pushing past the breakup point and staying there, for lead playing at least.) Getting satisfactory amp-generated distortion out of these amps usually requires a booster pedal, unless you plan on cranking one to the max and staying well into the breakup zone all the time.

As for sonic character, there are many flavors here, too. This is where your list of loved or loathed distortion sounds from your record collection comes into play. Which is the one for you? A phat, fuzzy distortion; a cutting, high-gain buzz-saw; a smooth, swelling distortion with a touch of front-of-attack compression; a harmonically-rich, saturated, high-gain distortion with lots of sustain and easy feedback; a thick, warm, woolly distortion with a spongy compression? Define it first, then look for an amp that does it for you. Anything can be a valid choice, it depends what you're after. If you define what you need for your style and your music, then you can try to avoid barking too far up the wrong amp tree if, for instance, you find you're being tempted by some of its features but the essential character of the distortion isn't one that really fits your requirements.

## SPEED AND TIGHTNESS

These are characteristics that you very likely haven't thought a whole lot about in the past, but will definitely have felt and heard. We've already examined them in relation to how individual stages or components contribute to (or detract from) both of them, but the proportion they make up of any amp's output plays a big part in shaping its voice.

When I say "speed" in this context, I mean the rapidity with which the amplifier circuit and speakers translate a note plucked on the guitar into a louder sound broadcast through the air (or, for that matter, down a line to a mixing desk or cab simulator, if you're DI'ing from an amp's output). Think of it as an amp's reaction time; within the circuit itself, engineers call it the "slew rate," but even without attaching any measuring devices, guitarists can hear its effect in the quality of the notes reproduced. We've already seen how an amp's power supply in particular can play a part here, its tube rectifier taking a moment to ramp back up to full power when the circuit is hit with a big signal at or near full volume. But other elements of the circuit itself can also contribute to this, such as the type and quality of individual components and even the type and length of wire used to hook them together. Certainly the speakers play a big part, as we'll discuss in more depth in Chapter Eight. With a slow response to the input signal the sound might be heard to contain a very slight (or sometimes considerable) blurring, at the front edge of the attack especially, and some lack of definition overall. Yes, we're only talking milliseconds here, but the difference can be noticeable, and even when it's subtle it can influence not just the overall sound of the amp, but the player's response to the feel of that guitar-and-amp interaction.

Let's be clear, though, I'm not saying this slowness is universally a bad thing. Listen to almost any great jazz guitarist playing amped-up in a recording from the 1940s, 1950s, or early 1960s, and you're likely to hear some of that circuit and speaker lag when they get into the fast bebop runs. It comes across as a slight slurring of notes—I'm thinking of the closing lines in Wes Montgomery's 'Besame Mucho' from *Boss Guitar*, or midway through the improv on 'Dearly Beloved' from the same album. There's no horrendous lag—it's slight, but it's detectible. I'm presuming he was playing Ampeg, Fender or Gibson amplifiers, but maybe not the largest models in the line, since he was in the studio. A big amp with a swifter power supply (solid-state rectifier, heavier filtering), output tubes with plenty of headroom in them, and responsive speakers might have kept up with nearly every note. In doing so, though, it very well might have lost some of the girth and texture of that sound—the teeth and hair—and might have been less appealing to the guitarist, and to the listener.

Listen to almost anything by Buddy Guy, but especially when he really gets ripping on one of his ragged-out Bassmans turned up to 12, and you hear the amp struggling to keep up. And he's not necessarily all that fast a player. You hear a lot less of that lag in much of Stevie Ray Vaughan's playing; he was usually using multi-amp combinations of some big, high-wattage models, and produced a sound that had a lot of clean bite in there, even amid the considerable breakup used for a lot of his lead playing. The lightning-speed riffs in 'Scuttle Buttin'' from *Couldn't Stand The Weather* sound tight and immediate, although the fills in 'The Things That I Used To Do' from the same album have a lot more slur and lag to them. He's clearly going for more of a trad Chicago blues feel on the latter track, and the compressive sound and feel are a big part of that.

With some playing styles, a slight lag in response and the compression effect that comes with it translates into extra touch sensitivity and dynamics, resulting in an amplifier that feels beautifully interactive. A little of this might work for the jazzer looking for that classic sound, or a lot of it sometimes works for the blueser. Rockers playing anything from classic Brit-rock to grunge might enjoy a feel somewhere in-between. Virtuoso country pickers, fusion players, shred fiends or thrash metal players who do a lot of fast, tight riffing are probably going to want a quicker response, which in turn offers the driving, percussive effect that these styles require.

This doesn't mean an amp's speed necessarily goes hand-in-hand with the speed of the playing style, but for obvious reasons the effect is heard more distinctly in fast playing. Listen to any of the really scorching leads from the likes of Dave Mustaine from Megadeth or the late Dimebag Darrell of Pantera and Damageplan, and amid the considerable filth you hear a swift, eviscerating response from the amplifier. No doubt Dime's 300-watt solid-state Randall Warhead had a little something to do with that.

Tightness and speed tend to go together, but they're not exactly the same thing. Amps that respond swiftly often spit out precise notes with great definition, but these are more the results of the amp's ability to handle and translate low and mid frequencies at upper volume settings, to which elements such as PI format, power tube type and biasing arrangement, and OT girth are all major contributors. Of course a preamp or tone stack that doesn't deal cleanly and accurately with its signal—even if its job is to filth it up—can also be the root of a loose, flabby sound. Speakers are major culprits too, and the classic combination of a vintage amp with under-spec'd OT and long-abused, under-powered speakers will give you the archetypal representation of this sound. You hear it most in farty bass and hairy mids, which, again, might be just what you are looking for if you're trying to sound like Buddy Guy.

As with speed, more tightness isn't universally going to be preferred over a little less. A looser, slightly rubbery sound can have a lot of soul in the right context and, again, it can often contribute to the feel thing, too. But anyone from your speed-picker to your jangle-pop arpeggiator will probably want a degree of tightness in the amp's response—and heavy metal players certainly want it in that thundering, down-tuned, low-string riffage. The faster, tighter amp will also very often suit players who generate a lot of their sound from pedals. This type of output stage frequently works best with preamp-generated distortion, where the job is to amplify all that grind and saturation from the cascading-gain stage up-front.

The combination of speed and tightness in an amp usually goes hand-in-hand with a firm low-end response, too. That is, you can pump a lot of lows through a preamp voiced to do so, but they will sound their biggest coming out of an output and power-supply stage designed for a fast response and a lot of solidity. In short, it takes more power to reproduce solid lows than it does solid midrange and highs, so amps that are predisposed to such characteristics are also more likely to have a firm, punchy bass response.

I have to emphasize once again that these are things you might feel as much as hear. If, after considering these descriptions and thinking it through for yourself, you believe you need a fast tight amp or a softer, more compressed one, you can narrow your search before you even plug in by seeking out models with the circuit and component characteristics outlined here. But the fact is these things aren't always promoted by the manufacturer, and many specs are never published. You might do just as well to try a range of amps that you feel will suit you, and try to get a feel for the overall response of each as you play your music through it, at the volumes you are likely to be using to rehearse, record, or gig.

If an amp just doesn't have the definition you require or doesn't seem to be keeping up with you, that's not something you can usually change in any major way with a tweak here or there. Move on. On the other hand, if the notes are coming out just a little too sharp and brittle for your liking, look for something a little looser, maybe with a little squash from a tube rectifier or a smaller, more vintage-styled OT. This also might mean you simply need to try a smaller amp, one that will strain a little more at the required volume, putting a little more cranked-up character into the tone.

If you already have an amp that you plan to stick with, but hope to get a little more speed or tightness out of it, there are a few little things you can do to move it in one direction or the other, and I'll cover some of these in upcoming chapters. You can't turn an extremely loose, squashy amp into a fast, tight one, but you can nudge the response in a number of ways, and that might be enough for you.

## TOUCH SENSITIVITY

To the three core characteristics outlined above, I would add another that might be present in varying degrees, and which isn't always inextricably linked to either a fast or slow, soft or tight, clean or dirty amp. This is something that many players refer to as "touch sensitivity," or simply as "touch"—best defined as a combination of interactive dynamics and responsive sensitivity to pick attack. Amps that possess this quality allow the player to determine the degree of breakup in the sound merely by subtle alterations of picking strength. They stay clean when you pick gently, but break up in increasing degrees as you pick harder. With the good ones, you'd swear the player had stepped on an overdrive or booster pedal or something, but it's just the amp reacting to the voltage change created in the signal by a stronger pick attack being translated through the guitar's pickup. Add to this the fact that amps with this property also react very well to changes in the guitar's volume control, and you have a surprisingly versatile sound coming from what might be a very basic, two-knob tube amp.

A high degree of touch-sensitivity makes for a very tactile playing experience, and an amp that's very much an instrument in itself, rather than just an amplification unit for stepping up the guitar's own sound. Many of the great blues, blues-rock, and classic rock lead players know how to make the most of this, and time and again you'll be amazed by the palette of sounds one of these guitarists gets from a guitar, a 20-foot cord, and a decent amp. And while players who use a lot of effects to generate a trademark sound might not need or even use a great degree of touch sensitivity in an amp, it can be a thrilling experience for any guitarist whose signal path is a little more straightforward.

## OPERATING CLASS

Having made it to this stage in the book, you'll know that all the sound-shaping factors we've looked at so far are affected by a number of elements within the circuit. Things like output tube type, biasing technique, size and quality of OT, the presence or lack of a negative feedback loop, the type of PI used, tone stack configuration, the number of gain stages in the preamp, preamp tube type, rectification and power filtering, speaker type, cap design and other factors all influence breakup point, distortion character, and speed and tightness. There's also that old bugbear, operating class, which in truth—at least as used by most marketing departments today—is already covered by these factors. But the class war (A versus AB, that is) does deserve a little more attention here.

"Class A" has been the hip phrase in tube amp circles for a number of years now, and a surprisingly high proportion of new amps released onto the market carry this tag. Whatever way you slice it, there's often a lot of deception going on behind this marketing tool, and without going into laboratory-grade analysis of operating class distinctions, it's worth knowing a little about what class A is, and isn't.

In the scientific sense, these operating classes were not devised to define a bad-better-best relationship between different types of guitar amplifiers. They are not distinctions of quality as such, in the way that food labels like "grade-A beef," are, for example. Two simple facts are worth nailing down in any discussion of this class war: 1) very few of the amps sold as "class A" actually are, when tested against the scientific definition of the term; 2) most amps that are broadly considered "classic class A" amps sound the way they do for many other reasons besides their actual or supposed operating class.

I covered the definitions for class A and class AB in Chapter Three during the discussion of output stages. You will probably remember that a big part of the scientific definitions of these classes includes measuring an amp's performance at maximum output *before distortion*. By definition, therefore, anyone talking about "the sweet sound of class A distortion" is categorically talking crap, to use the technical term. There is no validity in using a definition to describe a thing's core form of existence, then boasting about the way that thing performs when it is operating outside the parameters of that very same definition. The classic sound of the amps that we have commonly come to brand as "class A" has everything to do with the fact that they're cathode-biased (with a cathode resistor bypass cap installed, at that), have no negative feedback loop, and—more often than not—carry EL84 tubes, which break up sweetly and smoothly.

These three characteristics make for a sparkling, crystalline sound just prior to distortion, and a smooth, juicy, harmonically rich distortion when it does come. Aside from a change of tubes to 6V6s (which can also be juicy and rich when distorting), a tweed Fender Deluxe possesses the elements described here, and if you listen to a good one it has a lot of that smooth onset of distortion that has become associated with the breed. You can be sure that if Leo Fender had thought there was any benefit in advertising his smaller tweed amps of the 1950s as "pure class A" he certainly would have—and he would have been no more or less off-base than the vast majority of amp-makers who are doing so today.

If you read vintage Vox advertising in old magazines and brochures, not once do you find mention of the term "class A." You can be sure that Dick Denney, designer of the Vox AC15 and AC30, knew his onions as a tube-amp technician, so if he and Tom Jennings thought these amps' class was something to crow about, they would have made the most of it. The truth is, even these classic "examples of the class" are by definition operating outside of class A at many of the settings that we love them for, and perhaps even throughout their performance. You'll remember that while the tube biased in class AB shuts off for part of the signal cycle to share the load with its push-pull partner, the class A tube keeps working for the entire cycle and is therefore less efficient—its

efficiency being something close to a maximum of 50 per cent, in fact. The maximum potential output of an amp with four EL84s, such as the AC30, is 48 watts (12 watts per tube), which is rarely going to be seen without some very careful control of voltages and bias points, and an efficient and perfectly designed OT. Despite its name, though, an AC30 in top condition can put out close to 35 watts; pretty good going for such an amp, and way above half of its 48-watt potential. Class A? Hmmm …

Also note that two amps of the exact same model and year might be running at different classes at exactly the same settings on the volume knob, depending on how far their internal voltages and bias settings have strayed from original specifications. To point to any guitar amp and say, definitively, "Yes, that is a class A amp," you would first really need to have a good amp technician put it up on the bench and hook up some diagnostic tools. It's not something that's very often done by the average hard-working musician.

For a far more accurate use of the definition, look at the way the high-end hi-fi aficionados use the term. In the audio world, class-A power amps are sought out for their lack of distortion and their full-frequencied sound spectrum. They are almost universally extremely expensive units, too, often employing large and somewhat obscure tubes and over-sized OTs for a power output that is surprisingly low—the class A inefficiency element again.

If you are interested enough to probe the class distinctions more, plenty of good writing exists on the subject as it relates to guitar amps. Amp designer Randall Aiken contributed an excellent chapter on the subject to *The Tube Amp Book: Deluxe Revised Edition* by Aspen Pittman; Shane Dolman has some interesting things to say on the subject in a paper on the Sheldon Amps website; and a quick web search will very likely turn up a range of other articles.

The concluding message I have for you is this: before you let an amp's supposed status as "class A" be the ultimate deciding point in your purchase, remind yourself once again that the Marshall JTM45, plexi and 18-watter; the Fender tweed Bassman and Twin, blackface Deluxe Reverb and Super Reverb; any Soldano; many Mesa/Boogies; and so on and so forth and—yep—most Vox AC15s and AC30s within much of their operating parameters, are all class AB amps, and proud of it. Between them, they have also recorded the vast majority of rock's great guitar sounds.

## HIGH-GAIN AND CHANNEL-SWITCHING AMPS

For many players, high-gain and channel-switching amps are thought of as one and the same: you have a high-gain "lead" channel, and you use a footswitch to change to it from the "rhythm" (or "clean') channel. Very often in today's market they are the same thing, too, but they really didn't start out that way. Amp designers have been ramping up the gain since the 60s, and the early iterations of high-gainsters were born as single-channel amps. The original Mesa/Boogie, called the Mark I after the Mark II came along, was a non-channel-switcher, with dedicated inputs for its high- and low-gain circuits; when you were plugged into input 2 and dialed in for a lead tone, clean was only attainable by winding down the guitar's volume control. Same with the original Marshall JCM800 amps, and others. Channel switching came along—*a la* the Mesa/Boogie Mark II—two instantly-accessible channels dedicated to different voices, but the feature was in no way a prerequisite of the high-gain circuit.

Even today, with channel-switching well into its fifth decade, makers still produce dedicated lead amps with one channel, no switching, and a predisposition to *hot*. Fryette's Deliverance, Komet's K60 and Aero 33, and Carr's Bloke (though with a "slightly less crunchy" footswitchable option) are all dedicated overdrive amps, while Mesa/Boogie's Mark I reissue and used Marshall JCM800 models remain popular, too. Why would you want a lead-only amp in the age of handy footswitching? For some players, if you're going to go all out all of the time, or most of it at least, it just makes sense: no fussing with, or paying for, added clean channels that you aren't going to use; or, maybe you prefer the clean tones attainable by winding down your guitar's volume when plugged into a cranked high-gain channel. Either is valid, and both seem to suit plenty of players.

That said, you can get a whole lot more tone out of many channel-switchers today than you could in the old days, and plenty of convenience too. The fact that some channel-switching designs have, historically, compromised on one aspect or another of their tone (very often the clean/rhythm channel) doesn't mean that this predisposition is inherent to the breed. When a channel-switching amp is designed and built well—as Steven Fryette points out in his interview later in this book—the signal is going through nothing more than it would in a single-channel amp configured like either of the amp's individual channels, just a relay that selects between them, with no more signal loss than you'd get passing through a switch terminal. That said, some of the cheaper, more mass-manufacture-style channel-switching amps do make several compromises to get so much done at their price point, and tone is likely to suffer there somewhere or other. This doesn't mean channel-switching amps as such suffer from a lack of sonic depth and dimension, and you can find some with really outstanding sonic purity if you shop carefully.

Part of the challenge of swimming in the channel-switching waters also involves identifying what other features you need. Very often an amp's entry into that "footswitchable" door also brings other bells and whistles along with it: effects loops, switchable boost and other voices, and so on. Again, if these are ladled on at a low cost in an amp using bargain-basement components and don't-dare-drop-it build quality, there are bound to be compromises somewhere. If that's what your budget stretches to, and you really *need* all the extra features to get the job done, go for it. Otherwise, consider shopping for an amp that puts better quality into the minimum of features you can really live with, and you're likely to land greater robustness, of tone and of build. Or, if you want the best of everything *and* loads of features, save your pennies and be prepared to pay for an amp that delivers it all in top style.

In the realm of high-gain circuits in and of themselves, it's also important to think long and hard about the character of the amp-based overdrive tones you're hoping to achieve. All lead tones are not created equal, and even among the great ones there's a lot of variety. Are you looking for cranked-tweed or Marshall vintage overdrive, Dumble-esque smooth, über-high-gain contemporary California grind, or a jagged raw tone? Some versatile amps might be able to do a little of all of it,

but most likely you'll want to narrow down your selection to something that specializes in the go-to tone you're likely to tap most often. One good place to begin, as with so much of tone chasing, is by identifying the sounds of several known artists that you'd like to approximate, ferreting out some knowledge of what they play via magazine interviews and web chat room discussions, then testing amps that purport to achieve the tones of said gear. In any case, do your research and play as many channel-switchers in person as you can, to avoid the frustration of landing one that has a killer lead tone as claimed … just not a lead tone that suits your very specific needs.

## THE COST OF TONE

I often hear players bemoaning the cost of good, higher-end tube amps today, often while simultaneously reminiscing about the "good old days" when almost all major brands were hand-wired, carried quality components, and sounded like the best of today's boutique models "for a fraction of the price." But the passage of time forges its own rose-tinted spectacles, and the fact is that sentimentality and nostalgia often knock certain pertinent details out of view—such as relative wages of the day, or the necessity of adjusting that "fraction of the price" for inflation over 30 or 40 years. To my way of thinking, it's not so much that the prices of good tube amps have gone sky-high, but that a few guitarists need to learn to appreciate the quality that a higher gear investment buys you. (Or alternatively to appreciate just how much you can buy today for next to nothing, thanks to mechanized assembly and the price-slashing of mass-manufacturing.)

There's no doubt that a glimpse of an old Fender price list will get you drooling. A 1955 Deluxe for $129, a 1959 tweed Bassman for $339, a 1965 Super Reverb for $399. Or how about a 1968 Marshall JMP50 for approximately $350, or a Bluesbreaker for $600? If the numbers make you queasy, stop a minute to calculate for today's money: in 2014 the little Deluxe would be closer to $1,120, the Bassman around $2,673 and the Super Reverb closer to $2,908. The Marshalls are now a little above and below $3,000 respectively. And whadda ya know—for these kinds of prices you can get yourself a Dr Z Carmen Ghia head (the Deluxe of the late 1990s, and better built); Victoria 45410 (a tweed Bassman repro) comes in at around $2,500; and the price of the Marshalls easily buys you a gorgeous TopHat Emplexador, Mojave PeaceMaker, Germino Lead 55, or any of several others with plexi-like tones a plenty; it makes Marshall's own three-channel TSL100 look like a steal.

What's more, figures far smaller than these will purchase perfectly playable amps of the mass-manufacturing grade. The street price of a new Fender Blues Junior is in the $450 range (around $70 in 1960—unheard-of at the time for a quality 15-watt amp with reverb), and Reissue '65 Super

Reverbs can be found for some $1,400. Other impressive bargains in tube amps come from new models by the likes of Peavey, Carvin, Traynor, Laney, Ampeg, and so on. From the classic names among these, the designs and construction methods often aren't what they were in the heyday of the brand, but for pure bang-for-buck they are doing pretty well. Almost all amps under $1,000— and quite a few way over (other than very small boutique models and a few other exceptions)—are going to be made with PCBs (printed circuit boards) and mass-market-grade components, but that's what the price bracket demands, and plenty are still great-sounding amps. Along with the playable $195 Squier Stratocaster or Yamaha Pacifica, the good-sounding $300 tube amp is a miracle of the modern age of manufacturing.

Top rack or bargain basement, there's a lot more available in good, usable tube guitar amps today in terms of both price and variety than ever before. You don't have to spend a fortune to get a decent amp (without even taking into consideration the used market), but if tone, response and dynamics mean a lot to you, it's certainly worth examining just how much you can afford to spend, and learning exactly what the amps in those upper price brackets might do for your sound, and your playing. While the lower and medium-range amps can sound just fine, and even suit the needs of many professional players, your first experience of a really carefully designed and well built amp can take your breath away. Often there are extra degrees of depth, air, and harmonic richness to the sound, plus an element of touch-sensitivity that really makes the difference in your interaction with the instrument. And sometimes there aren't. But even if you don't feel you are "in the market," test drive as many really good amps as you can get hold of, and start to learn what kind of quality can often come hand-in-hand with gradations in price.

You'll recall my "cheap guitar into expensive amp" experiment from Chapter One. If anything, the majority of players willing to spend a couple of grand or more on their setup are usually inverting the principle I expounded there, and dumping the lion's share of their cash on the guitar. But if you want to appreciate the full glory of any expensive, hand-made guitar, you often need to put the same kind of cash into an equally exalted amplifier, new or vintage. If you have been playing mid-level gear most of your life but have finally saved up $4,500 for that dream guitar—which you think will make the world of difference to your playing through the same old $500 amp—consider hawking that too, and putting $2,500 each into a great guitar and a great amp. Shop long, and shop carefully. There are plenty of both afloat out there, at this kind of price, that would send many pros to their knees with sonic ecstasy.

If you want boutique quality at half that price, though, there's still a hell of a lot to be found on the used market. Here's one quick route to sound heaven for players in the market for a tuneful 50-watt guitar amp. Locate a late 1960s or early 1970s Bassman head (you should be able to get one for under $500, though there's no telling how prices can change in the future), invest $75-$125 with a good tech for new tubes and caps as necessary and a couple of ultra-simple mods, and put the rest into an empty generic 1x12″, 2x12″, or 4x12″ cab—depending on your needs—plus some decent speakers. Depending on tastes and requirements, a rig like this, set up properly, can easily rival many boutique amps costing three and four times the money.

Many, many tube amps of the 1960s/70s that have failed to become collectable, but were nonetheless hand-wired with circuits laid out on eyelet cards or tag strips that are easy to work with and modify, have the potential to be stunning amps with just a little care and attention. If the transformers and other general components are good, $120-worth of tubes, caps, and transistors—plus the cost of a couple hours of a good tech's time—can land you with a fine approximation of almost any amp under the sun. A Selmer Treble'n'Bass becomes a great Marshall plexi or Hiwatt Custom 50; a WEM Dominator becomes a hot little Vox AC15; a Traynor YGL3 becomes a Marshall crossed with a Twin Reverb, or just continues to sound great as a Traynor if put back into good condition. Compared to many larger "deluxe" amps of today, silverface Fenders, mid- and late-70s Marshalls (made with PCBs, but of a more serviceable type than used today), Hiwatts of the same era, and some of the less fashionable Gibson and Epiphone amps can offer amazing value … and that's not even getting into the real low-cost end of the market.

And as for that low end of the market … although they weren't made to the same standards, countless models from Danelectro, Silvertone, Valco (under labels such as Wards, Airline, Gretsch, etc), Alamo, Harmony, Kay and so on, can sound pretty fabulous in a grungy, freaked-out, lo-fi fashion when cranked up. Look for models with standard tube types—which you'll discern pretty easily either from the printing on the tubes themselves, a tube chart that might be glued inside the amp cabinet, or a schematic diagram of the amp's circuit—so that you don't have big hassles finding replacements, then just get them functioning decently with a minimum of attention or expense, play them, and enjoy them. These amps usually aren't worth spending a lot of cash on, or a lot of time modding and tweaking, because their basic components are generally of a pretty low grade. But some will really breathe fire when attacked with attitude, and many of the smaller ones make fantastic recording amps.

## TUBULAR ALTERNATIVES

To score some ferocious sounds for even less money, keep your eyes peeled for older tube PA and mono audio amplifiers going cheap. These days nobody has much use for a 30-watt tube PA, which distorts everything at any usable level and eases your vocals into a sleazy crunch at about 11 o'clock on the dial, but that $50 junker might make a stunning guitar amp. If it's got standard tube types and hefty-looking transformers, you're probably in business. Plug your guitar into a mike input and test it out as-is to find if there's at least a passable sound and the thing is functioning at all, then pay your money, tuck it under your arm, and head out the door.

If you spot something like this for sale that's going cheap, even with limited technical knowledge you can assess a few things pretty quickly that will at least give you an indication of whether or not it's a viable candidate for a guitar-amp conversion.

■ *Do the transformers look like a reasonable size and quality for the unit's supposed output power?* If so, they should also do a fair job of any guitar-amp duties. Guitar amps have rarely employed OTs that you could call high-grade in the broad scheme of things, and the same goes for cheaper, low-powered PA systems. In the old days, if a manufacturer made both, it was very likely sourcing its lower-powered OTs for guitar amp and PA amp duties from the same or similar off-the-shelf supplies. If you haven't seen a lot of tube-amp transformers, take a look at those on some standard but slightly older models from Fender, Marshall, Traynor, and others where they are pretty readily on view. Such makers used quality transformers—which usually means pretty large ones for their tube complement and rated wattage—and these provide a good gauge against which to compare the transformers on your prospective "cheap buy."

■ *Are the transformers clean and rust free?* If so, and if the amp is currently working, then it's probably in good enough shape to warrant a conversion. If either transformer is considerably rusty or corroded, leave the thing alone. The biggest benefit you hope to gain from a junker PA head is usable transformers and a chassis that's at least punched for some tube sockets, so replacing even one transformer makes the project impractical.

■ *What preamp tubes does it carry?* Look for the types that are still common today, and you won't have much trouble converting to guitar-amp specs. If the preamp runs on 12AX7s you're in business. If it carries another nine-pin type with at least the same pin-out—12AT7, 12AU7, 12AY7 in particular—they might be usable as they are, or can easily be converted for using 12AX7s with the change of a resistor or two. Even PA and audio amps with older octal preamp tubes are sometimes worth a try. The octal-base 6SC7, 6SL6, and 6SN7 will be the more common dual-triode types, and they can usually still be found in stock at good suppliers (although 6SN7s are getting pretty expensive, and more difficult to find). If you'd rather convert to a more conventional type like a 12AX7, the circuits of such amps can usually be rewired to accommodate if you punch a hole for a new nine-pin socket. The 6SJ7 pentode also offers interesting preamp possibilities, and you can still find a few stocks of these hanging around.

■ *What output tubes does it carry?* Anything using a 6V6, 6L6, 5881, 6550, EL34, or EL84 tube type is going to be a good bet. These are the best-sounding output tubes for guitar, and by sticking with the tubes the amp comes with you'll know you are staying within its power transformer's current-handling capabilities. Even if the thing carries an oddball output tube, there might still be hope. Write down the model number of the tube, and take it to your friendly local amp tech to ask if there's an easy substitution available. (You're going to bring them the PA or audio amp for conversion anyway, right? So let them know they're getting your business.)

If the tech can source a more common tube with the same pin-out (meaning the same configuration of pins as relates to internal connections), same or lower heater current draw, and same or very similar impedance, there's a good chance a substitution can be made, even if it means changing a cathode-bias resistor or fixed-bias setting to make things right. Alternatively, if you're tube savvy yourself, there's a ton of information online

Newcomb "gramophone-to-guitar amp" conversion.

about the operating parameters of less common tube types, and dealers you can search to assess availability.

In identifying your candidate for conversion, keep in mind a number of basic guitar amp topologies that you would hope to emulate. If the PA amp has a pair of nine-pin preamp sockets and two 6V6s in the output, you could be on par for a tweed or brownface Deluxe-type amp; if it has EL84s, then a Marshall 18-watt, Vox AC15 circuit, or Matchless Spitfire circuit might suit it. A PA with three nine-pin sockets and 6L6s will do any of the larger Fender tweeds, or a blackface without the effects. If it carries EL34s instead, make it a Marshall plexi. With three preamp tubes (or, more accurately, two in the preamp and one for the PI), you can even achieve a one-channel high-gain amp with cascading preamp stages.

If the amp sounds passable with a guitar plugged in as it is, but lacks a flattering tonal range for guitar, most likely changes will be needed in the coupling capacitors and the tone stack. These will have been voiced for PA applications, so changing to values and circuits designed to emphasize the frequency range of the guitar—by once again referring to some classic old schematics—should open up the sound entirely.

The first hands-on project I ever tackled myself involved converting an old Newcomb portable tube gramophone from 1960 into a tweed Deluxe. The chassis had two decent-looking transformers

(the OT in particular looked very much like the paper-wrapped Deluxe OTs of old, if perhaps a hair smaller), it had a miniature seven-pin single-triode preamp socket and nine-pin PI socket, a pair of 6V6s, and a 6X4 tube rectifier. I repunched the first socket for a nine-pin 12AY7/12AX7 as required by the Deluxe, and replaced the 6X4 with diodes to bring the voltages up to around 350VDC on the plates of the 6V6s, according to Deluxe specs. The rest was simply a matter of wiring in the very simply 5E3 circuit. It was a tight fit, and ended up a real rat's nest of a point-to-point circuit without a lot of attention to shielding or where high voltages, signal voltages, and heater current cross paths—but hey, the thing sounds fantastic. Breaks up just a little quicker than a tweed Deluxe, perhaps, and even without the tube rectifier it has plenty of sag. I still use the thing a lot for recording, and everyone who hears it is impressed with the "authentic 1950s tweed tone"—all for the $20 I paid for the original junker gramophone, plus about $20 in parts and tubes.

If you're tempted to go this route, start keeping your eyes peeled for prospective donor PAs, mono audio amps and gramophones on eBay and in pawn shops and junk shops, yard sales and garage sales. Anything that's especially complex is usually worth staying away from, as are many of the tube organ amplifiers out there that have extra features and multiple amplification circuits hanging onto each other. If the unit seems simple enough, is in fairly clean condition, and carries standard tube types, it's probably worth a try—especially if the price is right. In all of this process, of course, the most important step is probably to cultivate a relationship with a good technician …

## THE GOOD TUBE-AMP TECH

Do you know who your local guitar amp technician is? What kind of music does he listen to? What's his favorite color? Even if you don't have any work to be done right now—repairs, mods, conversions or otherwise—try to find out who in your area does the best work on tube guitar amps. If they working in a local guitar store, drop in and express your enthusiasm for the subject. Let him know that you respect what he does, and that you might have some projects in the not-too-distant future. But try not to get in the way or overstay your welcome; if he's a craftsman, he'll be busy. (More often than not it's a "he," though by no means exclusively.)

Even if you're in the market for a new tube amp, fully warrantied, you will probably need the guy's service one of these days, just for help with re-tubing and re-biasing or some other general maintenance. If you plan to hunt down a good, affordable used tube amp—or indeed a vintage classic—or to find a tube PA to convert, you will need the guy's help even more. Before spending your money on a used and possibly abused amplifier, discover whether a tech in your area is willing to put in some creative effort on your behalf to bring the old unit up to your own needs as a player. It's often worth trying to ascertain whether a tech is player-savvy, or is primarily a TV repairman who doesn't really give a fudge about how a guitar amp should sound, but needs the work because there aren't so many tube TVs around any more. Don't get me wrong, guys in the latter camp have often proved to be great amp repairmen and modifiers—but if you've got a guy who seems hell-bent on helping you maximize the headroom and minimize the harmonic distortion in your Marshall Super Lead, maybe he's not the right kind of tech for you … unless that was what you were asking for. In any case, figure out what you can get done locally before you invest in that salvage amp project, because shipping it to a good out-of-town tech will sure cost a whole lot more, not to mention the hassle of long-distance communication about issues and repairs, verses the convenience of face-to-face interaction.

I have come across no end of vintage amps that, once opened up, revealed entirely new circuits—spotless, beautifully wired-up and neatly soldered, to be sure, but hardly "vintage"—because an unsympathetic repairman felt it was simpler to replace all the vintage coupling caps and carbon comp resistors rather than test each individually for leakage or drift. Replacing all the old components for new units of the same value is certainly a straightforward way of ensuring that the circuit is at least functioning correctly, but if only two of the original Wima signal caps in your prized Vox AC15 are leaky, you don't want the whole bunch of them replaced with new Orange Drops. That's not to say you can't work with someone who would do such a thing: if a repairman at least has a broad technical knowledge, and if you develop an understanding of the compromises in components and circuits that sometimes sound best in guitar amps, you can work together to achieve your goals. Educate him a little, and let him educate you in turn.

In any case, track down and meet a few local techs, try to engage them in a little appropriate conversation without disrupting their work day, and, when possible, bring them some relatively minor jobs to get a feel for their work and their understanding of a guitarist's needs. At the same time, try to appreciate and respect the skill and knowledge that many of these professionals bring to the game. No one studies tube electronics at college any more, so the guys who really know their stuff are a rare breed. When you start planning that big used-tube-amp hunt, or that vintage PA conversion project, discuss it with them ahead of time, and ascertain whether or not they are willing to come onboard for the adventure.

The means of achieving great tube tone can come in many forms. Take in as much knowledge as you can, round up the help of skilled professionals where necessary, and enjoy the quest.

# CHAPTER 6

# Sizes & Requirements

**Big isn't always beautiful when it comes to tube guitar amps. It depends what you do with it.**

The key to making the most of any decent tube amplifier, provided it's in good condition, lies in finding its "sweet spot" for your particular style—which usually lives within a fairly narrow range on the volume dial—and then consistently using the amp at output levels that tap into this potential. Each model and design of amplifier hits this sweet spot at a slightly different setting, but with traditional-styled single-channel amps, as a rule you tend to find it a little under halfway up for clean playing, and a little past halfway for crunch and lead tones (or, sometimes, cranked all the way up for all-out mayhem). In either case, this is pushing things to the point where the output tubes are seeing a fairly high signal level, and this saturation is adding some texture and harmonic shimmer to clean tones, or some out-and-out distortion to the crunch and overdrive tones.

Much of what's been discussed so far in the book has involved identifying an amp's point of breakup and its distortion character. The key to using that, once you have identified it, is to be able to sit within or just either side of that breakup point in your own playing. You can probably see the lesson I'm framing for this chapter already, and it's easily summed up in a single sentence: "Use a size of amplifier that lets you reveal its sweet spot in your commonest playing situation." In short, this means using an amplifier that is big enough to compete with your drummer when turned up to halfway or beyond, but one that's not so big that you can't set it past eight o'clock on the volume knob without overpowering the room or the band, or both. In more cases than not, guitarists who heed this advice find they need to downsize their amps rather than upsize, and the general craze for smaller tube amps today is largely thanks to this kind of thinking. In some instances, though, you'll find your sonic nirvana lies in moving up to a larger amp, while finding a way of reining in its overall output level if you need that tone at manageable volumes.

## WASTED WATTS

I've known many players that owned very nice amps indeed, but never got the best out of them because they never played in a room large enough to let them crank the thing up. These guys saved their pennies for years, and finally bought the amps of their dreams: a metal-panel Marshall JTM100, a Fender Twin Reverb, a Soldano SLO, a Mesa/Boogie Triple Rectifier, maybe even "just" a Vox AC30. They brought the thing to the gig, and were heartbroken when the singer, or the bass player, or the sound engineer kept begging them to turn it down. They were even more heartbroken when, show after show, that gorgeous amp sounded entirely mediocre with the volume reined in to tone-stifling levels. If, instead of a 100-watter, they'd bought a little 15 to 30-watter with similar characteristics (I don't include AC30s in this "small" category, because of their surprisingly high volume levels), they probably would have been cruising in the tone zone each and every gig.

Plenty of these guys bought those big amps because in one gig out of ten they get to play in a large hall or theater or whatever, and that's where they figured they would really shine and make the most of all that power. Maybe so, but it's not worth sounding flat and constrained for those other nine gigs. If they'd bought an amp that sounds great for those small-to-medium-sized rooms, when that occasional big show came along, no doubt there would also be a big PA system with full monitoring to go along with it. Let the PA people do their job and ram your sweet little tone machine through their megawatt rig, and everybody will be smiling. Either that, or buy two amps, if you have the luxury of doing so—a Matchless DC30 and a Lightning, or a Marshall TSL100 and a DSL20—and size the amp to the room. Or, if you really prefer the tone of the big amp, regardless of volume, you find a way to make the volume side of the equation work … but more of that later.

Sometimes it's hard to put that macho big-amp mentality behind you, but if you do so when necessary you'll be a happier guitarist, I guarantee you. Remember, too, that these huge 100-watters came along in the mid 1960s when bands were moving into big arenas, but PA rigs were way behind the game, and struggling just to keep the vocals and drums loud enough. With the advent of efficient, loud, modern sound-reinforcement systems, guitarists didn't really need to be any louder than about the level of an unmiked drum set—and given good monitoring, they could even get away with less volume than that—but it was hard to give up those big stacks. Of course, they looked pretty macho too, and the "stack of stacks" was a major facet of the stadium rock show for years—and still is—whether or not all of the cabs are actually plugged in (hint: they aren't).

If you find yourself getting into the whole smaller-amp concept that I'm pushing here, and you develop a modest collection of two or three or more different models as a result … hey, what do you know, suddenly you've got yourself a big amp again. When that big-room gig comes along, you can now use two of these together, joined with a stereo pedal or A/B/Y box or something similar, to create a bigger sound that will also be more diverse and multi-textural than a single large amp would be anyway. Experiment with different combinations ahead of time to see which amps complement which others. You might pair an amp with a big bottom and shimmering highs with another amp with aggressive, juicy mids; or one with a punchy, tight, clean sound with another that is crunchier and compressed and breaks up more easily. Using two 20-watt 1x12″ combos pumps out the same power level as a single 40-watt 2x12″ and often the resultant sound is actually a lot bigger because of the added texture of two slightly different-sounding amps. Not that using two small amps will give you exactly the same performance as using one larger one, but in many situations the pair will give you a broader sonic palette to work with.

If you get a lot of hum you might need to try lifting the ground (earth) connection from one of the two amps. This is easily done in the US with a three-prong to two-prong adapter, leaving the grounding tag disconnected. Or, better and safer still, get a good-quality A/B/Y pedal to select between the two amps or simply to run both together safely, and find one that has both a ground-lift switch and phase-reverse switch for one channel. It'll do the job safely, and give you the bonus of matching two out-of-phase amps, too.

## WHEN YOU GOTTA GO BIG

All of this isn't intended to deny that there are some occasions when you might prefer a big amp. For one thing, there's nothing quite like the feeling of standing at the center of a large stage with your back to 100 watts of power roaring through eight blaring Celestion Greenbacks. All that air literally moves you, you feel it in your gut, and there are things you can accomplish with sustain and feedback at those sound pressure levels that just don't seem to happen in the same way with smaller rigs. But again, most of us, in most of our gigs, just wouldn't be allowed to turn that 100-

watt full stack up to levels where that magic starts to happen, so it isn't worth mourning the dream that can never become reality. Crank your 20-watter up to the right level, get a little closer to the amp, and you might feel it move you too, although it still may not be quite what you're after.

On the other side of the coin, many players who really do need a lot of clean headroom will, as ever, need 100 or 120 watts just to avail themselves of the 60 to 80 watts of power available before clipping. The same might go for players who get all of their overdrive and distortion sounds from pedals. If you need to play truly ultra-clean all the time, you can get away with that Fender Twin Reverb set at eight o'clock night after night. While you're just not going to hit the sweet spot of any large amp with its volume reined down to 25 per cent or less, you might get a pristine clean sound that works fine for those moments, while the template works great if you forge the majority of your more complex or overdriven tones from effects pedals. By the same token, amps that generate most of their distortion from cascading preamp gain stages often sound pretty decent with their master volume controls reined in; not quite as good, or as heavy and thumping, as they do with the masters up beyond noon, but still somewhat like themselves at least.

As for practical considerations in your big-amp/small-amp dilemma, it might simply be that "your sound" is one that only a particular large, high-output amp provides. If you're just not getting that in a smaller amp, then you'll need to find a way to make the appropriate big amp work for you. And that's a perfectly valid objection to the wholesale move toward smaller amps. You might get similar levels of natural tube-amp overdrive out of a 15-watter and a 50-watter and a 100-watter each turned to two o'clock on the volume knob, but—SPLs aside—the latter two will have a lot more low-end thump and a heavier, thicker body that you feel as much as hear. These things are usually evident even when you get each of the three said example amps to the same decibel level, either by using an output attenuator in the room, or by recording all there, and playing them back at comparable volume levels through good studio monitors. Sometimes you just won't be able to fake that big-iron sound and feel, even when your distortion is sweeter and more easily achieved from the small iron.

There has been a slight swing back toward larger amps in recent years, and I'm guessing two factors have contributed to this. For one, output attenuators have both improved, and have been more widely accepted as a viable means of volume taming. For two, some players who have given the small-amp thing a shot have found they just can't get the same big-bottle grunt from smaller tubes, lower-output amps, and/or smaller output transformers (as above), and have reverted to bigger amps, and the improved facilities to rein them in … more of which below.

## BIG VERSUS SMALL IN THE STUDIO

In the recording studio, the logic about small versus big amps applies even more—a "small amp" in the studio context could be half or quarter the power of a "small" one in a gig situation. On-stage, the attempt to reach an amp's sweet spot depends on what the band and the room size will tolerate. Working in the studio, as most of us experience it, will almost always involve a smaller room than even the coziest bar gig we've played, and on top of that—and even more of a factor in some cases—there is sensitive recording equipment to consider.

Some professionals in $1,000-a-day studios certainly do record with their full stacks roaring, but it's by no means a rule that even the big-name axe slingers always lug their big stage rigs into the studio. Many of these players, if they're telling you the truth (or if they remember), could reel off a list of much smaller amps they used for a variety of sounds on different tracks. The famous examples include Eric Clapton and his tweed Fender Champ (that 'Layla' tone, anyone?), Jimmy Page and his Supro Model 24, Brian May and his battery-powered "Deacy," Keith Richards, sometimes Pete Townshend, and even Jimi Hendrix, according to legend, and their respective small amps. The trend continues today, with countless name guitarists of all genres frequently using smaller amps in the studio than they would use out on the road. Luckily, too, there are better small tube guitar amps available now than ever before.

In the old days, small amps in the 4-watt to 15-watt range were generally considered "student" or "beginner" models, and even from the better makers these weren't put together with high regard to component selection—amps like the 12-watt Fender Princeton Reverb and 10-watt Vox AC10 being the exception, perhaps. Today, the makers of the better hand-wired tube amps recognize that many discerning pros are going to use small amps in the studio, and there are some stunning models available. The smaller of the hand-made options—what I'd consider the super-duper-Champs, all of which are far from direct copies of anything—include models like the Carr Mercury, TopHat Portly Cadet and Prince Royale, Dr Z Mini-Z, Cornell Romany, Cornford Harlequin, and plenty of others. There are also lots of extremely affordable low-watt tube amps from mass-market makers that provide great value, and often sound outstanding, thanks in part to the inherent simplicities of their design. The choice in slightly larger amps is even greater, although many of these get you quickly up to small-gig volumes.

The sub-10-watt format is a fun end of the vintage market to explore, too, and one that's usually more available to the musician on a budget. You can find smaller, single-ended b-list amps from the likes of Airline, Wards, Oahu, Supro and National for peanuts, often from Gibson for not much more, and these are frequently fantastic-sounding little studio blasters when you get them into good condition. Even many classics of this size are still within reach. You can occasionally pick up an early 1960s Vox AC4 for just a few hundred bucks (although prices are rising), and the slightly tattered tweed or blackface Fender Champ sometimes comes along at the same kind of money. Get any of these in front of a good microphone, and the sound can be enormous.

In any case—to get back on the topic—most of us don't even have access to studios of the size and quality that these guys were and are using, and more and more CDs are being produced in upgraded home studios based in basements, attics, and garages. Aside from having neighbors to contend with, a big amp often just turns to a boomy mush in a small room, especially one with low ceilings. In many cases there literally won't be enough cubic feet of airspace for the low frequency soundwaves to reach their full extent before they're reflected off the walls and ceiling, causing phase cancellation and tone loss.

It also takes some very good recording equipment and a lot of engineering skill to capture a big amp at its best; even then, you can damage some of the best sounding recording mics and overload plenty of sweet preamps while trying to accomplish the task. Lots of professional producers and engineers, and the guitarists who are smart enough to listen to them, record with much smaller amps even when they're working in big studios with rooms and facilities that might cope with high-wattage monsters.

A small amp opens up an enormous range of miking possibilities: the engineer can look beyond his rudimentary Shure SM57, Beyer M201 and Sennheiser 421 dynamic mics and break out anything from the Neumann U87 and AKG C12 condensers to the RCA 77 and Coles 4038 ribbons. Amps of more than 15 or 20 watts will blow out many of these sensitive microphones when you get them cranked up, but position them at the right distance in front of a Vox AC4, Fender Champ, Gibson GA-5, or TopHat Portly Cadet, and you can capture a huge sound, with loads of dynamics and a really flattering frequency range. Even louder amps than these 4-watt wonders—models like tweed Fender Deluxes, Marshall 18-watters, Vox AC10s and AC15s, and newer emulations of such—can be captured by many more sensitive mics without risk of damaging the equipment, as long as you're careful not to blast things at top volume, and don't try positioning ribbon microphones too close (they usually like to be 12-18≤ away to attenuate the lows a little anyway).

Even when cranked up, these small amps might sound a little lean to you in anything other than a bedroom-sized room, but into the mic and down on the track they will have impressive girth and punch. You really have to try it a few times to start to believe. The pleasing harmonics, punchy midrange, and richness of an amp being pushed hard, but without the mush or fuzz of a pedal, will often help them sit better with other instruments in the mix too. A big amp's sound often overwhelms the frequency range of a track as a whole, while simultaneously sounding like it has been compressed down to a blur. A smaller amp in the same context will tend to sound more open, airy, dynamic, multi-textured and fat. Put another way, the small amp ends up sounding big, while the big amp can sometimes sound very small. It's an exciting discovery that opens up a lot of possibilities; after all, who wants to drag around that double-stack anyway? Even if you're a player who has rediscovered the girth and tone of bigger amps, the smaller amp in the studio often does you the added favor of attenuating the low end somewhat, saving the engineer from having to filter it out while recording or mixing. Any experienced player will tell you that too much low end in your guitar track will only fight with the bass and kick-drum tracks, so often you don't want it there in the first place.

You also need to take into account the mechanics of the human ear—our perception of frequency in relationship to volume levels—and decide where you want the dynamics involved to be best perceived: in the studio live room, or in the living room, in the car, or on the dance floor. In the case of recording a large amp in the studio, for a heavy-sounding track in particular, the result will sometimes be that even the low ebbs in dB levels are pushing the equipment past their levels, while the aggressive portions are really flooring things. This allows less space for the light and shade of dynamics. But use a smaller amp, one that lets the mic and preamp be set so they're sensitive to subtler playing yet still capable of capturing the heavier attack without distorting, and you can bring a much more dynamic performance to the mix.

It's worth emphasizing again that using a smaller amp allows you a much broader selection of microphones, which means a wider palette of colors in the recording process. Any guitarist who does a lot of recording should put at least as much thought into mic and preamp selection as into perfecting the guitars-effects-amps chain. Some mics, even types that are perfectly good in certain situations, will turn your carefully crafted rig into an entirely different beast. Others might capture subtleties and offer a flattering frequency presentation that really brings "your sound" alive. It's magic when you find a mic that "simply" makes your amp sound as warm, rich, airy, and alive in the recorded track as it does in the room.

A good mic can fall into two categories: it can render your guitar-amp sound accurately, or it can color it slightly in a way that proves preferable to the "real thing." The good old Shure SM57 has undoubtedly recorded a lot of classic rock tracks, and often it's still going to be just the ticket for that punchy, aggressive part where the emphasized midrange gnarl is desired. With the smaller amp, though, you can try out other options, like the full range of condenser mics that are so sweet with vocals but distort too easily with loud guitar parts, or the ribbon mics that capture such a warm, natural sound in this application. Many mics in both of these categories are pretty expensive, but affordable options do exist.

Anyone who follows the market for studio gear will have noticed the plummeting prices of condenser mics over the past few years, thanks to the availability of cheap Chinese capsules. Some of these are even pretty good, considering their low cost. Even some ribbon mics—which you'd probably be most familiar with as the big, vintage RCA models or the Coles 4038 or newer Royers— are within the average home recordist's grasp. The Beyer-Dynamic M160 is a great-sounding microphone, which was reportedly often part of the multi-miking setup used to record Jimi Hendrix; and its simpler, single-ribbon brother the M260 (now out of production, I believe) can also sound fantastic on a small amp, and will sometimes turn up in the auctions or classified ads for just a couple hundred bucks or so. What's more, Asian mic manufacturing has now taken up the ribbon design big time, so various flavors of these are now available to the home recordist, too.

My own recording world came alive when I found a used STC (now Coles) 4038 for sale a few years ago. For me at the time, $500 sounded like a lot for a used microphone—but nothing else I had tried made my tweed Deluxe sound like a tweed Deluxe on a track, or my Matchless Lightning sound like a Matchless Lightning, so I added up what I'd spent on guitars and amps in recent years, and decided that spending a fraction of that to help them sound their best on record was really a small price to pay. I'm getting off track a little here, and I don't mean to send you off on any mad search for expensive microphones, but it all goes toward considering the entirety of the sound chain in any quest to perfect your tone—and when you are in the studio, that will include microphones, preamps, compressors, the recording deck or interface, and several other items. For a lot more on mic selection and recording techniques in general, look up *The Home Recording Handbook* by yours truly (Backbeat Books), or *Recording Guitar And Bass* by my friend Huw Price (Backbeat Books), which I edited and partly contributed to. It's packed with food for thought.

Ultimately the only way to work out whether a particular amp is right for you is to try it. Even if you still like to lug that 80lb monster in and out of the studio—and maybe it does the job for some tracks, sure—I promise you that a range of small amps will open up many more sonic possibilities.

If you still can't get the small amp/big sound concept through your head, look at it like this: you will be recording that amp through a microphone diaphragm that will be maybe a little over an inch in diameter at most, and probably much less than an inch, sending a sound down a thin wire to be stored digitally or magnetically, and eventually reamplified through household speakers that, these days, are going to have maybe a 6″ diameter at best, or through headphones or earbuds with speaker diameters of less than 0.5″. Listen to Neil Young's *Weld* album on a good pair of headphones, and it still sounds pretty damn big. The chain starts with a little 15-watt tweed Fender Deluxe, is captured by a 1″ mic diaphragm, and returns to you through 0.5″ headphone diaphragms… but what an almighty roar nevertheless. When it comes to recording, we often need to radically shift our perception of size to make the most of the job.

## FLAT OUT AT A WHISPER

Two major trends of recent years have combined to inspire a move toward lower output volumes from guitar amps. One is the move toward lower stage volumes, even on big-venue professional tours, which is frequently accompanied by the use of in-ear monitors. The other is the tectonic shift away from the large professional studio and into the home project studio (a trend that has also affected other aspects of the music business), which has sent countless players scrambling for ways of making their big amps quieter … without simply turning down the volume. Let's say you've already got a Vox AC30 that produces the sound of your dreams at two o'clock on the dial, but neither the neighbors, your family, nor your microphones are at all happy with the situation. The dream solution would be to find a means of retaining that same sound, but at a far lower decibel level. Seems unlikely, but there are in fact quite a few ways of doing this. Approaching the task from a logical point of view, you might imagine the possibility of squeezing that full-throttle power tube signal on its way to the speakers so that the amp is still running "cranked," but only a conversational level is coming out of the cab. Alternatively, you could always lock the thing in a padded room, so that anyone not locked in there with it hears no more than a muffled whisper at best. Sounds simple, and to an extent it is. These are pretty much the means that the majority of "cranked but quiet" amp components use to achieve their goal.

Some of these solutions come in the form of output attenuators, tube converters, simple half-power and pentode/triode modifications, "power scaling" systems, and isolation boxes. It's worth looking at each in some detail.

## OUTPUT ATTENUATORS

Want to run your amp near full-tilt, but send just a portion of that volume-creating wattage to your speakers? The output attenuator is the way to do it. Such units are placed between the amp's speaker output and the speakers themselves, and carry a large resistor or some form of reactive "silent-speaker"-type device to soak up a portion of the output power. The remainder is passed along to the speakers themselves, at a level determined by the user, usually specified as a stated reduction in decibels (reductions in steps of three seem to be common: −3dB, −6dB, −9dB, etc).

Attenuators have been around for some time, but they have become more popular in recent years, due either to the fact that they're now better and more reliable, or to the trend for lower stage and studio volumes (probably some confluence of the two). Some early units of the 1980s had a reputation for allegedly burning out their elements and, as a result, frying essential components within the amp to which they were attached. I don't know how often—if ever—this sort of meltdown actually occurred, but the chances of that happening with newer attenuators are minimal, as they tend to be extremely well-built, well-designed, sturdy, and reliable accessories. The differences between them nowadays have very little to do with whether or not one or the other will or won't damage your amp (in and of themselves, they should not), but whether they retain a satisfactory degree of the sound and feel of your amp played loud, at the quieter attenuated level.

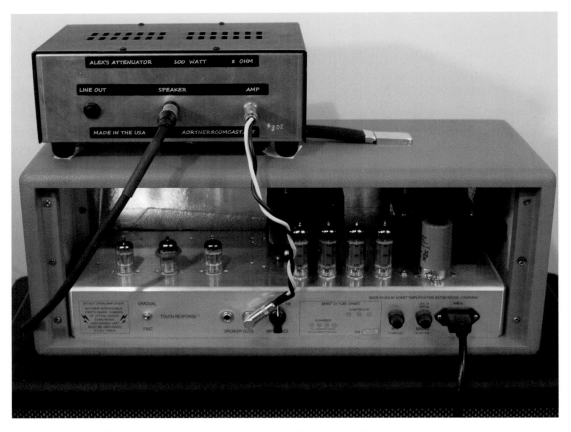

An output attenuator is used to reduce an amp's output power when connected between amp and speaker.

The obvious function of the attenuator is to bring big amps down to the volume levels of the small amps I've discussed in this chapter already. This opens them up to the same kinds of recording applications, enabling their use in smaller studios, with sensitive microphones, and so forth. Many players, though, have also been using attenuators a lot more for gigs, to knock off just 6dB or so, or to suit a large-room amp to a smaller room, or to drop their sound down a little bit at the start of the evening, when the room is empty, and then bring it back up to full output with the flick of a switch or twist of a knob—without changing the sound and distortion character—when the venue is packed and the bodies are absorbing more sound. Or, if you're mainly gigging in large rooms and don't need to rein in your volume for shows, an attenuator will help you get something close to your "live sound" in a smaller rehearsal room, where you might be getting the set together with just a vocal PA, no mics on the drums, and so forth. There are a lot of uses for the things, no doubt, and if you don't already own one, I'm sure almost every player reading this can imagine a situation in which a good attenuator would be handy.

They do, nonetheless, by the nature of their operation, have inherent … I wouldn't want to call them "drawbacks," but let's just say "elements of their function" that sometimes make your rig sound not *exactly* like a less-loud version of the same amp. The first is that driving your speakers at different levels obviously makes them perform differently; any speaker's reaction and interaction to and with the amp is a big part of the amp's overall sound, and these speakers sound differently when driven hard than they do when driven gently. This will be discussed in more detail in Chapter Eight, but speakers usually contribute a portion of the "broken-up" sound of any cranked amp's distortion content; speakers with high power-handling ratings usually still break up a little when played hard, and speakers with low power-handling ratings break up a lot. Reduce the signal running from amp to speaker, and clearly you will cut down on this "speaker distortion," and perhaps eliminate it entirely. For some sonic goals, speaker distortion is not desired anyway, so this could be another bonus of the attenuator. For others—classic rock'n'roll, vintage blues, garage rock styles— speaker distortion can contribute a lot to that over-the-top, edge-of-freakout overdrive sound of a cranked amp.

The second, perhaps less obvious, thing that comes to mind is that the human ear responds differently to the frequency spectrum at different volume levels. In short, even though the attenuator is allowing your amp to pump the very same output-tube distortion portion of its overall tonal palette to your speakers at a lower volume level, the mere fact of that lower volume will change the way your ear perceives the frequencies that make up the sound. Put another way, given a rig that isn't producing any speaker distortion at full volume anyway, the amp's tonal and harmonic spectrum will still sound "different" to you at 84dB than at 96dB, not simply "quieter."

Research on this subject published by Fletcher & Munson in 1933 determined—in simple terms, and among other things—that the sensitivity of human hearing fluctuates with frequency. We have a lot more sensitivity to frequencies toward the middle of our hearing range than we do to extreme lows and highs. With this in mind, it becomes clear why it takes a lot more wattage and a hefty output transformer and so forth just to help the bass player compete with the guitarist's cranked 30W amp grinding away at the midrange; why you get the firmer, tighter low-end reproduction from the guitar amp with the big, heavy OT; or why adding a few dBs to the high frequencies when mixing can bring out extra sparkle in an otherwise dull mix and really seem to make a track come alive. (A word of caution: this mixing practice can also prove very tiring on the ear after a while. Sometimes it can be better to reduce the frequencies you want to hear less of, and the others will stand out by comparison.) Frequencies above and below our peak sensitivity can be seen as existing out of our "comfort range," the higher frequencies in particular, and the brain strains harder to hear and decipher them.

Consider the Fletcher-Munson findings in relation to output attenuators, and you can see how your sound is still bound to change a bit merely because of the alteration of volume level, even with all other factors being equal (and of course they're not quite equal, given the speaker's own reaction to output levels). For an everyday comparison, try playing your favorite CDs at number two on your stereo amp's volume, and then at number eight. They are still characteristically the exact same songs, but certain frequencies definitely resonate more when you hear them louder. Many of the better attenuator makers claim they incorporate circuitry to compensate for our changing perception of frequencies at different volume levels, so you can expect them at least to minimize this somewhat. But even despite the possible drawbacks, a good attenuator can still have a lot to offer, and for many players it can provide a magical solution to a very pesky problem.

Some players worry about attenuators damaging their amps, but the better attenuators, as far as I can tell, have nothing in their own function that is inherently bad for your amplifier. The simple fact that you are likely to be running your amp harder with an attenuator attached (turning up "louder" to achieve the same volume level, but with a more "cranked up" sound) means that all components will be under more of a strain—tubes in particular—and will be liable to burn out faster. This is just the same as if you were playing in that large auditorium every night anyway, and were turning the amp up to the same higher volume without an attenuator. The amp is still pumping as much voltage through its system and running its tubes and transformers as hot as it would be when normally cranked, but the attenuator is converting a lot of that energy into heat to be dissipated through a large heat sink (or into mechanical energy in an alternative speaker motor, in the case of something like a Weber MASS unit or another attenuator using a reactive load), rather than sending it all to the speakers. As far as the amp itself is concerned, though, same volume levels means same wear and tear. If that's where an amp sounds best, many players figure that replacing output tubes more frequently is a small price to pay—or a large price to pay, but worth it. The fact that the amp doesn't sound as loud can make it easy to forget that you are still driving those tubes and components pretty hard, so anyone using an attenuator night after night should keep an extra sharp eye out for amp maintenance issues.

You can see how, used correctly, an attenuator should at least help the speakers see less wear and tear than they would at the end of a normally cranked amp. In fact this leads us to one of the other great uses for the things: when an attenuator is attached, the player has a much broader range of speakers available for use with a powerful amp. Your Fender Twin or Marshall plexi can drive a pair of Celestion Alnico Blues, or a little 2x10″ cab loaded with Jensen P10Rs, or you can run your Soldano SLO 100 through a single Celestion G12H-30. Just don't forget what you're doing and flip the dial to 0dB attenuation, or you could end up sending some expensive speakers to the re-coner.

There's another way of minimizing the attenuator's potentially false representation of the cranked amp+speaker distortion/tone relationship. If you have the luxury of attaching a different speaker with the attenuator than the one you would use without it—for example, a lower-power-rated, high-sensitivity model for attenuated playing—you will get back a lot of the sonic characteristics of a speaker pushed hard. It's a great way of leveling the playing field, and yields a setup that's both toneful at lower volumes and, once again, very interactive.

Excellent attenuation units are available today from a number of makers and, as I said before, they have improved dramatically in the years since 1980, when Tom Scholz's pioneering Power Soak was introduced. Even in the years since the first edition of this book came out, new makers have introduced several impressive new attenuators, some of which are pretty expensive, but the results are often worth it, if you've got it to spend in the first place. The first popular upgraded attenuator was the THD Hot Plate, and it's still in wide use today. Marshall's Power Brake has also been popular, as have units like the Dr Z Air Brake and Komet Airbrake, made under license by those amp makers, respectively, from the Trainwreck design. Others on the market include the Weber VST MASS and Load Dump units, the Alessandro Muzzle, the TAD Silencer, Alex's Attenuator (now made under license by Scumback), the Aracom PRX-150 Pro, the Tone King Ironman, and Swart Night Light.

THD's Hot Plate has been one of the most successful of these units. Like most, it incorporates a large resistive element, in conjunction with a network of capacitors and resistors that, as the company puts it, "adjusts the overall EQ as the volume is turned down, to compensate for the human ear's frequency response." As such, the unit is billed as being reactive, rather than just resistive. (To put this into perspective, a speaker is itself a reactive load and its impedance and frequency response fluctuate with volume, while those of a resistor remain constant.) The Hot Plate offers four preset reduction settings at −3dB increments, followed by a fine-tunable low-level setting, then a silent "Load" setting for DI-only or bench work. It also carries Bright and Deep switches with two settings each plus bypass, a line out with level control, and a passive noise reduction circuit. Large heat sinks help disperse all the energy that's absorbed at higher output reductions, and the noise-reduction circuit channels some energy into a light on the front panel that glows brighter the harder you play. Kind of a nifty feature—although there's a switch to bypass it if it gets on your nerves. Each Hot Plate model is preset to a fixed impedance level, and they're available in 2, 2.7, 4, 8, and 16 ohms.

The Air Brake/Airbrake, designed by Ken Fischer of Trainwreck Circuits fame, tweaked by Dr Z's Michael Zaite and Komet's Holgar Notzel and Michael Kennedy and manufactured by them under license, is a simpler affair. It has four levels of attenuation at preset increments (but user adjustable), plus a "Bedroom" setting that is fine-tunable from that point down to a silent load. It's a purely resistive load, and is ideally used with an amp's 8-ohm or 16-ohm output.

Weber's MASS is different from others I have encountered, in that it employs a small speaker motor rather than a larger resistor. In doing so it offers a truly reactive load that mirrors rather than merely mimics the way a speaker itself interacts with an amp's output stage (in a way a resistive load does not). It's also feature-packed, with a three-way Treble Boost, an Impedance switch to select 2, 4, 8, or 16 ohms, a High/Low Range switch to tape the continually variable output reduction via the Speaker control (a rheostat), and a line-out with three-band tone stack plus Volume control. With all this onboard, the MASS is well suited to both studio and live applications and a broad range of uses. That said, I wouldn't say, objectively, that it outwardly sounds a ton better than a purely resistive load. Weber's Standard Load Dumps carry a three-way switch for 4, 8, or 16-ohm load matching, a Bypass switch, and a rheostat for continual reduction of output level. The High Power and Mega Dump versions have a switch for 2, 4, 8, or 16 ohms; a rotary switch for bypass and incremental stepping down of the output, with a rheostat for extreme reduction down to silence at the last step; and a volume pot to govern the output level of the DI outs (paralleled to XLR and quarter-inch jacks).

Of the more recent units, the Aracom has won a lot of fans, and I myself have been particularly impressed by the Alex's Attenuator (now manufactured under license as the Scumback DBL). The thing just seems to do its job well, for less money than some of the more elaborate attenuators, and—with the amps I've tried, at least—delivers a good rendition of the cranked-up tone at a range of user-friendly volume levels. The Tone King Ironman is also very good, if more expensive. All of them sound best, though, when extremes of attenuation are avoided; to my ears, whether reactive or not, none of these units sound entirely like "your cranked amp but quieter" when you attenuate by more than 12dB or so. In fact, I find them starting to sound a little artificial past the −9dB setting, and pretty darn fizzy and constricted at −15dB or beyond. If you're in the market for one of these, try any you can get your hands on and decide what features you do or don't need. You are unlikely to be disappointed with any of the units I've mentioned, and I know there are others out there that many guitarists value.

That said, none offers quite the same thrill and exact tone as playing your amp cranked in a room large enough to take it ... while standing far enough away so your ears can take it, too. For reasons I've largely covered already, all the reactive elements and frequency-shaping networks still don't entirely account for the influence that sheer volume level—serious soundwaves moving through air—and the different sound of a speaker driven hard versus a speaker driven gently, have on an amp's perceived sound.

Here's a tip: if you're using an attenuator a lot with a particular amp, think about using it through a different cab with a lower-powered speaker, one that will reach that hard-pushed state quicker. For example, instead of a Jensen P12N use a P12R (25W instead of 50W); or in place of a Celestion Classic Lead 80 use a G12H-30, Alnico Blue, or G12H-25 Greenback. With the $200-$450 for the attenuator and another $50-$100 for the new speaker, this starts to add up to a lot of cash to make our big amp sound good quieter; you have to decide if a smaller amp would be a better bet. Or to get the best ratio of "maximum volume reduction to minimum unnatural tone," try coupling the attenuator with a low-efficiency speaker, and even one in a closed-back cab to reduce the multi-directionality of its projection. Going from a 100dB Celestion Gold in an open-back cab to a 97dB Greenback in a closed-back cab, with a good attenuator set to −6dB or −9dB, will take another −3dB off your output, with a perceived volume drop that probably feels even lower than that.

## TUBE CONVERTERS

These were something of a craze when they first hit the market more than a decade ago, seen most often from the THD brand. Tube converters most commonly take the form of a direct plug-in adaptor that, without modification to the amp, allows nine-pin EL84 tubes to fit in eight-pin sockets intended for 6L6 or EL34 output tubes. There are also versions to fit EL84s to sockets that normally hold 6V6s. These don't have a whole lot more output level than EL84s in the first place, but the thinking is that you might prefer the tonality of the latter, which is considered to have a crispy, compressed "British" flavor in some circuits, with slightly earlier breakup.

Tube converters redirect the EL84's pins to make the correct connections through those of the amp's eight-pin sockets. They also contain a small network of resistors to bring the voltages down to those required by the lower-powered EL84, and a bias resistor to change the format from fixed to cathode-bias. In doing so, makers of such converters universally claim that they change an amplifier's output from "fixed-bias class AB to cathode-bias class A." To prove or disprove that, you'd have to put a vast number of amps up on the bench and measure them for actual performance at maximum volume before clipping. But we can say this about their design: the converters contain a preset cathode-biasing resistor intended to be used with a wide range of amps, which can include designs running their output tubes' plates at 400VDC, 425VDC, 475VDC, or whatever.

Given what we've already learned about true class-A performance being critically tied to bias point, with relation to an output stage's operating voltages, it's hard to see how a single resistor value could manage this "class-A conversion" for such a broad range of amps. Also, these converters do nothing to alter an amp's inclusion or lack of a negative feedback loop (which, admittedly, has nothing to do with class distinction either, but is a major factor in the associated sounds of different class types).

Personally I think they're going a little too far with such claims, and would be better off just touting the sonic and volume-related changes that tube converters can offer—which, for what it's worth, can be considerable. The overall result is pretty impressive for the relatively low cost of the items. Given that the output tubes play a very big part in the sonic signature of any amplifier, inserting a pair of THD Yellow Jackets or TAD Tone Bones really can be "like getting a whole new amplifier," as THD's company literature states. A 50-watt amp in the Fender or Marshall style, with a pair of 6L6 or EL34 output tubes, will yield an output of around 20 watts with the Yellow Jackets in place. This can obviously bring a large-room amp down to bar-gig and studio levels.

Be aware, though, that the relationship between wattage and apparent loudness isn't a direct correlation. All else being close to equal (sonic character, speaker performance, cab type), a 20-watt amp still sounds significantly more than half as loud as a 50-watt amp, not less than. But the difference afforded by the converters definitely offers a quicker onset of output-tube distortion, and usually that's the real goal anyway. For the cost of a pair of converters, it's a fast track to a significantly different sonic signature. I must admit, though, I have tried these in some excellent 6L6 and EL34-based amps that only sounded fizzy and overly compressed after conversion to EL84s. In others, the Yellow Jackets and Tone Bones offered an excellent alternative. You shouldn't expect any amp you pop them into to be magically converted into an AC15, but they can make an interesting and useful volume-dropping or tone-altering option in many cases.

If you are really looking for a smaller amp with what is generally characterized as "the class A sound," and find yourself playing your larger amp with the Yellow Jackets or other converters installed all the time, I'd argue that you probably ought to sell the thing and get an amp that's designed from the ground up to do what you're looking for. The general principle for good, solid tone is to travel the simplest and most direct road that gets you there. On the other hand, if you love the sound you get with converters in place and wouldn't want to change it one jot, fine; or if you can only afford one amp, but need cranked-up sounds at very different volume levels and with different output tube signatures, that's OK too. Either way, converters are a cool product that can be a lot of fun.

## POWER-REDUCTION MODS

There are a number of modifications available, both simple and complex, to reduce an amp's output power. Some involve actual rewiring of portions of the circuit, and some involve no surgical intervention of any kind.

The simplest of these can be achieved with many fixed-bias amps carrying four output tubes in two push-pull pairs. By removing one tube from each side of these pairs (either the two inside or the two outside tubes, but never two from one side), the power of the amp can be approximately halved. Removing two tubes, however, also changes the impedance relationship between the remaining output tubes and the speaker, as seen via the OT, so ideally you will make another adjustment here too. On amps with multiple output impedance selections, drop the impedance by half at the selector when continuing to use the same speaker cab. If you're running a 16-ohm cab and you pull two tubes, switch your selector to 8 ohms; if you're running an 8-ohm cab, switch it to 4 ohms, and so on. Rather than a selector, some amps have dedicated outputs at different impedance ratings, so just re-plug the speaker connection to a different jack—same result. If the amp has just one output impedance, as is the case with most older Fenders, you can either run different speakers to create the desired load, or just tough it out. In truth, most Fender OTs will

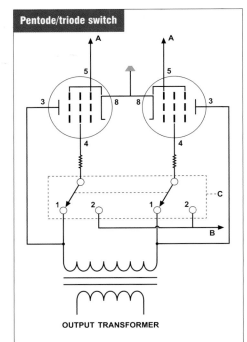

**Pentode/triode switch**

**OUTPUT TRANSFORMER**

**A:** From phase inverter

**B:** To DC high-voltage supply for screens

**C:** DPDT switch

**3:** Plates of tubes (6V6, 6L6, EL34 etc)

**4:** Screens of tubes

**5:** Grids of tubes

**8:** Cathodes of tubes

Switch Positions (for DPDT switch 'C')

**1:** Triode

**2:** Pentode

pretty easily tolerate an impedance mismatch going one step in either direction (ie, halved or doubled).

Frequency response and power might change somewhat, but you are seeking that anyway by pulling two tubes. If the result works for you, sonically, without an impedance switch, you are probably OK to go with it. Marshall amps are reputedly not as happy with an impedance mismatch, but fortunately the larger Marshall models generally carry impedance switches to match 4, 8, and 16-ohm loads. Some cathode-biased amps have half-power switches to knock out two of the four tubes, as used in many Matchless and Bad Cat models. Since the output tubes' bias is set in these amps by a permanent resistor that is usually tied to all four tubes, simply pulling two tubes would throw the bias levels for the remaining two way out of whack. What the switches do, though, is to add another bias resistor in series to increase the load as necessary, while also knocking two tubes out of the circuit. Clever stuff. You still want to drop your output impedance by half, though, to correctly match the load to the speaker you're using.

Despite the ability to compensate impedance-wise, this "pull two tubes" technique still doesn't instantly create, for example, a 50-watt amp that's exactly the same as the four-tube 100-watt version of itself in every regard other than power. The two remaining output tubes are now feeding a much heftier OT than most 50-watt amps would normally carry, so even when the amp is cranked up high there is likely to be less OT saturation in the amp's overall brew of distortion. Again, if you try this technique and the sound really works for you, who cares. The other side of the coin is that this bigger-than-standard "50-watt" OT (meaning the 100-watt iron) should give you fat lows and a firm response overall.

A trick achieved with a little more intervention is the pentode/triode switch (left), already used by a number of amplifier makers in the form of a "half-power switch." It doesn't exactly halve the power, and it changes the output tubes' tonal character in some other ways besides, but this mod is relatively simple, and certainly offers a faster path to output-tube distortion with a definite drop in volume levels.

The pentode/triode switch involves some fairly simple rewiring of the output tubes to make the pentode tube types think they are behaving as triodes. It doesn't actually turn them into triodes, but more "mock triodes" really. In any case, this triode mode makes the amp break up a little more quickly, and also induces a creamier, smoother, more midrange-dominant sound in the tubes. This can also be heard as a lack of sparkle and chime, with noticeably attenuated highs, so it doesn't suit every player's taste. Fortunately, the mod is simple and easily reversed, so things can be undone if you find you don't like the result. Personally, I have eventually removed the pentode/triode switching from just about every amp I've put it into for my own use, but plenty of other players dig it and like what it has to offer.

Be aware that this—like any internal modification—involves working around high voltages, so it should only be undertaken by a qualified professional amp tech. The work simply involves installing a sturdy DPDT (double-pole double-throw) on/on toggle switch, using one half of the switch for each side of the push-pull set. A single switch functions for two, four or six tubes, since the significant connections will be tied together. This switch lifts the output tubes' screen grid's connection to its DC voltage supply, and switches it between that supply (standard pentode mode) and a new connection made to the plates of the tubes (triode mode).

The work should take a good repair person about 15 minutes to complete, plus the drilling of an appropriate hole to mount the switch. This can sometimes be located in the hole for an extension speaker jack that you're not using, or if you aren't entirely sure you'll like the results, ask if the switch can be safely wired up "free-floating" first, so you can hear the results, then it can be drilled and permanently mounted if you are happy with it. Ensure that the switch used is rated for the kinds of voltages likely to be seen here (which are DC rather than the AC for which most such toggle switches are rated, but a high rating in the 240V ballpark with the ability to handle 5A or 6A of current should do the trick).

A technique dubbed "Power Scaling" by the Canadian company that first popularized it, London Power, requires a lot more surgical intervention, but provides a more thorough means of reducing power in the amp's output section across a steady, user-determinable range, while retaining the fully-cranked sound of the amp. Power Scaling circuitry works within the power section of the amplifier to scale down the voltages supplied to the output stage to yield a wide range of power levels, but all with the same relative breakup point and distortion characteristics as those achieved within the far narrower "sweet spot" of the original amp.

As circuit designer and London Power proprietor Kevin O'Connor puts it, Power Scaling "allows the output power of an audio amplifier to be dialed down from 100 per cent to less than one per cent." The circuit is available in a range of kits adapted to suit most existing tube amps, each of which should be installed by a professional, or at least by an experienced hobbyist with a thorough knowledge of the safe practices necessary for working around the high voltages inside an amp. Many production amps also include their own internal forms of voltage reduction, and you can find this feature in models by Mojave Ampworks, 65amps, Carr, Tone King, and others. Hall Electronics also offers a voltage-reduction kit suitable to a range of both cathode- and fixed-bias amps, and which has been popular with many players in recent years.

## ISOLATION CABINETS

If your concern is primarily about containing high volumes while recording—mainly, I suppose, to avoid annoying the neighbors, family members, your engineer, or whomever—there's another fairly popular solution to the problem: the isolation box. This is essentially a shrunken-down version of a vocal booth in a professional studio; a crate of the minimum size necessary, rendered as close to soundproof as possible, and loaded with a speaker and a microphone. Connect amp to speaker and crank up to whatever levels said speaker will handle, and the microphone inside the box picks up everything, while noise levels outside it are reduced to a whisper. Sounds simple, and in many ways it is. Commercial examples exist, or you can build your own with readily available and fairly obvious materials.

Isolation boxes don't offer much of a solution for practicing, unless you mike them into a mixer and play through headphones or monitors, which seems a pretty convoluted way around it, but they can provide a great recording tool in some situations. They might also provide a good way of taming a high-wattage amp in a big-stage situation with good sound support, if you're on a tour that likes to run everything through the monitors, or through in-ear monitors in particular. If you really need the sound of your amp cranked up high, unattenuated, miked-up through a roaring speaker, this is one way to do it. Of course that roaring speaker is unlikely to be the same one mounted in the cab the amp usually plays through—you might need to fit a smaller unit in order to keep the iso cab down to a manageable size.

Isolation cabinets have a range of drawbacks: they can be both boomy and over-compressed, because there is rarely enough air around the speaker to let the sound really breathe; they are difficult to either plan out or to acoustically tune, until you've built one, tested it, and perhaps discarded it for a larger or smaller box, which itself will be just another trial-and-error effort; and they make everything sound much like a closed-back cab, so a classic Fender combo sound is difficult to achieve.

They do, on the other hand, generally present high-saturation overdrive or over-the-top grungy amp filth pretty well, and usually work fine for hot rock leads or chunky, bottomy, rock power-chord rhythm parts. Another benefit of the iso cab is that, as well as keeping all the noise inside, they keep unwanted external noises out. In other words, while not bothering the neighbors, you can also record without them bothering you—same goes for street noise, screaming children, ringing telephones, and so forth.

Commercial examples often claim to get around the drawbacks of the DIY iso cab through some clever engineering, and some seem to offer excellent results. The AxeTrak is a compact version that comes all rigged up and ready to go. A more complex offering, Rivera's SilentSister has a clever "air labyrinth" built into the box, with separate chambers to let the mics and speaker "breathe', to the end of producing a much more natural sound from the cab. Demeter has offered an isolation box for many years, the SSC-1 Silent Speaker Chamber, as has Randall in the form of its simply-named Isolation Cab. Players have made their own throughout the years by using either temporary solutions like locking a cab in a closet full of blankets, pillows and other padding, or in a large flight case, or by building their own, along the most obvious lines imaginable.

You need a tough mic inside the box because you are not attenuating output level, just containing it. This volume-squelching solution doesn't allow the use of sensitive recording mics, as small amps or attenuators do. You also need a very high-powered but guitar-voiced 8″ or 10″ speaker (not something much in demand design-wise, although a few of the latter exist), unless you can build a box big enough to hold a 12″ and its internal baffle (more of which in Chapter Eight). The bigger the speaker, the more air space you need around it for a semi-natural sound. As simple as the concept seems, it's a tough item to get sounding perfect—but maybe perfect isn't absolutely necessary. A rough-shod DIY job is usually good enough for rock'n'roll, and will soon have you laying down some wailing, cranked tube amp sounds on your formerly anemic tracks.

Build a wooden crate large enough to house your proposed speaker with some air space on all sides, line with foam, embed a "floating baffle" (see Chapter Eight for more on how speaker cabs are put together) into the foam in one corner, lodge a sturdy dynamic microphone in the other (either just wedge it there or mount a short boom stand with some vibration-dampening material), close the lid, and wail away. I'm not walking you through this project in greater detail because the means of achieving the end are as diverse as you can imagine, and by the time you put extreme effort into designing and building the "perfect" isolation cabinet, you might as well have devoted your time to something more profitable, if you ask me. Slap together a box out of some thick plywood, chipboard or MDF, line it well, cut some notches for speaker wire in and mic cable out, and get to it. Usually you need to do a lot of lid on/lid off procedures to experiment with both speaker and mic placement before you get it right, and achieving a semi-natural sound almost always requires some EQ at the board.

The freedom of full-power playing and recording that these things offer can be a real kick, though, so this is usually effort well spent. In addition to being miked and tracked for recording, iso boxes have some other useful applications. Since identically-rated speakers in a parallel setup divide an amp's power output in half between them, you can use the box as a load for all sorts of applications: if you want to drop the wattage reaching a particular speaker cab by half—for either recording or live use—parallel it with an isolation cabinet carrying a speaker with the same impedance rating. Mike up the "open" cab, which can now be cranked a little higher, and you'll find you've taken a little of the excessive volume off the overall level. A little creative thinking reveals some other great uses for them.

In addition to bringing big-amp volume down to small-gig and studio levels, all of these avenues to quieter cranked sounds have another major benefit to them: your hearing is precious, and the less aggressively you assault it, the longer you'll have it. Plenty of great volume-reducing solutions exist, many of which retain all or at least an appreciable portion of an amp's original voice and distortion characteristics, and as such these products and techniques render sheer volume a purely quantitative phenomenon. When the quality of your tone is preserved—but at lower volume levels—you will very likely be a happier player in the long run, and hopefully one who can hear the playback too.

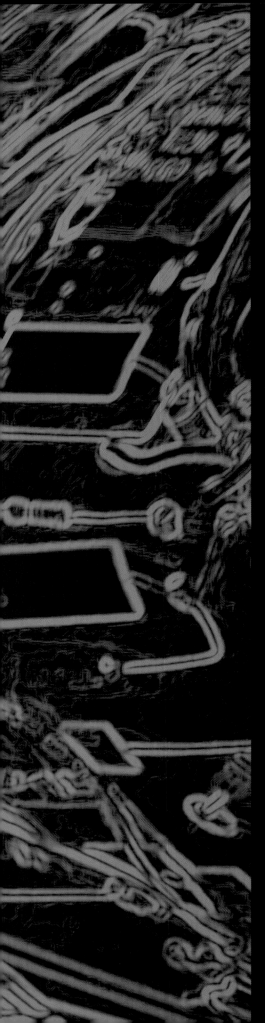

# CHAPTER 7

# Setup & Basic Maintenance

Just as a well-maintained car engine will run its best, a properly serviced tube amp will deliver its best potential tone and provide the best chance of trouble-free service. It certainly helps to know how everything works inside your amp, and how to spot problems, but also to know when it's time to call in the experts.

A full course on performing your own tube amp maintenance would require a book in itself, and there are some good ones out there already (see the bibliography/reference list at the back of the book). Within the context of this book, I would primarily like to outline the major maintenance issues that guitarists should be aware of, along with offering some basic setup and non-invasive "tune up" tips.

Even if your major periodic maintenance and repairs are going to be performed by a professional tech, it's useful to understand as much as you can of the basics of these operations. In this way, you can make informed decisions when a repairman suggests one surgical route or another, and you can also understand a good deal of what they say when explaining exactly what needs to be done, or offer options that require an informed decision from you, the amp's owner.

Let's look first at a range of issues that can be handled by any amp owner, along with some easy tips for maximizing your tube amp. Then we'll move on to outline what goes on in some of the more invasive professional repair jobs.

## TUBES

Plenty of players don't know the difference between a preamp tube and an output tube, but there's no shame in that. Here's the place to learn. Indeed, if you've made it this far in the book (paying even a little attention along the way), you've probably worked it out already.

If you have jumped ahead to this point and you're still not sure yet, here's the easy answer. In 99.99 per cent of amps made after the mid 50s, the preamp tubes will be the small tubes with nine pins emerging straight from the glass. They might be covered with silver metal shields, or "cans," which can be removed by hand, simply by twisting and pulling, or sometimes just wiggling and pulling. The output tubes will be bigger than these; in most cases where there's a tube rectifier, that will be bigger too (the main exception being smaller, older amps that carry a 6X4, which can be confused with some preamp tubes because of its small size). Three of the four main types of output tubes will have eight pins coming from a base that's wider than that of the nine-pin tubes, while EL84s will fit the same nine-pin sockets as used in the preamp, but will be nearly an inch taller than the typical 12AX7, the commonest type of preamp tube. An EZ80 or EZ81 rectifier tube, by the way, as seen in many smaller early Marshall and Vox amps, can also be confused with the similarly sized EL84.

There they are, in a nutshell. Now we can proceed to some slightly deeper identification and details.

I have seen countless old amps, and plenty of fairly recent ones, put up for sale with old, tired tubes that barely function and certainly don't bring out the best in the amp. This doesn't occur in your better guitar stores, where they will check over anything they're selling to ensure it at least performs its best, within reason. You find the rough jobs in pawn shops, less "hands-on" guitar emporiums, and classified ads. In many cases, there's a good chance the previous owner tired of the thing because it "just wasn't sounding as good as it used to," and rather than learning how to remedy the situation, it's been dumped. Tube replacement is something any player can undertake, with the caveat that some instances of output tube replacement will also require rebiasing, which needs to be performed by a professional tech if you don't already have such experience yourself. There really is no excuse for—and no economic sense in—dumping and replacing an amp that's getting tired, dull, and weak without first trying some fresh tubes in critical positions to see if the old baby livens up and starts to excite you again. You know, you're going to have to replace the tubes in that new amp eventually, too, unless you just keep selling them on and buying new amps just to get the new tubes that are in them. Which, of course, is insane; but it happens more than you'd like to know.

You can almost always change preamp tubes yourself, and, after tired output tubes, this is probably the second most common cause of an amp seeming to have grown lifeless or dull over time. Study the tube types in this book's Appendix, find out what tube types you've got in your amp (it will usually be printed on the tube itself, if not on a tube chart glued inside the amp's cabinet, or in the owner's manual), and keep a range of new and NOS (new old stock) makes on hand in the event of a failure. New old stock tubes, by the way, are tubes that were manufactured years ago—generally in the "golden age" of tube manufacture in the USA and Western Europe, where tubes are no longer made—but have sat on the shelves since that time, without having been used in an amp. They are old tubes but are not "used" in the truest sense. If they were manufactured without flaw in the first place they should be virtually as good as when new, even if they are 40 years old. Many players value NOS tubes because they represent a degree of manufacturing quality that is difficult to obtain in new tubes, although they can also be a lot more expensive than new stocks, and should be tested by the supplier to ensure they're not seconds or rejects.

Even if all is functioning well within the amp, try some preamp tube swapping just for the fun of it. Play a little with the tubes that are currently in there, power down and let them cool for a few minutes, then pop in a new tube, one at a time, and listen to the difference. It'll sometimes really surprise you, and as long as you are using the same tube type (ie, model) as that specified for the amp, or a type specified as a direct substitute, this swapping is perfectly safe for the amplifier. Note that this tube-tasting applies a little less to some modern, high-gain amps. In many of these, lower-gain modern tubes fit the bill just fine, because the amps have been designed around such tubes. Sometimes fitting an NOS tube—which might be sweet, rich and transparent, but perhaps also have much higher gain, as was the case with many great tubes of the past—can send the noise floor skyrocketing, and introduce squeals, oscillation, and other types of instability.

In addition to sampling different preamp tubes for their sonic variables, always carry one or two spare 12AX7s that you know are functioning in your guitar case's accessories pocket. Keep them boxed and wrapped in a little foam rubber or bubblewrap, and you'll be glad they're there when something in your amp's preamp goes "pop" during a soundcheck for that big gig.

To remove a preamp tube, first take off any shielding can that's present, as described already, then hold the tube firmly by its glass end and rotate slightly while pulling gently but steadily, and it should pop out in a matter of seconds (note that the tubes aren't actually screwed in place—the "rotating" motion is simply in order to ease the pins gently from the socket contacts). If it pops out too quickly, you should make a note to have your local tech re-tension (tighten) the tube sockets. To put in the new tube, you might want to lay the amp down on its face—or even, if it's the type carrying bottom-mounted tubes, balance it carefully on its top—so you can see the proper alignment of the tube pins within the socket. A tube's pins obviously have to go into the correct holes; fortunately, nine-pin tubes are made with a gap between pins number 1 and 9, so correct alignment isn't too difficult. Sometimes pins become a little bent, though, and forcing them blindly into what you think is the correct position will only worsen this, or snap a pin off entirely. Each pin on a nine-pin preamp tube goes to an essential connection within the glass bottle, so it will not work at all if you break a pin, and often the action of snapping off a pin cracks the glass and destroys the tube's vacuum anyway.

The procedure for removing output tubes is much the same, although you might need to let the amp cool down a few minutes more, as these bigger bottles are usually a lot hotter. Pull aside any spring-loaded retaining clip, or hold a Fender-style 6L6 clip aside with two fingers of one hand, while gripping the tube by its glass end and doing the wiggle/rotate thing as before. It'll pop out eventually, and again, if it does so without at least a little bit of a struggle, have those socket pins re-tensioned by a pro.

Aside from the very valid caution about burning your fingers on hot tubes, handling them too quickly after power-down—with, say, an oven glove or something—can be damaging to the tubes themselves. The elements within them are far more fragile when hot, and remain prone to damage or failure until they have cooled sufficiently. This is another reason why you should avoid jarring or moving your amp, without due care, when it's up and running.

Unless you are replacing a set of output tubes with a like-rated matched set—such as those provided by the Groove Tubes rating scale—you will have to rebias your amp when doing so.

If you plan on keeping the amp a while and would like to avoid rebiasing every couple of years when tube-changing time comes, try this useful bit of advanced planning: when buying tubes for a two-tube amp from a supplier of matched, tested tubes, purchase a quartet of matched output tubes rather than just the duet that you need. Pop in two of the four, have the tech set your bias, and away you go. When the amp starts to lose its luster 1,000 gigs down the road, just pop in the second pair from the matched quartet. If you are ordering tubes from the tester/supplier rather than choosing from duets and quartets in stock in a store, you can usually even request a matched sextet. The only downside is that you will be committing yourself to using the same tubes for the next few years, and if you're not excited by the tone after you pop in the first pair, you either have to stick with it, or bench an expensive quartet or sextet of output tubes. But if you are pretty sure you know what tubes you like already, this is a great way to save future rebiasing charges. Be aware, though, that after a lot of playing an amp's bias can sometimes drift from where it's been set, so routine maintenance might require a little bias adjustment even before your latest matching duet wears out.

Tube changing itself very rarely involves exposing yourself to harmful voltages within the amplifier. One exception to this is with the classic format of the Vox AC30, where you have to slide out the chassis to access both preamp and output tubes, and the same dangerous exposure to high voltages would arise with any amp that requires removing the chassis from the cabinet to change tubes (some amps, many old Marshalls for example, and plenty of newer models, have a screen or grille that must be removed to access the tubes, but this is just for "burn and bump" protection of fingers and tubes respectively. Removing these grilles rarely exposes you to the high voltage contacts within the amps.) The tube sockets on most amps are mounted for easy external access with the specific intention of making them user-serviceable, so in most cases tube-swapping is not a job that will expose you to any danger of electrical shock.

But still make sure you've read the Warning printed at the start of the book: the crucial point is that players without experience of working around high-voltage connections should not remove an amp's chassis from its protective cabinet. Inside the chassis there are many points within the circuit and power supply chain that will produce a large zap when touched by a grounded source—such as your finger. These points will be in different places in different amps, and might not even be in locations that you think will provide obvious electrocution hazards, so it's impossible to instruct you safely in identifying all of them here. And since we're all prone to occasionally slipping or dropping a tool, it's best not to even open up the chassis (that is remove it from the cabinet) unless you're already experienced in doing so. Filter capacitors can hold high-voltage charges a long time after an amp has last been switched off and unplugged (that's part of their job), so this danger exists even when an amp's power cord has been pulled from the electrical socket.

If you want to do a lot of taste-testing of output tubes—which, as mentioned, might require rebiasing each time—but don't have the technical experience to safely open up a chassis, there are a few products on the market today that allow the player to read and adjust bias without any exposure to the potentially lethal voltages inside the amp. Units such as the Bias Rite, Bias Probe and Bias King include a meter attached to a tube-socket-like probe. The probe plugs into any octal (eight-pin) output tube socket (replacing nine-pine tubes generally doesn't require any rebiasing), and in turn carries a socket into which you plug the tube to be measured. Of course amps that don't have through-chassis access to the bias adjustment pot, which is usually through a hole on the chassis" underside on most Fenders, will still have to be opened up to be adjusted. Many amps—including cathode-biased models (often those carrying EL84s), many tweed Fenders and repros of such, and others—don't carry any facility for bias, so you just pop in a new set of output tubes and go. Be aware, though, that in some circumstances a lot of these amps might still benefit from having a tech take a bias reading internally and adjust the preset bias circuit values as necessary.

The third, non-signal tube that many amps carry will be the rectifier tube. Plenty of amps since the early 1960s have used solid-state diodes instead of tubes for rectification, so your amp might not carry this tube at all. While such solid-state rectification was, and is, often referred to as "more reliable" than a tube rectifier, that's only marginally true. (Yeah, I know there aren't really "degrees of truth" … but stick with me.) Good tube rectifiers of the types manufactured back when tubes were still being made in the USA and Europe very rarely failed, and could last through many, many preamp and output tube changes, sometimes even the lifetime of the amp. If your amp's power supply seems to be functioning just fine and the rectifier tube in this position matches the type specified by the amp model (usually indicated on the tube chart) or is a direct replacement type, leave it alone. It's always worth keeping a spare of the correct type handy, though, as insurance against the day when the old one finally fails … probably in the middle of a gig.

Do bear in mind, though, that Fender tube charts from the late 1950s-60s in particular often lagged behind circuit changes inside the amp. Time and again you'll find a vintage Fender that carries a tube chart declaring one circuit, when in fact a look inside the chassis reveals that the amp contains the next upgrade, with different component values and sometimes even a different rectifier specified. A mismatch of rectifier by one type up or down—by which I mean a single step more or less powerful—will still usually allow the amp to function OK. But as a result it might be either weak and underpowered, with a distortion that's soft and too early, or too tight and cold, and running too hot along with it. In some cases, of course, the tweak provided by a different rectifier can be just what an amp needs to get it sounding the way you want it.

I have a tweed 1960 Fender Tremolux that follows the shortlived 5G9 circuit (the final variation before the Tolex amps), which specifies a 5U4GB rectifier tube. But the amp's power supply was designed for a 110VAC wall supply, and domestic power in the USA runs at around 120VAC, so the amp is a lot happier with a softer 5Y3GT rectifier tube installed. And by the way, this is another amp that carries the wrong tube chart: it says it's a 5E9-A, and in fact calls for a 5U4GB rectifier for that too, although the 5E9-A schematic specifies a 5Y3GT. Go figure.

Dropping your rectifier type down by a notch can be a good way of resolving the fact that a lot of vintage amps were designed to run on a lower AC voltage level than many regional domestic supplies are providing today. You can safely drop your rectifier type by a degree or two to provide lower DC levels to the tubes (but be aware that a fixed-bias amp with adjustable bias will need to have its bias level reset when you do). In many cases, though, it can be unsafe to swap up to a more powerful rectifier, because the higher voltage levels that will result might stress or even blow other components in the amp.

Dropping down by a rectifier type or two can also be a way of achieving a slightly "browner" distortion sound, without resulting in dangerous practices like using a Variac and risking blowing many crucial and expensive components within the amp. But of course the amps with which players typically want to do this—namely Marshall plexi types, in a quest to achieve that classic Edward Van Halen sound—carry solid-state rectification, so your hands are tied there, as there's no tube rectifier to swap anyway. In any case, do not use a Variac—a "variable AC" transformer—to reduce overall voltages to the amp, as done by EVH according to legend in order to achieve his famous brown Marshall sound. It's very much a "sledghammer to crack a walnut" approach to achieving that tone, and invariably results in some critical and expensive failure within the amp.

When I say that tube rectifiers can last many years, I mean good tube rectifiers. Some of the Russian, Eastern European, and Chinese factories are starting to turn out decent tube rectifiers now, but this wasn't always the case. Russian 5Y3s of the 1990s were often just rebadged 5AR4/GZ34 types that were not quite up to the power duties of, say, a Mullard GZ34 (nor anywhere near as sturdy), but were still a lot "stiffer'—that is, converted more of their given AC to DC, and did it quicker—than a quality NOS 5Y3GT. At first, that might sound like a good thing; but with rectifiers you want accuracy of specs so the tube produces the amount of DC you are looking for from its type, not an over-enthusiastic performance that gives you more voltage than your circuit desires. Some of the newer rectifiers like these can lead a 5Y3-carrying amp to run too hot, and a 5AR4-carrying amp to run a little cold. Many types were also prone to premature failure. I recall many years ago popping in two Russian 5AR4s in a row in a Matchless Lightning amp only to have each one, well, pop, before a quick dig through my box of NOS tubes turned up a slightly-used US-made rectifier that's still in service today. New makes from a reputable supplier might be tested, or should at least carry a warrantee of 60 or 90 days—which will usually reveal any tendencies toward premature failure—but many good NOS rectifiers are still available, 5Y3 types in particular, and a small investment now might last you as long as you own the amp.

I'm not a big fan of using plug-in solid-state rectifier replacements in place of the tube rectifier that an amp was designed for. In some cases, with a tech's supervision (or your own careful eye on the power supply and amp circuit's performance, if you have the experience), the higher DC voltages that these supply might help an amp perform in a different desired manner. But there are relatively few circumstances where you are going to want such a change. One exception is with the Copper Cap rectifier replacements from WeberVST. These are made with a resistance network that duplicates a tube rectifier's voltage drop and sag characteristics, so they can often make a reliable like-for-like replacement for an original tube rectifier, especially if you can't find a reliable tube, and the cheaper ones you're using keep failing on you. Weber makes Copper Caps to replicate the voltage levels, sag, and warm-up characteristics of a wide range of popular tube rectifiers, and they are certainly worth checking out. Otherwise, if you're looking for a tighter sound, more headroom, and higher operating voltages overall, you might want to shop around for a different amp.

## TUBE TOPOLOGIES

While your amp might contain anything from two to six or even seven preamp tubes, they will all be performing slightly different functions. Let's look at the most common positioning for these on a few popular amps (along with their partners in the output and rectifier stages), with a view toward knowing which will have the greatest effect sonically, and which are largely functional rather than tone-shaping. Note that the first amp examination, of the 1960s/70s blackface and silverface Fender reverb type, will carry a little more information than those that follow it, because many of the details of preamp tube recommendations and so forth apply to a broad range of makes and models, and would only become repetitive. So even if you don't own such an amp, the information in this first example might be of use to you.

The blackface and silverface Fender "reverb & tremolo" amps that the company manufactured from 1963 to 1982, and has reissued again recently in a number of models, remain extremely popular amps. They are the benchmark for this breed of traditional, non-high-gain amp with onboard effects, and a lot of other makers follow their circuit and tube layouts closely, or at least partially.

Any of the models in this series that carries the word "Reverb" in its name—including the Deluxe Reverb, Twin Reverb, Super Reverb and so forth (with the exception of the Princeton Reverb)—

**Fender Super Reverb Reissue.**

will also carry six nine-pin preamp tubes, or rather five preamp tubes and a PI (phase inverter) tube.

As you view the amp from the back, the first two 12AX7s from the right perform similar jobs. In fact these are usually labeled for 7025 tubes in such amps, but this high-quality variant of the 12AX7 is difficult to find today, and many new makes of tubes that are labeled as such are really just 12AX7s anyway. A 12AX7 (or European ECC83) is a direct replacement here, and that's what you'll probably end up with. Each of these tubes provides the first two gain stages for its respective channel: tube 1 belongs with the "Normal" channel, and tube 2 belongs with the "Vibrato" channel (the reverb & tremolo channel). As the effects are all on the second channel (tube 2), which also has a little more gain because of an extra triode gain stage after the reverb circuitry that channel 1 lacks, most players use this channel and ignore the Normal channel. (It's not a "high-gain channel" in the modern sense, but there's a very slightly hotter signal happening there.)

If you own such an amp yourself, this points you toward a few interesting possibilities. You can simply pull tube 1, which not only adds a little more gain to tube 2 but prevents you burning up a good tube that you're not using anyway; or, if your amp is of the less collectable silverface types, you can have a tech put a useful mod into the Normal channel (or do it yourself, if you have that experience). A few popular options for this include changing it to higher gain via a "tweed Deluxe" or "Marshall" style mode, giving its tone stack a Marshall-esque voicing (all described by Brinsley Schwartz in the Deluxe Revised Edition of Aspen Pittman's *Tube Amp Book*, and elsewhere by other authors). You can also make it into a switchable cascading-gain stage feeding into channel 2, but that's not a favorite of mine—if you want that kind of thing, buy an amp that already does it better. There are plenty of channel-switching amps that cost less than a good used silverface Fenders.

It's also very simple to modify the amp so that the effects run on both channels, which is worth doing if you are putting a different sound or higher gain into channel 1, so you can use an A/B footswitch to jump between them. Once this channel has been modded to run through the reverb and tremolo, it's also going through the third gain stage that channel 2 uses, which means these two channels are no longer out-of-phase with each other. You can now use a short jumper cable between channel 1's input 2 and channel 2's input 1, and blend the two voices.

If, like a lot of players, you are primarily using channel 2 on a Fender like this, socket 2 is where you put the sweetest preamp tube in your collection. A quality tested new tube or a good NOS type will make the most difference to your tone when placed here. Once again, if you don't use channel 1, remove the tube from the first socket and save it. If channel 1 has been modded for a tweed or Marshall crunch and lead sound, put another good tube there if possible (but check for one that is low microphony, too. You can easily check microphony by installing a tube, turning the amp up to a medium-low volume level, and—with the tube shield still off—tapping gently but directly on the tube using a pencil. Many will amplify just a little bit of a tapping sound through the speakers, but if it's excessive—particularly with a ringing or rattling sound along with it—you've got a microphonic tube. Some tubes will start off fine, but become microphonic after being used and exposed to vibrations within the amp, so you might find yourself performing such checks on tubes that have already lived in your amp a while. If you have a high-gain mod in that channel, an NOS tube won't be of as much benefit as it might in channel 2, because you won't make the most of its tonal subtleties, and its inherently high gain might be a little over-the-top. But a tested, low-microphony tube will be worth finding.

If you want a lower-gain sound in either of these channels—to avoid overdriving the preamp stage so you can push the output tubes for a fatter output-distortion sound, for example—you might use an NOS 12AY7 here, which tweed amps routinely carried, or a good NOS 5751. This is a trick that a lot of players have used, notably Stevie Ray Vaughan, to add some extra beef to their Fenders.

Position 3 carries the reverb driver. By definition, this would seem to be less tonally critical than the tubes providing the channels' first gain stages, because it will only impact on the proportion of the signal sent through the reverb effect. But Fender's reverb circuit from this era—while sounding great—demands a lot from the 12AT7 tube in this position, running the parallel-joined plates at upwards of 430VDC in some models. A sturdy, tested new 12AT7 will help keep your reverb running trouble-free for longer, and one with some good tonal properties will improve the sound of the reverb effect itself. NOS 12AT7s are usually a lot cheaper than good NOS 12AX7s, so this might be the place to try one out; you should still try to get a tested example to use here, though, since such high voltages might induce early failure in this position. If you don't use the reverb at all, which is probably rare if you own such an amp, you can pull this tube and save it, too.

But you can't pull tube 4. This tube devotes one triode to the signal pick-up stage following the reverb, and the other triode to the third gain stage for channel 2 (and also for channel 1, if you have joined both channels through the effects). The first half of this tube affects the quality of the reverb sound somewhat, as well as its noise level, but the second half is tonally critical to the entirety of channel 2's signal, because both the wet and dry signal (meaning with and without reverb) pass through here. Typically tubes further along in the circuit are involved in lower-gain stages, and so aren't as prone to inducing noise. Tubes that prove noisy in the first two positions when you rap the cab with your knuckles will sometimes work just fine here (again, you can isolate the microphonic tube by tapping each individually with a pencil as described above). If a tube is both noisy and not a very nice-sounding example to begin with, just ditch it (or save it for emergency repairs), but if it's a sweet NOS tube that you hate to throw away because of a little microphony, this might be one place to put it to use. Otherwise, just source a good-quality, tested new make; you don't need to pay for a high-gain tube in this position. Fender blackface and silverface schematic diagrams will list this as another 7025, but you will probably substitute it with a 12AX7.

Another 12AX7 stands in position 5 (this time its labeled that way by Fender, too), and this one powers the tremolo circuit. This tube's job is purely functional, not tonal in any sense. It drives the tremolo circuit and makes that light-dependent resistor oscillate (pulse). No signal passes through it, so you can save some money on your tube choice here, as long as the thing functions reliably. Again, if you never use the amp's tremolo, remove the 12AX7 here and save it for a rainy day. You'll have noticed by this point that if you only use channel 2 (the better sounding, higher gain channel in these Fenders) but with no reverb or tremolo, you can pull a total of three preamp tubes. Most players buy such amps partly for their great vintage effects, though, so you probably won't want to be so stingy about the tubes just for the sake of it.

This sixth "preamp" tube is in fact the phase inverter, which in the blackface and silverface Fenders is another 12AT7. The signal does of course pass through here on route to the output tubes, but it is a less tonally-critical tube than those providing the first two and the third gain stages. It's definitely worth seeking out a tube that is functionally of a high quality, though, and of all the possible locations, I'd place a tested tube here. If you can source a tube with good balance between both triodes, that's a good thing too, because you want each of the 6V6 or 6L6 output tubes (or pairs of) to receive as close to the same signal level as possible. This usually isn't easy to determine, however, and at the moment Groove Tubes is the only company I know of that offers tested, balanced PI tubes—at a pretty hefty price, at that—but it might be worth it to some players. You can also safely substitute a higher-gain 12AX7 here if you want to push the output section a little harder, to induce a little more break-up.

It's often said that you should replace the PI tube whenever you replace output tubes, but good preamp tubes will usually last a lot longer than any kind of output tube, so I really don't see a lot of logic in that. I suppose it would be one way of insuring you've got a fresh PI, rather than trying to track down a faulty one, by trial and error, when your amp starts sounding dull and toneless (or stops functioning entirely). But ditching the PI every time you change output tubes could also lead to throwing out a lot of good tubes for no reason, and good tubes are getting expensive. Also, these Fenders subject the PIs to lower voltages than they do the 12AT7 in the reverb position, for example, so a good one should hold out for many years, everything else being equal.

The next two tubes along in these amps are the output tubes (or next four tubes, in the case of a Twin Reverb or Showman Reverb). In Deluxe Reverbs or Princeton Reverbs, these will be 6V6s, and in the larger Fenders they will be 6L6s. There are plenty of options for sonic adjustments here, by selecting tubes with characteristics you hope to emphasize in the amp, but these are covered in more depth in the Appendix on tube types, as well as in the promotional literature of retail tube distributors. (And remember the tips earlier in this chapter on buying multiples of matched output tubes and saving rebiasing costs.)

If your amp carries a third but slightly different-looking large octal tube, this will be the tube rectifier. In Fender amps from this era it's always located on the far-left as you view the amp from the back. A number of Fender amp models use silicone diodes for rectification rather than a tube, and you won't see these at all; they are inside on a small circuit board located near the power transformer. As mentioned already in this chapter, odds are that a rectifier tube that is currently functioning will keep functioning for years to come. But if you're buying a used amp, it might be worth checking that the previous owner installed the correct type of rectifier tube, and consulting an experienced tech if the amp seems to be underperforming because of a suspected mismatch in this department.

The tube layout on this Marshall JMP50 follows the same topology as the larger tweed Fender amps, but it appears reversed because these are "top-mounted" tubes rather than "hanging" tubes, as on the Fenders. The same applies to a JTM45 or any similarly formatted vintage-style Marshall head. If you want to apply this layout to a late 1950s Fender Bassman, Twin, Super, Bandmaster, or similar, just turn the Marshall upside down. This applies to both vintage originals and reissues of Marshalls and, in reverse, Fenders.

Starting from the far left, the first ECC83 (a European equivalent of the US-made 12AX7 or 7025) provides the first gain stages for each of the two channels, with one triode of this dual-triode tube devoted to each channel. This is the most critical preamp tube in the amp in terms of tone, so this is the place to install the sweetest tube you've got. These amps were issued with great British-made Mullard ECC83s, and few tubes sound as good as these in an old Marshall. They are hard to come by, but if you can lay your hands on one—even a used but functional example—it's worth

**Marshall JMP50.**

putting to use here. Avoid any microphonic tubes in this position, though, as it has the highest input-to-output gain of any stages in the preamp, and any noise here will be amplified to unacceptable levels. As good as they are, some old, used Mullards (or other old tubes that have seen a lot of service) will have become noisy over the years, and you will probably need to save them for other duties, if not scrap them altogether.

Tube 2 is another ECC83, which works as the second gain stage for both channels, preceding the cathode-follower tone stack of these Marshalls (and tweed Fenders). This is another tonally critical position, although not so critical as position 1. A good new, tested tube will provide decent service here, or else use the second-sweetest NOS tube in your collection. Microphony is a little less of an issue here than in position 1, but a noisy tube will still make itself heard.

These amps contain just three preamp tubes, so our third little bottle takes PI duties. Even after Fender switched to lower-gain 12AT7s (ECC81s) in the 1960s, Marshall was still using its 12AX7 equivalent, the ECC83, in the PI of this design derived from a late 1950s Bassman. This drives the output stage a little harder, and is part of that heavy crunch for which these amps have become known. You can use an ECC81/12AT7 here if you want to tame your Marshall a little, but most players will want to stick with a quality "83/AX" type tube. Although the signal passes through this stage, functional stability and side-to-side balance are more critical here than top-notch tonal considerations. Unless you have a crate-load of great NOS tubes at your disposal, use a good, tested newer type here for reliability and save your really sweet-sounding Mullard, Brimar, RCA, GE, Telefunken, or whatever for other applications.

The next two big bottles along (or four, in 100-watt amps) are the output tubes; these will be EL34s in vintage Marshalls, or sometimes 6550s in US-distributed amps of the late 1970s and early 1980s. Early JTM45s following the same layout will carry either KT66s or 5881s, a US-made 6L6 equivalent. You will usually need to bias these. Many early Marshalls originally had no bias adjustment pot, although many have had one added over the years to maximize their performance. If yours has no adjustment facility, just pop in a good new pair of tubes and you're away. Everything after the JTM45 has solid-state rectification, so there's no tube rectifier to consider here.

Many smaller modern amps, like this Fender Blues Junior, generally have a single channel, but can be pushed to crunch and overdrive levels because of their combination of a master volume and a series of tube gain stages. The tube layout here follows the order of other three-tube Fenders of old, but their functions differ somewhat.

The first tube is the first gain stage, followed by volume control, then gain makeup stage from the second triode of that 12AX7. Tube 2 uses its second triode only, as a gain makeup stage following the tone stack and before the master volume. Its other triode is unused. The third 12AX7 is the PI. The reverb is driven by a solid-state circuit, and rectification is solid state, so the two EL84 output tubes are all that's left here.

Pity the person who has to pay the bills when it comes time to replace some tubes in a crate full of glassware like this one (right, bottom). The 150-watt Mesa Triple Rectifier Solo Head has so many big bottles in the back that it has to squeeze the smaller preamp tubes into a second row down the middle of the chassis. Let's look at the latter first, since that's the pattern we've followed so far.

Ideally you need to remove the output tubes to get at the preamp tubes, which are all 12AX7s, so let's proceed as if we have done so (in this photo, you can just see the silver can shields of these 12AX7s hiding behind the third-through-sixth 6L6s from the right, between the transformers). This Mesa's signal flow appears reversed from that of a Fender, because the chassis is mounted tubes-up (same as the classic Marshall head). Viewing from the back, the first tube on the left provides one triode as a first gain stage for all channels, and another as a second gain stage for the clean channel. Half of the second tube provides a gain makeup stage for all channels, while the other half is used as a first boost stage for channels 2 and 3 (crunch and lead).

**Fender Blues Junior.**

As this is an extremely high-gain amp, it's important to use a reliable, low-noise tube in any early gain stages, especially those that will be shared by all channels. Any noise created here will be increased dramatically as the cascading-gain preamp boosts the signal further down the line, so you want a good, new, tested tube with minimal signs of microphony. This isn't the best place to use expensive NOS tubes, either. Good versions of these are usually somewhat higher-gain than standard newly manufactured 12AX7s, but this amp produces enough gain as it is with a good standard tube in place. The extra gain from a hot NOS tube will also increase the noise floor, and the trade-off isn't usually worth it. Actually, some of the same rules are going to apply to most positions in this amp's preamp: use good, reliable (ie, tested) new tubes that are as

**Mesa Triple Rectifier.**

low in noise as possible. As for tone, use your choicest example for tube 1 because all channels will benefit, and your next sweetest for tube 2.

Sonic considerations are less crucial with tube 3, which uses both triodes as further boost stages. Sure, you still want this tube to sound good, but this one's job is to crank up the grind factor, so any subtleties that would shine in position one might be lost here. Tube 4 uses each triode as the buffer for the FX send and return respectively, so functionality is more important than tone, and likewise for tube 5, which is the PI.

Most modern, high-gain, channel-switching amps follow suit as far as preamp tubes are concerned (though not necessarily with the precise positioning), which is good news for your gear budget. Expensive NOS tubes are largely overkill (and sometimes even detrimental, due to the noise considerations), so go for good, new, tested types, which should only cost you $8-$15 anyway, if you shop carefully: you're going to have to blow the budget when you replace those output tubes.

The six slimmer octal-based tubes to the right side of the amp are the 6L6 output tubes. Mesa ships amps with its own in-house tested versions of modern-manufactured output tubes, and recommends the purchase of a set from them when replacement time comes. The company goes some way toward almost necessitating this by excluding a bias-adjustment facility on these amps; to get a quick, easy replacement match without the help of a tech and a tube tester, the player needs to buy six new matched tubes from Mesa Engineering. If you are into sourcing your own supplies regardless, a tech could help you find other 6L6s that would approach the same bias requirements as the Mesa set that your amp currently carries, but doing this with four or six matched tubes (Dual or Triple Rectifier models) could require a lot of hit-and-miss testing.

High-gain amps of this type usually benefit from output tubes that lean towards the firm and tight rather than the soft and easily compressed. All the distortion and compression is coming from the preamp, in fairly precise user-determined degrees, so the output stage really just needs to amplify what it's given. In a big 150-watt stadium blaster like this, or even the 100-watt Dual Rectifier models, these tubes simply want to take what the preamp gives them and make it a lot louder. The same principles apply to most amps with high-gain preamps, those from Soldano, Peavey, Crate, Bogner, Engl, modern Marshall DSL and TSL models, and so forth. Again, go for new, tested, matched tubes, and seek out firm, bold versions of these for the best punch and definition.

Mesa's theory is that the slight feel of compression and touch-sensitivity offered by a tube rectifier can be a boon to even a high-powered rock amp such as this, so here they give you three of them to meet the demands of the power supply in this 150-watt amp. These are the three big Coke bottle-shaped octal tubes to the left of the amp. For a firmer, faster, tighter sound, there's a switch to bring in solid-state rectification. Players on a tight budget might be tempted to duct-tape that switch into the SS position if it ever comes time to replace these tube rectifiers, but they certainly offer another sonic alternative, and they should last a long while. Most amps in the Triple Rectifier's league will just carry solid-state rectification, which is the norm for the fat, firm lows and fast response required of the big rawk sound.

## TIPS FOR HAPPY TUBES

I've already discussed the importance of letting tubes cool down before handling them, both for their sake and the sake of your fingers. It's equally important to let them warm up adequately before putting them into service. The filaments, or heaters, within the tubes take anywhere up to 30 seconds to warm up enough to let the tubes do their job safely and efficiently. Once that full operating temperature has been reached, the boiling of electrons off the cathode that constitutes the tube's amplification process can go on with minimal stress on its components. But if this flow of electrons is demanded by the arrival of a high-voltage DC current before the low-voltage AC current has heated the filament, the cathode can be damaged. This will rarely mean instant failure, but over a period of time it could seriously shorten tube life.

The reason that thoughtful manufacturers design tube amps with both power and standby switches is not merely so you can flick the latter for instant playability after warm-up, but specifically so the warm-up can happen safely. The power switch sends the full AC wall-outlet power to the amp's power transformer, but the standby switch, when off, blocks the high-voltage DC current supplied by the rectifier—tube or solid state—from getting to the tubes until they are ready. With both switches in the off position, you plug in your amp, flick on the power switch, and give the tubes a good 60 seconds to heat up. Most can reach their safe operating temperature a little quicker than this, but a little extra never hurts. When you flick the standby, the DC current surges instantly to the hot-and-waiting tubes, and away you go.

Many types of tube rectifiers provide a natural warm-up to the preamp and output tubes, because they themselves deliver their DC supply only gradually as their own filaments warm up. This is why many amps with tube rectifiers—Vox AC15s and AC30s, tweed Fender Deluxes, Champs and so forth—don't carry standby switches. They aren't necessary, from the perspective of keeping the tubes' cathodes happy. But many others that carry tube rectifiers do also carry standby switches. I guess a little extra warm-up never hurts, but a standby is also useful for bringing an amp from silent to roar-ready at the start of a gig, or for sending it back to snoozing during a set break without having to go through the entire cool-down/warm-up thing again. Also, some tube rectifiers reach maximum performance more quickly than others, so it's still a good idea to give your tube-rectified, standby-equipped amp 60 seconds or more before you bring it fully to life.

I've already talked about the increased potential for damaging a tube's internal elements when they are still hot. But even when cool, these components can be harmed by excessive physical shocks. Don't lie awake nights worrying about this kind of thing—tubes are often a lot sturdier than we might expect, and decent ones can stand up to a lot. At least they aren't the fragile, sugar-glass dainties that early promotions for solid-state amps would often have us believe. But do what you can to minimize bumps and jolts and a rough ride in general.

Whenever possible, avoid using castors on a tube amp, and don't add them to a combo that doesn't have them already. Those little wheels might seem like a great way of getting your 80lb Fender Twin Reverb across the 200-foot gym floor to the sock-hop stage (pardner), and they probably are; but roll it on out the back door, down the pot-holed alley, and through the gravel parking lot, and you could be taking months off the life expectancy of those expensive 6L6s. Sure, big amps are heavy. If you aren't blessed with a full-time roadie, get the drummer to help you carry it in. Wheels on a combo or other tube-carrying amp are never a good idea. On a big speaker cab, hey, no problem. And a combo inside a professional-grade, padded flightcase with castors on the case shouldn't cause any grief either.

Another thing that can help keep your output tubes happy is a set of spring clamps or retainers.

Small octal tubes like 6V6s usually don't need these, but bigger 6L6s, EL34s, 6550s and others that are mounted hanging under the chassis rather than pointing up above it can sometimes work themselves loose through the sheer force of gravity, and ultimately plummet to their deaths in the bottom of the cabinet. This is also sometimes a sign of loose tube socket contacts, which is something else I'll address later in this chapter, but a useful remedy in any case is a set of tube retainers. These come in two main types: a design with two long springs and a little "hat" that is pulled tight over the tip of the tube, or the traditional Fender clamp that looks like a miniature bear trap and holds the tube in place by gripping its plastic base with a row of teeth cut into each of two arched steel springs. The former is a little more foolproof, but either usually works pretty well. With some amps, especially those with externally mounted tube sockets held in place by self-tapping screws rather than bolts, any user can install these. If you need to get at the nut of a bolt that runs into the chassis, or work inside the chassis for any reason, you will want the help of a pro, unless you are fully experienced with draining filter caps and working around high voltages.

Another useful type of spring clip is available for EL84s too. These hook onto eyelets mounted at the sides of the tube socket's retaining clip, so they are installed much like the larger types described above. As well as keeping the tubes from dropping out of the amp, tube retainers can help maintain the electrical connection between the tube's pins and the socket contacts—but if these are particularly loose they should still be tightened by a pro.

Another thing that helps to keep tubes happy is keeping them cool. This applies to the big bottles again, which get especially hot during extended use. Simply ensuring adequate ventilation is one way to start. Never close off any rear or underside access to the tubes, because these will be points for cooler air to flow in and warm air to escape. If you back an amp right up against a wall or a padded surface or something—to achieve a particular sound while recording, for example—or enclose it in a crate or a small closet with a mike to create a makeshift isolation booth, you will seriously impede that crucial air flow, and risk blowing an output tube.

Amps that run hot, or perhaps aren't designed with good natural ventilation, or especially those with four or six output tubes, might even benefit from the installation of a small fan to help keep the air flowing. A properly installed fan can dramatically improve tube life, and should theoretically help keep the amp running and sounding better during normal daily use, because it will minimize the heat stress on tubes and other components. A good tech should be able to install such a fan in almost any amp, and it is usually a simple, reversible mod that can be removed when it comes time to sell that precious vintage model. A range of small box fans designed to run inside computer enclosures are suited to the job, and many can be run at lower-than-spec voltages too, which will make them go a little slower and quieter. If extreme quiet is required for some recording situations, a switch can be installed to disable the fan as desired.

## SPEAKER SENSE

Careful and correct handling of speakers is also worth some consideration. A speaker swap is something any player can do themselves, provided the amp is switched off and has been given a few seconds to cool down (and to let the filter caps drain via the OT and through the speaker, if applicable). Removing a speaker is pretty straightforward. The ins and outs of why you'd want to do this—even if a current speaker isn't blown—are covered in Chapter Eight, along with a lot of discussion of speaker types. But undertaking the work is very simple. First, disconnect the leads from the + and − terminals. If these are slide-on clips, hold the terminal mounting in place with one hand while wiggling the wire and clip gently side-to-side with the other until it slips loose. If this isn't happening, you might need to gently widen the clip closure with a small jeweler's screwdriver; or some clips have a tap at their center that needs to be depressed to let them come free. If de-soldering is required to undo the connections, first place a piece of card or other flexible but sturdy material under the clip mounting board (between the clips and the speaker cone) to prevent blobs of hot solder from dropping onto your precious speaker cone and damaging it.

Once the clips are free, loosen the retaining bolts or nuts to free the speaker frame from the baffle. I like to do this in the same manner that you tune a drum, by gently slackening off the first bolt a turn or so, then slackening the bolt opposite that one, working on pairs of opposite bolts across the speaker until all the bolts are loose enough to remove them easily with the fingers. This helps to prevent any compression strain or warping in the speaker frame (or "basket'), which might be caused when an overly-tightened driver comes loose unevenly, perhaps with a thick gasket pressing against it as it feels more give on one side than the other. Once all the bolts are out, hold the speaker by the magnet (at the back) and wiggle it gently to see if it lifts free of its own accord. Sometimes the paper or rubberized cork gaskets that cushion the speaker frame against the wooden cabinet baffle get a little sticky over the years and hold to the baffle like glue. If the thing doesn't pull free with a gentle tug, you'll have to consider whether you want to risk tearing the baffle in getting it free—especially if this is a vintage amp or a particularly precious speaker. Sometimes a little gentle prying with a wide, thin implement helps to get it loose (no screwdrivers, please), but if that doesn't do it you might consider leaving it be, or seeking professional help, unless it really is a junk speaker or one with a blown cone that needs major repair anyway.

When lifting a speaker free from a cabinet, always handle it by the magnet—and gently even then. If you are lifting a speaker that's magnet-down on the floor, hook your fingers under the edges of the metal frame and avoid touching the paper cone at all. What starts as a little crease or dent can grow into a larger flaw or tear after the cone has felt 50 watts of power for a few hours.

Installing a new or repaired speaker is pretty much the reverse of the procedure used to remove one. Screw down the bolts or nuts until they are just finger-tight, then bed them down just another half or three-quarters of a turn—a turn-and-a-quarter at most if they feel particularly loose—with the appropriate tool, working with opposite pairs across the speaker again (a far more important technique while tightening down than while loosening). Be aware that the first bolt tightened might feel just a little loose again by the time you've tightened the last, due to the slight compression of the gasket, so this might require a further quarter of a turn.

Reconnect the leads running to the amp chassis or the cab's speaker jack, being careful to observe the polarity, and you're done. If it's a new or reconed speaker, go through the warm-up and break-in procedures described in Chapter Eight. Any periodic user-maintenance of an amp should include checking and gently tightening loose speaker-mounting bolts, so give these a feel pretty frequently to see if they need attention. It's better to have to keep retightening them periodically than it is to force them down so tightly that they'll never budge, which in the process might warp the speaker frame. Even if this doesn't cause a speaker to fail, it'll impede your tone by twisting the speaker cone out of alignment as it vibrates; not a sonically desirable thing.

If you have an amp that arrived without a speaker connection, or you need a new one to go from head to cab, it's crucial that you always use the correct type of wire for connecting speakers to amps. This will be something similar to the high-quality, heavier-duty wire used for speaker connections in good hi-fi systems—something like Monster Cable will do just fine. Never—honestly, never—use a guitar cord to connect a speaker cab. It will "work" in the broad sense, sure, and at first it might even sound just about OK—especially if you've never heard your setup the correct way. But the added impedance of the guitar cord's shield, in particular, will put an enormous strain on the amp's OT, and in turn its tubes. The whole output stage will work too hard, and something will very likely blow in time. And believe me, the amp will sound a lot worse than with a proper speaker cable. It might take some listening, but the wrong type of wire—and that added impedance in particular— will restrict the amp's volume and frequency range, and just choke it off a little in general. Don't do it, and carry a spare speaker cable if you're a head-and-cab user so you don't put yourself in an "emergency situation" where you use a guitar cord in a pinch because you've shown up at the big gig and can't find the speaker wire in your bag.

If that does happen, and you haven't had the foresight to include a spare, here's what you do: cut a piece of two-core lamp wire, long enough to do the job; remove the quarter-inch jack plugs from each end of the spare guitar cord you would have been tempted to use, and attach them to the electrical wire, making sure you maintain the polarity relationship at each end so that one side of the two-core lamp wire goes to the tip connection of each plug, and one goes to the sleeve. Instant speaker cable. And although it has arrived from a non-musical source, an 18-gauge lamp wire will make a much better-sounding (and safer) connection than that guitar cord would have. Of course this might mean getting your hands on a soldering iron—unless you're good at improvising (twisting short-cut leads together, taping them up maybe)—which is why you should also carry a soldering iron in your gig bag. But if you're the kind of person who remembers the soldering iron, you probably won't forget the speaker cable. Still, the electrical wire improv is a good solution—you can always make up your own speaker cables from decent-quality general-use electrical wire.

## USER CHECKS

Having mentioned tightening your speaker bolts as a matter of routine maintenance, there are plenty of other things you can tighten while you're at it. In short, anything that's screwed or bolted down should be checked occasionally. This includes: all chassis-mounted transformers, such as the power and output transformer, choke, and reverb transformer; tube sockets; speaker baffle; rear cabinet panels; chassis mounting bolts; nuts retaining jacks and switches on the front and back control panels; set screws that hold control knobs onto pot shafts; the nuts under these knobs that hold the pots firm in the control panel; and anything else I'm forgetting. Don't try to force any of these down so tightly that you'll never have to tighten them again—doing so can dent whatever surface they are mounted on or into—but just make them firm, which should render their related component rattle-free in the process. And don't forget the handle. Tighten that too. You and your amp will both be glad you did.

Some amps will emit a low-pitched electro-mechanical hum that can be difficult to trace, until you think outside the box, as it were, and discover that it's simply the loose power transformer vibrating against the chassis because of all the voltage surging through it. Tighten it down. I checked over a blackface Fender Vibrolux Reverb amp recently that was in stunning, virtually untouched condition—except that the output transformer was just hanging by a turn or two of screw thread. This $2,750 amp was about to become a $1,500 amp in a gig or two when the vibrations finally revolved those screws another couple of turns each and the original OT divebombed towards the reverb pan, taking out its tube and speaker jack connections with it. On many amps those things are held by just two self-tapping steel screws; check them frequently, and tighten as necessary, so your priceless vintage OT doesn't become an expensive paperweight.

There are plenty of places on any amp—combos especially—where you can identify and eliminate noisy buzzes and rattles with just the help of a screwdriver or socket wrench. Speaker frames can rattle against baffles, baffles can rattle against cabs, back panels can hum and buzz, even loose handles and hardware can kick out loud vibrations that sound like something a lot more serious and expensive than they really are.

Many screws and nuts that are prone to vibrating loose can be held in place with a small dab of superglue. Place a drop where it will bind the screw head to the metal mounting surface beside it. If you ever need to intentionally remove this screw or nut, a muscular twist with the right tool will quickly snap the super glue, but it should help to withstand vibrations for a good while.

You can also often track down the source of a dead channel or faulty effects stage, or an entirely dead amp, by learning a simple procedure. If the amp itself is entirely silent, first follow this sequence of seemingly obvious but often ignored checks. Confirm that the amp:

**1** is plugged in
**2** is switched on (pilot light on?), power and standby on
**3** has all speaker wires connected
**4** has a guitar connected to it. Guitar cord OK?
**5** has the volume up (and tone knobs up—some block signal)
**6** has a functioning (un-burned-out) fuse

If all of this checks out, and you've not forgotten to turn up your guitar's volume or plug in your pedalboard's power supply, you can proceed to the tubes. Although good rectifier tubes are usually reliable for many years, this can be one simple cause of an amp where the lights are on but no one's home. If the pilot light is lit but you're getting no sound from the amp, and the other checks above are all OK, try a fresh rectifier tube. In such a case the AC voltage is still entering your transformer, and being passed from the PT's heater winding to the pilot light and the tube heaters, but is not being converted by the rectifier to the high-voltage DC supply that the tubes need to make sound. A bad rectifier will often signal itself by popping fuses frequently, then eventually by popping itself in a fairly obvious manner, but some die quietly at switch-on one day when least expected. Always remember to look here if all else seems fine with the amp. Solid-state rectifiers, by the way, almost never go bad; but if and when they do, it's a job for a tech.

Rectifier working fine? It's time to move to the preamp tubes. Select a preamp tube that you know for certain is functioning, not just "a new one"—they can often be faulty right out of the box—and replace each preamp tube in the amp one at a time working from the first gain stage until you locate the bad one. Surprisingly often, amps that make no noise when plugged in and turned on will be remedied with a fresh tube in one position or another. If you run the gamut through the preamp and still no sound, pop in a functioning pair of output tubes. These usually don't die an entirely silent death simultaneously, but it needs to be checked. Also, logically, a tech would troubleshoot an output stage first, because any problem there would nullify signal from anywhere in the preamp, but it's easier to run through the preamp first, and that's a more likely source of a popped tube, too. You don't need to bias the new output pair or anything, just plug them in to see if you get any sound.

If none of this succeeds, take the amp to your local repair shop. Nine times out of ten, though, or more if you're lucky, these procedures will get to the bottom of the problem. I can't count the times I have been about to pull a chassis and begin diagnosing "major problems" simply to discover that my guitar is still plugged into the amp I'd been using to record the previous track, or something like that. Likewise, a huge proportion of older tremolo/reverb amps sold as "reverb not working" or "faulty tremolo" just need a new tube in the reverb or tremolo stage. When I was first learning to work on my own amps, the tech at my then-local London guitar shop told me my non-functioning tremolo more than likely needed a set of new signal caps. Having ripped the amp apart and put new caps and resistors in the entire tremolo circuit, I found it was just as throb-less as ever once I got it back together. Then on a whim I popped in a new 12AX7, and that got it sounding all Twin Peaks again in a jiffy. I'm not sure where that guy trained … or maybe he just wanted to teach a lesson to an upstart guitarist who thought he could repair his own amps. Again, carry a fresh preamp tube, or two, in your gigbag, plus a spare set of output tubes and a rectifier tube.

## PROFESSIONAL JOBS

There are several elements of amplifier repair, maintenance, or modification that are best left to a professional, unless of course you have experience working inside amps and, in particular, are fully aware of the safe practices necessary when working with high voltages.

### Filter caps

The highest voltages present within a tube amp are found coming off the rectifier and at the live terminals of its filter capacitors, so you definitely don't want to mess with these unless you know exactly what you are doing (which involves, in part, correct procedures for draining these caps of any residual high voltage, and keeping them drained while undertaking the work). The electrolytic capacitors that perform filtering duties are inherently short-lived compared to the majority of other components in the amp, apart from the tubes. Most quality electrolytics have a lifespan of at least ten years, and some might still be functioning reasonable well after 20 years … in which case, they are well due for replacement, just to be safe. Over time, the dialectic from which electrolytic caps are made dries out and becomes ineffective, and these caps no longer do their job. At best, this will lead to a noisier amp with flabby lows and some "ghost notes," where an odd-order harmonic seems to follow the notes you actually play. At worst, a dried-out cap will blow entirely when a voltage surge hits it, and possibly take out other components along with it.

Any amp you acquire that is 20 years old or more and still carries its original filter caps really should have these replaced. If the amp is working and sounding fine, hey, you might be tempted just to go with it for a while and keep your fingers crossed. But many amps acquired used are up for sale in the first place because a previous owner hasn't played them for a while. These 20 or 30-year-old amps might seem in decent condition because they were only ten-year-old amps when the previous user put them in the closet. Heavy service after a long rest (and the inherent drying out that this usually involves) will almost certainly lead to a blown something or other after a few gigs or rehearsals. A re-cap isn't very expensive, and quality new caps will only bring your amp back to spec and get it sounding its best, not alter its core tonality, in the technical sense (although it might sound different afterward than it did before—more like it did new, in other words—because the new caps should tighten up the sound considerably if the previous caps were extremely old and even failing). Get it done sooner rather than later, and both you and your amp will be happier for longer as a result.

The exception is with some vintage amps that have greater value to collectors than to players. If you find one of these in totally original condition, you might want to consider selling it on at a profit to someone who is building a collection more than seeking a gigging tool—or store it safely as-is to be sold on a rainy day, preferably after its value has risen further. I have replaced the large filter caps in a number of vintage amps that I've been using for my own playing over the years, and while it's always a little heartbreaking to do so, it brought these amps back to life, and put them back in the studio or on the stage where they belonged. Personally I think it's more tragic to leave a great tone machine on the shelf for fear of tampering with an "original component', which is an inherently expendable, short-lived part anyway, than it is to yank out that part, put in a functioning new one, and get that amp out where it can be played and heard. Others might disagree.

## Signal caps

These non-electrolytic capacitors that make up a large portion of what's going on in your amp's circuit can also age poorly and fail, but they don't have the inherently short lifespan of your filter caps, and might last the lifetime of an amp if you're lucky. (The lifespan of a decent amp, by the way, is usually longer than that of a player—although some parts will inevitably be changed over that period.) When these capacitors fail they become leaky, which will cause the amp, or a particular stage of the amp, to malfunction or at least perform below spec. When this happens, they need to be replaced. The same thinking applies with these as with the dried-out filter caps.

If it's a vintage amp that you intend to play, it will be heartbreaking to pull a couple of original yellow Astrons from your tweed Deluxe or mustard caps from your plexi; but if these are leaky coupling caps between a preamp and a PI, or a PI and the output tubes, you just can't leave them in there. Replace them with signal caps that are as close to original value, type and composition as you can find, put the originals in a bag to save for a future owner, and get playing that amp again. (Having the faulty original parts available in the event of a future resale of that amp can sometimes even increase its value.)

The good news is that one leaky signal cap doesn't necessarily mean they are all leaky (technically the same applies to filter caps but, as these have more limited lifespans anyway, rather than just replacing three leaky filter caps of five from the same era, you might as well yank them all while you're in there).

Leaky signal caps can be identified using a meter, which is most likely to be done by a tech who suspects a fault at that stage because of some aspect of the amp's performance. Other adequately functioning stages and non-leaky caps don't need to be replaced at the same time, however old they may be.

Some techs, maybe the ones who either aren't players or don't have much respect for the values of vintage amps, will just pull all the signal caps and replace them with new Mallory or Orange Drop supplies—or even more generic parts, if you're unlucky—because it's easier to solder in eight little caps than to diagnose and measure two or three that might be leaky. If your amp is at all old or has any vintage value, tell your tech you don't want any major component replacement such as this undertaken without first discussing it with you—they should measure and replace only if absolutely necessary, leaving any functional original components in place. Some techs might argue these signal caps are by no means "major components" and your amp will run better and be quieter if you just go ahead and replace them all. Simply reply that you really like the look of those tubular blue "Molded" caps inside your 1964 Fender Super Reverb, and you want as many left in as is humanly possible.

By the way, remember that the high voltages that are stored at the larger filter caps, even when the amp is unplugged, can pop up at many points in the circuit when touched by a tool or a finger, so this is another job for an experienced tech.

## Resistor replacement

This isn't something you specifically go looking for, but very often when a tech opens up an amp to diagnose a fault, the source will prove to be an aged or blown resistor. It's a simple job in itself, but requires diagnostic skills to pinpoint the flaw in the first place, and the ability to measure a resistor. The dropping resistors in the power supply of older amps will frequently need to be replaced. Often the originals will look scorched or heat stressed, if not blown entirely; they were big resistors in their day, but not big enough.

Don't sweat it much if the tech needs to replace a couple of crispy-looking 1-watt carbon comps between the big filter caps with some newer, higher-spec 2- or 3-watt resistors. (Something to be aware of is that although a resistor's "value" in ohms determines how much resistance to voltage it puts up in the circuit, its wattage determines how much voltage it can handle without burning out. Resistors in the majority of the amp's preamp and tone-shaping circuitry are generally just 1/2-watt types, though sometimes 1-watt, while those in the power supply are often two, four or more times that.)

On the other hand, you might discuss the possibility of further resistor replacement in advance if you are putting in a vintage amp for servicing. If a tech is checking and measuring a suspect preamp stage, and finds a few carbon comps that have drifted upward from spec value by 10 or 15 per cent, he will often just replace those as a matter of course. To the tech that's a legitimate diagnosis and a valid repair, even if it's not the main source of your amp's woes. But those resistors might have drifted their way up there years ago, and often that timeworn change in value can be a part of the warm, loose "vintage mojo" of a classic amp. You might consider specifying in advance, in congenial tones, that you'd rather not have any components replaced that have merely drifted somewhat off-spec, rather than failed entirely, at least not without discussing their positions and implications with you first.

Stopping the job to consult you might incur a higher bench charge for the repair, and that's only fair, but if you are still trying to keep an old amp roadworthy—while maintaining some vintage value and vibe at least—rather than propping it up in a museum, you might decide that's a few extra bucks worth paying.

If some of the old carbon comps really do need to be replaced, you should specify that the tech should locate other new or NOS carbon comps of a similar look to replace them, if maintaining at least a modicum of originality is important to you. As with signal caps, as discussed above, some techs will just pull all the old resistors from a troublesome stage in the amp and replace them with "quiet, reliable" ugly blue metal film resistors or something of that kind. If you've got a JMI Vox AC15 or a 1959 Gibson RTV GA-80, you probably don't want that.

## Tightening tube sockets

Yes, it's the high-voltage thing again (as is the case throughout this section). Tightening or "retensioning" tube socket contacts is a simple enough procedure, but some of these contacts will be hardwired to the big filter caps, which can mean a big zap. This job is one your local repair tech should perform any time you bring in an amp for routine maintenance or a general tidy up, but if your tubes—and power tubes in particular—are becoming unusually loose in the sockets, you can specifically request a retensioning. This isn't just a matter of tubes falling out of sockets (the spring retainers you installed yourself will have solved that); when contacts stretch open over time, the electrical connection weakens, and this can lead to noisy crackles, at least, or periodic, even terminal output failure at worst.

Your tech will insert a flathead jeweler's screwdriver alongside the outer edge of each circular pin contact in the socket, and gently close the gap slightly. A little contact cleaner dabbed on the pins of a tube that's then inserted and reinserted a couple times (to spread the cleaner across the socket contacts) can help matters too. If contacts are badly worn or bent, the tube socket will need to be replaced. Not a major job at all, but another one for a pro.

## Cleaning pots and jacks

In theory this is simple enough that any guitarist could perform it, even a drummer maybe, but any amp that requires you to access the guts of the circuit to get at the pots' lubrication holes will also need to have the filter caps drained first for safety's sake, and that's where the pro comes in—so the pro might as well do the entire job. Crackling pots will be cleaned with a quick squirt of tuner cleaner into the hole in the body, followed by a few quick rotations of the shaft to spread the love. In addition to cleaning dust and grit, the tuner cleaner leaves a lubricating trail that will help keep the pot working smoother for longer. Jacks, on the other hand, will be cleaned with contact cleaner, which excludes the lubricant because you don't want any contact-inhibiting surface left behind here.

## PT and OT replacement

These are among the "big jobs," but replacing them is relatively straightforward, so you don't need to panic. Wiring in a new output transformer only requires making about half-a-dozen solder connections, and possibly drilling a few new holes in the chassis if a replacement with the same mounting configuration can't be found. A new power transformer will require a few more connections, but not all that many. The trick in both of these jobs is in sourcing the correct replacement part, which any good tech should have the skills to do.

Most recent-era amps will have direct replacements available from the manufacturer; and well-made, precisely-spec'd replacement PTs and OTs are available for the more popular vintage amps from a range of manufacturers. A blown OT on a 1960s Fender, Marshall, or Vox can be a real heartbreaker, for sure, but it shouldn't put the amp into retirement. Suppliers like CE Distribution (Antique Electronic Supply on the retail side), Hoffman, New Sensor, Mojo, and others have good replacements for many models from these makers. High-end transformer manufacturer Mercury Magnetics has an impressively broad range of replacements made from plans drawn up after careful analysis of original vintage parts. Majestic Transformers in the UK does the same (they have a great collection of vintage Vox transformer specs). Some other transformer manufacturers will occasionally sell a one-off for a repair, if your tech can spec out the requirements precisely and have them match it with a unit they already manufacture. Shorted vintage transformers can sometimes even be rewound, which is worth looking into if you are desperate to maintain as much original material in the amp as possible.

In any case, don't panic. If you merely want a good-sounding, functional amp that's ready for action again, the job shouldn't cost you all that much. A good, US-made replacement OT for a 15 to 20-watt amp should only run you $30-$40 plus labor, a PT around $50. Figure $70-$90 for a PT for a 100-watt amp, and $60-$80 for a good OT. Prices for Mercury Magnetics' Axiom Tone Clone series can run pretty high—around $225 for a vintage-style AC30 replacement OT, for example—but the company has an excellent reputation for quality and accuracy to original specs. It's worth bearing in mind that, back in the 1960s, Fender, Marshall and Vox were rarely buying the most expensive transformers they could find—quite the opposite really. But the quality of iron used in transformers at the time was generally better than that which is supplied for routine manufacturing today, so the old transformers had a leg-up in that sense.

Repairing a vintage amp with anything other than an exact replacement OT might change its sound slightly, but if it's a good transformer with comparable size and specs, you might have to listen very closely to notice. If your valuable classic model has a weak-looking little paper-wrapped OT, that's probably what you should put back into it, even if you could "improve it" with a larger, sturdier OT for the same price. On the other hand if your amp is a good player but of little collectible value, this is an area where you might make an upgrade if the part is going to be replaced anyway. Lots of players fit heavier OTs to 35-watt 1960s Fender Pro Reverbs, Bandmasters, and Vibroluxes, for example, to give them the firmer lows of a 45-watt Super Reverb. A similar step-up to heftier iron can benefit many amps.

A new PT should affect your amp less, sonically speaking, provided your replacement transformer supplies precisely the same high-voltage level to the rectifier. The original specs of most vintage amps are pretty easy to track down these days, and your repair tech should be able to match the numbers pretty easily to keep your tubes running at the same DC levels. If an upgrade is desired, the tech can find you a PT that handles a little more current—rather than putting out higher voltages (you want those numbers the same in any case)—so it will run cooler for longer. If an amp with a newly replaced PT comes back sounding either too tight, harsh, and sterile or too soft, squashy, and easily distorted, there's a chance the new transformer is either putting out too much or too little AC respectively to the rectifier.

Even if you have a great tech close at hand, do your own research before or during any repairs, and learn what you can about the availability of replacement parts that can keep your old amp close to spec. You might need to let your repairer know that you don't mind paying a little more or waiting a little longer to get that vintage-accurate or upgraded signal cap, carbon comp resistor, or OT. Decide ahead of time whether the goal is to maintain the exact sound—and sometimes look— of your amp, or to use the opportunity of a blown part to upgrade it, and work together toward the chosen goal.

# CHAPTER 8

# Speakers & Cabs

If you wonder why they've got a whole chapter to themselves, just consider this: your guitar and amp simply can't make a sound without speakers—and the wrong ones can ruin your sublime tone.

The speakers that you feed an amp through, and the cabinet they're mounted in, play an enormous part in determining your rig's overall sound, but they've long been criminally unsung heroes in the tone story. Plenty of very good players get wrapped up in all the potential ingredients that contribute to their tone—pickups, strings, wood types, effects, preamps, tubes, power amps, and so forth—without pausing to consider where the sound eventually comes from. Simple: your speakers. Whatever components play a part in the signal chain that shapes every note you play, the humble speaker is still what takes the sound to the listener, or indeed the microphone. Even in DI recording, guitarists and manufacturers alike go out of their way to include realistic-sounding "speaker emulators" in the process or product; we're used to the sound of an amp played through speakers, and anything other than this tends to sound unnatural—not quite rock'n'roll.

Experienced amplifier designers have long declared that your speakers and cabinet are together responsible for 50 per cent of your tone, but the speaker is often the last thing a player considers in an effort to overhaul an unsatisfactory sound. Replacing a stock speaker with a different type, even of the same size, can sometimes alter your amp's sound more than any other single component change, and it can be the quickest, simplest, and potentially cheapest way to convert a mediocre combo into a tone machine that sounds great and even feels easier to play. It's also a great way to tweak an already good amp into a more appropriate tone zone for your own style and sound.

But it's not always just a matter of installing a "better" speaker, so knowing a little about the general tonal characteristics of a number of speaker types, and their popular uses, can prove valuable to any guitarist. And of course the cabinet type and design will itself play a major part in shaping your sound, so let's take an overdue look at the whole ball of wax after the output jack.

## SPEAKER TYPES

Speakers—sometimes called "drivers" to differentiate the functioning units themselves from the cabinets they come in—are available today in a broader range of makes and types than ever before. But you can split guitar speakers very broadly into two categories: "vintage" or lower-powered types and "modern" or higher-powered types. Within these they can generally also be divided into "British" and "American"-sounding units. I should say right up front that these lines are extremely arbitrary, imposing genre for the sake of genre really, and I can hear some speaker techs shouting at me already. Most larger manufacturers working today produce a range that covers all of these semi-imaginary

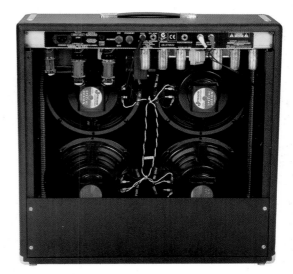

categories, as well as plenty of speakers that have their own voices and blend the best of all worlds. Still, the distinctions are commonly recognized by a lot of players, and they provide a handle to latch on to when exploring the broad range of types out there, used and new.

## Vintage and low-powered

In the 40s, 50s, and early 60s, guitar amps rarely carried speakers rated higher than 15-30W power handling, and indeed guitar amps in the early days rarely put out more than 30 watts (not many speakers manufactured in those days could handle even that much power). Speakers this size were fine individually in the recording studio, or in multi-driver cabs at dance hall volumes, but push them hard and they started to "break up," in sonic terms, adding a degree of speaker distortion to the overall distortion of the amp itself.

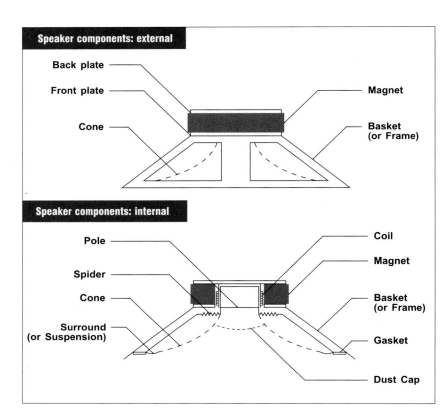

Speaker distortion, distinct from amplifier distortion, occurs when a driver is pushed to its operating limits, when the voice coil and paper cone begin to fail to translate the electrical signal cleanly, and thereby produce a somewhat (or sometimes severely) distorted performance. Put simply, the paper cone begins to flap and vibrate beyond its capacity, and introduces a degree of fuzz into the brew. As with an amp's tubes, push its speakers harder than they were designed for and distortion is the result. Of course in some cases we like it that way.

If you still aren't clear about it, here's a means of visualizing the concept of speaker distortion versus amp-generated distortion. Imagine two different amps: amp A is a 60W Mesa/Boogie MkII with a 100-watt Electrovoice (EV) driver, running with the cascading gain preamp cranked, but the master volume down to about 2 out of 10; the sound you hear is definitely distorted, but that's coming entirely from the amp—the speaker is operating well within its limits. Amp B is a 15W Vox AC15 running flat-out into a 15W Celestion Alnico Blue speaker; the sound you hear is part distortion from the floored amp, and part distortion from a speaker hit with very nearly more power than it can handle... and the result is a wilder, more textured, even somewhat uncontrollable sound—but a great one, by many standards. Swap the speakers around and the Vox is still giving you output tube distortion, but no more speaker distortion because the big EV is easily standing up to its peaks of power, even when they spike up above 15 watts. The 60-watt Mesa/Boogie is now giving you high-gain preamp distortion plus some speaker distortion from that 15-watt rated Alnico Blue. If we keep the Boogie's master volume down around 2 we're probably OK—but crank it up much higher and we're going to risk blowing the speaker.

As guitarists found themselves in bigger and bigger venues, requiring higher clean volume levels, amp builders sought out more robust speaker designs which would add minimal distortion artifacts to the sound. But these cost more than the cheaply built, lower-rated drivers, so even when they were available, they weren't universally employed. JBL's upgraded 12″ D120F and 15″ D130F, designed by Harvey Gerst, were available as long ago as the early 60s. Based on the standard D120 and D130 used mostly by the hi-fi audio industry, they had enormous alnico magnets, sturdy cast-metal frames, larger voice coils and, as a result, had higher power rating than almost anything available (Gerst has said they would handle from 35 to 60 watts, although JBL literature of the day claimed 100 watts power handling). These were an expensive upgrade, though, and usually only the pros and rich kids could afford them—and even they didn't always feel like splashing out. The "F" in the model name, by the way, stood for Fender, JBL's biggest customer and an occasional distributor at the time. Many stories have it that surf-guitarist Dick Dale helped design these speakers, to improve the Showman amps he was also purportedly helping Fender design around the same time, but I've also been told that Mr Gerst never met Mr Dale—nor even heard from him—during the design process, so that seems unlikely.

Price and availability aside, a lot of players who weren't seeking absolute "clean clean" enjoyed the edge, bite, and apparent compression that a little speaker distortion added to their sound, and lower-powered drivers—with all their gorgeous inherent "flaws"—quickly became a big part of the foundations of the rock'n'roll sound. In the USA, Jensen was far and away the most respected—and for a time most used—manufacturer of lower-powered speakers, and their 12″ P12R (15 watts), P12Q (20 watts) and P12N (30 watts), and 10″ P10R (15 watts) played a huge part in the signature sounds of classic amps from Fender, Gibson, Ampeg, Silvertone and others. Each of these models has its distinctive characteristics, but together they are broadly characterized by bell-like highs, somewhat boxy but rather open and transparent mids, and juicy, saturated lows, to the point of flapping, farting out, and giving in to all-around low-frequency freak-out in the lesser-rated models. All of which—short of the extremes—combines to produce great, sweet, tactile clean sounds when driven a little, and barky, succulent overdrive when driven a lot.

All were built using alnico magnets, paper cones and paper "formers" around which the voice-coils were wound, which universally prove essential ingredients in the vintage driver formula. Depending on costs and availability, most of the same manufacturers also fitted units from brands like Utah, Oxford, CTS and others, which more often than not shared some of the Jensens' characteristics (provided they were alnico-magnet designs), but were rarely as revered by players.

Players have raved for years about the great sound of alnico-magnet speakers versus ceramic-magnet units, and while the science behind this is difficult to quantify, there is certainly a little something to it in some cases. As used in speakers, and in some vintage-style pickup magnet assemblies, alnico is generally regarded as the "musical magnet." There are different types of alnico, but the one used for speakers is almost exclusively alnico 5—an alloy of eight per cent aluminum, 14 per cent nickel, 24 per cent cobalt, with a little copper (around three per cent) and a large percentage of iron to hold it all together. Thanks to the relative scarcity of cobalt—and high prices from the early 1960s onward—it's also an expensive alternative, especially when you need to gather together enough of it to manufacturer a big magnet for a high-powered driver.

Roughly speaking, alnico speakers tend to be musical, sweet, and harmonically rich without much harshness. These characteristics have a lot to do with the fact that alnico magnets compress smoothly and gradually when a speaker is driven hard. "Ceramic" speakers—so-called because their ferrite magnets are created using a ceramic process—are characterized by muscular, aggressive, punchy performances. Both of these are generalizations, of course, and either type—if well designed—can also possess elements of the other's characteristics. In the early days of ceramic magnets, the material was chosen for use in speakers because it was relatively affordable. This also meant ceramic was the magnet of choice for heavy, firm, high-powered modern speakers, where a big magnet was required to get the job done. A 50oz ceramic speaker magnet, for example, as required for a good low-end response, costs only a fraction of what a similar-sized alnico speaker magnet would cost. Just as the cost of alnico was skyrocketing in the early to mid 1960s, the ceramic technologies were advancing considerably, and you see a corresponding phase-in and phase-out of these two different magnet types at this time.

But for all of alnico's supposedly magical properties, many ceramic-magnet speakers still offer what plenty of players view as tone heaven. The lauded Celestion G12M and G12H-30 carried ceramic magnets (and still do in their reissue forms), and the "C" series ceramic Jensens found in slightly later vintage Fenders are still great-sounding speakers.

There are plenty of good speaker options afloat today. Many of the more popular Jensen models—both alnico and ceramic—are available again from the Jensen Vintage Reissue range offered by the brand's new owner, the Recoton company of Italy. These capture at least some of the originals' tonal characteristics, even if materials are not 100 per cent exact matches between the new and old units (although alnico magnets are used on the "P" models). Eminence—which evolved out of CTS—also builds a number of vintage-styled drivers, and has many excellent-sounding speakers in its broad new Patriot and Red Coat range. Eminence is also the manufacturer behind many own-label speakers from Kendrick, Fender, and others. The smaller builder WeberVST offers some highly respected vintage-repro units and versatile original designs.

In recent years, John Harrison's California speaker-servicing company A Brown Soun has introduced its own version of classic alnico and ceramic drivers to the market in the form of the Tone Tubby range. These are made with sturdy yet light hemp cones, and offer the sweetness, texture and responsiveness of the best vintage speakers, but with a fatter low-end and greater power-handling capabilities. Carlos Santana, Eric Clapton, Billy Gibbons and plenty of others are already swearing by these Tubbies, and virtually everyone who tries them seems to be converted... if they can afford it. Both the ceramic and alnico Tone Tubby units I have tried myself were amazing-sounding speakers: plummy, smooth, warm yet defined, with a chocolatey richness—they just seemed to sum up so many of the most appealing factors of analog sound, and made me want to play my guitar for hours. Without a doubt, it's getting to be a competitive market out there.

## British vs American

Over in Britain, Elac, Goodmans, and Celestion were building 10″ and 12″ speakers that weren't a world away in design from the Jensens of the USA. Using pulp-paper cones and alnico ring magnets to achieve power handling conservatively rated at from 12W to about 20W in the early units, these appeared most famously as the Goodmans Audiom 60 and (Celestion-built) Vox G12 "Blue Bulldog" in the Vox AC15s and AC30s of the late-1950s and early 1960s. By far the more famous and highly sought-after of the pair, the Celestion unit has sweet, rich, musical mids, and appealing (though not over-intense) highs. It doesn't have tremendous low-end reproduction, but offers an extremely flattering tonality overall, and great dynamic range. When pushed, the Blue has a midrange growl that really flatters the guitar. In short, it's one of the most beloved guitar speakers of all time. It was (and in Celestion's very impressive reissue form, still is) a highly efficient speaker too, offering 100dB (measured @ 1W/1M—which means that's how loud one watt sounds at one meter from this speaker), versus figures ranging from less than 90dB to around 96dB for similar Jensen units, or 97dB for a Celestion Greenback. This means that a pair in a 2x12″ cab topped with a 30-watt Vox AC30 chassis makes for a pretty gutsy combo, despite the apparently low wattage numbers on paper.

Celestion evolved the G12 into the ceramic-magnet G12M "Greenback" in the mid-1960s (rated at first at 20W, and later 25W). At this time these speakers were generally found in multiples of four inside the classic Marshall 4x12″ cabs that helped broadcast the rock message to the masses in ever larger arenas, at ever greater volumes. The Greenback is warm, gritty, and edgy, with a none-too-firm bottom end but plenty of oomph when tackling the output in numbers, especially in a closed-back cab (and remember, four of them together can take 100W, and better share the low-frequency load without flapping out). This speaker, as much as any amp, typifies the "British sound" sought after by so many blues-rock guitarists. In the late 1960s and 1970s the slightly higher-rated G12H took on a heavier 50oz magnet (as against the M's 35oz) to give a tighter low-end response, but otherwise carried on with the Brit sound tradition. This speaker was a step in the direction of other modern, high-powered drivers, but was still only rated at 30 watts. Fane, too, deserve an honorable mention for some good-sounding lower-powered speakers they have produced over the years, as well as for the sturdy drivers that helped give many Hiwatts, for example, their legendary big, bold sound.

## MODERN, OR HIGH-POWERED SPEAKERS

As many higher-powered guitar amps evolved to cope with the larger concert halls, amp-makers sought speakers that could take the full punch and transmit it relatively uncolored, as undistorted as possible. All contemporary manufacturers offer a few models of this type, but early classics usually came from more specialized manufacturers, such as the American makers JBL, Altec, and Electrovoice (EV). JBL—as discussed above—helped to make early 100W Fender Twin Reverbs and Dual Showmans into some of the loudest combos in the States, while EVs were Randall Smith's preferred choice of speaker to take the brunt of the cascading-gain blast in his compact (1x12″) but powerful early Mesa/Boogie combos. JBLs present firm lows, a rounded midrange with an edge of bark and nasal honk, and ringing, occasionally piercing highs. Various popular EV models down the years have tended to be muscular, balanced, and aggressive, while still very musical and fairly "hi-fi" in a guitar context. They translate the amp's sound rather than imparting much of their own character, and remain the top choice for a number of rock soloists. They can handle a lot of power, and they are heavy speakers along with it.

Today, most of the larger speaker manufacturers try to perform all tricks. Celestion's Classic Lead 80 and G12H-100, a number of Eminence models, some Jensen Mod series models, and others offer the similar power-handling capabilities and firm-yet-musical response in bigger amps. A handful of speakers in each of Eminence's new Patriot and Red Coat ranges can handle upwards of 120 watts and 150 watts. Most of the newer neodymium-magnet speakers—introduced by

Celestion in 2001, but now available from Eminence and Jensen—also offer high power-handling capabilities, and inherently firm low-frequency reproduction along with it.

While an ability to handle massive power levels sounds like a desirable characteristic for any speaker, you might already have perceived the trade-off: some firm, robust drivers barely flinch when hit with the full-whack from lower-powered amps like, say, a Fender Deluxe Reverb, a Vox AC15, or a Matchless Lightning 15—all of them great recording and club amps—and it means the tone resulting from this partnership can be somewhat tight, dry, and sterile. This brings us back to that old speaker distortion … in many circumstances we like it, and when it comes to achieving a characterful semi-clean, crunch or distortion sound at lower volume levels, it can be a real boon. Some of these sturdy speakers, though, are surprisingly supple and responsive, and many players using small amps find they do a great job of translating exactly what the amp is doing for them tonally. As ever, it all depends on what you are trying to achieve, and your music and playing styles. For mega-watt rockers, who need firm sounds on the big stage, for either bold clean playing, high-gain distortion, or gut-rumbling low-string riffs, the advent of high-powered drivers was—and remains—a godsend. They are more or less a must for this type of music.

While classics in the alnico camp—such as the Jensen P10R, P12R, P12Q, and P12N, and Celestion Alnico Blue ("Bulldog")—tend to be sub-30-watt drivers (aside from the Jensen "N"), it's not impossible to build a high-powered alnico unit. It just takes a lot of alnico and a firm cone. I have seen the JBL D120F and D130F rated variably at 60 watts or 100 watts; the EV SRO was a powerful alnico; and Britain's Fane still offers a 12" alnico-magnet speaker rated at 100 watts, the Axiom AXA12.

## EFFICIENCY AND SENSITIVITY

While relatively few guitarists put adequate thought into the general "sound" of their speakers, even fewer consider the effect that speaker sensitivity—in other words the speaker's efficiency in translating wattage into sound—will have on the volume of their amp. As stated elsewhere in the book, the speaker plays an enormous part in determining the sound pressure levels (measured in decibels, or dB SPL) that an amplifier is capable of producing, and is as important a spec as the amp's wattage rating in generating that thing we call volume.

Sensitivity is not related in any way to power-handling ability. There are 15-watt speakers rated at 100dB (measured @ 1W/1m), and 100-watt speakers rated at 94dB or less. The relationship of these differing efficiencies to your amp's volume is critical: every doubling of an amp's power creates only a 3dB increase in output. Hit our illustrative 100dB 15-watt speaker and a 97dB 100-watt speaker in turn with the signal from, say, a good 12W tube amp, and the lower-powered speaker will give you twice the audible volume (and probably sound better in the process if you're a rock'n'roll fan, with more speaker distortion and coloration added to the brew). Hit the pair of them with a 60-watt Mesa/Boogie MkII cranked to full, and the sensitive 15-watt speaker will blow; it's important to remember that high efficiency does not equate to high power-handling capabilities. But stick in one of the new Celestion Century neodymium speakers, rated at an astonishing 102dB and capable of handling the Boogie's full 60W, and you've got a loud little combo. Other sturdy, high-end drivers from JBL and EV also have very good sensitivity ratings, as does Fane's alnico Axiom speaker, rated at 101dB.

What all this means is that you can make your amp of choice far more muscular by fitting a speaker (or speakers) with a higher sensitivity rating—for example, converting a 20-watt combo fitted with a Celestion G12M-25 "Greenback" (97dB) that just won't cut it at gigs into a club player's dream by changing to a 100dB Celestion G12H-30. As much as this would seem to be universally a "good thing," a more sensitive speaker like this might make your much-loved recording combo too loud for optimum studio use. Alternatively, you just might prefer the sound of its original, less efficient driver (or find equal reason to swap down from a loud, sensitive speaker to a juicy, softer, insensitive one, which virtually acts as its own output attenuator). Referring back to our beloved tweed Fender Deluxe, Tremolux, and the like: these originally came with Jensen P12Rs and P12Qs, which weren't highly efficient volume producers, but they sounded delightful.

Amplifier power, speaker efficiency and the human ear's perception of increases in sound pressure level combine to make the whole "less loud/more loud" situation pretty confusing sometimes. Regarding amplifier power, there's an oft-quoted truth that it requires twice the power, or wattage, to produce just a 3dB increase in volume. That means jumping from a 50-watt amp to a 100-watt amp has the same effect as changing the speaker in that first 50-watt amp from a 97dB driver to a 100dB driver. A speaker change such as this certainly increases an amp's perceived loudness, as I've said—and changing from an even less efficient vintage unit at, not uncommonly, around 90dB or 93dB to one of 100dB increases it even more. But it doesn't make the amp produce twice the volume, as you might have assumed jumping from a 50-watter to a 100-watter would have done. Of course that 100-watter will usually provide a better bass response and more headroom overall, so the change in its reproduction of the guitar's frequency range relative to the way the 50-watter reproduces it will also affect the difference in performance between the two.

So far we've seen what a huge, and often underappreciated role a speaker's sensitivity plays in the sound level stakes, but other factors have a great effect on perceived volume. Different types of perfectly good tube amps playing at exactly the same wattage outputs, attached to the same speaker cabinets, will sometimes have different perceived volumes, even when a sound meter is showing you they are achieving precisely the same dB level. This is because many intermingling elements of an amp's sound—its texture, dynamics, compression or lack of, the character of its harmonic distortion, the point at which it breaks up at certain frequency levels and holds firm at others—will all affect what the human ear hears as the amp's "bigness of sound" (you can tell I'm a real scientist). A driving, compressed, warm-sounding, midrangey performance might not sound as loud as a tight, shimmering, jangly performance with ultra-firm lows and some eardrum-piercing highs, because the way the latter crosses the human ear's pain threshold gets our attention. On the other hand, the former might sound as if it has "more meat on its bones," and be more appealing along with it.

All of which is to say, a label like "45 watts RMS" (meaning wattage measured by the standard root-mean-square, the most common mathematical formula for determining wattage levels) might define an amp's output capabilities—and it's probably the best means of doing so that we have—but it doesn't mean every such amp will have the same perceived loudness turned to the same points on the dial. Myles Rose writes well on this subject in his article "Power Modeling: Amp Volume Shell Game" in the Deluxe Revised Edition of Aspen Pittman's *Tube Amp Book* (Backbeat Books).

Again, speakers have a lot to say in that whole equation, but the fact that you can easily swap speakers between cabs and combos and further tweak your sound through the variable of efficiency, and not just tone, means that the speaker part of this equation can definitely be under your control.

## SPEAKER SIZE

Size matters, but bigger isn't always better. The vast majority of guitarists pump their air via 12″ speakers, but plenty of great combo amps carry 10″ drivers as well: the tweed Fender Bassman, Vibrolux, and Super Amp; the blackface Fender Tremolux, Vibrolux Reverb, and Super Reverb; the Vox AC10 and the Matchless Lightning 15 210; many of the cool Dr Z combos; and the vintage Marshall 18-watt Model 1958. A few great combos carry 15″ speakers, namely Fender's tweed Pro, brownface Vibrosonic and blackface Vibrosonic Reverb. All of the above—including countless combos and stacks carrying 12s—are stunning guitar amps.

It's a common misconception that 10s are inherently "bright and trebly," while 15s are "bassy and woofy." It ain't necessarily so. A decent 15″ speaker designed for guitar amp use will be capable of producing as much audible treble as any 10″ driver—or at least more than you probably want to hear anyway, at full whack on the Treble control. It just might not be perceived the same because its overall balance of frequencies will be different (for example it might have warmer, fuller lows to couch those highs). On the other hand, a pair of 10s offer more speaker-cone surface area than a single 12″, and are capable of reproducing a more solid, forceful fundamental, provided their frequency response dips to the lowest-produced notes on the six-string guitar.

As much as anything to do with frequency response, the impact of cone size centers around attack and response times—that is, the delay between plucking a string on the guitar and the speaker getting audible airwaves into motion. At one end of the scale, 10s have a faster response due to the shorter distance the cone has to travel and the fact that there's less of it for the wattage to move, which results in crisp, articulate notes and a speedy attack. This can also translate to more lively seeming highs, though not necessarily more high-frequency content as such. At the other end of the scale, 15s—with their much larger, deeper cones—are slower to get moving and pumping the air, the result being a slightly less articulate attack. As you would expect, 12s fall between the two, offering a good compromise. We're talking tiny fractions of a second here, but it all contributes to the resultant tone. Singly, 10s do have trouble giving enough oomph to your lows, while 15s can get too flappy for some playing styles—which was the very reason Mr Fender changed his Bassman from a 1x15″ to a 4x10″ in the mid-1950s. It's seen as a classic guitar amp today, but the change to a 4x10″ succeeded in making it a better bass amp in its day, too.

Not all speakers of the same diameter have the same cone depth, either. The 12″ JBL D120F, for example, has a cone that can appear surprisingly shallow on first viewing. The shorter travel of a shallower cone both helps it withstand signal surges and also tends to make the driver "speak" with great articulation—and those old JBLs are extremely articulate speakers.

For all the reasons given, the 12″ has attained the broadest appeal of all speaker sizes. Even so, a quick look at the actual surface area of different speakers and speaker combinations can be informative—and it's a way of learning just how much air different speakers are capable of moving. For example, many players will look at a 2x10″ cab as somehow being "wimpier" than a 1x12″, but add up the numbers and there are some surprises in store. If we flatten out the cones of each speaker type, and assume their depth is approximately equal (which they are not, but for comparison purposes this makes life easier), the total surface area of the cone of a single 12″ is

113.04 square inches, while that of two 10s is 157 square inches. The total surface area of a single 15″ is 176.6 square inches. More unusual combinations throw up some interesting numbers: a cab with 1x10″ + 1x12″ = 191.54 square inches; one with 1x8″ + 1x10″ = 128.74 square inches. You can see from this that a pair of 10″ speakers will push about 50 per cent more air than a single 12″, and that adding even a single 8″ to a single 10″—an unusual combination, perhaps, but it's the kind of thing seen occasionally back in the 1940s/50s—makes that combination bigger than a 12″ too. The 1x10″ plus 1x12″ combination (something Gibson revived recently) offers a lot more surface area than a single 15″, fits a fairly compact cabinet if necessary, and blends the articulate response of a 10″ with the beefy growl of a 12″ (provided you select a speaker with a beefy growl, that is). Food for thought.

## BUYING USED SPEAKERS

The classified ads, pawnshops, and online auctions can sometimes be great places to pick up used speakers to try out—and occasionally some vintage units will pop up for surprisingly reasonable money. But while the slogan "buyer beware" attaches to any used musical equipment, it carries even more weight where speakers are concerned. You can pretty much assume that any really old driver you pick up is about to blow; even if it isn't, factor that eventuality and the cost (and potential sacrifice of both tone and value) of a recone into your buying budget. If you are getting some quality used speakers for a steal—or even just some interesting oddballs—they're certainly worth trying.

You might get years of flawless service out of some old drivers you picked up for a few bucks. On the other hand, you might pay top dollar for vintage Jensens or Celestions, only to have them blow, days after installing them. I've known plenty of players who bought old amps that had been sitting around untouched for years, only to have the seemingly flawless speakers blow on them after just a little playing. Years of storage in an environment that's either too dry or too damp, exposure to sunlight, excessive heat or cold, and other factors can put wear and tear on speakers when they aren't even being played. If some pawnshop owner or back-alley repair store is offering you a pair of functioning 1960s Greenbacks or P12Rs for $50, yeah, definitely, pay him your money and give them a try. But if you're considering paying $300-$500 for the same—which can be the going value in vintage circles—don't be too surprised when one starts to fart out or develop a voice coil rub after a couple of weeks, necessitating a reconing and an instant devaluation. And if, alternatively, they continue to operate flawlessly for years, be very surprised, and overjoyed. That's what we'd all hope for, but there's a good reason so many old and vintage combos on the market contain reconed or replacement speakers.

Bargains can sometimes be had in odd, little-known makes and types from the 1950s and 1960s—lesser-seen Jensen alnico models pulled from organs or old console stereos, or even long-lost brands made to similar specs. If you can grab some of these for a few bucks, for use in vintage-style amps in particular, you don't lose much by trying them out, and you might be pleasantly surprised. Oh, and here's a tip: how many times have you seen guys who are "in the know" about speakers set an old driver down on its magnet and pump it up and down by the cone to "check if there's a voice-coil rub"? Well, don't do it. If the speaker doesn't have a rub already, you can pretty quickly cause one by "checking" them in this way. Mount the thing in a cabinet, play it gently at first, then a little harder if it sounds fine up to that point, and you'll quickly know if there's a rub or not. If you don't have a guitar or amp handy and want to know that a garage-sale or pawnshop speaker is at least functional, touching a 9V battery very briefly to the + and—terminals on the speaker should produce an audible click in the cone. This tells you at least that the voice coil isn't open or shorted.

If you buy an old speaker (or amp, for that matter) that has lots of promise, but just doesn't sparkle as you think it should when you play through it—perhaps it sounds muddy, hairy or just dull—the thing might just need a little drying out in the right atmospheric conditions. This also applies to speakers or amps that you've had in storage yourself, in a basement or garage where they might have been exposed to airborne moisture. A few days' rest in a dry environment can bring soggy drivers back to life, and the tonal results are often startling. Read the interview with Michael Zaite of Dr Z later in this book for an excellent tip on accelerating this process.

If you have acquired a vintage amp that still has its original, unreconed speakers, it might be worth putting these into storage in a safe place where they won't be exposed to extremes of temperature or humidity. Load the amp with some good reproduction or reissue types that match the originals in approximate tone and performance—or try something slightly different if you're looking for tonal or volume improvements along the way (you're saving the originals, so nothing to lose here). That way you can get back to gigging and recording without fear of cutting a hefty percentage off the value of your amp every time you blow a speaker. If, on the other hand, the way the amp sounds now, with its original speakers intact, is the tone of your dreams, hell, keep 'em there. And hats off to you. These things were made to be played, not tucked away for some rainy day that comes after you're in the grave.

## BUYING NEW SPEAKERS

Any quest to purchase new speakers poses its own set of difficulties. It's much like trying to find the best replacement pickup for your guitar: unless you are buying a direct replacement for a similar driver/pickup that you already own, you often can't test drive these things enough to determine that they'll work just right in your own rig. If you have a friend who uses them and you can connect your amp to his/her cab, great. If a local guitar store stocks a combo or cab that carries the same units, that's good too; let them know they'll get your business if they let you bring in your own amp and guitar to test them through the speaker in question. And when you decide you do like those drivers and you want to order some, buy them through that store rather than going online just to save a couple of bucks. Building good relationships with dealers can be really useful to a guitarist on a gear quest, and these people are going to start shutting their doors to you if you continually audition products in their showrooms before buying them mail-order to save a little money.

If you just can't find operational examples of the speakers in question to perform the desired test drive, a little more guesswork comes into play. Read the specs thoroughly, and try to gather opinions from any source you can find (speakers get reviewed in the guitar magazines less than amps or guitars, but online searches often turn up some professional assessment or other). Eventually, if all the stats and opinions continue to uphold your own inclinations toward those speakers, you might just have to pay the money and take your chances.

I would, however, advise that players read online "user reviews" with a grain of salt—not only regarding speakers, but any piece of guitar gear—because people are often, if not always, predisposed to like and praise something they have already laid out the cash to buy. It's human nature; they want both to convince themselves it was the best purchase, and entice others to join them, and these factors often skew such "reviews." Even so, they can be very useful for gauging a general flavor of a piece of gear, and frequently users will tip you off to certain flaws or inconsistencies in the equipment that certainly won't turn up in the manufacturer's promotional material.

Many players aren't aware that new speakers generally require a breaking-in period, too, much like a new engine in a car needs to be run in. Fresh out of the box, they might well sound a little tight, dry, and constipated. They could also be prone to early failure if you bolt them into a cab, switch on the amp, crank it up to ten and hit them with everything you've got straight off the bat.

A brief break-in period applies to vintage-style speakers in particular—and I'd want to give it a little extra effort with any expensive alnico drivers like Celestion Alnico Blues, Tone Tubby, Webers, the alnico Jensen Vintage Reissues, and so forth—but all speakers should benefit a little from this.

Mount the speaker into the cabinet, handling it by the magnet to avoid poking a finger into the edge of the cone, and tighten down its screws or bolts until they are just finger-tight, then perhaps another quarter or half-turn tighter with a screwdriver or wrench. Turn the amp's volume down, switch on, let it warm up, then turn the volume up just about 20 per cent of the way and—without playing the guitar yet—let the slight background hiss and hum run through the speaker for a couple of minutes to warm up the voice coil. After this, start playing gentle but firm clean strums on the guitar, perhaps barre chords up and down the neck that get the speaker pumping on the full frequency range of the instrument. Don't do any hard, single-note leads yet, which might bias it toward a narrower frequency band.

Do this rhythm playing for a good ten minutes or so, turn the amp up a little more, and play some general stuff to your own taste for another few minutes (nothing too distorted yet). After that, you're pretty much there. The speaker won't be fully "played-in" in the sense of achieving its full sonic glory—that takes many hours of signal consumption, which usually means a few weeks, even months, for players who can't be at it all day long. But it will be nicely warmed up and out of the danger zone, and ready for you to give it what you've got. With vintage-style speakers in particular, a warm-up of a few seconds at power-up, where you just let that hum run through the voice coil without playing anything, is always a good idea.

## SPEAKER CABINETS

If speakers are too frequently ignored, the cabs people put them in are even more neglected. Cabinet design and resultant tonality could make a book in itself, but there are a few major factors and formats worth understanding to begin to pin down your requirements. These include open versus closed-back designs, the size and particularly the depth of the cabinet, the use of single or multiple drivers, cabinet wiring, baffle construction, and wood types.

### Open vs Closed Backs

Simply bolting a piece of wood across the back of a cabinet or leaving it open can be one of the single greatest tone-influencing aspects of a speaker cab's design. Open-backed cabs (which would more accurately be called "partly-open-back") accentuate the higher frequencies, with a wider, more "surround-sound" dispersion—basically because very little of the sound is prevented from leaving the back of the cabinet. They generally offer a broad, well-rounded, transparent, and relatively "realistic"-sounding frequency delivery. Their low-end response, on the other hand, tends to be somewhat attenuated: this is because of the partial phase cancellation that results when sound waves from both the front (driver pumping forward) and back (driver pumping backward) of the cab reach the listener—or microphone—at the same time. This isn't usually enough to cause any really alarming phase cancellation problems, but it does influence the overall sound signature of open-backed cabs … sometimes for the better, sometimes for the worse. The nature of low-frequency waves makes them more prone to elimination by phase cancellation, so in the case of the open-backed cab, these are the notes that soften up first.

The same phenomenon means that if you stand anywhere but straight in front of an open-backed combo, it's likely to sound louder (though less bassy) than a similar but closed-back amp, with a more "omni-directional" sound projection. Again, depending on your requirements, this can work for or against you.

Closed-back cabs offer greater emphasis on the low end, with a more directional sound projection that comes straight out from the front of the speakers. Sometimes this is accompanied by slightly spongy, compressed-sounding mids and slightly attenuated highs. A closed-back cab will also be relatively quieter than a similarly loaded and powered open-back cab if you stand to the side or, obviously, behind it. As well as their tonal properties, some closed-back designs also help the speakers work more safely within the realms of their maximum power-handling capabilities, and in fact can actually increase these figures. By supporting a speaker cone's movement within the cushion of air present in a close-back cab, the design provides its own damping, and helps to prevent extreme cone "excursion" (or travel, the back-and-forth motion of the cone) at high volume from overly stressing the cone. This is a big part of the reason that Marshall mounted those four underpowered 15-watt Celestion G12s in a closed-back cab in the first place. The design helped to cut down on speaker failure—along with accentuating the firm lows that had previously been difficult to achieve—and helped to make the high-powered rock amp possible.

There are other alternatives between the fully-closed or the "open" back. Fancy "ported" cabs have more often been a thing of the hi-fi world, but some makers have brought them into the realm of the guitar amp over the years. These generally involved cabinets with backs that are largely closed, but contain some form of opening—usually called a "vent" or "port'—that is tuned to help maximize the desired resonance and frequency response. Sometimes such cabs are even ported through the front, using an actual hole or tube mounted into the baffle, or the space between a "false baffle" and the one that carries the speaker itself.

Some pioneering amp manufacturers played with such designs many years ago, Leo Fender being a notable example. The elaborate ported-double-baffle design of the early Fender Showman amplifiers was intended to create a bass-reflex system to vent the low-frequency soundwaves bouncing around inside the box in harmony with the sound presentation coming from the front of the speaker, with a minimum of phase cancellation. Although these cabs were relatively short-lived (they were costly and complicated to make, for one thing) their design was largely successful in achieving its goals, and made these Showmans extremely loud, firm-bottomed amps with just a single 12″ or 15″ JBL speaker onboard.

Some contemporary makers are using Thiele-Small parameters—a set of calculations that can help to acoustically proportion a cabinet's size to maximize the performance of a particular speaker—in order to design carefully tuned, ported cabs. Dr Z uses these principles for its Z-Best cabs, which combine elements of a Showman-like double-baffling format with Thiele-calculated porting; and the Tone Tubby speaker company also uses the parameters for the porting in its semi-closed backs. Other makers lean toward closed-back designs but leave a lesser portion of their cabinet backs open to let the speakers—and the sound—breathe some, in a bid to avoid the sometimes constricted, compressed sound of a fully closed cab.

In a nutshell, you can think of the "open-back" sound as the gritty, edgy, full-throated wail of a Fender tweed Deluxe; the bright, bold twang of a Twin Reverb; or the juicy, sweet mids of a Vox AC30. Think of the "closed-back" sound as the bowel-rumbling blast from a Marshall plexi, or the foundation-rattling roar of a Mesa/Boogie Triple Rectifier stack. The ported cab blends elements of the two, retaining open midrange and shimmering highs, but with a firm, muscular low-frequency reproduction.

## Single vs Multiple Drivers

The number of speakers in your cab obviously plays a big part in determining how much air you're going to move, but other aspects of how running through a 1x12″, 2x10″, or 4x12″ will affect an amp's tonality are less obvious. To understand this concept thoroughly, you need to understand a little about phase cancellation, and how multiple drivers of even the exact same model will project slightly different soundwaves into the same air. The more drivers you have in one cab, the greater the potential for phase cancellation.

Guitarists encounter this phenomenon far more when recording than when playing live, since a microphone placed at a single point in space is then capturing soundwaves coming to it from slightly different directions in a multi-driver cab. But the phenomenon still contributes to the characteristic sound of a 2x12 or 4x12 and so forth, with frequencies from different drivers arriving at the ear at very slightly different points in time, creating a smoothing and rounding-off effect that influences the total presentation of that cabinet. Drivers of the same exact make and model can even react slightly differently to the signal being fed them (they are not such precise instruments, actually) and this further compounds the phase issues.

I don't mean to make this sound like a bad thing, and in fact it's often part of what makes some multi-driver cabs have a certain magic to them; there can be a natural smoothing of some harshness or some woofiness that might be there if otherwise left unchecked, in addition to the greater air mass moved and the increased power-handling capabilities of two 12s verses just one, and so on. The overall effect is usually heard as a slight "blurring" of notes, which sometimes contributes to a fatness and texture that is flattering, and which has certainly contributed to many classic recordings. On the other hand, in some circumstances this can fight against efforts to achieve tightness and definition. You don't need to understand all of the science behind it, but simply be aware that putting two Celestion G12H-30 drivers in a cab instead of one doesn't simply do twice the amount of exactly the same thing. The speakers' interaction—both acoustically and electrically—comes into play in a number of subtle and sometimes unexpected ways. Also, while two speakers will push more air than one, they split the amp's output equally. Whereas the speaker in a 50-watt 1x12″ combo gets all 50 watts, the same amp in its 2x12″ variant gives 25 watts to each speaker. The two speakers will be pushing more air, and hence the overall volume levels will be higher, but the amp isn't delivering "more power" as such.

As with every other element of the grand palette of amplifier variables discussed in this book, the main thing as a player is to remain open to the fact that the variables exist at all, and to audition as many of them as you can before coming to any hard and fast conclusions about your own optimum rig.

Some makers take advantage of the complementary interaction of two or more speakers in a cab by mixing entirely different types of drivers. Matchless uses one juicy, soft Celestion Greenback and one tighter, brighter Celestion G12H-30 in its D/C-30 cab, with excellent results. Mojave Ampworks combines a Celestion Alnico Blue and a G12H-30 in many of its 2x12 cabs; the ceramic speaker gives punch and a fat low end, while the alnico unit offers a plummy midrange, silky highs, and a lot of sweetness overall. Taking the principle further, the designers at Trace Elliot selected a Celestion Vintage 30 12″ and a 10″ Vintage 10 for the original Gibson Super Goldtone combo, and it helped to create a great-sounding amp.

This mixing-and-matching is something you can try yourself. If you are tempted to replace both speakers in a twin-style cab, try replacing just one first. That might be enough to change the sound for the better, and the mix of speaker types might make for a richer, more complex sound besides. Of course, always mix speakers of the same impedance—that's something you do not want to mix-and-match. It's also worth trying to use two speakers of roughly similar sensitivity. An exact match here is useful if you are trying to blend equal proportions of each, but a slight mismatch in efficiency can still yield an interesting tonal combination.

A prominent British amp manufacturer once told me he thought Matchless's use of a 97dB Greenback and a 100dB G12H-30 was pointless, because the "H" would drown out the Greenback, which is a full 3dB weaker. He was right in the technical sense, but not in the actual sense. Two speakers that are mismatched, but not too extremely so, can still work interestingly together, and even if they aren't contributing equally to the amp's sonic presentation, the unequal blend might carry just the desired sonic proportions. Any long-time Matchless D/C-30 player will tell you this: the 100dB Celestion presents most of the body, punch, and low-end tightness, but there's a clear edge of juicy Greenback texture riding in there right along with it.

I was once seeking the perfect cabinet for my own boutique-style 4xEL84 amp, and just on a whim decided to cut a new baffle in order to mount one 12″ Celestion Alnico Blue and one 10″ Jensen Vintage Reissue P10R into a cab I already had. The Blue is another loud 100dB speaker, and the P10R has a sensitivity rating of only 95dB (all, again, measured @ 1W/1M). You would think the 12″ would totally eviscerate the 10″ to the point of rendering it pointless; but the result was unexpected—that cab had a lot more sparkle, dimension, and texture than it did with the 12″ Blue alone, plus a really tasty element of speaker-nearing-freakout from the struggling Jensen when it was cranked up. It surprised the hell out of me, but that's the way it was.

Interestingly, replacing the Jensen with a 10″ Celestion G10L-35—a slightly firmer, more efficient 10″—decreased the cab's overall appeal, to my ears (although the G10L-35 was a great little speaker, used by Matchless and many others, but sadly discontinued for some reason). Of course I also know that with a different amp, the sonic results might not have been so flattering, and the speaker combination might not have worked well together at all.

Try your own mixing and matching, of speaker types, sizes, and so on. You might not want to buy new speakers to try this at random, because it's a very hit-and-miss process that only proves its successes through trial and error (unless you know a particular manufacturer has already had success with the combination). But if you already have a range of drivers lying around, or can borrow them from different amps and cabs, it's worth giving it a whirl, and even cutting yourself a new test-baffle where necessary if mixing sizes appeals to you too. Use your ears and your head, follow the speaker wiring diagrams given later in this chapter if necessary, and see what happens. Some wild mixes can even work out well: maybe two 8-ohm 10″ speakers in series together (for 16 ohms), then paralleled with a 16-ohm 12″ for a total load of 8 ohms. The single speaker would receive half of the amp's wattage, as would the pairing of the 10s (meaning they'd get only 25 per cent each), so the sets would likely have quite different breakup characteristics, depending on their power ratings.

Mess around, and see what you discover. Remember, though, if you're doing a lot of on-the-fly experimentation with speaker swapping, you need to switch your amp off entirely and put your guitar down before you go around back to disconnect speaker wires. Not a lot of guitarists realize it, but the high-current/low-voltage signal present at the amp's speaker out can create an electrocution hazard under some circumstances, especially when the guitarist is connected to the ground via the guitar.

Related to all of this, with any multiple-driver cab, there's another factor that has its say in your sound, namely wiring.

## CABINET WIRING

We're talking about series versus parallel wiring here, or indeed a combination of the two. This can be a very complex issue (heard that before, right?) but it's not hard to comprehend at least enough of the subject to know roughly how it effects your tone. All speakers interact with the amp's output transformer and, via that, its output tubes, to create different degrees of damping and resonance according to matching impedance and how hard you're driving them (very roughly speaking). Although speakers all carry a nominal impedance rating—usually 4 ohms, 8 ohms, or 16 ohms for guitar drivers—their actual impedance constantly fluctuates during use, rising considerably when the speaker is working hard. For this reason, the way you wire together two or more speakers will affect your tone, because the degree of their interaction also affects the way in which this fluctuation occurs.

Speakers wired in parallel tend to damp and restrain each other somewhat more, offering a slightly tighter response and smoother breakup—all of which is highly desirable in some circumstances. Speakers wired in series tend to run looser, with less damping, resulting in a more raw, open sound—which is, yep, highly desirable in other circumstances. If you have a 2x12″ or 2x10″ cab with two 8-ohm speakers and an amp with 4-ohm, 8-ohm and 16-ohm outputs, you can test it both ways and decide which you prefer. Two 8-ohm speakers in parallel will create a 4-ohm load, while in series they'll create a 16-ohm load, so set your amp accordingly.

Be aware, though, that if one speaker in a parallel set-up blows, the other will keep functioning. The amp (specifically the output transformer) will remain safe for a time, but you should switch off pronto and replace the blown speaker. When one speaker of a series-wired pair blows, your output

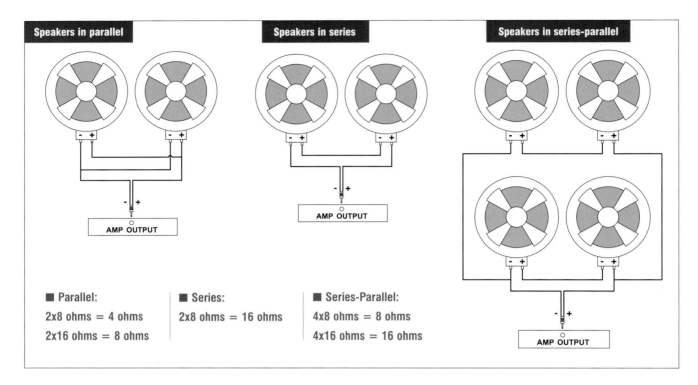

**Parallel:**

2x8 ohms = 4 ohms

2x16 ohms = 8 ohms

**Series:**

2x8 ohms = 16 ohms

**Series-Parallel:**

4x8 ohms = 8 ohms

4x16 ohms = 16 ohms

will die instantly because each speaker relies on the other to complete the signal flow—so dive for that power switch before your OT starts to fry. This is most likely why Fender wired all of their earlier multi-speaker cabs in parallel, rather than because of anything to do with tonal differences between the two arrangements. That said, a tighter, smoother, more restrained response was probably desirable to most early amp designers. Now that we appreciate distortion more than the old fellas used to, the little bit of looseness and wildness offered by a pair in series can sometimes be just what we're looking for.

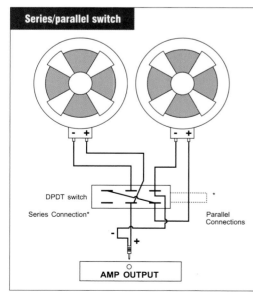

**Series/parallel switch**

The switching arrangement shown in this diagram requires a sturdy, high-rated on/on DPST switch (something in the range of 6A 125V/3A 250V will do), and some extra speaker-grade wiring. Rather than fixing the series or parallel configuration directly at the speaker's own connection terminals, the connections are brought to the switch, and reconfigured according to setting. After you have completed wiring it up, mark each side of the switch casing with a Sharpie or other permanent marker so you don't forget which way is which. Remember, the switch bat (or switch tip) points in the opposite direction from the internal connection it is making between terminals.

*Switch tip is in the series position

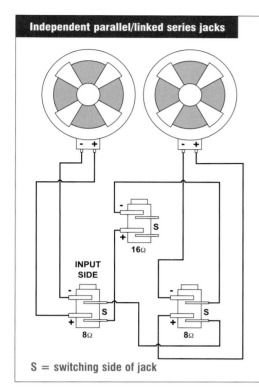

**Independent parallel/linked series jacks**

INPUT SIDE

16Ω

8Ω     8Ω

S = switching side of jack

Here's a cool little mod that I've put onto a number of my own speaker cabs, especially those with mix-and-match speakers of different characteristics that I tend to use a lot for recording in addition to gigging. By using a backplate with three input jacks, the cab can be wired so that a separate speaker cable can tap each of two speakers individually, or can automatically tap both together in series for a load that's double the impedance of each individual speaker. Because many amps have multiple outputs of a single impedance—the Fender amps with a 4-ohm impedance in particular—with a cab carrying two 8-ohm speakers, you can, for example, run two speaker cables, one to each individual jack, for a parallel connection and a 4-ohm load. You can then use the same cab if you have multiple, selectable OT taps on the amp, or another amp with a 16-ohm output. Or, especially for recording, you can just use one speaker or the other with a smaller amp with 8-ohm output, to capture that individual speaker's sound without the potential blurring effect of its partner. This is also a quick way to wire a single cab for stereo use, or you can run two amp heads into a single cab. There really are a lot of uses for this simple configuration.

Makers also use a combination of wiring formats both to create desirable effects and to correct impedance matching. The classic Marshall 4x12 cab is the most obvious example. With four 16-ohm speakers, wiring pairs of two together in series (a 32-ohm load), then wiring each pair together in parallel to the amp's output, yields an impedance match of 16 ohms. It also provides a best-of-both-worlds sonic result—a little damping, a little looseness, and at least a pair stays in circuit if one speaker blows.

If you have the option (that is, if you have the speaker combinations available to you and the multiple output selections on an amp to test it), try a range of different wiring configurations for yourself. You can even add a series/parallel switch or multiple jacks to a speaker cab to make its wiring—and the resultant impedance load—switchable. As long as you've switched off your amp and disconnected it from the cab (or internal speakers, if it's a combo), there are no dangerous voltages present in the speaker wires or on the speaker tab connections themselves, so you don't need any amp-maintenance experience to try these simple mods for yourself.

## BAFFLE CONSTRUCTION

The "speaker baffle" is the board at the front of the cabinet in which a hole has been cut to enable speakers to be bolted to it. The way in which it's fixed to the cabinet, as well as its thickness and the material it is made from, will also affect the overall sound of any speaker cab. Thinner, more loosely fixed baffles will vibrate more, creating wood resonance and standing waves that add to the sound of the speaker itself. Vintage cabs, as a rule, tend to be built this way more than modern cabs, although of course any modern reproductions of vintage amps follow the same formula. That said, many vintage British amps used very rigidly fixed baffles, so those are exceptions too.

The classics of the lighter-baffle breed include Fender's tweed amps from the 1950s, most revered in the form of the 5E3 Deluxe, the 5F6A Bassman, and their brethren. These are built with "floating baffles" attached to the cab's front panels by only four bolts, a pair at the top and bottom of the baffle. When cranked, the whole cab begins to sing—and the amp reacts much more like an instrument in itself. For the right style of music, this can sound great. In other circumstances, the tone can be perceived as woolly or blurry.

Fixing the baffle tightly to all sides of a sturdy, thick-wooded cab tends to restrain baffle resonance, while transmitting more acoustic speaker energy through the interior of the cab itself, and translates a greater proportion of the pure speaker tone into the resultant sound. In general this can mean a somewhat more controlled response and tighter, fuller lows. A lot of modern makers use this format to create punchy, firm-sounding cabinets. Even vintage British classics like those from Marshall and Vox had baffles that were more tightly affixed than the 1950s Fenders, and this contributes to their sonic signature. When Fender moved from screwed-on baffles to baffles that were glued into notches in the cab panels in the 1970s, they took the principle a little too far, at least for the ears of many guitarists. These cabs can sound a little stifled and constipated—and the particle-board baffles that the company had already been using for a number of years didn't help much.

## WOOD TYPES

The kind of wood from which the cab and baffle are built can make a difference too. Broadly speaking, plywood and chipboard offer a firmer box and less cabinet resonance than do solid woods (or less and lesser, respectively, if you prefer). This can be desirable for some designs, where the amp builder has factored in precisely what is wanted from the amp and drivers, and doesn't want too much unpredictable cab vibration and wood resonance to get in the way. Cabinets built from sturdy, quality, multi-laminate plywood can offer some of the best punch, note definition and overall frequency presentation of any cabinets out there, so it's false to throw the ply cabs into the same pile as, say, a laminated-top acoustic guitar (compared to one with a solid spruce top) or cheap laminate-covered furniture.

Solid wood cabs, usually built from pine, red cedar, or similar soft woods, as used in the early Fender and Gibson cabs, offer a more uniform, musical resonance and, well, a woodier tone. To some ears this can be slightly indistinct and unfocused; to others, it is sonic beauty incarnate. Either way, it's a contributing factor to some of the greatest sounds of rock'n'roll history. The material that you cover a cabinet in can even affect its sound; primarily, it dampens down the resonance of the bare wood somewhat. Many hobby builders have framed up their finger-jointed, solid yellow pine cabinets, and plugged them in for a test-drive before covering, to marvel at their sonic splendor. Time after time, plugging in after gluing down that Tolex or tweed and letting the whole thing dry for a day yields a slight but detectable shift in tonality.

## GOOD, BETTER, BEST?

So which of all the above is best for you? Of course only you can decide. Little of what we have covered here—vintage vs modern or American vs British speakers, fixed vs floating baffles, series vs parallel wiring—is a "better/worse" dichotomy. It's all a matter of choosing the right tool for the job, and the one that best suits your sonic tastes and playing style.

The importance of all this lies, as ever, in understanding the vast range of tonal choices available to you. Never ignore the major role that speaker selection and cab design play in the tonal recipe, and you'll be better able to achieve the results you want from your amp. Experiment, mix-and-match, and see what you can come up with. Whereas previously you were convinced you needed to lay down another wad of cash for a vintage Marshall half-stack to get the sound your band requires on a couple of tracks, you might discover that injecting your 15W Orange AD15 through the studio's in-house closed-back 4x12″ pulls off an impressive JTM45 impersonation—while distorting a lot quicker and sweeter, and being easier to record too. Or that Fender Deluxe Reverb that just isn't up to some of your larger club gigs might suddenly speak up for itself a little louder when you swap its generic-sounding and inefficient Utah or CTS driver for a 100dB Celestion G12H-30.

Creative amp-makers—the ones whose amps we all dream of buying—consider speaker choice and cabinet design a big part of the overall job of designing any new model of guitar amplifier. They know that the choice of these elements will greatly impact the overall sound of the unit, and will necessarily affect decisions made inside the chassis and circuit too. Really thoughtful designers will simultaneously be considering diverse elements like speaker selection, gain stage voicing, output tube type and bias format, output transformer type, and more, while putting their new baby together. In other words, the whole ball of wax—and speakers and the cabs they ride in are pretty large chunks of wax in themselves. In the enormous picture of mix-and-match components and stages that the guitar amp represents, the speaker and cab are the final variable, and one of the biggest. Other than, of course, you—the player.

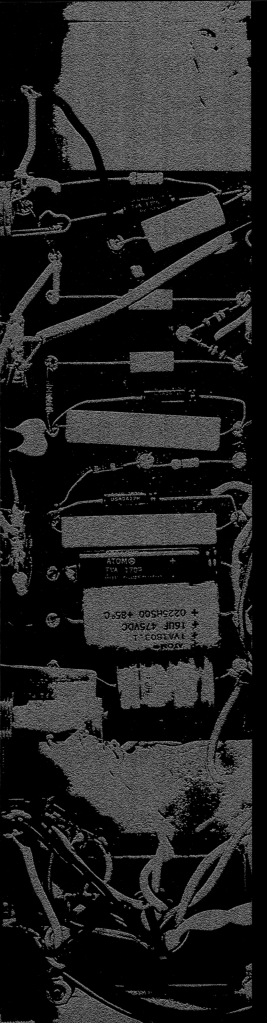

# CHAPTER 9

# Building An Amp

**Why fork out all that cash on a handmade "boutique" tube amp when you can make one with your very own hands? (Read this chapter and then decide on your answer.)**

t occurred to me in the course of writing the rest of this book that all of this delving inside tube amps might give some guitarists the urge to build one themselves. The project outlined in this chapter is based around a great-sounding design called the Two-Stroke that I put together to be a pretty simple job for first-timers and to emphasize a number of points that have been discussed throughout the book. You will already need to have developed some basic soldering skills and an understanding of how to strip and dress leads properly and read layout diagrams and so forth in order to make a success of it. But anyone who has undertaken basic hobby-style effects projects or other amateur electronics should be capable of stepping up to a tube amp like this one. If anything, this design is simpler than most of the effects pedals out there, and that's part of the beauty of it— and one of the reasons it sounds so good.

Before proceeding, please consider this advice: I strongly suggest that—unless you are already very confident with tube-amp circuits, soldering, safety issues, parts specifications (including understanding power and output transformer specs and applications—you approach this project by purchasing one of the available kits. At the time of writing, the official Two-Stroke amp kit is supplied by tweed übermeister Mark Baier at Victoria Amplifier Company. It is available as a full kit with comprehensive instructions, or as a completed amp built by the good folks Victoria themselves. You will find that this is not a "low-budget" option, but neither is anything about it low budget: parts are top quality, sourced from US suppliers wherever possible, and the cabinet is a stylish and exclusive item that really stands out. In short, the results are entirely in line with the standard products manufactured by this company, one of the world's best-respected makers of vintage-style tube amps. There are other amps made to designs and formats very similar to the Two-Stroke available from other suppliers, which your research will no doubt uncover. The most familiar of these is an affordable option that still offers the challenge of building your own tube amp, even if many of its components are offshore, import-grade parts—parts commensurate with its price, in other words. You might also decide to build a different low-wattage tube amp kit for your first DIY project, anything from a tweed Champ to a tweed Deluxe or even a Marshall-style 18-watter. If so,

## WARNING! PLEASE READ THIS

This tube amp kit-building project is to be undertaken by readers solely on the understanding that they do not plug in or switch on the amp—incomplete or complete—until it has been securely and correctly mounted in the speaker cabinet, with the protective upper-back panel secured over the chassis opening. Potentially lethal voltages are present in guitar amps, even when they are turned off and unplugged from the AC wall outlet. Electrolytic capacitors store high voltages that can still be harmful and even lethal, long after an amp has been switched off and unplugged. If your kit amp (or DIY project) does not power-up correctly and function properly when first switched on after mounting it in the cabinet and securing the back panel, consult a qualified professional for troubleshooting, repair, or assistance. Do not attempt to remedy the problem yourself, as the amplifier will now have received a high voltage charge that might still be present after it is powered down and unplugged. If your amp works after completing the building project, but fails some time in the near or distant future, again, do not attempt to diagnose or repair it yourself. Seek professional help.

The author and publisher of this book assume no responsibility for any damage whatsoever to persons or property that may result from readers undertaking work on their own amps. Please read the warning in the introduction at the beginning of the book for other important cautions.

**Prototype Two-Stroke combo, in tasty "charcoal" Naugahyde.**

these instructions won't directly apply to your work, but should provide a good "walk through" of some useful techniques for amp building.

If you have the kind of experience outlined at the start of the above paragraph, you can also source your own components from the list provided and go at it from scratch, a rewarding effort in and of itself.

In any of these scenarios, you should note that the author and publisher of this book take no responsibility whatsoever for your efforts in building this kit, or for the results achieved. **We provide no support service**, and will not reply to questions asked in that regard. The Two-Stroke project has already been successfully completed by hundreds of readers of the first edition of *The Guitar Amp Handbook* and, in short, it works. If you complete the project and your amp doesn't work, it won't be due to a flaw in the project, but rather a flaw in your execution or in one of the components sourced for the build. If this sounds harsh, my sincere apologies, but I'm sure you can appreciate the author and publisher's inability to put adequate time into offering phone or email support of a DIY project such as this.

## THE AMP

In basic terms, my Two-Stroke amp design is an 8-watt, all-tube, single-ended combo with tube rectification and a straight-ahead control layout consisting of volume, tone, and three-way boost/voicing switch. This description hides a lot of pretty cool tricks though, and as simple as this amp is, it compiles a lot of stuff we have encountered in these chapters.

The Two-Stroke in this *Updated And Expanded Edition* has evolved somewhat from that of the original edition. The circuit is essentially the same, other than a handful of minor component-value tweaks that I've brought in over the years as one or another minor improvement occurred to me, but the format has been altered somewhat. The original cab and speaker complement of one 10″ and one 8″ was fun and provided some interesting sonic breadth, but after playing that amp at higher volume levels with several fatter, humbucker-equipped guitars, I began to feel that a single 12″ speaker would maximize the circuit's potential, allowing more midrange girth and a firmer low end with the volume maxed out (the smaller speakers can fart out a little—or a lot—under such circumstances, which is kind of a cool vintage-fried thing in itself on some occasions, but not universally desirable).

In addition, although the original Two-Stroke's dual-single-ended topology was cool, I found myself preferring the tone of a single 6L6 for 99 per cent of the situations in which I wanted to get the upper power range out of the amp. Put another way, the effort of building up this amp as a dual-single-ended architecture—with all the added components, effort, and expense that entails—proved quickly redundant when I found how good it sounded with the single 6L6, which was crisper, more detailed, firmer in the lows, and more "big amp in a small package" overall. A single 6V6 can still be substituted to cut the output by about half, and achieve more compression and quicker distortion, and you can still sub in an EL34 or KT66 for different flavors of the amp's full power potential.

Aside from these two significant changes and a handful of less noticeable ones, the amp is essentially the same—although, in fact, *better*, which was the object of updating these features in the first place. Here are some of its interesting points and features:

**1** This is a true class A amp, thanks to its single-ended nature, and therefore is rich in even-order harmonics—a real sweetie, in fact.
**2** While the "base design" is built around a 6L6 output tube, the way in which these tubes are individually cathode-biased means you can use a wide range of output tube configurations:

  **a** One 6V6 for approximately 4 watts
  **b** A single EL34 or KT66 for approximately 9 or 10 watts
  **c** A single 6K6GT for a soft 3 watts

**3** The extremely simple preamp design is intended to emphasize output tube distortion at higher volume levels, and to provide a "cranked-up" sounding sweet spot at levels that are great for studio recording, the home player, and smaller rehearsals.
**4** The volume control has a wide, smooth travel. It doesn't jump from whisper to roar at around ten o'clock like so many similar designs do, but gives you a range of lower output levels with good headroom up until a little past the halfway point—so plenty of bedroom practice and home-studio levels—then segues into crunch and lead tones from there.
**5** A three-way boost/voicing switch acts on the first triode's cathode-bias resistor configuration and its related bypass cap to offer three levels of preamp drive and voice, without interrupting the signal chain in any way and, therefore, without any tone-sucking whatsoever. This switch takes the amp from blackface-style shimmer and twang, to fat tweedy raunch, to bright plexi-like crunch without introducing any artificial modifiers to the signal chain, or the tone.
**6** The one 12AX7 that provides the preamp's single gain stage and the driver for the output stage can be swapped for a 5751 or 12AY7 to yield a smoother amp, or just changed for a different make of 12AX7/ECC83 for easy "low variables" preamp tube taste-testing.
**7** Because the circuit is extremely well voiced as it is, the single Tone control is enough to take you from darker/warmer to brighter moods, and it also contributes to the gain functions of the preamp, passing more signal level on to the output stage at higher settings.

**Victoria Amp Company's rendition of the Two-Stroke, as a kit or a fully-constructed combo.**

**Inside the chassis of Victoria's rendition of the Two-Stroke**

# AMP-BUILDING PARTS LIST

## ■ Output Transformer

Good options at the time of writing include:

- Hammond 125ESE output transformer
- ClassicTone 40-18031 by Magnetic Components Inc.
- Mojo15WH from MojoTone

A different OT can be used, as long as it is a properly air-gapped transformer intended for single-ended use, rated for approximately a 15-watt output, with a primary of approximately 4k ohms to 6k ohms into an 8-ohm secondary (ideal for a 6L6, but if it also has a 4-ohm secondary, you might plug your 8-ohm speaker into that when using a 6V6—let your ears decide). Other primary and secondary ratings will work—tell your transformer supplier what type of amp you're building, with what tubes and speaker load, and see what they suggest. Heyboer, for example, will sell custom and one-off transformers to order.

## ■ Power Transformer

Good options at the time of writing include:

- Mojo760 from MojoTone (or 760EX for export voltages).
- Weber 125P1B (part #W022772)
- P-TF22772 from Antique Electronics Supply

You might find several others. If you are providing/building your own chassis and mounting dimension aren't a concern, any PT intended for use in a tube amp and with the following specs will do. Primary: 120V (240V UK); secondary somewhere between

310V–0–310V and 330V–0–330V center-tapped (rated for at least 70mA–80mA); center-tapped 6.3V AC filament supply at 4A; 5.0V AC rectifier filament supply at 3A. Even if you don't understand these numbers yourself, they will help a distributor or transformer manufacturer supply you with the right part. Be sure to check that the transformer will mount correctly on the chassis you select.

## ■ Chassis

If you are getting your own parts, a chassis from any reputable supplier that's made to approximate a tweed-era Fender Princeton-type of layout will do the job nicely. If you have metalworking skills and the right tools, you can make up your own chassis entirely from scratch. Hammond makes a wide selection of suitable steel and aluminum enclosures, and something in the range of 14" long x 6" wide x 3" deep will do (in fact the width can be anywhere from 4" to 8" or more). Any chassis supplied with a kit designed for this project should already be fully drilled and punched to spec.

## ■ Eyelet board, insulating card, and brass grounding plate

Again, if you are getting your own parts, eyelet boards made for use with 5F1 and 5F2 tweed Princeton-type amps adapt nicely to this. If you already have amp-building experience, you can make up your own circuit board from a range of available materials, or lay it out between terminal strips.

## ■ Resistors

You can use a mixture of carbon comp and carbon film to keep noise a little lower, but honestly, a little noise never hurt anyone so I'd consider just going with all carbon comp (preferably do use carbon comp where I have noted here). Note that although resistors are color-coded, you very rarely (if ever) have to order according to color code—just specify the value:

- 68k (1-watt) x 3
- 1M (0.5-watt) x 1
- 1.5k (1-watt) x 2
- 1k (2-watt) x 1
- 100k (0.5-watt, preferably carbon comp) x 2
- 220k (1-watt) x 1
- 10k (5-watt ceramic) x 1
- 500-ohm (10-watt ceramic) x 1 (often 470-ohm is more readily available, which works fine)

## ■ Capacitors

- *Electrolytic*:
- 25uF/50V x 2 (or 25uF/25V is fine)
- 22uF/500V x 1 (anything from 16uF to 22uF will suffice)
- 16uF/450V x 1 (anything from 16uF to 22uF will suffice)
- 8uF/450V x 1
- *Signal*:
- 0.022uF x 2
- 0.0047uF x 1
- 500pF x 1
- 0.47uF 400V axial x 1

## ■ Miscellaneous parts

- 1M audio potentiometers x 2
- power switch (heavy duty SPST) x 1
- mini on/off/on SPDT toggle switch (boost/voice) x 1
- 1/4" plug for speaker leads x 1

- 1/4" switching jack (input) x 1
- 1/4" non-switching jacks (outputs) x 2 (or switching can be used)
- screw-secured control knobs of your choice x 2
- fuse assembly
- 1-Amp fuse, slow-blow 1.24"
- pilot light assembly, jewel, and bulb
- ring terminal for grounding to tube socket bolt x 1
- terminal strip (3 lug, 1 ground) x 1
- power cord
  (In the UK this will end in a fused three-pin plug—the standard 13-amp fuse that comes with most plugs is fine at that point, since the amp is internally fused anyway.)
- power cord strain relief x 1
- rubber grommets (9/32" diameter grommet for chassis-hole diameter 3/8") x 3
- nine-pin ceramic tube socket x 1
- eight-pin ceramic tube socket x 2

### ■ Tubes:
- 1 x 6L6 (plus 1 x 6V6 and 1 x EL34 as options)
- 1 x 12AX7
- 1 x 5Y3

### ■ Hookup wire for connections
- solid-core cotton-braided 20-gauge black and white (2.5' each). Solid-core wire with other types of coverings can be used (PVC, for example), but cotton braided wire is easy to work with because the covering can simply be pushed back to expose the desired wire length, and it doesn't melt with excessive heat from soldering, as PVC often will.
- shielded single-lead cable (Belden or other quality brand) (1')

- a couple inches of shrink tubing, diameter sized to fit your shielded wire, above (you will have extra)

### ■ Speakers and hardware (as suggested for Two-Stroke-style combo):
- Any good 12" speaker of your choice will do the trick. A Jensen reissue P12R or P12Q or an Eminence Legend works well for a traditional vintage Fender-ish tone. Alternatively, several other selections from Celestion, Eminence, Scumback, WGS and others will work great.
- speaker wire (1')
- speaker mounting bolts and T-nuts (if cab isn't supplied with prepared baffle) x 4

### ■ Assorted hardware
- nuts and bolts for tube socket mounting x 8 each
- nuts and bolts for circuit board mounting x 2 each
- nuts and bolts for OT mounting x 2 each
- nuts and bolts for top-mounted
- ("tweed" style) chassis mounting x 2 each

### ■ Tools required
Soldering iron (25 to 40 watts), solder (resin core, ideally around 0.032" in diameter), small and large flat-head and Philips-head screwdrivers, small wrenches (spanners) in a range of sizes.

### ■ Cabinet
Any kit provided should come with an appropriate cabinet or, alternatively, instructions and diagrams for building your own. If you are getting your own parts for this project and plan to build your own kit, a cabinet made from 0.75" plywood or solid pine made to the dimensions of at least 16" high x 20" wide x 10" deep will suffice. Or mount the chassis in a small "head" cabinet to use with almost any extension cab.

For the combo cabinet, make the baffle of quality plywood stock with a nominal thickness of 0.5". A front-mounted baffle works best if you want to keep it a compact combo, as per the prototype example in the book. Mount the baffle to 1"x1" battens affixed along the sides of the cab. If you're building your own cab, test the positioning of the speaker and the completed chassis (or at least a chassis with transformers temporarily mounted) to ensure you are allowing for enough clearance between speaker(s) and transformers. Alternatively, you can custom-order a 5E3 tweed Deluxe-sized cab from any of a number of makers and have its control-panel cutout done to suit the size of the chassis you are using.

**Note: for non-US readers**
1' (one foot) = 12" (12 inches), which is 30.5cm.
Half an inch (0.5") is 1.27cm.

In short, this is an extremely versatile little amp, and it's a real gem for recording and just jamming in circumstances where you want to get your tubes really singing, but don't want to crack the plaster. Think of it as a tweed Champ with more; or more accurately, a tweed Princeton with more. It's not a mile away from that 50s classic and other tweed-era American single-ended amps. It's a simple circuit. There isn't much in the way of your signal getting from input to output, so it really lets you hear what the tubes and components are doing. To make it any simpler, you'd have to skip the volume and tone controls (I did consider this). Also the boost switch, instead of rerouting the signal path through further gain stages, as it does on a lot of amps, functions by simply manipulating the bias of the preamp tube. It's an old trick, and used by a range of amp-makers in one form or another, but it's a very good one. The result is an extremely tactile, touch-sensitive amp that responds incredibly well to your playing; even at pretty high volume settings it cleans up as you ease back on the pick, then really roars when you dig in. Shades of distortion can be controlled easily from the guitar's volume pot, too. The sound of this little thing cranked up to anywhere from about 9 to 12 really is phenomenal; it conjures images of some of the most desirable vintage tube amps of all time—tweed Fenders, early Marshalls, Voxes—but at levels that any room, and any ears, can deal with. Most of all, I think the "less is more, simplicity is king" philosophy is what draws me to this as a great project, and makes it a fun players' amp in general.

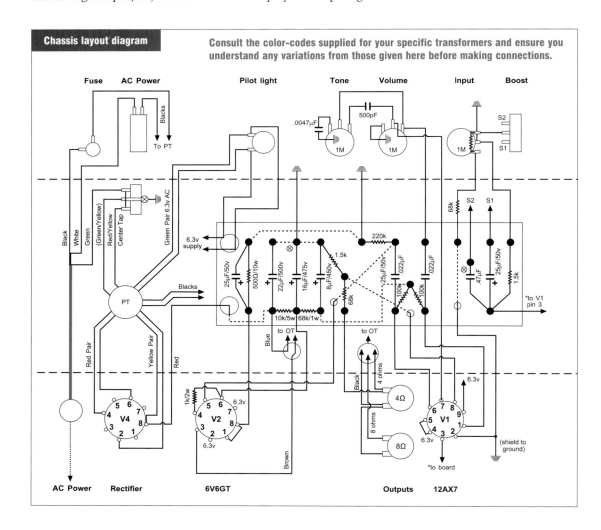

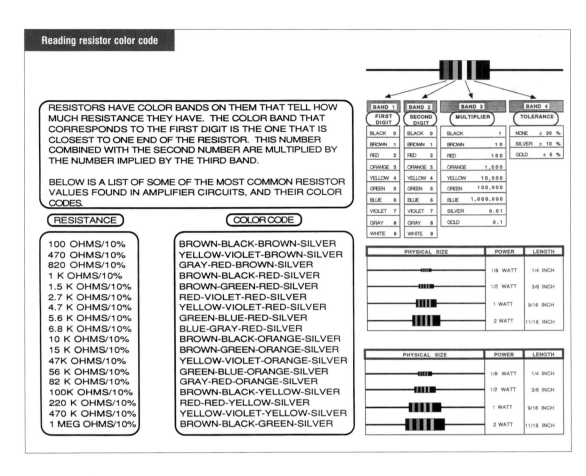

**Reading resistor color code**

RESISTORS HAVE COLOR BANDS ON THEM THAT TELL HOW MUCH RESISTANCE THEY HAVE. THE COLOR BAND THAT CORRESPONDS TO THE FIRST DIGIT IS THE ONE THAT IS CLOSEST TO ONE END OF THE RESISTOR. THIS NUMBER COMBINED WITH THE SECOND NUMBER ARE MULTIPLIED BY THE NUMBER IMPLIED BY THE THIRD BAND.

BELOW IS A LIST OF SOME OF THE MOST COMMON RESISTOR VALUES FOUND IN AMPLIFIER CIRCUITS, AND THEIR COLOR CODES.

| RESISTANCE | COLOR CODE |
|---|---|
| 100 OHMS/10% | BROWN-BLACK-BROWN-SILVER |
| 470 OHMS/10% | YELLOW-VIOLET-BROWN-SILVER |
| 820 OHMS/10% | GRAY-RED-BROWN-SILVER |
| 1 K OHMS/10% | BROWN-BLACK-RED-SILVER |
| 1.5 K OHMS/10% | BROWN-GREEN-RED-SILVER |
| 2.7 K OHMS/10% | RED-VIOLET-RED-SILVER |
| 4.7 K OHMS/10% | YELLOW-VIOLET-RED-SILVER |
| 5.6 K OHMS/10% | GREEN-BLUE-RED-SILVER |
| 6.8 K OHMS/10% | BLUE-GRAY-RED-SILVER |
| 10 K OHMS/10% | BROWN-BLACK-ORANGE-SILVER |
| 15 K OHMS/10% | BROWN-GREEN-ORANGE-SILVER |
| 47K OHMS/10% | YELLOW-VIOLET-ORANGE-SILVER |
| 56 K OHMS/10% | GREEN-BLUE-ORANGE-SILVER |
| 82 K OHMS/10% | GRAY-RED-ORANGE-SILVER |
| 100K OHMS/10% | BROWN-BLACK-YELLOW-SILVER |
| 220 K OHMS/10% | RED-RED-YELLOW-SILVER |
| 470 K OHMS/10% | YELLOW-VIOLET-YELLOW-SILVER |
| 1 MEG OHMS/10% | BROWN-BLACK-GREEN-SILVER |

| BAND 1 | BAND 2 | BAND 3 | BAND 4 |
|---|---|---|---|
| FIRST DIGIT | SECOND DIGIT | MULTIPLIER | TOLERANCE |
| BLACK 0 | BLACK 0 | BLACK 1 | NONE ± 20 % |
| BROWN 1 | BROWN 1 | BROWN 10 | SILVER ± 10 % |
| RED 2 | RED 2 | RED 100 | GOLD ± 5 % |
| ORANGE 3 | ORANGE 3 | ORANGE 1,000 | |
| YELLOW 4 | YELLOW 4 | YELLOW 10,000 | |
| GREEN 5 | GREEN 5 | GREEN 100,000 | |
| BLUE 6 | BLUE 6 | BLUE 1,000,000 | |
| VIOLET 7 | VIOLET 7 | SILVER 0.01 | |
| GRAY 8 | GRAY 8 | GOLD 0.1 | |
| WHITE 9 | WHITE 9 | | |

| PHYSICAL SIZE | POWER | LENGTH |
|---|---|---|
| | 1/8 WATT | 1/4 INCH |
| | 1/2 WATT | 3/8 INCH |
| | 1 WATT | 9/16 INCH |
| | 2 WATT | 11/16 INCH |

| PHYSICAL SIZE | POWER | LENGTH |
|---|---|---|
| | 1/8 WATT | 1/4 INCH |
| | 1/2 WATT | 3/8 INCH |
| | 1 WATT | 9/16 INCH |
| | 2 WATT | 11/16 INCH |

## BUILDING IT

Let's get started. This amp is so simple that the layout diagram virtually tells you all you need to know about soldering the thing together, but a few tips will help you minimize mistakes and backtracking. If you already have a kit or your own parts at hand, read through all of the building instructions before beginning even the first step of actual assembly, because there might be a point relayed later in the process that makes an earlier step clearer in your mind. Remember, the following is just my own run-through of the project for educational purposes: if you're purchasing a prepared kit, the supplier's instructions should supersede any advice given here. (If, on the other hand, you have the experience to source your own parts and build from scratch, this should provide adequate guidance.)

The order of work will involve assembling the circuit board first and attaching some of the flying leads that will go between there and the chassis-mounted components, then installing transformers, potentiometers, jacks, switches and so forth in the chassis, and finally mounting the semi-assembled circuit board and wiring it all up. The time it takes to complete the assembly of the amp will vary, of course, depending upon your skill level and experience, but most people should be able to have this amp up-and-running in a weekend.

## CIRCUIT BOARD

We'll start by "dry mounting" as many parts as possible to the eyelet card (circuit board), then soldering these into place once you have double and triple-checked to ensure they are all in the right locations. Position the eyelet card as per the diagram, with the two large eyelet-less pass-through holes at your left, and the four to the

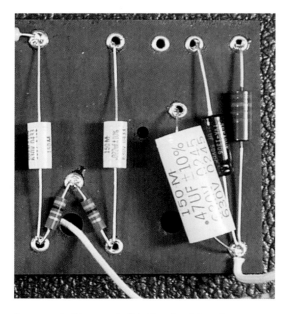

Components 'dry-mounted' in the circuit board.

bottom. To fit the components to the eyelet board, prop the board on woodblocks or similar at a slight angle, with the top edge higher than the bottom so there's some clear space between the underside of the board and your work surface. Double-check the value of each resistor and capacitor as you take it from the bag (capacitors have the value printed right on them, as do the larger power resistors).

Measure, cut, and bend all component leads and connection wires at right angles before inserting them into the eyelets, and insert all component leads into any eyelet containing more than one connection before soldering any into place. (With the leads bent at right angles, and the eyelet board propped up at an angle as described, most resistors and capacitors should hang in place well enough.) Pay special attention to wire connections made at the underside of the board—indicated by dotted lines in the layout diagram—and don't forget to measure and place these too, as appropriate, before soldering. You will also need to measure and attach some of the flying leads going to various components, playing safe by leaving them longer rather than shorter and trimming more precisely later. Other leads will

be attached to the components first and connected to the board later, so read on to note some of these.

In some cases where wires are to be attached to a chassis-mounted component first and then to the eyelet board after the board is in place, try to solder just enough to adhere the other capacitor/resistor leads to the eyelet, but leaving a gap to insert final wires, and complete soldering later as required. Note that my prototype, which appears in the photos here, differs slightly from the final, correct design for this amp (and from any kit that will be offered) and that the diagrams should be considered the final reference for building. One of the purposes of a prototype is to feel your way around the design as you build an example from scratch, and to learn ways to improve the construction technique as you go. This prototype does follow the exact circuit, but a few components will be mounted differently on the "correct" model in order to save space and improve the flow of the design. Also, the prototype's chassis is one adapted from an off-the-shelf chassis designed for a different amp, as well as carrying the "Mark I" dual-single-ended output stage and mix'n'match speaker complement; the kit's chassis will be punched and sized more precisely to the task, although it will still be of this type and construction, and of the same approximate size.

Instead of placing the largest filter cap first at the left of the board, we begin with the cathode-bias resistor, which leaves just enough clearance for the lamp assembly in most chassis. Your 22uF electrolytic cap now goes next to this, the 16uF follows, and the 8uF follows that in terms of power-supply flow. If physical space on your board is tight, you can position the 8uF cap on top of the 16uF cap, as long as its connections are going to the right place.

When dry-mounting the large filter capacitors (and some other components), note where you can use the excess lead length on the grounded side of these in particular to run under the board and complete a grounding connection that's shared with another component, rather than using an entirely new length of wire. You can also use the excess lead from the 16uF cap at the center of this filtering chain to go to the bottom-left corner of the brass grounding plate, where it will be soldered to make the ground connection for all these caps. Bend these at gentle right angles so the leads run from the cap through the eyelet from above, then under the board to the relevant adjacent eyelet, hooking up into that one to join the lead from the next component.

Before soldering anything in place on the board, be sure to insert the small circuit board mounting bolts into the appropriate holes, which will be difficult to access after components are soldered into place. One hole is located approximately below the third eyelet from the top-left corner of the board (if you've adapted an off-the-shelf 5F2 chassis), and the other just below and left of the single eyelet a third of the way down from the top edge toward the right end of the board. Insert the bolts thread-first, then screw a nut up onto each to secure it temporarily while you proceed with your work.

Now, once you have double and triple-checked your component placements and connections, you are ready to begin soldering. Start at the left end of the board. Preheat your soldering iron well, then place the tip into the desired eyelet so that it makes good contact with both the eyelet and all component leads inserted into it. After a few seconds of heating (three to five seconds usually does it, depending on the strength of your iron), touch the end of a length of solder to the joint and let it flow. Each eyelet might take a little more solder than you would have expected—an inch, maybe two—but don't give it so much that it's going to start seeping under the eyelet and potentially form a short against another eyelet or wire run. Once you have a shiny, silver liquid pool, pull the soldering iron away and—holding the components steadily in place if necessary—let the solder cool thoroughly, which will take a few seconds in these eyelet connections. A good solder joint will look silvery and shiny; poor joints

(called "cold joints") have a hazy, almost matte-like gray-ish finish to them. Cold joints might work OK to begin with, but they are inferior connections and will be more prone to loosening over time. Best to re-heat the joint and let it cool again to a shiny silver appearance.

Work your way along the board from left to right, remembering to leave any eyelets that will receive further wires with an adequate gap in the solder, or no solder at all if they are awaiting multiple connections. Solder at the other end of the respective components should still hold everything in place while you move along with the work.

To save space, we are going to mount our lone 68k resistor directly from the input jack's positive lug to just one of the three eyelets in this triangle on the board, from where a wire will run under the board to the input of the first preamp tube. When you come to soldering in the 0.47uF and 25uF/50V bypass caps that are the third and second components on the right side of the board, be sure to leave room in the upper eyelets so that later you can add the wires to the opposite poles of the SPDT switch, which will eventually connect these to ground (or leave them open, depending on the switch selection).

We'll use a length of shielded cable run under the board to go from the eyelet where the 68k resistor will eventually be connected to pin 2 of the nine-pin preamp tube socket. The end at the resistor's eyelet will connect from underneath the board, and the other end will come up through that large, eyelet-less hole near the bottom-right corner of the board. Measure a length of this shielded wire to reach to the far side of the chassis hole where the nine-pin socket will go, which is approximately where pin 2 will be. Strip one end so that both the plastic coating and the stranded shield are cut away to a length of nearly 1/2", then strip the positive wire at the center to a length of a little under 1/4" (ie, not as far as the shield has been cut back). Twist and tin (melt solder onto) the thin "positive" wire at the center, then insert a 1/2" length of "shrink tubing" over the end and position it to cover the place where the shield has been cut away, and hold it above the hot barrel of your soldering iron until it shrinks to a snug fit. The idea here is to cover any stray wires emerging from the cut braided shield, so they won't accidentally contact anything else. Strip the other end of the wire without cutting the shield, then loosen the braided shield until you can pull the center "hot" wire and its own insulated sheath out from within it by about half an inch, twist the braided shield together and tin it. Strip the positive wire about 1/8" and tin it. Insert the prepared wire through the guide hole in the circuit board so that the end without any exposed shielding reaches the eyelet near the input jack, hook enough positive wire up into that eyelet to prevent you from letting it slip away when you eventually attach the 68k resistor, and solder it into place.

## PREPPING THE COMPONENTS

When the board is complete, set it in place in the chassis without mounting it yet. If you're building from a kit or a pre-punched 5F2-sized chassis and circuit board (or similar), you will find its position by consulting the diagram, and by lining up the two mounting holes in the board with the similarly-spaced holes in the chassis. If you are preparing your own chassis to drill and punch, be sure to position the board where it won't interfere with other components that might protrude considerably, such as larger switches, the socket for the pilot light, and so forth. We will now test-mount the other components: switches, jacks, sockets, fuse holder, lamp assembly, transformers, and so on. All of this work should be done with the chassis resting on the workbench with the transformers down, open-side up, and the tube sockets toward you.

For the boost/voice switch, you might need to snap the small tab off the washer that comes with it, if a tab exists. Mount this switch vertically in the control panel, which means its external bat (or "switch tip") points either to the top or the bottom edge of the panel when thrown, not side-

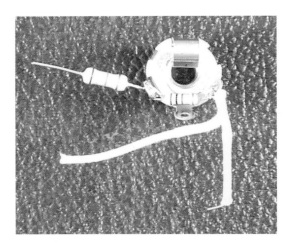

**Input jack wiring.**

to-side. Mount the volume and tone potentiometers so the three terminals on each point toward the opening in the chassis (that's the bottom edge of the control panel into which they're mounted, when viewing the panel face-on). Mount the OT with the secondary leads (those going to the speaker jacks) coming out from the side facing the bottom edge of the chassis. (Remember: many OTs will have to be fixed in place before the circuit board is finally mounted, because one or both of its mounting bolts often lie beneath it, but we are not permanently mounting it yet.) Now you have the correct distances to measure the remaining flying leads from chassis-mounted components to the board. We will cut these, solder a connection to the component but not the board, and eventually remove them all again, pulling the wires with you through holes for components that mount externally (namely the tube sockets).

When soldering the resistors to the input jack (these are notoriously tricky little devils, even for some experienced amp builders) try to observe carefully the positioning as suggested in the photograph. Remember, you will need to keep the 1M resistor back out of the way of the plug that will be coming into the jack, and the 68k needs to be at the correct angle to reach the board, with not so much lead length retained that you can't aim it into the eyelet, but not so little that it's

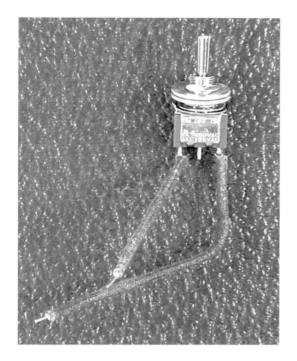

**Boost switch prepped out of chassis.**

"stretched" to make the connection, and will break easily if the jack shifts or rotates in use. (You'll hopefully have taken care of some of this already with your dry run). You might need an alligator clip or some spare tools to prop the 68k in position at the correct angle while you solder.

Cut a length of black signal wire to go from the input jack's grounding terminal—that's the top terminal of three when the jack is mounted in its hold with its positive plug contact pointing inward and toward your left—to the center terminal of the boost/voice switch, and another to go from the same grounding terminal on the jack to the first eyelet in the top-right corner of the board, which is the ground connection for the top lead from the preamp tube's cathode-bias resistor. (Note that the wire used in the prototype is white; the color doesn't matter as such, but consistency of color between signal stages at different points, ground, and power-carrying wires is usually desirable, and will help you keep track of what's doing what when you start to get everything in place.) Solder these in place at the jack only for now. Cut lengths of black signal wire to go from

the bottom terminal on the boost/voice switch to the second-from-left eyelet at the top of the board, and from the top terminal on the switch to the eyelet positioned about 3/4" below and left of that, where the top lead from the 0.47uF signal cap is connected. Solder these in place at the switch only.

Measure a length of white signal wire to go from the eyelet at the top of the first 0.022uF cap to the right-hand terminal on the volume pot, and another length of white signal wire to go from the same pot terminal to the center terminal on the tone pot. Solder these in place at the pots, but not the board. Cut the leads of the 500pF cap so that it extends between the center terminal of the volume pot and the right terminal of the tone pot, hook the ends, and solder it in place at each pot (leave a gap in the center terminal on the volume pot, where we will connect the shielded signal wire later as one of the final points of assembly). Scrape a patch on the back of the tone pot with the pointed edge of a screwdriver or other tool. Clip and bend the leads on the 0.0047uF signal cap so that one end connects to the left terminal on the tone pot, and the other crosses to the scored patch on the pot housing. Solder each in place; be aware that it might take a while for your soldering iron to develop enough heat for the solder to flow on the pot housing. If your iron is less than about 30 watts, you might need to buy or borrow a larger iron for this and a few other similar connections, although it should work given enough time to heat the area (note that significantly larger irons might produce too much

**Pots wired up out of chassis.**

heat for some of the smaller components, so don't use it throughout the work). When you have done this, you can remove the potentiometer assemblies, input jack, and boost/voice switch from the chassis.

Now it's time to measure the wires from the transformers and cut them to length. These will be a lot easier to strip, twist and tin once you have pulled the transformers free again and the chassis isn't in the way of your wire stripper. Don't leave a whole lot of slack in the transformer connections, but enough so they aren't pulled extremely taut when finally soldered in place. Also, be aware that you will be using a lot of the spare wire lengths from these wires to complete many of the DC voltage-supply and heater supply connections in the amp. These wires are of an appropriately heavy gauge for these tasks, and most transformers come with more than enough to make their own required connections, so set the spare lengths carefully aside as you proceed.

Here's how you go about preparing the transformer connections:

## Power transformer
The 6.3V AC heater supply wires (usually green, but check the wire codes for your specific transformer) should be twisted tightly together and run first to the pilot lamp assembly, where one will connect to each of the two terminals. The

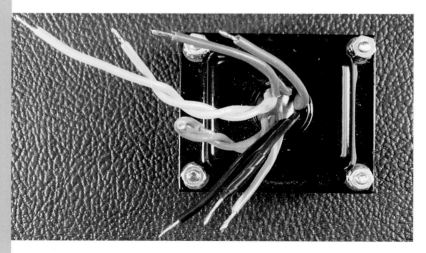

Power transformer with leads cut, tinned, and twisted.

pilot light runs on the same 6.3V AC supply that feeds the tube's filaments. Cut these wires at the correct length to reach the pilot light socket's terminals, then measure another length of the twisted green pair that's left over so it runs from the lamp terminals (note there's a pair of holes in each terminal) down along the bottom surface of the chassis to the approximate locations of pin 2 and pin 7 on the central eight-pin socket, which is the socket for the 6V6/6L6 (the octal socket furthest left when viewing the chassis from the back or below is for the rectifier tube).

Remember: you aren't soldering any of these yet, just measuring and cutting them while the components are temporarily in place, so you can strip and tin them after the transformer is removed again. You will want to keep these filament supply wires tight against the chassis throughout their run, to avoid inducing noise into any signal wires they cross paths with. (By the same token, elevate any of the latter as necessary to keep them out of the way of the DC supply, and where the two cross paths, try to cross at right angles to minimize contact.)

Next, we'll need yet another new length of wire to take us to the 12AX7's heater connections, so twist the two 5V AC rectifier heater wires (usually yellow) from the PT tightly together, measure them to pin 2 and pin 8 of the rectifier's octal socket, the socket further left on the chassis as viewed from the back or below, and cut them there. These wires won't really need to hug the chassis like the 6.3V heater supply because they are the left-most current run in the amp, and no signal path comes even near to them. Now you can twist together the spare yellow pair and measure them from the 6V6 socket's pins 2 and 7 to the 12AX7's pins 4/5 (which will be joined together by the heater supply wire) and pin 9. Run this twisted yellow pair down tight against the lower surface of the chassis again and back up to the nine-pin socket, splitting them towards their respective pins only on the final approach.

Twist the two wires delivering the 330V(+/–) AC current (usually red) and run them to pins 4 and 6 on the rectifier socket. These are the high-voltage AC supply from the PT that the tubes run on, which will be converted to DC by the rectifier tube. The red/yellow wire is the center tap for these (often indicated as "0" on the wiring diagram), and will be grounded at your main grounding point, so cut it at that length. (Again, consult the wire code diagram for your chosen power transformer; many of these codes are universal, but some might vary, especially on transformers with added options). If your heater supply also has a center tap, often a green/yellow wire, that too will be grounded at the same place you grounded the 330V supply's center tap (consult your PT's wiring code and spec sheet).

All that remains now are the two black wires, which are the AC input to the PT. One should be cut at the far tab of the power switch, and the other at the near tab of the fuse holder. You are finished measuring the PT connections now, but leave the transformer in place for the time being to help prop up the chassis while the OT wires are being measured. If your transformer has other wires for options you aren't using, cap these off with some heat shrink or electrical tape to safely and securely cover any potentially exposed wire, and wind them up to secure out of the way. You can even cut these fairly short before capping them off, if you are confident you will never need to use them.

## Output transformer

The black wire from the OT is the common negative lead. Run it from the OT's secondary side through the centrally positioned grommet hole—on the standard 5F2-style chassis it's the middle of the three holes, about 3/8" in diameter, toward the lower edge of the chassis—and directly to the first speaker jack it encounters and cut it to reach the jack's grounded terminal. Cut another short piece of the leftover black wire to run from the grounded terminal of the first speaker jack to that of the second.

There are some alternative OT wiring options here, depending upon which speaker and tube

combinations you expect to use most. If you are working from a kit these connections will be clearly explained according to the provided OT; if you're using another OT be sure to consult and digest the wiring codes for that product, and check with the manufacturer if you have any questions about which wire goes where. With many OTs, you might want to connect a different secondary tap to each of the two speaker output jacks in order to present a better match to the output tube used. For example, if you've got an OT rated for both an 8-ohm and a 4-ohm output from a 6L6 into the primary, you would use the 8-ohm output with a 6L6 installed, but re-plug your single 8-ohm speaker into the 4-ohm output in stead when using a 6V6 in order to correctly match the tube's impedance. In truth, these impedance matches aren't always entirely precise—as you can guess from considering that OTs designed for use with a single 6L6, for example, might have primaries of anywhere from 4k to 6k ohms or so—so many will tolerate a little mismatch in either direction, and you can use your ears to determine which output you prefer, in most cases. If you're only using one output from the OT's secondary (one "positive" wire in addition to your black "negative" wire), or your OT only *has* one, you can use the second output jack as an extension-speaker jack, or just omit it entirely.

To prepare the OT's secondary, take the positive wire(s) that you want to use through the grommet hole on the far right and cut them to reach the terminals on the output jacks. Cut any remaining unused secondary wires to approximately the same length as these (who knows if you or someone down the line might want to provide options for other speaker combinations?), cover the ends individually with electrical tape then wrap them together with a little more, wind them up, and bind them tightly with a small cable tie.

As this is a single-ended OT, we have only two leads from the primary to deal with. Your OT might have multiple options for this too, so consult the manufacturer's info (with reference to what has been discussed earlier in this chapter) and decide which you need. Many, on the other hand, will just have one wire in from the output-tube's plate, and one from the B+ connection in your power supply. Take these wires through the left-most grommet hole; cut the OT's connection to the power supply at a length that comfortably reaches the eyelet that forms the junction of the positive lead from the first large filter cap and the left-side lead from the large 10k/5W dropping resistor. Take the other wire in an arc over the top and side of the output tube's octal socket so that it comes down at pin 3 from above, bent at a right angle, and cut it there.

That completes our measurement of the transformer connections, but we still have some connections between tube sockets that we need to prep some wire for. Cut a length of solid red wire from the leftover PT leads to run from pin 8 of the rectifier socket to the eyelet that forms the junction between the positive lead from the first large filter cap and the left-side lead from the large 10k/5W dropping resistor—the same place where the OT's blue wire will be connected. Cut a length of the same gauge power-supply wire (whatever you have available) to run from the next eyelet in the power chain—the junction between the second filter cap's positive lead, the right-hand lead from the 10k/5W dropping resistor, and the left-hand lead of the smaller second dropping resistor (68k)—to pin 4 of the 6L6 socket. This wire and the other red wire from the previous eyelet to the rectifier will be soldered to the board from the underside last thing before final mounting.

The white signal wire from the underside connection to the eyelet on the upper edge of the board that forms the junction of the second 0.022uF signal cap and the 220k resistor (red/red/yellow/gold) should come out through the hole near the center of the bottom edge of the board and reach pin 6 of the 6L6 socket. You might have left this long when soldering the board, so cut it to length now, but don't solder it in place yet. Cut a length of black signal wire to go from pin 8 of the 6L6 socket to the cathode

resistor connections, which will be the eyelet at the lower end of the large, white resistor at the lower-left corner of the board (and its 25uF/50V bypass cap), and solder it in place at the tube socket only.

Cut a length of white signal wire to run from pin 1 on the 12AX7's nine-pin socket to the eyelet where the lower lead of the first 0.022uF signal cap and a 100k plate resistor are connected, and cut another length of white signal wire to run from pin 6 to its similar connection at the next eyelet along (you will want to give these enough slack to arc them up and out of the way of any filament wires in the area). Cut a length of black wire to run from pin 3 to the first eyelet on the bottom-right corner of the board. Solder these three in place at socket pins 1, 6 and 3 respectively, but not yet at the board. The white signal wire that runs under the board from its underside connection to the junction of the 47k negative feedback resistor and 1.5k cathode resistor at the center of the board should come up through the second wire-pass hole from the right and be cut to reach pin 8, but don't solder it there yet.

This completes all the component and wire-length prep. Remove all the smaller components from the chassis, then remove the circuit board, then the transformers. Strip, twist and tin all of the spare pieces of transformer lead that you have cut to length, and set them carefully aside to prepare for final assembly. Tinning these wire lengths before mounting them in place makes the stranded wires easier to handle, and prepares you for a better solder joint in general. The solid-core wires used elsewhere, on the other hand, don't need to be tinned in advance.

## ORDER OF ASSEMBLY

Once all leads are measured, trimmed and tinned, and the eyelet board is complete other than final connections, this is the order in which to put it all together:

■ **1** Insert the rubber grommets into the holes where the OT wires will pass through, then insert the OT bolts through the chassis from the inside (ie, heads inside, threads outside) and hold them in place with a couple of pieces of tape while you position the OT and tighten down the nuts, with a lock washer for each. (Procedures, number of holes and number of grommets needed might vary with different chassis.)

■ **2** It's probably best to install the circuit board before mounting the PT, as the chassis will be easier to handle without all that extra weight at the left end. Before doing so, though, take the red wire that you've prepped to go from the first filter cap to the rectifier, run it through the large (eyelet-less) guide hole in the lower-left corner of the board, and solder it to the appropriate eyelet connection from the underside. Take up the wire that you prepped to run from the second filter cap to the 6L6 and solder it—from the underside—to the eyelet carrying the positive lead of the second electrolytic cap and the junction of the two dropping resistors (there is no guide hole for this

one). Now pick up that loose piece of twisted green filament wire that you've also prepped, and thread enough of it through the guide hole in the top-left corner of the board so it will comfortably reach the terminals in the lamp assembly. This positioning will help keep these filament supply wires down tight against the chassis and out of the way.

■ **3** We're going to have to strip the end of our power cord anyway, so we'll use some of the spare PVC sleeving as spacers for the eyelet board (waste not, want not). Cut two 1/4" pieces to go over the sections of bolts between the circuit board and the insulation card beneath it (that's the extra piece of card the same size as the eyelet card, but with only the mounting-bolt holes in it), and two 1/8" pieces to go over the bolts where they pass between the insulation card and the chassis, to balance out the height needed for clearance over the OT bolt heads. The insulation card beneath the board is extremely important: it

The back of the Victoria Two-Stroke, fully assembled.

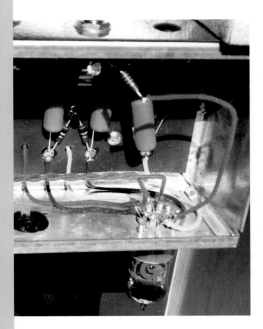

**Connections to the preamp tube socket.**

keeps your contacts throughout the board from shorting out against the chassis! Some types of circuit boards, however, don't use (or require) such insulation, but it's crucial with the old-style Fender eyelet board.

■ **4** The mounting bolt under the negative lead of the 16uF filter cap will have been put in place before you soldered that cap in position, so insert the other bolt through the small hole midway down the board to the right side and push one of your homemade 1/4" spacers onto each bolt. Slip the insulation card over these two bolts and spacers, then insert an 1/8" spacer onto each bolt under that. You are now ready to fit the circuit board into the chassis. This is one of my least favorite jobs of assembling this type of amp, because it's always a little tricky holding the board and insulation card together with the little bolts and spacers in place while you semi-blindly get those bolts through the two little holes in the chassis. Watch from the underside until you see the ends of the bolts approach the holes, and finesse them through as best you can (note that the bolt protruding through the right end of the chassis will come out very near to the OT, but should just clear it). Put a locking washer on each end, then a nut, and tighten them down. Another advantage of using the PVC sleeving from the power cord is that it has a little elasticity that helps to lock things down in place, without having to over-tighten those little bolts and distort the fiber circuit board. Tip: you might have locking nuts with your kit or self-sourced supplies, and these are useful in that they hold tight to their position once secured in place. If these are not available, a drop of Super Glue, Krazy Glue or

similar will help to lock down little nuts that might eventually twist loose from the vibrations inherent in such amps. If you or your repair tech eventually needs to remove the nut to service a particular component, a firm twist with the appropriate wrench will easily snap the glue bond.

■ **5** Pass all the wires from the OT through the appropriate grommets now, before the other components start to get in the way. Solder the power-supply wire from the OT's primary to the eyelet where the positive lead from the first large filter cap is connected. If this eyelet is already too stuffed with leads to fit this in, you can make a little hook in the wire, clamp it around the filter cap's thick positive (+) lead near the eyelet, and solder it in place there.

■ **6** Hold the brass grounding plate in place over the holes at the reverse side of the control panel, insert the boost switch and input jack through them, and tighten them down to hold the plate in place. Use the sharp edge of a flat-head screwdriver or other tool to scrape a rough patch in the grounding plate at a position between the hole for the two pots and slightly to the lower edge of the plate, and scratch another near the far lower-left corner of the plate. Now solder the ground connection from the output tubes' cathode-bias resistors/caps to the spot between the pots, and from the large filter caps to the spot in the lower left corner. As with soldering the potentiometer housings, you will need a lot of heat here, so use a more powerful soldering iron if necessary. You might also want to use the tip of a heat-resistant but non-metallic (ie, not heat absorbing) implement to wedge between the chassis and the grounding plate at its left end to "decouple" the plate from the metal of the chassis, which would only absorb heat from your iron and slow down this soldering job. Be sure to get good ground connections with both of these.

■ **7** Solder the loose end of the 68k input resistor to the third-from-right eyelet at the top of the board, being careful not to let the wire coming from the bottom of the eyelet slip away. Now make the connections between the jack and the boost switch, and the boost switch and the board.

■ **8** Insert the volume and tone pots (terminals up), and solder the signal wire from the volume pot's right terminal to the fourth eyelet from the right.

■ **9** Time to install the tube sockets. Mount them starting from the right, the eight-pin sockets in particular, because it's easier to get at that back nut to tighten it without another socket in the way to the left of it. You need to mount the nine-pin socket so pins 3, 4 and 5 are nearest you (ie, nearest the open edge of the chassis), and the eight-pin sockets so that pins 1 and 2 are nearest you, with the notch in the guide-post hole pointing slightly toward your right. During this mounting, place the ring terminal under the right-hand nut of the nine-pin socket. The grounded end of the shielding from the cable connected to pin 2 of the nine-pin socket will attach to this.

■ **10** Position the PT through the cut-out with all of its trimmed, prepped wires protruding from the top, and tighten down all mounting nuts except for those at the top-right corner nearest the

The 500pf cap linking the volume pot to the tone pot.

power switch. (This transformer might come with two nuts per bolt; if so, tighten down the nut with integral lock washer first, then put the spare nut over that to keep it tight.)

■ **11** Locate the three-terminal/one-ground terminal strip, and run a length of bare bus wire (pulled from a spare piece of signal wire or the

Components soldered into the completed board.

trimmed end of one of the large filter cap positive leads, with insulation stripped off in either case) through each terminal in succession, hook it onto each of the outside terminals to hold it in place, and solder it to all three. Put the grounding tab of this terminal strip down over the final PT bolt, and tighten down the nuts to hold it firmly in place. This is a tight space—which is one of the reasons we haven't installed the fuse holder, power switch, or lamp assembly yet—but you need to get a good grip on your wrench and really bed this down into the chassis, because this is a crucial grounding connection. Work carefully, because you don't want to slip and damage the terminal strip.

■ **12** Solder the center-tap wire from the PT's 330V supply to the far terminal on the strip, and the center-tap wire from the 6.3V supply to the center terminal.

■ **13** Install the lamp assembly, then solder one wire from each in the twisted green pair from the PT to one hole in each of the tabs, and do likewise with the twisted green pair of filament supply wires coming up from the guide hole in the upper-left corner of the circuit board. The rest of this twisted green length should run down along the underside of the chassis to the center eight-pin socket (the one for your 6L6/6V6). Make the connections there as per the diagram, and follow on from there to the nine-pin socket with the twisted yellow wire (or whatever you used for the remainder of your heater connections to the 12AX7). Remember to keep these wires hugging tightly down against the chassis. When you reach the nine-pin socket, one wire will need to go through the holes in both pins 4 and 5 and be soldered to both (you might need to twist these pins gently to help the wire through) and the other wire to pin 9. With these filament runs completed, it will be easier to reach the other connections.

■ **14** You can now make the majority of the rest of the connections as per the layout diagram—obviously apart from the OT secondary connections to the outputs, since we haven't

mounted those components yet (just keeping them out of the way for now to make the other connections simpler). Check through the entire layout diagram carefully before making any solder connections, in order to plan your work in the most logical way, then solder harder-to-reach wires first, and save those toward the open side of the chassis for later. Try not to solder yourself into a corner.

**a** Remember to connect the red DC supply wire from the lower left corner of the circuit board to pin 8 on the rectifier socket when you are also making the solder connection for one of the twisted yellow wires there.

**b** Regarding the shielded wire that protrudes through the guide hole in the board, solder the twisted, tinned shield to the ring terminal on the right mounting bolt of the preamp tube socket and the positive wire to pin 2. The other end of this shielded wire has already been capped off, and doesn't connect to anything. This arrangement provides shielding protection to the signal at the early stages of the amp, without creating a ground loop, which might occur if both ends were grounded.

**c** Now prepare another length of shielded wire to run from the tube socket to the volume pot in the same way you prepared that one. Connect the shield-less end to pin 7 of the nine-pin socket. Now bend the left-hand terminal on the volume pot toward the pot body, and score a patch on the body near that point to prepare for a solder connection. Run the twisted, tinned length of the signal-wire's shield through this pot terminal to the body of the pot, and solder in place at both points. Solder the positive wire to the center terminal on the volume pot. (Again, only one end of this wire's shield should be connected to ground.)

**d** Complete the rest of the connections between components that we have mounted so far, using the spare lengths of wire you trimmed and prepared earlier.

■ **15** Once all the other board connections have been made, install the two output jacks. Make these connections as per the diagram, not forgetting to connect the wire from the board to the positive terminal of the speaker jack nearest the board to complete the connection for the feedback loop. After you have made the connections from the OT secondary to the output jacks, as discussed earlier, it's a good idea to use an indelible marker or sticky labels of some sort to help you remember which output is which, if you are using two different taps from the OT's secondary for 4-ohm and 8-ohm outputs, for example.

■ **16** Strip, twist, and tin the three individual wires within the sheathing of the power cord, and run this through the hole in the underside of the chassis, give it enough length to reach the fuse and power switch positions, snap the strain relief clip onto it and pop it into place in the hole. Solder the power cord's green wire to the left terminal on your three-terminal grounding strip.

■ **17** Mount the fuse holder and power switch. Solder the power cord's black wire (blue in the UK) to the side terminal on the fuse holder, and one of the black PT wires to the terminal at the end of the fuse holder (note that there is no polarity to

the two black wires going to the input—or "primary"—of the power transformer, so either one can be used for either connection). Solder the power cord's white wire (brown in the UK) to the left terminal on the power switch (with the terminals pointing upward toward the open side of the chassis) and the other black wire from the PT to the right terminal.

■ **18** You have now made all of the solder connections and completed construction of the amplifier, so here is the most important step. Double-check all of your connections, for both correctness of component and connection, and for good solder joints. Then triple-check them. I know this will seem tedious, and you will be itching to try out the amp, but this due diligence will pay off, and it's not that complicated an amp to go over—there are only so many things to check! Occasionally I find something I have forgotten to put in, or a connection I have reversed, and you need to correct this now before you get 350 volts DC surging through the circuit (for an explanation of the voltage levels present in this amp, see later under "Voltage Readings"). Done it? Promise? OK...

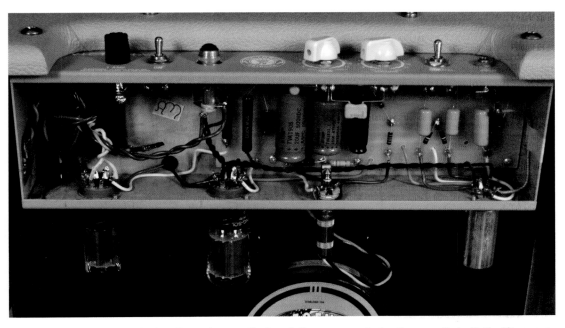

**The Two-Stroke completely wired up. Remember: use the layout diagram or any instructions supplied with the kit you are using as your final reference.**

■ **19** Put a 1-amp fuse in the fuse holder, then bolt the chassis into the speaker cab (either one supplied with the kit, or one you have constructed yourself). Mount the upper back panel to the cabinet to enclose the chassis, then plug in the speaker(s). Insert the tubes; be gentle with this, as the socket contacts haven't seen tube pins before, and they might be a little tight at first. Set the volume control to minimum, the boost switch to the center position, and the tone control to about halfway. Ensure that your power switch is in the off position, and plug in the amp. No sparks, pops, sizzling sounds, bad smells or smoke clouds? Good.

■ **20** Switch on, and just let things warm up for a couple of minutes with the volume still at 0. After 15 or 20 seconds at most you should be able to hear a slight hum through the speakers. Even so, leave it alone a while longer to let the caps, tubes and speakers warm up gently.

■ **21** Plug in a guitar, wind the volume up to just 2 or 3, and play gently. The output level here should be fairly low, and the sound should be clear and clean. Sounding OK? Play this way for a few minutes, then roll it up to 4 or 5 and play for a good five or ten minutes. If all is still well, test out your boost switch positions, and play with the tone control a little. If the amp is still happy, give it a couple extra notches on the volume and play some more.

■ **22** Enjoy your amp … you deserve to after putting in all the work!

## PROBLEMS?

This is a simple design, and—in kit form at least—uses high-quality components, so there is very little to go wrong. If you have checked and rechecked all of your connections against the diagram after completing both the circuit board construction and the assembly of the chassis as a whole, the amplifier should fire up first time and work smoothly. There will be a little hum in the speaker, as this is inherent in single-ended amps, but it should be reasonably quiet even so—quieter than many vintage single-ended amps, at least.

If your amp doesn't work after allowing a brief period for warm-up, follow the troubleshooting checklist in Chapter Seven and eliminate all of the obvious possibilities as described. If this doesn't solve it, the beginner or novice builder MUST NOT open up the chassis. Don't even remove the back panel. The amp has now been plugged in and switched on, and the filter caps will have built up a high-voltage charge. Take the project and diagrams to your local amp tech, who will know how to discharge the caps safely and should easily be able to diagnose any faults within your build. In fact, they'll probably tell you this is the easiest amp they've had to work on since that 1956 Fender Champ walked in the door last month, find the problem in a few minutes, and send you on your way.

If you have built this amp from a kit supplied by a third party, check any enclosed documentation regarding parts warranties and the availability of spares, should the problem come down to a faulty component. Modern capacitors, resistors, potentiometers and so forth—along with tested tubes—are generally very reliable, but parts do occasionally fail when they are first hit with high voltages, even those from good makers that have passed a quality inspection before going on the market.

In general, though, this amp should offer years of trouble-free service. Output tubes might need to be replaced every year or two depending on how frequently you play the amp. That said, you can buy vintage amps of this size that have their original tubes still functioning well, so results will vary. Preamp tubes will last perhaps five to ten years on average, but possibly a lot longer than that. Filter caps won't need to be changed as a matter of routine maintenance for up to 20 years, although premature failure does occasionally occur. All of these are the same routine items of maintenance required by any good tube amp, and can be undertaken by your local amp tech—if you haven't learned to perform such operations yourself 20 years from now when it's time to renew the electrolytic caps.

*The author and publisher of this book are not equipped to provide any servicing on amp projects described here, and will not be available to answer technical questions that might arise. This is a project taken on the reader's initiative, and the author and publisher advise that in the unlikely case of any problems or failures, a local qualified amp tech be sought for service.*

## VOLTAGE READINGS

Readers with experience and understanding of the safe practices involved in working inside "live" tube amps might be interested to check some voltages within this amplifier to ensure everything is running to spec. Beginner and novice builders can take the amp to their local tech to have the same done, and it should incur only a minimal bench charge. Taking such readings involves working within the amplifier with the back panel off while it is plugged in and switched on, so I can't emphasize enough that this is an operation for an experienced professional only (the points raised in the warnings printed with this chapter and at the beginning of the book apply especially to this matter). Because the amp's power transformer converts the incoming AC wall voltage to a higher level of AC voltage (around 320V to 330V AC), which the rectifier then converts to an even higher DC voltage, there are much higher voltages present inside the amp than the 120V (or 240V in Europe) going into it from your domestic supply. These voltages are highest at the far left of the power-supply filter chain—the point from which the OT and output tubes are supplied—and lower toward the right end of the chain and the rest of the circuit, because the dropping resistors have reduced the voltage for the preamp supply.

You should be seeing from 340–360VDC on the plates of the output tubes (pin 3), around 300VDC +/- on the grid (pin 4), and from 140–160VDC on the plates of the 12AX7, (pin 1 & pin 6, but more easily measured at the junction of the wires from each of these pins and the near side of the 100k resistors on the board—ie not the side where the two resistors join together, but the

opposite side of each). Within these ranges, this amp will sound its best as per the design. It will be extremely dynamic and touch-sensitive, with a chewy, rich texture and a lack of any discernible harshness.

If your measurements are a few volts below or above these, don't worry—the amp should still sound great; a few volts here or there within this range doesn't make an enormous difference to the sound and character of the amplifier. If it's way outside the range in either direction, you might want to have a tech investigate it for you with a view toward possibly changing some of the power supply dropping resistors. If it's just slightly outside this range (so long as it's not way high on the output tubes plates—say not beyond 380-400V DC—or much above 350V DC on the grids), but it still sounds great to your ears, feel free to leave it that way. In any case, if you've put all the correct resistors in the correct positions, you should find that it falls within the 340–360V range etc. That variance, such as it is, will be due to the discrepancies in local power supplies and the tolerances between different 5Y3 rectifiers and dropping resistors in the power supply—each of which can be surprisingly inconsistent.

Note that many Russian-made 5Y3 rectifier tubes supplied with kits might be somewhat inconsistent and, in particular, are likely to supply DC voltages that are a little—or even quite a bit—higher than spec. The amp should still function fine and sound great, but it might be worth investing an extra $10-$15 in a NOS 5Y3 to bring the voltages down to the 350V mark, and putting the Russian variant away as a backup.

Amp-building can become addictive. If you enjoy this project, there are plenty of others out there that offer further challenges and different tones. Tweed-era Fender amps have inspired a lot of the kits that are on the market, and there are some more original designs available too. An internet search or general perusal of the tube amp bulletin boards will usually turn up a number of suppliers. Have fun.

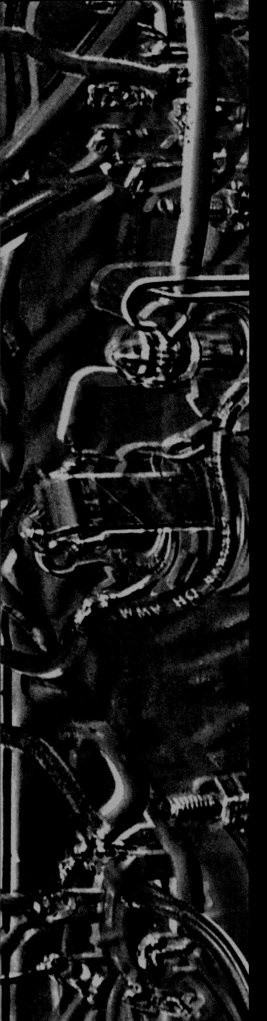

# Meet the Makers

**Author Dave Hunter talks to 10 top figures in the guitar amp-building world—Ken Fischer, Michael Zaite, Mark Sampson, Mark Baier, Victor Mason, Reinhold Bogner, Brian Gerhard, Steven Fryette, Holger Notzel, and Mark Bartel.**

# Ken Fischer of Trainwreck Circuits

Ken Fischer is considered by many guitarists to be one of the finest amp-makers and designers of our time. After a diverse early career, he eventually set up his Trainwreck Circuits amp repair service in Colonia, New Jersey, in 1981. In 1983 he built the first Trainwreck amp; by the late 1990s, ill health had forced him to largely abandon making amps himself. I spoke to Ken in 2005 for the first edition of this book. He passed away on December 23, 2006, at the age of 61, after suffering complications relating to chronic fatigue immune dysfunction syndrome. Given his status in the amp world, I wanted to let Ken's words here remain as originally transcribed, although some observations regarding current events will clearly be out of date. Ken Fischer's designs remain on the market in the form of the Komet 60, Concorde, and Songwriter amplifiers, the Komet Airbrake attenuator, and the Trainwreck-licensed Dr Z Air Brake attenuator.

### Can you tell me a little bit about how you got started with guitar amps?

Oh, we've got a long, involved story going there. When I was 12 years old, we moved to Colonia, New Jersey, where I live currently, and my dad met a guy who lived a block down who was a Lockheed electronics engineer. He had big radios and stuff and he had hi-fis. When I got interested in electronics he would give me parts and this and that … it was like, "Hey, I'm going to teach this boy electronics." So there I am working on Marantz and McIntosh amps and all this stuff. He'd draw me little schematics and teach me how to read that stuff, and I'd play with electronics.

### Great stuff to learn to work on.

Yeah, and you've got this Lockheed engineer who was a top guy in electronics at that time. So I started out with that, then I wanted to play the organ. But my parents had bought this house out here and they didn't have a lot of money, so they said, "Pick an instrument that's not so expensive." So I wound up with a guitar. I got a hollow Kay electric so I didn't have to have an amplifier with it, but since the dealer was a Kay dealer I eventually got stuck with a Kay amplifier, and they weren't too thrilling. You don't see Kay amplifiers on the collectors' list.

So I said, "Hey, I know how audio stuff works. I've been working on Marantz and McIntosh and Harmon/Kardon amps." So I started making some guitar amps. Then as I got older I went to school and started learning electronics. A little later I took a course at RCA (RCA had a school that was not supposed to be affiliated with them …). Jess Oliver, the co-founder of Ampeg, he and I took the same course at RCA, but at different times. It was basically an engineering course, minus all the other courses you didn't need, like language and stuff like that.

I went into the Navy and became an aviation anti-submarine technician. Then I got out of the Navy and went down to Washington DC and did two things down there. I was a professional dry cleaner, and I did TV and radio repair for Diamond TV, which had about five or six stores located through the Virginia, Maryland, and DC area. This was very early on during the Vietnam War—in the early 1960s, before it was even an official war—and I was going down to Walter Reed Hospital in DC to fix TVs and things, where guys had been coming back from the war with arms blown off, legs blown off, all kinds of things. I was one of the few repairmen who would go into those wards, because guys would go in there and just lose it. But I said, "Hey, these guys are just men, and I want to help the¶m out."

Then when the riots started happening in the early 1960s I moved back to New Jersey. I had all this money saved up from working two jobs, and I'd gotten into motorcycles down there, so I got myself a motorcycle. I thought I'd take a year and just cruise around on my motorcycle and have fun and whatever, and when money started running thin I'd get a job.

That happened, and then I saw an ad in the newspaper: Ampeg Amplifiers in Linden [New Jersey] was looking for assemblers. So I went down there and got interviewed and told them I could do all this stuff. They asked if I could play an instrument—because Ampeg liked to hire guys who could play an instrument—and I could play the guitar. So they said, "OK, start work next week. You're hired." So I was there on the final assembly line, about the second week I was working there, and a bunch of Gemini IIs were coming down. You'd put the chassis in and the reverb tank in, and do the final soldering. I said, "Hold it, man. These amps have got a mistake in them." The guys next to me said, "What do you mean? We worked on these amps last week, they must have made a change."

I said, "This wouldn't be a change, because it's a wrong value resistor. It wouldn't make the amp function properly." I went to the supervisor and told him they had a wrong value resistor in there, and he said, "How would you know that?" I told him I could read the code and it's wrong, so he should get an engineer out here. When the engineer came out, he said, "You can read the color codes?" So I told him about the RCA course, and he said, "That's what the vice president of the company took. You know electronics, you're a tech. Why are you out here working on the assembly line?" They had a tech that was leaving in a week in the final assembly room, where they check out the amp; a certain percentage of the amps don't work, of course, so the final-test tech's job is to fix them. They moved me down there, and on my first day they had a pile of over 100 amps in the corner that needed fixing because they'd been getting backed up. They said, "You're probably not going to keep up so you're just going to make the pile bigger, but if you eventually figure out how to work you'll be OK."

Two weeks later I'd not only fixed every amp in the place, but the 100-amp pile was completely gone. Their jaws just dropped. When you're fixing amps that come in like that, it's a lot harder than fixing amps that once worked. If an amp once worked, you at least know it was wired right. When it's not working from the start, you could be trouble-shooting for everything. After that, they had an opening in engineering, but they didn't want to lose me in the tech-repair job. So they made me an engineer, but part of my duties were to fix the amps in the final check stage.

So I wound up doing that. Everette Hull, the president of Ampeg, recognized that I was pretty talented, and whenever one of his personal friends would come in—an artist or someone—he would have me work on their amp. Ampeg was always full of major artists, because don't forget, we did all the jazz guys and the country & western guys: Ernest Tubbs & The Texas Troubadours, Lionel Hampton, Dizzy Gillespie, all the guitarists. The Tonight Show was in New York, so we got Barney Kessel, Herb Ellis, Tony Mottola, we had guys like that in there day-in-day-out.

Everette Hull said to me, "When one of these guys comes in, you stick with him all day and make it right. Whatever it takes to get his amp right and make him happy, that's what you do. Then at the end of the day when he says, "How much?" you tell him it's on the house. And if he tries to give you a tip, don't accept it." He had this thing about quality and pleasing customers.

### There's a lot to be said for that.
Sure. That's one of the ideas that he really impressed me strongly with. Some of his ideas were absolutely stupid. For example, when The Beatles and The Rolling Stones were out, he was saying things like, "Rock'n'roll doesn't swing, it never will, it's not musical, and we will not ever make anything for rock'n'roll." And he was proud of saying that, because his guys were playing bebop, jazz … and Everette himself was an excellent musician.

So I worked there for a couple of years and learned what the corporate structure was, and that was not so good. Then when they sold the company, the guy who was going to be in charge of me, he had a masters degree, and had worked making electronic door chimes. He would make up printed circuit boards for me, and I'd say, "Hey, Murray, this will not work. You've got your output line running right next to an input line… it will just oscillate."

And he'd say, "Hey, who's the masters-degree engineer here?"

"You are, Murray."

"Make it!"

So we'd make it, and what does it do? It oscillates. The day the deal was signed, he becomes my boss, and I quit. I was still into motorcycles, so I just rode motorcycles and did bike repair for a number of years.

And Trainwreck, by the way, was my motorcycle handle. Because I was a little bit wild in my riding style.

### When did you get back into amps?
Well, the US government put huge tariffs on imported motorcycles to try to save the US motorcycle industry, urged by Harley-Davidson really, so that business slowed down a lot for me. I didn't want to go back to dry cleaning, so I decided to repair amplifiers. I put a couple of ads in local newspapers, set myself up as a business, and in 1981 I officially became Trainwreck Circuits.

This was a tough area because there were a lot of famous shops where the famous musicians would go when they'd come and play New York. Within one year, they were all complaining that I had stolen all their business. Because when I started Trainwreck I said, "There's no bench charge. Come in and I'll give you an estimate, and if you don't like the estimate take the amp out. No problem." Everybody else had a bench charge, besides anything else they'd do, as soon as you walk in the door. I didn't have an hourly rate, either. Because let's say this guy has a $40 hourly rate, and he's a blockhead, he doesn't know what he's doing. I bring him a Fender Twin, and it takes him ten hours to figure out what's wrong with it. He's going to charge you a shop charge of $400 plus parts. OK, if you bring your Fender Twin down here and I fix it in 15 minutes, and I charge you the same $40 that he would charge for an hour but I only worked 15 minutes, would you feel unhappy? So that's the way I worked—because I developed a system at Ampeg of troubleshooting amps, I could work like that.

I got to the point where I had a separate guy whose job it was to take the chassis out of the cabinets. I'd fix the amps, and he'd put them back together, because my time was more valuable, whatever. So it was like that. I got this reputation that I could fix amps while guys waited, so I was getting amps from Boston down to North Carolina. Guys would make appointments—I'd say, "Come up here, I'll fix the amp while you sit and wait," and no other place would do that.

### That's a pretty good deal.
Yeah. And the other thing I'd do is, any part I changed off that amp, I would give it back to you in a bag. So if I tell you the output transformer is bad on your Marshall, I'm not taking the good one out and stealing it and changing a ten-cent resistor. You'll know it's bad, because you'll have it in a box and you can go and have it checked if you want to. Because I found out that was a big thing that was going on. Where are you going to get a used, working condition Marshall output transformer from? Because no one's going to take their Marshall and say, "Take the output transformer out and give me something inferior …"

When did you get into building the first Trainwreck amps?
It was around 1982, and I was friends with a woman who was working directly under Ahmet Ertegun at Atlantic Records in New York. They had an artist they were recording, his name was Caspar McCloud, and he was one of the two original John Lennons in Beatlemania at the Winter Garden. Alternate shows were done by

Marshall Crenshaw, and I worked on his amps. Marshall was down here several zillion times in the old days.

When Caspar came here from England he was going to bring his Voxes, and they said, "Oh, we've got amps here, you don't have to worry." For Beatlemania they got him a Vox AC50 head, which he didn't like as much as his AC30, but it worked. So in any case, Caspar comes down here and says, "I just did an album for Atlantic Records and they bought me a Mesa/ Boogie ..." I never had a problem with Mesa/Boogie amps, don't get me wrong, but it doesn't sound like a Vox. But one thing that Mesa/Boogie had that Vox didn't have was high gain. He liked that for the solos, but he didn't like the master volume and he didn't like the 6L6 sound, he liked EL84s. He wanted me to build him something, and I told him I don't really build amps, I just repair them, but sure, I could build him something, whatever.

So I made a prototype from a stripped-out old Super Reverb chassis I had and mounted some transformers, and put two EL84s in it. He came down and I said, "Of course the amp I would make you would be twice as powerful, but this is the basic premise." He loved it, so he said, "Make me the full-size one. By the way, what are you going to do with this one?" I said, "Oh, it's just old junk parts, you can have it."

So in January 1983, the first real Trainwreck done from scratch on my own chassis was Caspar's Liverpool 30, Ginger [Ken gives all his amps individual names, as we'll see]. That amp's still around, after 22 years—it's owned by a guy who works as a detective in New York City. I wasn't planning on making any more. I was making a lot more money repairing amps and selling tubes than I would be spending all that time building amps. And what can you sell them for? The first Trainwreck sold for $650 and it took me several days to build it, whereas I was making a $1,000 a day fixing amps.

### But I'm guessing the word got around ...
Yeah. Caspar would play the amp in the studio, and guys would say, "Hey, what kind of amp is that?" Before you know it, they'd be saying, "I want one. Build me one." I told them they'd have to wait, because I had 50 Marshall heads stacked up awaiting repair, and 20 AC30s. I couldn't even move, because I used to have corridors stacked with amps waiting to be serviced. Tweed Fenders, Hiwatts, all the old 1930s/40s amps, I could work on anything. So I told them they'd have to wait. I started building more amps, but I always thought it was just a part-time thing. I brought the price up to $1,000.

In 1984 I added a model called the Express. There was a guy I became friendly with, I was always servicing and modifying his Marshalls. He said, "I like EL34s, and I like the Liverpool sound, but can you do something a little more aggressive and crunchy?" So I made the first Express for that guy. Through the years I'd raise the prices a little bit because the cost of parts would go up and so forth. So they'd be $1,200, then $1,600, then $1,800.

Then in 1990 I decided I was going to make a series of amps kind of based on the Vox amps, but not a Vox clone, because I don't do clones of anything. I started

doing the Rocket amp, and then I got chronic fatigue immune dysfunction syndrome in 1988, so my health was terrible at this time. I was still doing repairs, but on the basis that I couldn't promise it for any particular day, because I might spend a day in bed. I would always be going to doctors and they'd be diagnosing things, and they still don't really know what it is today. Then other things started happening with me: I got a GI [gastrointestinal] bleed, I had a stroke, and whatever.

So I made one Rocket for myself, just as a prototype, then a friend of mine played it and wanted one. I'd gotten four transformers when I ordered the prototype because I wanted to see how consistent they were, so I built a second one for him, then I ended up building a total of about 12 of them—but I don't really count them, because I give them names instead of serial numbers. So if you give me the name of an amp, I can tell you what model it is, what it sounds like, everything. If you give me a serial number off an amp, that doesn't mean anything. I used to put in my brochure: "You wouldn't give your children serial numbers. Neither would I." Whatever, it was advertising.

So that's what happened. But I eventually got so sick that I said I couldn't do repairs any more, period. Although I do for some famous rock stars, because I have an agreement that the guys bring them down here and get the parts for me, and I'm not going to box them or ship them. So I've been doing that for Mark Knopfler just now, and working with Metallica, and Aerosmith, and Ritchie Sambora, because he's a Jersey guy. Billy Gibbons was the first famous guy to buy a Trainwreck, back in the 1980s. It's just easier for me to deal with guys like that because they appreciate, "Well, do it if you can do it ..."

### And they've got other amps to play meanwhile.
Yeah, they can get by. And they can afford to send a guy down with the amp, which most ordinary guys can't do. I designed amps for these two guys down in Baton Rouge, Louisiana, the Komet. And I did the Komet 80, which was a recent limited edition of 20 KT88-powered amps. And we're doing an Anniversary 60, which we'll do 30 pieces of with hardwood cabinets and maple "V"s and the rest of it.

### Any idea how many Trainwrecks you made over the years?
I don't count them, because I think it's a total jinx. I have a record book with every Trainwreck I ever made: the name of the amp, the year it was built, what kind of amp it was, what tubes it left with, this that and the other thing. And I could easily count them up, but it's not that many. If I was to guess, roughly, I'd say there were probably 100 Trainwrecks in the world.

### What do you think about the fact that they have become such collector's items?
That's kinda nice and bad at the same time. People say, "Hey Ken, you started the boutique thing." I get that all the time, but I say, "No, I didn't." The guy I truly believed started the boutique amps in the modern sense was Howard Alexander Dumble. He had amps out way before me, and it seems his amps and my amps are the

ones that are now the high end of that market. You know, a guy just paid $28,000 for an Express. Though if you're lucky you can still spot one for under $20,000. But that was kind of nice, although it never benefited me, because I never charged anything like that for an amp. If I sold an amp to a guy for $650 and he turned around and sold it for $20,000 that didn't benefit me.

People tell me it benefits me, because of the fame and so forth. But I don't like to think that way. When people call me up and say, "Hey, is that the famous Ken Fischer?" I say, "You're talking about my dad. He's dead." When people call me an "icon" and stuff, I hate that. The only term I will go with is "guru" because a guru is a teacher, and I like to share knowledge. So yeah, I will go with that.

But anyway, when the amps started going up, that was kinda cool at first. But what's happening now is that they've reached the price point where two things happen. First, a lot of real musicians can't afford them. So the guys who get the amps aren't really great players, but they have money and they collect stuff. They like to have the '59 Les Paul, this that, they've got to have a Dumble, and they've got to have a Trainwreck. And then the amps just sit around. When I made my amps, I always thought of them as something to make music, to make the world better, make people happy.

### That's the beauty of it.

That's the beauty. That's why I liked making amps, compared to dry cleaning or whatever—which is the dullest business in the world. Oh, jeez, not another "I spilled wine on my dress," you know? Anyway, they became so expensive that when they resell, they don't go to musicians. That's why I went along with the Komet amp thing, because I wanted to get amps down to a price where somebody could actually afford them.

And of course if a musician does get his hands on a Trainwreck, he'll probably be afraid to take it out and gig it, in case they spill beer on it or it gets stolen or something.

Yeah, that's the second thing I was going to say. I talk to a lot of guys who've got Trainwrecks from me, and I say, "Still using it?" And they say, "Oh, no no no! My old Strat, my old Les Paul … No, I take a Line 6 and an Ibanez to a club …" Something like that. "I wouldn't bring my '59 Les Paul and my Trainwreck to a club." So they're getting kind of reserved. Occasionally one gets on an album in the studio or something, but that's about it.

### That's kind of sad.

Yeah. That, to me, is negative. But that's the way it is with vintage guitars, or collectable amps. People are afraid to take it out. I like things to be out there making music. I sold an amp in 1998 to this one guy who was a great guitar player, and I sold it to him for $5,000 less than I could have got for it, just because he was going to play it out. I said, "If I sell you this amp, are you going to play it out?" He said, "Yeah." The other guy who was going to buy it was a lawyer. It was going to go into the music room in his mansion. He said, "I've got the room all soundproofed and I go in there and turn it up, and my wife doesn't complain." I thought I'd rather lose the

$5,000 and have the amp played out than have it sit in a room with one guy.

The other thing I used to do is I'd go to a club and hear one of the guys playing an amp of mine, and I'd hear maybe it needed output tubes or something. I'd say to the guy, "You know, that amp needs new output tubes." And he'd say, "Yeah, I know, but I just got married … I've got these expenses …" Yada yada, you know. Then the next time they were playing I'd go to the club and pop in a new set of tubes. He'd say, "I don't have the money for these." But I'd say, "It doesn't matter. It says "Trainwreck" on the amp. It's got to sound the best." You know? That's the way I've always felt about equipment. And like I said, I have to give Everette Hull a lot of credit. He made some mistakes, not embracing rock'n'roll and so forth, but I really did like his attitude for treating people fair. He always said, "You don't have to cheat people to make money."

### It would be nice to see a little bit more of that going on today.

Sure. You know, when people bought Trainwrecks they always had the privilege of trying it for two weeks. Originally I sold them to people who would come down here and buy them because they were local guys, and then when I had to start shipping them I'd tell them, "When the amp is ready, you send me the money for the amp plus the shipping and I'll send you the amp. In two weeks, give me a call and if you don't like the amp, send it back and I'll refund not only the price but the shipping both ways. I'll pay for everything, so you haven't lost a penny." Because I don't want anybody to ever say, "Oh, I had a Trainwreck and I didn't like it, and I lost $100 on shipping …" Or stuff like that. So that was my policy—but of course I never got an amp returned in 22 years.

Several years back I instituted a policy: any Trainwreck amp out there has a "triple-your-money-back" original purchase price guarantee. So if you've got a Trainwreck and you don't want it any more, send it back to me and I'll look up the original purchase price and refund it triple. Everybody cracks up on that, because I'm offering maybe $3,600 back for an amp that's worth $20,000. So I think I'm the only company in the world that's got a lifetime triple-your-money-back warrantee.

### So you're still waiting for one to come back, I guess.

Yeah, that would be nice. None have come back, but I've had people over the years ask me to give them an amp, for an endorsement deal or something, but I never did endorsements. I never gave away amps.

Me and Billy Gibbons were having it out once because he borrowed my amp just to use it, and it was supposed to come back to me, and I'd named it after my grandmother, Sarah, who had died. It was my personal Express amp. He used it for two weeks and he called and said, "I've got to have this amp." So I said I'd build him one just like it, take a couple of months. And he said, "No, you don't get it: this one. I collect amps. I know one sounds one way and the next will sound a little different. I've got 45 JTM45s down here and each one's different."

So we went back and forth for a while, because this one was named after my grandmother and all, and I consulted with my family. They said, "Well, Grandma liked music; if it's your amp it's just going to sit in the basement, but if Billy Gibbons uses it it's going to be on records and a lot of people are going to hear it." So I called him and said, "Yeah, you can have the amp." So the next day, by overnight FedEx, I got this check—not from his manager or his record label or someone—but a personal check with his personal address and everything.

**He didn't want to wait for his manager to pay up.**
No. He didn't want to lose that amp. But I've had a lot of interesting stuff with musicians. I used to know Jonny Z [Zazula], who was a big promoter on the East Coast, and just before *Ride The Lightning* he would bring Metallica down here and I'd work on their amps. They had these 50-watt Marshalls that were actually pretty terrible—one fawn one that was awful. Because they didn't have any money in those days, and they didn't have very good amps.

**Let's get inside the amps a little more. What were some of the design goals that contributed to making Trainwreck amps different?**
Ooh, there are a lot of them. One thing is that I stayed away from printed circuit boards. There are good-sounding PCB amps out there: in simple amps it doesn't seem to make that dramatic a difference. In fact when I worked at Ampeg, my favorite Ampeg was the B-15NF, which was the printed circuit version of the B-15. So it's not like I'm prejudiced against printed circuits in that way. But when you get amps with channel switching that get very complex and stuff like that, and they use printed circuits to make them sound consistent, to me it just sounds consistently bad, because everything is exactly on the same plane—even if you've got a dual-sided board and whatever—they get all inductively and capacitively coupled up and screwed up and whatever.

But all that goes even beyond what my basic philosophy is, and that is to keep it simple. The less components inside the amp that will do the job, the better the amp will sound. An analogy I used to make, back in the days when they used cassette tape, was if I made a copy of a tape, that's copy one, then dumped that onto another tape, now we've got copy two; then I take copy two and put that onto another cassette and that's copy three. Just keep going down the line like that, and by the time you get five or six times away from the original, what happens to the sound? It degrades, it gets noisy, detail goes away. Things just go missing, small subtle things will disappear.

Same thing with an amp. You're using capacitors, resistors, potentiometers, and the more you go through, they will do something—everything's got a loss factor associated with it. Every extra piece of wire you put in an amp's got a loss factor. So, for example, if you want to put a switch in to jump one value of capacitor across another to change the value, that works fine. But you've got to realize that even when that switch is open, you've got the two leads going out, they act as antennae, they act as this and that. So that's one of the things. Simplicity.

Another thing is actually selecting components for the way they sound, and wire for the way it sounds.

**You put a lot of thought even into wire selection?**
Yeah, a lot of thought, and a lot of experimenting. Will the solid core sound better than stranded wire? And if it does, is there a difference between thick-stranded and fine-stranded? Does it sound better with polyvinyl-chloride [PVC] insulation? Does it sound better with irradiated polyvinyl-chloride insulation? Teflon insulation? What brand of potentiometer, carbon-comp resistors, carbon film, metal film—what are their benefits, what are their pitfalls. And a resistor that's used in a power supply circuit will sound different than when it's used in a preamp circuit. Stuff like that. And especially, neatness in wiring counts. And wire has a polarity, which most people don't know. If you take a guitar cable and plug it into the amp one way, then you take it out and plug it in the other way, your guitar will sound different. Putting tube shields on and off will change the sound of the amp. The color of the insulation on the wire, the pigment they add to the covering material of the wire, can change the dielectric absorption of the wire. So these are like the microscopic points that I get into.

My friends say, "Hey, you're the detail man. You get into all the little points ..." And I say, "Yeah, but that's what I do."

**And I guess that makes the difference, too. It's easy enough for a tech to look at a schematic and build an amp, but the difference in quality must come with the details.**
Oh, there's a real classic example I use for that. Get a Clyde McCoy Wah-Wah, an early Vox wah like Hendrix or Clapton would use, and get a new Jim Dunlop CryBaby Wah-Wah. Every component value in the wahs and the schematic is completely identical. So why does the old Clyde McCoy Wah have a much more vocal sound than the new CryBaby? It's exactly the same schematic. So it's got to be in the details, in the components.

So I can take a schematic from any amp and just change some parts, and make it sound like a completely different amp.

**What has turned out to be your favorite wire?**
It depends on what I'm doing. Certain stuff works well in certain spots. On the Trainwreck amps it was solid-core with PVC insulation. Solid-core wire's fast, but non-irradiated PVC is slow. But I'm using such short pieces of wire—because I want to get a certain speed, or what they call "slew rate," and there are a number of ways of getting it, but wire's part of the sound. But because PVC-coated wire is like coating the wire with American cheese, when you solder it the insulation just falls away—that's a very very hard wire to work with. The irradiated PVC doesn't melt so fast, but the non-irradiated—which is the one I liked—most people can't work with it, because they don't have the soldering technique to get the wire to solder without melting the insulation.

So when I did the Komet amp for the guys in Baton Rouge, those guys wanted to use Teflon wire because with Teflon you can put a torch to it and it doesn't burn. But Teflon-coated wire is stranded, and to get the Teflon onto it they extrude it, and extruding Teflon will not work with copper, so either they nickel-plate it—which is very uncommon—or more usually most of your Teflon wire is silver-plated, which changes the sound again, because silver's a better conductor than copper. And there's the skin effect—because the silver's on the outside and high frequencies travel on the outside—with Teflon on top of it, which has a very low dielectric coefficient so it doesn't absorb stuff from the wire ... You can make a very shrill-sounding amp very quickly with Teflon wire, if you're not careful what you do with the rest of the circuit.

So they wanted to use Teflon wire, and I just made the amp so it would sound real good with Teflon wire. So Holger, who is one of the co-owners of Komet amplification, said, "I'm going to build one and I'm going to use the wire that you use," so I gave him the brand and the specs and colors I would use and whatever. He went to build one and I said, "It's going to sound awful. It's going to sound dark, it's not going to sound clear." He didn't believe me, because he was thinking of how a Trainwreck sounds clear and so forth.

He built it, listened to it, and said, "Yeah, you're right. This wire sounds awful on this amp." I said, "Yeah, I voiced the [Komet] amp using Teflon wire. I voiced my [Trainwreck] amp using the wire I was using."

I use aluminum chassis because they conduct better. I always see in guitar magazines where guys who aren't engineers are arguing whether aluminum really conducts better, or whether it's just myth. And they say, "Well, Marshall didn't use aluminum chassis for the JTM45 because it conducted better, they used it because it was easy to work with." Sure, but people who are using aluminum chassis today and getting them manufactured for them—like Dr Z amps, that are all aluminum chassis, Trainwrecks, and Komet amps—they're getting them cut on a laser machine, which will cut anything, so they're not using aluminum because it's "easy to work with." It could be aluminum, stainless steel, titanium, whatever. Doesn't matter whether it's "easy to work with."

The chassis goes to ground, and all ground currents eventually go back through the aluminum chassis. Iron steel or mild steel—as Fender was, and Marshall would be later on—that's a different chassis. What actually happens is, negative flows to positive, so actually all the currents first flow through the chassis, and they flow out of the chassis through the circuitry—through the power filters and then eventually back into the chassis. But the current actually comes out of the chassis, and the chassis is the main conductor in your amp. Aluminum conducts better than steel. Does that make it a better chassis?

Depends on what you are going for. If you're going for more fidelity and a faster response, yeah, you want aluminum because it's a better conductor. If you're going for a traditional sound, Fender never used aluminum, they always used steel, so if you are going to make yourself an amp and you want it to sound like a Fender, by all means use the steel chassis. It's not like one's better than the other in an absolute respect, it's a matter of whether it's better for what you want it to do.

And there are a lot of things I've found that I just don't think work for anything. Like metal-film resistors—I've never heard an amp with metal-film resistors that didn't sound harsh. A lot of guys will say, "But they make

the lowest noise." Oh, absolutely, they're far lower-noise. Carbon film is lower-noise than carbon comp, but metal film is way lower noise than either one of those two. Yeah, you can get less noise, but you won't get as good a guitar tone. That happens also with a lot of the really high-end audiophile caps. The guy makes himself a guitar amp, and it really sounds like it should be used for acoustic guitar or stereo, rather than electric guitar.

And the circuit board you make it on ... you could make it out of phenolic like some of the old Marshalls, fiberglass, Alexander Dumble has made a lot of circuit boards out of wood, and he likes the sound he gets out of a piece of, say, rosewood for a circuit board. And that's valid too.

But my amp is ... keep it simple. And for the high-gain amps, the one with a really high-gain response, like the Express or the Liverpool, it's "keep it near the point of instability." There's another analogy I can use here: what makes an F-16 or one of these really high-performance jet fighters able to turn so fast and be able to do all these wacky maneuvers and stuff? They're basically unstable and if they didn't have a computer onboard to help, the pilot wouldn't even be able to fly the plane. It's the instability that let's the plane, in a fraction of a second, roll 180 degrees and make a 90-degree turn at the same time. When you go into planes like a 747 where you want stability, because you don't want some jerky movements there, you make the plane very, very stable. If the pilot has a heart attack, even it it's not on autopilot, it will fly for miles before anyone realizes it. But if you do want to turn it, it'll take you two-and-a-half miles to do so.

### Your amps are more akin to the hair trigger.
The hair trigger on those jet fighters, yeah. And when you start getting complex harmonics, that's what you need to make an amp sound complex. The more stable an amp becomes, the less complex it is. If you're actually going by the audiophile definition, the amp should be "transparent." Which means whatever you put into the amp is exactly what should come out, nothing more, nothing less, only louder. But a guitar amplifier not only amplifies, it's a tone generator.

If you want to plug in a guitar and it has this and this harmonic, but you want more harmonics in your sound than the guitar itself has, you've got to generate them in the amplifier. Or in some cases, you have harmonics that are coming out of the guitar, but the guitar amplifier isn't quick enough to capture them and reproduce them. With a guitar amp, you want to capture all those harmonics, plus add to them, and that's what makes a great sound.

Hi-fi guys have a term for that: "euphonic." They say, "OK, it's a euphonic amp, but it's not accurate." A lot of hi-fi guys would not want the amp to change the tone, so a guitar amp is a completely different type of audio amp; all other audio amplifiers are designed to keep distortion down and just reproduce what's there.

One of the problems with all of this stuff in modern times is that, with solid-state amps being used most, a lot of the best brands of components—resistors, capacitors, tube sockets, potentiometers, and whatever—have gone by the wayside, and you've got to use whatever is available and make it work the best you can. And the tubes are the same thing. Everybody knows that if you put "new old stock" tubes in the amp it will sound better than with any of these Chinese or Russian-made tubes.

### Do you have a favorite preamp tube of all time?

That depends on the amp. Telefunken made a great 12AX7, but they made a smooth plate and they made a ridged plate, or waffle plate. Fender amps tend to like the smooth plate. Trainwreck amps really don't like either one in the first position. The Komet 60 amp that I designed likes the ridged plate, but the Komet 80 likes both the ridged plate and the smooth plate.

Then you've got Mullard from England, their tubes were always changing. They made a long-plate version early on, then they made a short-plate version. What most people really don't know is, most of the 5AR4s you ever see out of Europe are all the same. If it says Amperex Bugle Boy, Mullard, Telefunken—maroon base, large black base, small black base, brown base—they were all made in the same place. It's interesting to me because people will come to me and say, "I want a Telefunken with a metal-banded base, because that's rare." And I say, "OK, you're going to have to pay me this much for it versus this much ..." But it's the same tube. That base didn't make the difference, the only difference was on the plates inside: the ones with the straight edge on the side of the plate, the ones with four notches on the side of the plate, and the ones with seven notches. Those were the only three variations they made. The bottoms varied a lot, but for the actual internal guts, there's only three variations.

### Where were they made?

They were made by Mullard, in Britain. When they have the Mullard codes etched in the glass, that's how you know who made them.

### Are there any components that you hear being talked about in tube amp circles these days that are perhaps over-hyped?

Well, people get very hyped up about transformers. They'll say, "This transformer's the sound of this amp, this one's the sound of that amp ..." and whatever. And that is true to an extent, because you have different core materials used in different transformers at different times and different winds, a certain thing that makes a Marshall sound like a Marshall—which was their propriety, they know it and I know it, but I don't give it out because I don't want to help people clone other people's amps, you know?—but sometimes people get too twisted up on that. I can take an average-sounding transformer and make a great-sounding amp out of it. The output transformer is more critical, but the power transformer makes a difference, the choke makes a difference, all the iron on the amp makes a difference.

Or you can take a really great transformer and use it wrong, and get a bad-sounding amp. There was a magazine article about why, if the JTM45 was copied from the Fender Bassman, did it sound different. And one of the differences was the output transformer. So one guy said, "I took a Marshall output transformer and put it on my Fender amp, and it still sounded like a Fender amp, so it couldn't be that." Of course he was using a blackface Fender, not a tweed Bassman. It's completely different, though, because if you take the output transformer out of your Fender and put it on a Marshall, it'll definitely sound different. That's just not a proper way to judge anything. It's like, if you can put the same size tire on two cars and say, "It still feels like the same car." There's other things involved, you know?

The RS transformer that they used on the original Marshall had different primary impedances than the Fender transformers used on the four-ten Bassman. Fender had an M-17 core, which is a lower grade of metal, compared to the M-6 core which was a very good transformer used in hi-fi, with grain-oriented steel and so forth. And the first Marshall amps were M-6 cored transformers. Vox used two cores, they used M-50 and M-40—they used two grades, because Vox used 13 different transformer companies over the years. They got their transformers wherever they could. Albion was of course the best one they ever used. But the M-50 and M-40 was a very low grade of core.

So transformers get to be a big, big issue with these guys. They say, "If I get an output transformer like Jim uses, my amp will sound like Jim's amp." No. I used to change Trainwreck output transformers all the time, because I'd like to experiment and stuff. It's part of the sound, but it's not as critical as people make it out to be. They're always searching for the magic bullet, and actually it's the culmination of a lot of different things. I used several different transformer companies, and several different core materials. I'd just give the company the spec and then I'd build the amp, and if I didn't like the sound of the transformer I didn't use them. So Trainwrecks are floating around out there with a lot of different output transformers, and when I first started building them and it wasn't going to be my vocation or whatever, I was just using off-the-shelf transformers, like Marshall did at first.

Then in 1989 the company that was making the off-the-shelf transformers I was using most often, but not exclusively—StanCore, Chicago Standard Transformer—stopped making those transformers, so I bought up all they had left of those to get me through a year with a few spares. Then in 1990 I had about six to eight prototypes from different companies and chose one of those off the bat, so the first amp in 1990 had a transformer from another company, and that was custom-built to my specs—power output, the whole works. But since 1990 I might have used ten, 12 different transformer companies here and there. What matters is how I spec them, how I design the transformers to go with my amps.

### Do you have to guard those specs pretty carefully?

Well, yeah, some guys do try to get a hold of them sometimes. One guy out in the Midwest was making transformers for Trainwreck amps, but then I had them revise the output transformers and make a few that were really high-end, with M-6 cores and so forth, for some 40-watt hi-fi amps I was making. Then when the old guy died the sons got the company, but they weren't really engineers like their old man. To make some money, they advertised that they had made transformers for all these different companies, and one name they mentioned was Trainwreck, so guys were calling up and saying, "I want those Trainwreck transformers." But since the sons didn't know what specs they were looking at, they made up the transformers from the latest revision, which was for the hi-fi amps.

These guys were getting their transformers and saying, "Are you sure these are the output transformers Ken Fischer uses, because they really don't sound right ..." So that's what happened there.

Another thing that happened to me was, another of my transformer manufacturers had a new sales guy, and this company Two Rock called up and said they wanted 50 of my Trainwreck output transformers. Normally there's a proprietary number on a custom-spec transformer and the company will only provide them to the guy that originally ordered them, but this guy thought they had my permission and whatever, so he sent them 50 of my transformers. When the owner of the transformer company found out he called them up and said, "That was a proprietary design," and he notified me that they already had those 50.

Well, they had a guy who had a Trainwreck, and they opened it up and copied it, and put those transformers on, and they were saying it sounded even better than the real thing and all of that. Then a guy who bought one brought it down to me because he wanted to compare it to the real thing, and you know, it sounded nothing like one of my amps at all. Not even close. It was a horrible-sounding amp. The transformer didn't help them at all. I got to hear two or three more of their amps and they weren't any better, and then they came out with a Dumble copy. You know... guys who have talent, they design their own amps.

**It all seems to come down to the fact that, if you don't design the amp with every component in mind, and fine-tune it for those specific parts, it's still going to sound like a different amp.**

Right. Exactly. They were using a brand of power filters that I would never have used, and they were using some Formica kitchen-counter board for circuit board. That's really whack, because this stuff is designed for kitchen-counter tops, it's not designed for characteristics of how it handles electricity, particularly when it's handling high voltages. But that's the way it goes.

My own basic principle is still "keep it simple." When techs see inside a Trainwreck for the first time, they say, "There's nothing in here ..." I say, "That's right." I'm not putting down anybody else's amps, because I'm not into that, but when I see triple and four-channel amps, how could they possibly sound good with all that circuitry and all that switching? And when I did switching, by the way—because I did that with modifications to people's amps even though I never did it in Trainwreck amps—I always used relay switching because those LDRs (light-dependent resistors) and other switching devices, they really extract a big toll on the tone.

People say the trouble with relay switching is that it's noisy, you can't switch back and forth without getting a pop in the speaker. But I'd make channel-switching amps for people out of Fenders and whatever, and they'd make no noise in the speaker at all. If you put your head against the chassis you'd hear the relay clicking inside, but you wouldn't hear any other noise other than that. A lot of times I'd use dual relays that were timed, and I'd cut the circuit at one point a hundredth of a second different than at another point, and that prevents the pop. It's just a matter of timing the relays.

### Again, it's in the details.

Yeah. I'll give you some more details. Like, when I was designing the Komet amp, Holger wanted it with a Fender jewel-type pilot light, which can burn out or is subject to jolts and mechanical shocks and whatever. I'd always used a neon pilot lamp in Trainwrecks that had a 50,000-hour lifespan. But he said, "Well, I like the Fender-type jewel, because people can screw it out and put in a different color or ..." You know, so, fine. Another thing, I always like the Switchcraft jacks better than the plastic Cliff jacks from England, because I get much better reliability with the Switchcrafts. Holger likes the plastic jacks so we've got Cliff jacks in the Komet, but I find after a while when you pull the cord out of the input you get crackling noises, because in the Cliff jacks the shorting pin doesn't make a good contact. Then you have to open up the amp and clean it all up. That never happens with the Switchcraft jacks.

So you can compromise an amp in that way, too. Although in other areas we didn't compromise and we went way overboard, like using ceramic tube sockets with 24-carat gold-plated pins, audiophile grade sockets made in Japan. We're using custom-made 2-watt potentiometers with the tapers that we want, and airplane-grade aluminum for the chassis, so it's just as strong as a steel chassis—and we're not even saving any weight on the chassis, because it's so thick. It's a great chassis, it's all laser-cut, and it's powder-coated on top of that. They're very nicely made amps, but those are two little compromises that I wouldn't have made.

### Are there any other amps around today that you admire?

Most of the amps are copies. Like, I could say, this guy does a good copy of a Marshall or that guy does ... Well, I think Victoria does a good copy of an original Fender tweed, even better than the Fender Reissues that they have out. But I admire people much more when they have designed their own amp, even if they're out of business now. Like Jim Kelley, he designed his own amp. As far as what I would call really elegant engineering, I'd have to say Dumble. I have to preface this by saying that Dumbles can be inconsistent. When Dumble decides he's going to make an amp for an artist and do it well, then you get all top-notch components, and when you get a Dumble that's done right, there's nothing out there like it. None of the guys who have ever copied Dumble amps have ever copied a good-sounding Dumble. The thing is, Dumble had amps that he just threw together and sent to Kitty Hawk in Germany for the European market, and they stink. But when you get a really good Dumble ... It's a completely different amp than mine, but they do what they do, and my amps do what they do.

I've never spoken to Alexander Dumble, but I speak to his friends and he speaks to my friends, and I know he would never copy a Trainwreck, just like I'd never copy a Dumble. I'm probably the only guy on the planet who could make a Dumble that would sound like a Dumble, and he's probably the only guy who could make a Trainwreck that would sound like a Trainwreck, but we're not going to do it. There's that respect.

When I worked at Ampeg in the 1960s there was that kind of thing going on. Leo Fender owned Fender until 1965, and Everette Hull owned Ampeg until a little past 1965. Fender was selling a lot of amps, but we had Ampeg, and from Everette Hull on down, we said, "We're not going to make a copy of a Fender amp, because we're Ampeg." And I knew people who worked at Fender, and they said Leo would never make an Ampeg copy, even though he knew the [Ampeg] B-15 was a better bass amp than anything he had. He had too much pride. Same thing with Dave Reeves and Harry Joyce from Hiwatt and all those British guys. Hiwatt was not going to make a Marshall clone, and Marshall was not going to make a Vox clone.

Today, I think what's basically happened—and there are good and bad sides to this—is that there's 18,000 guys out there making a Marshall copy or a Fender copy, and now it's really popular to make Trainwreck and Dumble copies, because that's what sells for the most. The bad thing is, there are a lot of lousy clones out there that don't sound anything like the original amps. The good thing it is that they all need parts and tubes, so they keep the demand up. If it wasn't for these little boutique companies, I think all the major amp makers would just love to go all solid state and be done with the big transformers and stuff. And it keeps the interest in classic amps alive. The bad stuff is, I don't see any innovation.

When a guy is copying an old tweed Fender and thinks he's copying 1950s technology, which was actually licensed by Fender from Western Electric—it's technology that's really from the 1930s and 1940s. This is 2005; you should be able to come up with something new already. I come up with new stuff all the time. I designed the Liverpool and the Express and so forth, and people ask me, "If you were building amps today, would you build the same amp?" And I say, "No." For one thing, they were designed back in the day when you had really good tubes, and they don't sound good unless you keep really good tubes in them. Also, they don't work with modern speakers, they work with speakers that were available in the old days. The Komet would be an example of an amp that's a good-sounding design, but it was designed around components that are available now.

Mike Matthews over at New Sensor is a friend of mine, and he'd just had some new tubes come in from Russia when I designed that amp, and the preamp of that Komet is actually designed around the long-plate spiral 12AX7. So that amp sounds good with Russian long-plate spirals, the Winged-C Svetlanas made in St Petersburg. That's all you ever have to put in those amps to keep them sounding good. The thing is, if you put new-old-stock tubes in those amps, do they improve? Yeah, they do. But it'll run and sound good with the Svetlana tubes. When Aerosmith used their Komet on their album, they were using the stock Russian tubes. When Bon Jovi did the Bounce album with the two first Komets they had, they were stock tubes, just the way they came from the factory.

The thing is, people don't know how to do tube curves when these new tubes first come out—draw the load lines, and figure out what's going to make the tubes sound good and be linear. Probably what I'm trying to say is, guys aren't learning electronics, they're copying. Do they actually know what's making this amp work? No. They're just copying the circuit.

**And when you can't get the same parts any more that the originals used, the amp's going to sound different anyway.**
Yeah. But we can compensate for that. In five years of production of Komet amps now, we've already gone through a lot of different suppliers as one type of electrolytic cap gets discontinued, or we've gone through three different makes of resistors, the 2-watt pots got discontinued so we went up to Precision Electronic Components in Canada and had 2-watt pots made to the old Allen-Bradley specs of molded hot-carbon composition tracks and stuff with stainless steel backs and metal shafts. We don't use any Taiwan controls. All the hardware on the chassis is stainless steel with lock nuts, so we do stuff like that and, yeah, the output selector we were using, which we loved, was made by Ohmite, an 1,875-watt rating for a 60-watt amp. Would you ever kill that output selector switch? Never. Bush passes his tax cut, Ohmite moves to Mexico, and the Mexicans don't know how to cook Bakelite at the right temperature. We get the Ohmite switches from Mexico with the Bakelite body, put it on the back, and as you tighten the nut the Bakelite falls apart, it just crumbles.

**Nightmare.**
Yeah, so now we had to find a new switch. There's always something, and the people who were making these types of controls and switches aren't making them any more, because high-voltage electronics is becoming obsolete. In the old days that wasn't the case. When I worked at Ampeg, the same parts we used in the 1950s we were getting in the 1960s. They were American parts companies, and they didn't change. These days, one day they're made in the United States, the next day they're made in China.

Like Celestion, good old British speaker company, now made in China. When they first started coming over, people were saying, "Well, these sound pretty good." But of course they were shipping all the cones over from England. What's going to happen when those are used up? They're not going to keep shipping materials back and forth, they're going to make cones in China, so we'll have to see how they sound then.

Now since Bush has been in power the US dollar has just been going down, down, down. So what the Chinese and Russian tube makers are doing is, so they can still sell them to the US for the same profit, of course they're just going to be making the tubes cheaper. Because we're not going to pay double the price for the tube. And these countries don't care, because it's not even a big part of their industry any more.

*I guess we'll see a constant decline in those areas, because there's never going to be a market that will keep a large manufacturer afloat.*
Nope. It's getting that way. I didn't think tube amps would last this long. It's reaching a point now, with Bush in here for four more years, I think we're going to end up with the economy so bad that it's going to be a frightening thing.

*Let's look at a more cheerful subject. Can you recommend any "best buys" in used amps for the readers?*
There are amps out there that are bargains, but some of them are not bargains the way that they came from the factory—but with 20 minutes of working with it you can make it a great-sounding amp. I just recommended one a short while ago to Mark Knopfler: a Selmer Constellation 20. An early 1970s Selmer, printed circuit board, two EL84s, two channels, volume, bass, treble, two Goodmans 12″ speakers. Don't worry about it being a printed circuit; if you're into the Pete Townshend sound, this is the Townshend sound at a volume level you can actually use. It's the loudest you'll ever get two EL84s to sound. That's a great sleeper amp.

Sometimes you don't like the amp itself, but you can strip it out and make it into something else. Like a Sound City, they had good transformers. Or if somebody's going to sell you a Sound City half-stack for $500 you'd be crazy not to buy it, because the pre-Rola [pre-1970] Celestion 30 speakers in that cabinet are worth $350 a piece. Stuff that Ampeg made, even, like the R12-R Reverberocket that used 6V6 output tubes and all octals in the preamp: that was Everette Hull's one effort to make an amp a little bit more Fendery.

You've got to keep in mind that Everette Hull hated rock'n'roll, he hated distortion—even when the blues guys would play distortion. Amps were not to be distorted. So those R12-Rs had blue Jensens in them, 6SN7 and 6SL7 octals, which are always nice, fat-sounding tubes. That amp would be a great indie-rock machine. Ampeg made it for a short while and all the jazz guys were complaining, "What's wrong with the new Reverberockets? They break up too early." So Everette Hull converted them back to 7591 [output tubes] because people were complaining. But if they had marketed them as a rock'n'roll amp they probably would have been very successful.

*And when you see one of those for sale, it's usually going pretty cheap.*
Oh, yeah, they're not that much, and they are great little amps. They are absolutely a better amp than an 18-watt Marshall, and those have been bringing in like $6,000. You could get an Ampeg R12-R Reverberocket for $600 or less, and it's a great-sounding amp. Things get crazy. The 18-watt Marshall is a cool little amp, but soundwise it's not anything near a $6,000 amp. They're a good-sounding little amp, sure, but there aren't that many of them, so all of a sudden people decided to make them a $6,000 amp.

And what about a Vox AC10? Why isn't a Vox AC10 that expensive an amp? A lot of them had Albion [transformers] on them, but the thing that was bad on

them was they had crappy speakers. You put a good pair of speakers in there, and they are great-sounding amps. They are at least as good as an 18-watt Marshall combo. There are also a lot of Gibsons that were OK—and mostly I hate Gibson amps, although the early GA-40 was a good-sounding amp. But there was a model a little later that had that little fixed-network tone filter; I'd just clip those out and put in a jumper, and the tone quality increases by a factor of three. Suddenly it's a pretty good-sounding amp. The thing looks like one big ceramic disc cap with four leads coming out of it. Pull them out, and the amp sounds great.

Then there are a lot of amps from Valco that were pretty good, or the Harmony 415—particleboard cabinet, but it does come with two Jensen C12Rs. It came from the factory with two Mullard EL84s, and just plugging straight in it doesn't sound like that much, but plug an overdrive into it and it's a killer-sounding amp. And the Jensens they used in there were painted black, so people don't recognize them as Jensens. And that's an amp that's selling for $75 or $100, maybe $150.

An overdrive I actually like a lot is the Menatone Blue Collar. Put that into the Harmony and it sounds great. I had a Marshall 18-watt combo down here that I was working on for a friend, and we put a guitar straight into the Marshall, then into the Harmony combo through that Menatone pedal, and it just devastated the Marshall. So there you've got $300-worth of amp and pedal killing that $6,000 Marshall. We put the overdrive into the Marshall and it sounded fine, but it still didn't sound as good as it did with the Harmony. So there you go.

*Are you still designing circuits?*
Oh, sure. I'm designing amps all the time … Just little amps to play for myself, or amps I'll end up giving away to friends or whatever. What I always liked about electronics, and about amp design, was the innovation. I still enjoy finding that little thing in a circuit that just makes the difference. Like, back when I went to school at RCA the guy always told us to be creative: "Don't just follow the book." It's like, there's guys who can write songs, and there's guys who can't write songs—it's the same with electronics. I come up with clever little ideas all the time, and I have a little logbook where I log all these ideas. I have a little circuit where you can change the bias on a cathode-biased amp without even changing the cathode resistor; I have over 100 master volumes for amps … all kinds of things. I like inventing stuff.

*Do you think you'll ever publish all your own circuits?*
I don't know. I've got a lot of things that might help a lot of guys out, but at the same time I don't like to reward amp builders who aren't coming up with their own ideas, who just want to copy stuff. Guys will call me up and ask for stuff, and a lot of times I'll help them out if I know what they're going to do with them, and they'll respect what I give them. Like Dr Z, I've told him some of my ideas and he has built some things from circuits I've given him. Like a little amp I designed called a Dirty Little Monster, a single-ended amp, and Joe Walsh wanted a couple of those for recording. Joe Walsh has been using

two Dirty Little Monsters, and Dr Z built them from my circuits. But when Dr Z came out with his own single-ended amp it was different, a single EL84 at 4 watts, so I know I can trust the guy and give him something, and

he's not just going to call it his own. He does very original designs himself, and that's why we get along so well. And the other thing is, he's actually an engineer. He knows what he's doing…

# Michael Zaite of Dr Z Amps

**Michael Zaite founded Dr Z amps in 1988. Based in Maple Heights, Ohio, just outside of Cleveland, the company has grown to be one of the world's biggest manufacturers of hand-wired tube guitar amps. Dr Z amps are known for their simplicity, originality, and quality of construction.**

### What got you interested in amplifiers in the first place?

My dad was a TV repairman in the mid-1950s. I'm 53 years old, so in the 50s [as a child] the basement of my parent's house was kind of like my workshop. There were tubes everywhere, so I grew up around all of that. I certainly had an interest in electronics and my dad was always very helpful with it, so it came very easy to me. I went on to get a degree in electronics, but unfortunately in the 1970s when I went to school they didn't teach tubes. It was kinda like one page in a book, then, "Let's move on to transistors…" But fortunately I had a background in it.

### Were you playing the guitar already yourself?

Actually I was a drummer. My parents were always pretty good about having practice at my house—if you remember those days of basement bands from when you were a teenager—and the guys would leave their gear at my house. Oh boy, I did some unauthorized modifications, I can tell you that, to quite a few old Fenders and Silvertones and whatever was left at my house.

So I started learning like that. Then I worked in medical electronics for quite a few years, doing sophisticated stuff. But I always liked amps and started to do some repairs for a lot of friends that were blues players here in the Cleveland area. And you know how those blues players are; they had some great old vintage amps, so I worked on old Marshalls and old tweed Fenders. Just retubing them and setting the bias. Nothing special. But I certainly got amazed by the tones and the sounds of these rich-sounding amps. I got to thinking, "This ain't so tough. I think I could build something like this."

### When did you build your first amps?

It was around 1988/89—that was when I started prototyping amps. Then I got one into the hands of Joe Walsh. He went to college here in the Cleveland area—I'd known Joe for many years. We'd passed each other in certain situations, and I knew his manager real well, David Spero. I told David I had an amp that I thought Joe would really like, and he said, "Well bring it to me, I'll give it to him."

This was when the Hell Freezes Over tour was getting together. Joe was going to use some AC30s, and he actually did use a couple of them on the *MTV Unplugged* Eagles show prior to the tour, because they did an electric tune or two at the end. And one of those AC30s went up in smoke, which they were notorious for doing. You know, they're an English amp so they can be pretty unreliable, but when they work they can sound incredible. So, I knew Joe's tech and I got a call from him, and he said, "You know, Z, Joe brought in that amp you made and he was carrying it in his arms like it was a baby. He said, "A friend of mine made this for me, and I want to use this on the tour.'" And the rest was history. David called me, and I had to get another rig set up to use as a backup on the tour.

Financially, it didn't do a whole lot for me, because with tickets being $185 a seat for the Eagles show, I went to about six or seven of the shows … Most of the people there had multiple pagers and cell phones on and whatever—they weren't guitar players, is the point I'm trying to make. So it didn't do anything but make me feel in my heart that it could work. I said, "I think I've got something here." With that in mind I kept working and developing.

### It seems like by the late 1990s you had developed a pretty solid reputation.

Sure. I'm going into my 17th year now, so it does take some time. And I kind of like the slow growth that I've had, because the way I've modeled and run my business has as much to do with the success I've had as my electronic chops. I mean, I'm OK, I'd learned this stuff so early on that it seems almost second nature to me. It doesn't seem that amazing.

Well, one of the things I appreciate a lot about your amps—and I believe other players appreciate—is that there's a lot of simplicity there, from all angles. It's clear from the control layouts that you're aiming for simplicity, and the circuits themselves are very uncomplicated too. A lot of players have come to realize that can contribute to a great sound.

I think the less that's in-line, the better an amp can sound. And that's one thing I learned early on with the Eagles tour. Joe had 22 guitar changes during the two-set

Hell Freezes Over show. And Joe didn't need to be going back and tweaking his amp between each one, so you've got to have a base amp that will allow a Tele to sound like a Tele, and a Rick to sound like a Rick, a Les Paul to sound like a Les Paul. Not over-process the sound, but just give a nice, broad bandwidth and let the player's fingers be the manager. Just amplify it. Make something that's reliable, and simple, and bring it in at a great price.

That's my basic principle. There have certainly been some people that have meteorically risen in this industry—with this neat little thing or that neat little thing—but they sort of pigeonhole themselves a little bit, with this type of sound or that type of sound, or going toward one type of musician. One thing that really expanded my business was when country players started playing my stuff.

**Sure. I noticed that Brad Paisley has been using your amps ... And that's not commonly a "boutique amp" market.**
No, it's not. A lot of guys that I talk to in this industry don't even try to pursue that area, and I say, "That's fine, leave it for me. I'll fill it." It's funny, because country players today are a little different. They're not playing Peaveys any more. They're going for a more modern kind of tone, and they like to experiment, too. And man, they're great players—and they like to buy stuff. They're not like a blues player who's got this old Fender that they've had forever and that's all they need. So that's really opened up for me. Boy, there are pockets in the United States where there are really, really big fans of that music. They're the NASCAR fans of the world. You go there, and they really listen, and they support their artists…

**And the players you're talking about are obviously excited about making some really good sounds.**
Right. They certainly are.

**Along with the simplicity, are there any other design principles that you live by?**
I kind of brought with me into my designs some background in medical electronics. I was a General Electric engineer and, as un-fancy a subject as it might be, I certainly put a lot of work into my chassis designs. I use 90-thousandths aluminum chassis. I chromate dip them for increased conductivity. And it really does make a very breathable, alive base for the amp to be built on. It's a very good grounding platform.

One thing with doing CT scanners or MRI scanners, a lot of time patients are on some type of life support system or respirator or whatever while they're being scanned, so there can't be any ground currents, you know? You can't zap somebody while you're trying to take a picture of them. So that's always been something that was rooted in my thinking, something that I learned from medical electronics.

And another little thing that I think helps my amps is capacitors—the coupling caps. The company that makes the old Orange Drops now, SBE, they're way out in Maine somewhere, and what I ended up doing was formulating an older-style cap that was no longer in production, as they moved on to faster and more powerful caps. I kind of liked the sound of an older-style cap that they made, so I had them build them for me in large lots. So that eliminated deviation from amp to amp, because these caps were all built the same day, and they all had extremely tight tolerances on them. I didn't have to say, "Why does this one sound a little different? It's a little brighter, it's darker, it's a little harsher …" You know. That kind of took one of the variables out of the scheme.

**That certainly is a variable with some other hand-wired amps, if they don't have a consistency of components.**
Sure. And sometimes that's something that works for you, but often it works against you.

**What type of signal caps are those?**
Actually they are the old 417 caps, and they're polyester. They're not polypropylene like the newer chemical designs of the foil-type caps are. To me they sound a little bit more like the old banana-yellow Astrons that sound so wonderful in amps. Those were old wax-impregnated caps, and they're kinda highly carcinogenic to build, so they no longer make those. But there's a little more warmth, and a little more subtlety to the sound of these polyesters. They're not quite as immediate. Some of the polypropylenes, to me, are just a little too transient. That adds to a little ear fatigue, it adds to a little harsher response, where these polyesters are a little more round, a little smoother, a little slower, and I just found that I could work with that, incorporating it into the rack of my designs.

Because that's a very critical component. All you've got is resistors, capacitors, and pots. Tubes of course, but on the inside of the amp, those are the three major components. That's what's doing the rolling off, or letting pass, and proceeding the signal on to the next stage.

**Any other types of components you believe highly in?**
I do use carbon films. I just find them to be a little bit on the warmer side, and there's a lot of "shot noise" in the old carbon comp resistors that are in the older Fenders that guys swear by. But I don't know, I just don't like that much baseline shot noise.

The old carbon comps are nice, you know, the old Allen-Bradley and stuff like that [the Allen-Bradley company invented the carbon comp resistor in 1935], and a lot of people use them. But there is an element of shot noise … There's little holes inside of them, that's part of the carbon composition, and you hear what they call shot noise, or white noise, that little "ssshhh" kind of sound. When they're attached to a plate, that gets amplified. It's really only affected in high-voltage circuits, or plate circuits, where you've got 200 or 300 volts across them. They're not as bad as cathode resistors or any kind of voltage divider; where you just have AC signal you're not going to have that [shot noise].

I know some people talk about them being most effective in high-voltage positions because that's where they have the potential to distort, and to contribute some warmth to the circuit... But at the same time that's going to be noisier too, isn't it?

It seemed that way to me. I was generally building a little bit more modern of a design, so I didn't have to worry about trying to eke as much gain as I could out of a "Betty Crocker" [standard] design—a tweed Bassman or Marshall 50-watt, where a lot of these guys took their beginnings. I basically take a clean sheet of paper and design an amp, from input to output. Of course I look at the history, I look at the old stuff. I read—just like an artist goes to an art museum—to see how the old masters did it, but I certainly try not to be influenced by that, or have it affect me in my designs.

Having some sort of an original sound certainly has made my growth a little slower, because at the beginning of the boutique market, everyone was asking, "Does it sound like a Vox? Does it sound like a Fender? Does it sound like a Marshall?" Everyone kind of wants to hear something that they're used to hearing or that they want to hear. And I would say, "Well, it's got a little bit of all of those in there, but it's a Z amp."

*It's gotten to the point now where every guy and his brother can build a tweed Deluxe-type amp, and I can't count the people selling you Bassman clones, so hopefully having a more original direction would keep you in there for the long-haul.*

Right. And you saw the ebb and the flow of that as the pendulum swung to different styles. There were people doing the tweed reproductions, and doing it very, very nicely ...

*Sure. Victoria and so forth ...*

Exactly. And then it kinda went into the Voxy thing, and it seems to be in a Marshall phase right now. But you're always fighting that ghost. And that's something I would not want to do: the ghost of Leo Fender, you know? It's like, no matter how good it is, some guy is going to drag in some dog-eared Bassman and it's going to smoke that amp. Those old Jensen speakers, the way everything has been played for years—it's like an old guitar. It just resonates, it has a sound. Something new is going to be tight, it's going to be a little more constipated in its tone, and that magic is just not going to be there.

*Are there any components that you feel are over-hyped?*

A lot of guys seem to be using these really high-end caps, Solens or whatever. To me, where I draw the line is that I want to build an instrument, I don't want to build and amplifier that's like a stereo—a high-fidelity type of amp. I still want to build an instrument, something with a little character to it. And I find that when these guys start using gold chassis and pure oxygen[-free] wire and all these really expensive resistors and really expensive capacitors, the more they spend, the worse they sound, to my ear. You're not making an amp to reproduce prerecorded music, you're making an instrument to make music. I find that some of the little warts and quirks, some of the lesser components, when married together correctly give a better output.

*That's the magic, isn't it? And that's why guitars sound great. Leo didn't build a Bassman to go to 12, really, he built it to sound good and clean at around 5; part of the magic is what comes in when you go past 5 and those warts and quirks come out, as you put it.*

Right, exactly. But also, Dave, I don't want to appear to be dissing anyone. I take my hat off to anybody that does the same thing that I do, because it's not easy. They do what they do, and there is a group of people who are kind of enthralled by that, and they like that high-end thing. They buy high-end this and high-end that, and they're impressed with that and want to spend their money with that, and that's of value to them, so that's great ...

*And as ever, part of the beauty of music is its diversity. These high-end amps work great for some people, and they make beautiful music with them.*

Yeah. Great. I like to paint with a little bit broader brush, and try to suit my equipment to the wider base of musicians that are available. I've got 13 or 14 models in my line now.

*I have been impressed by how the Dr Z line has grown. Is there any amp that you are proudest of?*

I don't know ... maybe the little Carmen Ghia, that was the first amp I ever sold in any numbers, and I still sell those in incredible numbers. I've made thousands of them in my years.

*It's a very affordable amp.*

Yeah, and I've kind of kept it that way. And it's really unique—there's not another amp that has circuitry similar to that, I must admit. It does use some kind of awkward designs, or different designs if you want to call them that. But it's a nice little two-knob amp, and if you get a guy who can play, that's all he needs.

*Players who really use the dynamics of an amp seem to be the ones who appreciate simpler amps.*

Right. Set the tone control to where it sounds nice with your guitar, set the volume to however loud you want it to be, turn around, close your eyes, and just play. And not worry about "where's my midrange set, do I have my fat boost out, do I have my treble up..." The worst thing for me is when I see a guitar player up on stage and he's fuddling around with his amp every song, twisting this and turning that. Man, just get into the music. Who cares! It doesn't matter if you make a mistake or you do this or do that, it's the spontaneity of the music that matters and not the clarity and fidelity of what you're trying to reproduce.

*Of other people's amps that you have run into in the past, is there anything that comes to mind as a hidden gem?*

Probably one of the greatest amps—the pawnshop prize—is the old Gibson GA-40. It's the old Les Paul amp, and it was made through a lot of years. But some of the earlier ones, the ones that were done in tweed, they had a Jensen in there and they kind of went against the tweed Fender Deluxes, and I'll tell you what: they go from a crystalline clean to an almost Marshall-like bark. You can pick them up from time to time, and I really look out for those. I've done a lot of work and service on them, and that's one little gem.

**Gibson made some great amps early on, although they went through some strange phases over the years.**

Yes they did. But they made lots of those, and they can be found now. They're pretty nice.

**I find that Dr Z amps are not only very original as a line, but there's a lot of originality from one model to another. The Carmen Ghia is one kind of amp, then the Route 66 and its smaller brother, the Z-28 ... those are very different amps again. That little Z-28, with only three knobs, has an amazing range of sounds to it ...**

Yeah, it's so sweet. The thing that forced me into that design was those tubes—the Electro-Harmonix 6V6. I got some of those, and I said, "Man, these are some sweet-sounding tubes, I've got to incorporate these into a design." They're readily available—which good 6V6s weren't for a while—and they're very inexpensive, and boy, they're pretty rugged. And I really like the way they sound. They captured a pretty nice-sounding tube when they designed that.

**Do you have the difficulties with EF86 preamp tubes that some makers and players have experienced, like the problems with microphony and early failure rates?**

Not really. I guess I'm at a little bit of an advantage. There's a guy named Eric Barber, he wrote for Vacuum Tube Valley—great editor, great designer—and then he was hired by [Russian tube manufacturer] Svetlana. Svetlana wanted him so they could take him to shows and hold him up and say, "Look, we've got Eric Barber!" In this esoteric tube industry, it was quite a name for them to have. I hooked up with Eric, and I told him what I wanted to do with this EF86. I wanted to use Svetlanas, and I wanted to use a current production tube. One of my little things when I design an amp is that I want to be able to call up and get 100 of these tubes tomorrow. And it's also a thing for the player who gets the amp, so he doesn't have to go search high and low for a Telefunken such-and-such or the amp will never sound as good.

I talked to Eric and he gave me some pretty nice insight into how their tube was developed and how it operated, so we kind of co-opted a tube design, and he put it up on Svetlana's website for a while. With that, I was able to take a $5 or $6 EF86 and, because it was designed correctly, I didn't have the microphonic problems that other manufacturers had trying to use an EF86. I didn't have the squealing and high-gain problems, and the burning-out of the tubes, because I kind of picked the brain of a guy who knew a lot about it, and he was very, very willing to help me.

Basically, that little formula I use on the Route 66, and the Z-28, and the KT45 and the Delta 88 provides four platforms that I'm able to use different output tubes in and get four different amps, but basically with that same

premise from the shared preamp. The nice thing about the EF86 is that it really looks for a nice, high-impedance output, so I was able to dial in that cool little tone stack that I have and not have to worry about any recovery stage, just take it right to a phase inverter. I could get what I needed from a very simple, two-tube preamp.

**I always like the sound of those EF86, but they just seemed to be problematic.**

The nice thing about those, and something you might not realize, is that the EF86 can handle about a threefold peak-to-peak input, and it stays remarkably symmetrical. Now, when you overdrive a 12AX7 triode, they all have a type of asymmetrical response, where they kinda clip at the top and the bottom stays somewhat sinusoidal. That sound signature is what you hear, kind of a bulky midrange response with a little bit of a brightness to its timbre. It's nice, you know, it's what we've heard for years and years, but it certainly is a signature sound and that's what a 12AX7 gives you.

The EF86 has an incredibly symmetrical output, so whatever you put into that amp comes out the other side of that tube. It has the ability to add an incredible amount of gain if you want it to, but it stays sinusoidal, so it works incredibly well with pedals. There was one point in time where you'd feel like there was a new pedal coming onto the market every five minutes, and they were all pretty cool. These guys had done a nice job. But sometimes they would work with some amps and not with other amps. But boy, a Route 66 or any of those EF86-based amps that I did, it sucks that in like a straw. I mean, it sounds like the pedal's inside the amp, not on the floor.

**And then you're moving things on to the output stage where all the nice tube overdrive is happening anyway.**

Exactly, all that third-order harmonics, all that real sweet, thick, rich harmonic distortion occurs. And it gives the pedal some body. It doesn't sound just like a germanium transistor any more, it gives the sound some thickness to it too.

**Are those Svetlana EF86s available on the general market?**

Yeah, I buy them by the hundreds. They are on the market. Tesla made some for a while and they were nice, but they stopped. I don't know what other current manufacturer did make them. But what I understand through Groove Tubes is that they were trying to get other manufacturers to make EF86s again, so hopefully that's something that will bring a little more variety to the market.

**It fascinates me that you have used ultralinear output transformers on the Route 66, the SR Z-65, the 65/45, and the Delta 88.**

What brought me to that was, I'd gotten a couple of old Sunn chassis in the early days, when I was starting to play around with amp design and was working on circuits. I'd picked up a couple of broken Sunn amps, and they were ultralinear. I thought, "Wow, this is kind of novel." I did a little research on it and found that they work very well with any of the KT—"kinkless tetrode"—family of tubes: KT66, KT77, KT88. They were kind of designed around ultralinear applications.

I put a pentode in [my design], an EL34 pentode, and found that it does generate a little bit of negative feedback between the screen and the plate, so that no negative feedback was needed in the amp. I could do away with a negative feedback circuit and get an amp that was pretty harmonic, but still had a little bit of hum suppression and background noise suppression that negative feedback gives you. So I started experimenting more and more, and found that with the KT66 it was really interesting, and boy, with the 88 it's really exceptional. I was able to nail a pretty nice output-tranny design that was perfect for the 88, and they feel right at home. The advantage of it is the screen and the plate track very linearly—as the plate voltage starts to sag, as you push the amp harder, the relation between the screen and the plate stay the same, because the screen voltage sags by the same amount. So that's the linear portion of the ultralinear transformer. It keeps that screen open and forming a band of electrons, and it keeps them very constant.

I found I could get a nice distortion with these ultralinear amps, but also have a nice articulation.

**That's a big part of what players see in those amps.**
Yeah, you always have a double-tracked kind of sound. You have this articulated sound and you hear each note, but also there's a nice bloom of airy distortion around the note, so it almost sounds like a double-tracked kind of thing. Tubes tend to last a little longer this way, and they're very, very happy.

**And yet when Fender tried ultralinear OTs in their high-powered Twins, for example, the sound fell flat as far as most guitarists were concerned.**
My experiments found that a tetrode—a 6L6 beam-powered tube—doesn't really work very well ultralinearly in a guitar amp. And one other problem that the engineers at Fender didn't realize was that there is a generation of negative feedback already being produced in the output stage, and then they left the really suppressive negative feedback in their phase inverter that they used in their other 6L6-type amps.

**Which was a pretty heavy amount of negative feedback in the silverfaces anyway.**
Exactly. So then you've got this almost constipated, very sterile-sounding amp that's way, way over-corrected, and there's not much harmonic content. It almost sounds solid-state-ish. The more experiments I did with 6L6s I just couldn't get a 6L6 tube to really sound good in a guitar amp that was ultralinear. It just kept its teeth—it always had this "biteyness" to it, that no matter how much distortion or pedals or whatever you put in front of it, it would never soften that up.

I think the trick in getting ultralinear designs to work was more or less trying to find the right tube to use with the right transformer, and then to design the phase inverter or the driver circuit to complement that. When I did all those, you know, no one listening to my amp goes,

"Oh, that sounds like an ultralinear Fender." I certainly had a lot of problems early on, as you can imagine. Sixteen years ago, people were going, "Ultralinear Dr Z amps man, those sound like those Fenders, and the late Seventies Fenders sound like shit …" you know. I had to battle that a little bit, but these people hadn't even heard the amps. I saw the results and said, "This is creating my own voice, this is what I want to do." If I'd just wanted to use a soft EL34-type transformer like a Marshall, it would have sounded like a Marshall, and that was not what I was trying to do.

**It certainly achieved the goal for you of getting a unique sound. And it also opened up a constant string of questions on web boards about your use of ultralinear OTs.**
Oh, sure. And here's a little secret. Some of the earlier Trainwreck amps that my friend Ken Fischer built used ultralinear trannies. Now, he tied the ultralinear legs back, but they were Dynaco 470s, which was an ultralinear 4k tranny that works pretty nice with four EL84s or two EL34s. It's a great, great transformer with nice compression and good sound. That was the same tranny that Sunn used, which was kind of how I got hooked onto them, initially. I was looking at the things and going, "Man, these are Dynaco trannies…"

There was a guy somewhere in Ohio, I believe, that was making them as replacement Dynaco kit parts. And boy, he wasn't real receptive to selling parts to me in any kind of number or price break. He was pretty guarded about it, so I kind of circumvented it and designed my own and went my own way, which was certainly a little bit more expensive than I would have wanted to do 16 years ago, but of course it's paid for itself quite well through the years.

**Probably a good thing in hindsight.**
Oh, sure. But at the time I'd have to bite the bullet and get 50 of these trannies, then hope I'd sell 50 amps.

**I know you put a lot of thought into speakers and speaker cabs, and you developed your own 10" speaker a few years back. How did you come to do that?**
I looked into developing my own speaker, and I kind of hit the wall with the 12". I'd get them, and I'd listen to them, and I'd go, "Eh, it sounds OK," you know? But the thing I do, is I fit the model speaker into the specific amp that I'm selling. Which means I use [Celestion] Greenbacks, and Vintage 30s, and G12H-30s and Bluebells [Alnico Blues]. So I use those four variations of speakers in various models trying to get the best that I can get. Now, there's no one 12" speaker that's going to sound like all four of those. I decided it was kind of frugal trying to design just one speaker to sound like these four, and why try to design four different speakers when these already exist, and I'm having difficulty just copying one to my liking?

**And they're pretty good speakers.**
Yeah, and nobody doesn't like a Celestion. They look at the back of the amp and they see a Celestion, and they

go, "Wow, man, a Celestion—quality." Or whatever that Celestion says to someone. So I wormed my way into Celestion, England, and purchase speakers direct from them, and as long as I satisfy the minimum number of speakers that I need to order, I get them very reasonably priced, and get good quantity and quality. So I'd kind of been stuck that way.

Then I said, "So how about 10s?" There was a [Celestion] Vintage 10 that I used in an early amp and I kind of liked it. It certainly wasn't everything I wanted, but it had a nice kind of "high-cholesterol" lead tone. The notes were fat, it was cool for leads, but it just didn't have that spanky tone that I like in 10s—that's the reason you buy 10s. So I worked with Eminence and said, "Man, I really like that English cone, and the dust cap, but I think I'd like to get a little more magnet, get a little more juice out of the speaker. Let's try a few things." And boy, two or three iterations landed me a speaker that I just really loved. I stayed with that, and have for many years. I've sold 5,000 or 6,000 of them, I guess, I don't know. I order a couple of hundred just about every quarter, so I go through them. I knew I liked them, and as soon as people heard them they said, "Wow, these sound great. They sound like 12s…"

One other thing I do that kind of makes them sound a little better is, when the Eagles were out on tour, I got to see a lot of the shows and went backstage and stuff, and Clair Brothers was doing the sound. Clair Brothers is quite a substantial sound company, and they design their own cabinets and have engineers and all. So one day I was looking at the side-fills with a flashlight, and I was looking inside the bin and saw something weird. This one engineer came up and said, "Hey man, what're you doing. Stay away from there!", you know. So I introduced myself and told him who I was, and he was like, "Oh, OK, cool." We sat down and started talking, and basically what they use is lens technology. If you think of the idea of a front-loaded horn, you've got a driver and then you've got a distance through that horn that make for a specific projection of sound. This lens focuses the sound and allows it to project a little bit further before it disperses, and you're able to project the sound and make different throw-lengths for the cabinets. Every one was kind of different. To try to fill an arena, they had different focus points for their speakers so that not one spot is the ideal spot to listen to the band. They tried to fill the room as much as possible.

I thought that was a novel idea, almost like the old Fender Tone Ring. Fender would use a 15″ and add a Tone Ring to it, and boy the speaker would sound like an 18″ then. So basically that's what I do. I take my 10s, and use a lens baffle over the baffle, and I basically add about an inch-and-a-half to each 10. They kind of sound like 12s. They have the projection and fullness of frequency of 12s, but the nice compact size of a 10.

### But they probably still have a quicker response.
Yeah, they're still bullet-fast. For fingerpicking styles and those kinds of things, they're still very dynamic and real nice. I did make sure, when I designed my 10″, I made it a little bit more linear than the Celestion speaker. The Celestion Vintage 10 always seemed to be a little bit too nasal, just a little too much midrange. I took that out, I thought, "Let my amps controls control the tonation of the speaker."

I increased the bandwidth, certainly clipped the end, so you get a nice smooth top end, and a full bottom that doesn't sound too fidelic, you know. But make the midrange kind of linear, almost hollow. And if a guy wants to boost the midrange, he wants to put a Tube Screamer in front of it or whatever, fine. It actually works a lot better than being overly midranged.

So that's what I did, and I incorporated the lens technology, and I'll tell you what: you take one of my little 2x10″ combos and it really cuts through the band. Here's something I have been telling people over the years. If you ever go to a jam, go back to the furthest wall from where the band is set up and listen. I'll bet you a dollar to a donut you're going to hear the Z amp so clear and so much in the mix, you're going to be amazed. And that's the projection of that amp. It just kind of cuts through a room like a hot knife. It's not overbearing, but it's very finite. That's where so many people say, "Wow, Dr Z's Maz 18 is so damn loud." It's not that it's so damn loud—well, it kind of is for a two-EL84 amp—but there's more to it than just that: the cabinet, the speakers, the way it's put together, just tries to optimize everything it has in really giving a nice-projecting amp offstage.

### It proves how important the speaker is to the design of a good amp. You can build a great circuit and stick a real duffer of a speaker in there, and you've ruined the thing.
Right. The speaker's so critical. I think that's where a lot of guys kind of miss the boat, because that is the final transducer. That's what you hear, so it's very important that you have the right speaker. More so than having new-old-stock tubes or this, that, and the other thing. If you can't couple it to the right speaker and get the most out of the amp, then you're never going to get it.

### I often suggest to players looking to change their amps that a new or different speaker will make the single greatest sonic change from a single component.
Yeah, exactly. You're going to hear that the most. You could put another 12AX7 in there and go, "Ooh, listen to how textured that midrange is." You can sniff a cork and try to say all the adjectives that you want to say about the response of a Telefunken or whatever, but gosh, it's so subtle, and it gets lost in the mix, and it's not anything—besides putting it down to tape—that you're ever really even going to notice for your $80 or $100. Find the right speaker for the amp, a speaker that you like, and that will make a big difference.

Generally speaking, for low-wattage amps I like high-efficiency, low-wattage speakers. Those seem to work the best. You get the most coloration and contribution from that kind of speaker, if it's a low-wattage amp. But if it's got a good efficiency, wow, you can hear it, and it really sounds nice. And then the opposite is true with very percussive or high-volume amps, you're better off with a little higher wattage, but less efficient, so that as you push the amp the speaker kind of pushes back, and it sounds in harmony with itself.

**So few people seem to consider a speaker's efficiency rating, even if they are considering its power-handling capabilities and other specs.**
Right. And efficiency's probably more important, because that's where the harshness comes in. That's where the frequencies are that you can't get rid of, or you have to turn the amp up so high because the speaker's so inefficient that it starts to muddy up the amp. So it's a matter of marrying up the right combination.

**Any practical tips you can offer us?**
Here's a great one. Speaker cones are weighted and measured in grams. It doesn't take a whole lot of weight difference to really throw a cone off from sounding the way it should sound. Now, when you store an amp, the worst thing you can do is put it in a damp basement or in a situation where it's going to be able to wick up moisture. It's amazing how a speaker can do that, and now all of a sudden you have a dull, dud-sounding speaker, because it doesn't take much water to throw it off. It's amazing how just a few drops of water can really change the response and characteristic of a speaker.

So what I do when I store speakers—and I've got tons of them, I buy all kinds to try—is you get the little silica bags that come with electronics components, you throw one of those in the box, close it up, put that speaker away for a little while to let that silica soak up all the moisture of that cone. And you'll be amazed how wonderful that speaker sounds after the moisture's been taken out. It's nice and dry and reedy sounding, and now you've got a cone that responds the way it was supposed to, with this earthy tone to it that's just unbelievable. People use hot guns, they do this, they do that, and boy, you just never really get them right. But just put a couple of those little silica bags in and just leave it be, and it's such a natural way of wicking the water out and drying the cone out nicely, without overheating the surround.

That's a little secret that I tell people, and it's amazing. You can take an amp—you find an old Twin Reverb or something somewhere and it just sounds dull and dead—and it's the speakers. You take a little time and dry them out, and the amp will come to life.

# Mark Sampson of Star Amplifiers

Mark Sampson founded Matchless Amplifiers in 1989 with Rick Perrotta. The California-based brand became one of the best-known lines of the "boutique" tube guitar amp revolution. Then, during a temporary halt in production in 1999, Sampson parted from Matchless to begin designing amplifiers for Bad Cat. He founded Star Amplifiers in 2004, and has also designed models for the SMF line sold by Star's distributor, Sonic Machine Factory.

**Tell me about how you first got interested in amplifiers.**
What first got me started was that I was in a band when I was like 14, and my dad and I made an amplifier out of an old tube radio. That sparked an interest, but I didn't do much with it. I eventually quit the band and got into cars and racing and all kinds of vehicle-related things in Mason City, Iowa, where I grew up. I started playing again in the late 1970s and needed an amp, and I just couldn't get the sound I was after. I had enough background in electronics that I just started modifying my own things and experimenting.

That went into buying old broken and defective things from the back of stores and trying to figure out what broke on them and why, and modifying them, and it evolved from there.

**When did it start to look like you'd get your own amp business out of it?**
In the early 1980s I started buying and selling gear when I was in a band again, and I was making more money buying and selling gear than I was at my job fixing cars. I quit the job and started doing the buy-sell trade full time. It kept morphing into more electronic technician things than it was buying and selling, because at the time there

weren't very many people that knew British amps real well in the States, and that was primarily what I was focused on. There were some guys that were into Marshall, but the Voxes—nobody wanted to deal with them, and now I understand why. They're not easy to work on, but I like them so I cut my teeth on them.

**Is that part of how you developed the Matchless sound?**
Yeah, Vox was a huge influence. But I've been influenced design-wise by a lot of other things. Sonically, I like the thing that EL84s do: the compression, that kind of "scranggg …" sound it does. That's the only tube complement and setup that'll do that. But in terms of American design, it's kind of like comparing an American muscle car to a British sports car. In the American muscle car you can ignore the red line and even go beyond it, and it'll just make more power. With the European car, don't do that. It'll work brilliantly up to its red line: 200rpm beyond, it destroys itself.

I enjoyed working on Fenders and Gibsons and even the weirdo little Valco amps. There were a lot of engineering flaws in those, or I guess you could argue whether they were flaws or just price-point guidelines. But they could always be improved, and I admired some of their clever circuitry. Some of those guys were handed a cost and a marketing concept first, and told, "Now back into it from this point." That's harder engineering than when you have an open template with cost being no object.

### And they made some pretty good-sounding amps out of what they had available at the price.

That's right. You recap them and put new tubes in them, and some of those amps are stunning.

### How did the Matchless template come about?

I moved to LA in January of 1989. I had been living in the Midwest and buying and selling and modifying amps for people, and I was doing so much work for people and flying out to do a lot of session work—coming in to consult on guitar sounds and modifying amps to try to get the sound they were after—that I was making more money flying back and forth, after I paid expenses, than I was doing my business in the Midwest. So I just moved out here [to LA].

Soon after I moved I ran into Rick Perrotta. Rick always wanted to build an AC30 that wouldn't break, and after being out on the road and seeing the rigors of the road I could see there was definitely a need for that. The original concept behind Matchless was basically to build a roadworthy amp that sounded good, but the "roadworthy" was the stress, initially.

We found that there are almost two separate lines of thought. They can be parallel or non-parallel, in terms of sonic character and design reliability. It was easy to implement good sound with design reliability. Design reliability is more foundational in terms of electronics. So once we got it where we thought the platform was not going to break, then it was easy to tweak the sound.

### Did you find pretty quickly that the point-to-point wiring you became known for was the most direct route to doing that? Did you play around with a lot of other formats first?

No, we didn't. Basically, because I had done so much work on amps by that time—and Rick Perrotta had a background in it also (he was managing a studio, but he was a tech on the side too)—we knew that with a circuitboard type of format, when you're on a tour, in and out of a bus and so forth, even the best ones will break. You have to be careful with them, you know. We just felt like it was more roadworthy [to do it point-to-point]. That was the concept, and also if it did break it was easier to fix because you could find the flaw, you know.

### And your amps are literally point-to-point, of course—meaning the components connect directly to each other rather than having a circuitboard as a go-between—as opposed to some other forms of wiring that get referred to as point-to-point, such as turret boards or tag strips or eyelet cards or whatever.

Right. The circuit almost pictorially follows the electron flow path.

### Did you home in on components through a lot of trial and error, or was there a process to it?

I was just curious about how things sounded. That started in the early repair element of my work, but I also found out that you can't ignore anything. The one thing you think isn't going to sound any good is going to come back and bite you in the butt if you don't pay attention to it. You've got to try everything, and anything that's new, I try it, so I would at least have a handle on what it's about. Even if I think it's going to sound bad, and the company's got a horrible history not making products that work for what I design, I will still try it because you never know when you're going to get surprised.

### Speaking of what does and doesn't work, there's a lot of myth afloat in the tube guitar amp world. Is there anything out there being hyped today that you feel just doesn't add up, in tonal terms at least?

I'm a real pessimist regarding anything that has an advertising plan. I just have to try it. Everybody has their marketing shtick, and they're all the same. I have to use the same advertising and marketing tools as they do, and that stuff is just hype, you know? And audio products are the worst. They get really slick marketing and graphics guys to draw up slick ads, and you get this product that costs thousands of dollars and you try it and you go, "I've got a 1950s piece of junk thing that sounds way better than this has ever thought of sounding." The [new] thing is more complicated and has all these features, but who cares—it doesn't sound any good.

We're kind of digressing into the digital modeling thing, but that's OK. I have two lines of thought on that. On one hand, it looks like it's the natural course of evolution for guitar amps. On the other hand, it's a huge sacrifice. So I guess my challenge to the guys who do the digital modeling thing is, "Look, you've got to improve it …" It's not good enough to have a palette of 69 colors if they're all just shades of gray.

### That's a great way of putting it. And look at the best pro players over the years: not many of them needed to step on 50 radically different sounds over the course of a night's show.

No, it's usually a handful—less than six sounds.

### Which you can get with a couple of pedals and maybe a couple different amps, if that.

Right. But the thing is, if an industry—and this is a broad statement—doesn't garner interest among the young generation, you are dooming the industry at the end of the generation that's leaving it. I thought the hotrod industry was going to be dead, but the sport tuner cars have basically revived it and kept it from going into extinction, and that's a good analogy.

I have a 15-year-old son who, without my prodding, decided he wanted to play guitar, and he's playing guitar in a band. I use them as a beta group to gauge their reaction to things. It's more interesting for them to have all the different sound capabilities. Like, with the digital modeling thing, you can point out the [shortcomings in the] tone to them, and they just go, "Yeah, so?"

It forms the question in my mind, "Is it really that

important to them, or have I focused so much under the microscope that I'm missing the big picture?" I do what I do and I'm not going to change it, because it's been successful, but the question it leads to is, "Is the market actually changing? Or is it because they have so little time and so many things they have to do in their time nowadays, as opposed to 20 or 30 years ago, that they're willing to trade that off without a second thought, because of the ease of just hitting a button and getting a new sound, whereas we'd have to go get a new amp, plug it in, and wait for it to warm up.

***That's a very valid consideration. And you have to ask yourself, how much is the audience going to notice the difference by the time you get it onto a CD or out into the crowd in the middle of a full-band gig?***
And that raises another thing: they would almost rather keep it entirely digital. Just take a USB cable right out of the amp and go straight into the computer to record it. They don't even hear what they're doing until it's mixed and quantized and harmonically perfected. It's an eye-opener to me. I wouldn't go that way, but I see all the professional studios doing that, too, so it really is a trend. How that affects guitar amps, I think that remains to be seen. Because from the most expensive down to even the cheapest professional studios, they all have one good amp. Unfortunately it's a smaller market, and everyone's fighting over that smaller piece of the pie.

***And that studio-sized amp has also become the main amp for a lot of players who used to play a 50- or 100-watt amp, but now realize that a 15- or 20-watt amp is all they're going to get much use out of.***
Unless you're playing stadiums and auditoriums, a 100-watt amp is not a usable amp for most settings. It's too loud.

***That has become part of the learning curve for guitarists as much as for amp-makers. Realizing it's just not going to sound good if you're sitting at 2 on a 100-watt amp, as opposed to 6 or 7 on a 20-watt amp.***
Sure. Speakers always sound best when they're pushed, so if you can push the speaker and cut the dB level at the same time, you end up with a better tone at a lower volume.

***Some of your most popular amps of the past used EF86 preamp tubes, but you have stopped using them with Star. Why is that?***
Well, I still like that tube. It's just a tube you have to deal with. And this will tie in to our discussion about the younger people. They don't understand microphonic tubes. It's like, now microphonic tubes are way more important in terms of warranty than they were ten years ago. Ten years ago people would just go, "Oh, that's a microphonic tube. As long as it doesn't go off and start oscillating on its own, I don't care. Rattles a little bit, doesn't matter." But that's not acceptable any more, and the EF86 of course is notorious for rattling. There are ways to design it where you can eliminate part of it or a

great deal of it, but when you turn the amp up to ten and you tap on the top and hear a rattle, they [newer players] perceive that as a problem. Well, it's just an inherent design feature of the tube. It's part of its nature, but you can't convince people of that any more.

***They want you to send them a quiet one, and that's impossible because quiet ones don't exist.***
Yeah, because they all do that. You can get your design to the point where they won't oscillate, but they all rattle. You make a tube with the three grids in that small bottle, and it's bound to happen.

***How have your design goals evolved with the new line of Star amps?***
It's the same thought process of trying to make an amp that's roadworthy, that's not going to break and that sounds great, and to get as many features into without it becoming cumbersome and hard for the consumer to use. Because the dirty little secret with a lot of guitar players is that they have a much bigger ego than the rest of the band, with the exception maybe of a solo lead vocalist. So they don't want to admit that they don't know what a knob does, and I find that a lot. I find it even at the pro level. And it's OK, you know, especially on an amp that has 20 knobs. You go, "Oh, man, this is dizzying even for a designer." And what I typically find with some of them is they'll just have chalk marks or tape marks on the amp, and if they need to vary it they turn a knob just a little bit, and that's their tone.

So they're effectively using an amp that maybe even has shelving or parametric EQ, and they're presetting everything. That's kind of my whole marketing idea: give them a handful of knobs that do something effectively, and limit it so that it can't sound bad no matter where you set it. Because some of the amps that do parametric EQ, you can get some incredibly bad sounds out of them. You have to look at the whole system and how it functions as a unit: the speaker you're using, the cabinetry, the type of tubes, and then the circuitry coupled with it.

With Star amps, I'm just trying to get a great two-channel amp that's footswitchable, where you can get an amazing clean sound and an amazing distortion. That's what my process was with the current model we're shipping, the Gain Star 30.

***Which takes things a step beyond your former approach, because you used to be very minimalist regarding features and channels—although a DC30 had a few knobs on it.***
The DC30 had nine knobs. I think the current thing we're building has ten. But the difference is, and this was a chronic complaint, is they wanted to be able to switch the two channels. You could do it with an A/B box, but you had a common master on that amp, so you were stuck. That's one of the things we have tried to address with the Gain Star; it's two channels, with the master on the channel that distorts the most. The clean channel is designed to be clean most of the way up, to get good tone and good harmonic content at the same time.

*I was very interested to see that Gain Star design come out, because it has always seemed to me that Mark Sampson was a designer who bucked against the footswitchable lead format.*

Well, you know, if I was to follow my own personal philosophy I wouldn't do this. But at the same time, the analogy I draw is, I could be the best buggy-whip maker ever, but if no one needs them—or the market isn't asking you for them—what good is it? So I'm basically just trying to respond to the market. I took all the comments and the feedback and the emails over the years and looked at them, and said, "What's really lacking in a point-to-point amp is that—footswitchable channels. No one really has an amp like that."

We do have several different models of single-channel amps that are much more minimalist than that one. So I've still got some of that core in there, but if the market's asking for blue and you give them green, your competitor's going to give them blue and you're going to be out.

*Like you said with regard to your son and his bandmates and their modeling amps, you really do have to assess what the younger players want to play, and try to give it to them, from the perspective of good business sense at least.*

Right. And in contradiction to my own statement, sometimes if you create a great product the market will follow that. Sometimes you have to lead and sometimes you have to follow—the trick is knowing when.

*And if you create that great product, you still have to get people to hear it.*

Yeah. Because if you just simply follow what the market says, always, you're never going to be a leader. At some point you have to put a stake in the ground and say, "This is what I do, and it's great because of 'X.'" Whatever "X" is.

*You're still a huge fan of class A designs, obviously.*

Oh yeah, for guitar amps I think they're the best. They give the best harmonic content. In terms of numbers and power, it's lower, but who cares—it's just as loud. I can make a needle move on a meter and it says 50 or 60 watts, and I can make the same needle move at 30 watts, but when I put a dB meter in front of it and the 30-watt one is louder, who cares? Because nobody's looking at the needle, they're listening to it, in real life.

*I think that's a factor that surprises a lot of people. When you first started building DC30 amps with Matchless, or when people were getting into AC30s 20 years ago when they really became a craze, they were looked at as small amps by a lot of people.*

Sure, when you've got a Marshall full-stack that you're going up against. But nobody needs that any more. With modern PAs and huge high-power MOSFET power amplifiers, it's just not needed, even for the great big stages. And you couple that with the stages now, where everybody's after the clean look, and—since the size doesn't matter—the smaller amps make a lot of sense.

*And of course a Marshall stack was never three times as loud as a Gain Star 30 or a Matchless DC30—it just looked it.*

And it projected a little further. But my point would be that it doesn't really matter, if you're going to put a microphone in front of it anyway. Just let the soundman do his job.

*I've always had the impression that you put a lot of thought behind many of your major components, such as the output transformers. How much work went into that process?*

A lot. Part of my background is audio, and part of it is guitar amps. Even though they're cousins, they are very distant cousins, and as I said, they are diametrically opposed, but they are cousins. When you understand what makes one work, then you can understand what makes the other work. It all started in a quest for tone back in the early 1980s; trying to find something that sounded great, and then trying to understand why it sounded great—why it did what it did, how it interacted with other components ... Which was actually, in the end, more important than what sounded great. I spent a lot of time just dissecting transformers. Especially when one would die and I knew that I was going to replace it anyway, I'd cut it apart to see how it was made, and why it broke.

So I ended up reverse-engineering tons of old British output transformers, and the American ones too. The American ones are more formulaic than the British. British engineering always tends to be a little more esoteric, with problems that are created by being esoteric and trying to be better. You can apply that to pretty much everything the British make versus the Americans.

But it just started on a quest for tone and what sounded better. And you can't ignore any element, even to the point of how they bolt down and which way: whether they lay down, or stand up, are horizontal or vertical, and everything.

*Obviously there's a lot of convention on impedance ratios and so forth, but I understand that you have bucked against those rules on occasion, such as with the Matchless Lightning OT, where the primary impedance is a lot lower than the standard 8k ohms that most makers go with.*

Yeah, it's a little high for most companies, but it depends on which book you look at, you know? Over the years I have collected a huge library of tube design books and of the engineering on the design of the tubes themselves. I was fortunate enough to meet a guy, shortly before he died, who was a retired JBL engineer out here near Pasadena. He was in his eighties, but he was still the go-to guy for the JBL engineers when they got in a jam. He had a sixth-grade education and was self-taught, which speaks volumes about schooling and all that kind of thing. I mean, he was the guy that 16-years-of-college guys are calling for the answer. He taught me a lot, and when he died I went to the auction and bought a lot of his design books, and literally filled the car with them.

The impedance that's correct for a pair of EL84s is really very subjective. You can use one formula and come up with an exact number, but you can alter the formula—which is equally correct—and come up with another number. The plate impedance on a pair of EL84s should be 10k to 6k, or even up to 12k, but they all work. It's just, what do they sound like, where does it distort, and how does it distort? And there are so many forms of distortion in that: you've got phase distortion, frequency distortion, distortion where the curve becomes nonlinear... All of that affects the sound, but in the end most people really don't care, because all they care about is what it sounds like.

Now with audio, all of that's really important because people buy things by the specs, not by their ears. So the specs become important in the audio market, not in the guitar amp market.

***It sounds like you're saying it really comes down to a lot of listening and testing the variables.***
Yeah. I have a test bench that I use—although it's packed away right now—where I can mount up to six output transformers with one big rotary switch, and I just listen to them back-to-back. And there's another knob where I can plug in up to four speaker cabinets, so I can listen to six different output transformers with four different speakers at the switch of a knob. That's really how you've got to do it, because if you take the time to unsolder and resolder to listen to something, you lose your frame of reference, especially if somebody comes in and starts talking to you. So I do those things when there's no one around, after everybody's gone home. I shut the phone off and go into design mode, which is a whole other process than running a business.

***That raises a whole big chunk of the mythology about guitar amps in general. People talk about one type of speaker or tube or what-have-you being better than another, but often they're comparing apples to oranges when they make that statement.***
Yeah, statements like that are very hard to dissect, because for someone to say, "My rig sounds better with the JTM45 than the tweed Bassman." Sure, your rig sounds better for you like that, but that statement won't even apply to the next guy because of the way he holds his pick, or the way he attacks the strings with his fingers. That affects the tone as much as anything else. And also the room you're in, what pedals, what cords he's using, what speakers he's using with it. Even though you could say those two amps, an 5F6A Bassman and an early JTM45, are virtually identical—and I have taken the plexi panel off a JTM45 and it does drop on a 5F6A Bassman, they didn't even change the layout—but they are apples and oranges, and you can't compare them like that.

The trick is to add different types of fruit. I don't want to be a great apple, or another type of apple. I'd rather be a papaya or a mango. But there's a huge risk in that, which is why a lot of manufacturers don't go there. Nobody bats a thousand, but you've got to try to establish your own identity.

***And, with regard to that, guitarists—despite sometimes being "wild rockers" and so forth—are often extremely conservative characters.***

Oh, there is no truer statement. They want to be different like everybody else ... For all the ballyhooing about how radical they are, if they've had some success they want to stick with whatever their formula was. The ones that are open to experimentation are really the most fun to work with. Especially the guys who have done a lot of studio work, and they see the amount of variation that's required to actually stay successful and stay working.

***That's one arena where an appreciation of some different sounds will do them some good.***
Yeah, one day they've got to come in and sound like Jimi Hendrix, then the next day they've got to sound like Duane Allman or Ricky Skaggs—who knows? And they've got to jump quick.

***Any hidden gems out there among used or vintage tube amps that you can turn the readers on to?***
The hidden gems are the ones that, when you plug them in they sound bad, but they are tube amps made in the 1950s or early 1960s. They don't sound good because they need service work; generally they need new capacitors, especially filter caps, and new tubes. Gibson amps have been the most overlooked; they're as well built as a Fender, but they used filter caps that were notorious for failing. To a one, they fail. So if the amp doesn't blow the fuse, you'll get a beat frequency of 60 cycles out of the wall. It's not pleasant.

The other ones are the early Ampegs. They're ignored a lot, and they usually need the same thing: filter caps. And a lot of the Valco amps. Everybody's overlooked the Valco amps, the Supro, Montgomery Ward, Sears Valco amps. Those amps, when they're worked over, can sound really good. And that's pretty much the problem; you have to know how to work them over, change pretty much every cap in the amp, and retube it. And sometimes they need a little bit of reverse engineering. Sometimes they need some help.

Those Valcos are really overlooked, always have been, and probably always will be. Because you need to know what you're doing and be able to do it yourself, or pay someone else to do it, and their value isn't that high, so it does limit the market.

But a Gibson GA-40 Les Paul amp from the 1950s is an amazing sounding amplifier.

***And probably a third of the price of a tweed Fender Deluxe.***
That's pretty close. They're sold more as an accessory for your Les Paul guitar now than they are for use as an amplifier. They used the same blue-bell Jensen speaker as the tweed Deluxe, and depending on what variation you've got, some of them had a pentode preamp that just squashed beautifully, great tone. They have a great vibrato when they're working right. And they're ignored. Meanwhile a tweed Deluxe, no matter how bad it is, it'll sell.

## Mark Baier of Victoria Amp Company

Mark Baier founded Victoria Amp Company in Chicago in 1994 as the culmination of his own quest to locate a 'new' amp with the build and sound of a vintage tweed Fender. Victoria has grown to be the clear leader in the market for hand-made, precisely spec'd reproductions of Fender designs from the 1950s, but has also branched out into more original designs in the new millennium.

***I know you initially got bitten by the tweed bug as a player. Tell us about that.***

There was a confluence of a lot of different things that were happening. I initially got interested in electronics from a purely intellectual point of view, from trying to figure out what made my Apple computer work. At one point about 12 years ago when I was a stockbroker, we had just upgraded our server system and I found myself staring at the guts of this thing going, "Oh God, how does this thing work?" So I started getting interested in electrons at that point, just trying to figure out what made them move from point A to point B. And at about that same time I got back into the guitar after taking a hiatus to have a career.

What really pushed me into the pool was that one of my buddies out in DeKalb, Illinois, which is about 70 miles west of where I'm at, he had this old silverface Fender Deluxe Reverb that we'd used all throughout college; and one day I called him up out of the blue—it was kind of ironic I called him up then—and he said, "You know that silverface Deluxe Reverb? I just threw it in the dumpster last night. I was playing it and all of a sudden it made a loud noise and smoke came out of the back of it, so I figured that was the end of it and I threw it out."

So I said, "Damn it, go take it out of the dumpster!" I made the trip up and picked it up, and proceeded to take it apart and find out what was wrong with it. That was my first introduction to actually getting my hands dirty. After having done that and seeing what they were all about, it just naturally progressed and turned into a hobby, which was a lot of fun and satisfying intellectually. It occurred to me at the end of the day, after I'd built all these project amps and read all these books and determined what it was that made the old amps sound the way they did, that I probably wasn't the only schmuck out there that wanted something like this in a brand-new amp.

The truth of the matter is that when I went to buy myself a new amp, when I reintroduced myself to the guitar world, nobody was making them the way I expected them to be made. Having played all those vintage Fenders as a kid and as a performer, to go out into the real world and find out that they weren't building them the same way, that was kind of a bitter pill.

***Did the notion to build them yourself hit you pretty quickly?***

I was just building them for myself, and a light went on: "My God, I've invested all this money …" because I'd invested in chassis and so forth, and I wanted to build my own amps kind of as a hobbyist, because I'd figured out that I could do it. By that time Aspen Pittman had introduced the first *Tube Amp Book,* and it had all those schematics and layout drawings in it. Unless you were a hard-core tech you'd never seen a layout drawing before. I looked at that and thought, "This shows you exactly how to build this amp…" The only thing missing from everybody who wanted to build amps was the chassis. I had enough money to buy the chassis, and I had a buddy who was a sheet-metal worker and he made some chassis. One thing led to another, and it was just kind of a hobby that became a vocation.

***Why did you center your business on the Fender tweed models?***

Because they're simple and they were amplifiers that I'd used as a performer. Back before they became vintage instruments, they were used amps. I couldn't afford a new Super Reverb, but I could afford that beat-up old Bassman in the corner. The new Super Reverb was $500 or $600, but that used Deluxe or used Bassman or whatever was only a couple hundred bucks. Nobody wanted them. Remember how everybody used to paint them black?

***Sure. Kids were ashamed to be lugging their uncle's old tweed "electric suitcase" to gigs.***

Yeah. I bought them because they were affordable, and when I was looking at the aspect of building an amplifier, they were simple to build. There's not a lot of parts in them, and it's just a fortuitous accident that I discovered the simplicity of the circuitry is really what has a lot to do with the tonality of the amplifier. The less resistors and caps you put in the way of the signal path, the better it sounds.

But the reason I settled on the tweed stuff in the first place was just that they were easy to build. You take a look at the schematic of a tweed Super then look at a Super Reverb—if you're just getting your feet wet the one to start with is the simpler of them. Then when the company became viable, it was all about providing a viable alternative to the vintage amplifier. When I first started out, that was when the tweed thing was hot as can be, and you couldn't touch a tweed Bassman for less than $2,000 or $3,000. Well, you can buy one of my reproductions for half that. At the time, that was not the case in relation to the blackface amps. In 1994 you could still buy a blackface Super Reverb for under $1,000. You'd pay me more to make that amp. Now, that may or may not be the case. I think things have swung the other way, and the blackface stuff is escalating.

## Give us some of the keys to the "tweed mystique."

There are so many little intangibles. First off, I think it's the simplicity and the elegance of the circuitry. If the design is sound, the fewer components you've got in the way—theoretically—the more purity of tone you're going to have, the more dynamics you're going to have. The more the varying of your pick attack—which creates a different signal voltage on the grid of the first tube—will be able to be translated through the rest of the circuitry.

Things like the way the cabinet is built, that old bunny-hutch cabinet construction—I'm not going to say it's an infirm cabinet, but when you take a look at the tweed cabinet construction next to a blackface cabinet, it's pretty obvious that the blackface is a little stouter and a little sturdier. But that makes a difference sonically as well, so the relative "looseness" of the tweed cabinet is responsible in part for the amp's sound. It acts as a passive radiator of sound in some ways, it vibrates a lot more. So I think that's part of it—I think the whole vibration of the amplifier has a lot to do with the way an amp responds, and with its dynamics. You can go into an old Fender or one of my reproductions of an old Fender, and "thonk" on one of the coupling capacitors—tap it on the board—and hear it through the speakers [the author does not recommend doing this yourself; read and observe the Warning at the start of the book].

It's very lively, it's very microphonic in that way. It's my sense that when you're playing and the whole thing is sympathetically vibrating, you get kind of this vocal character that you're never going to see on an oscilloscope, but the heart and soul of that kind of vibe is lying at the heart of this electro-acoustic, psycho-electric phenomenon, or whatever you want to call it.

## Which I think is a big part of what people really dig about tweed-type amps.

Yeah, they really do seem lively. Another little intangible is the material that's used to mount the components, that black vulcanized fiberboard. It's not an ideal substance to mount high-voltage electrical components to, because it will allow some voltage creep across it when conditions are right, so it's very lively in that way. Modern fiberglass boards don't allow for that voltage creepage to get across. And I think that also plays a part among the little things that make those amplifiers compelling.

## Overall, there's a magic in these amps that is hard to put your finger on.

And a lot of that magic is due to what, by modern standards, are design flaws engineered into those amps. It's in those little quirks that that "magic zone" may lie. Certainly the circuitry itself is very important, the classic Western Electric circuit designs [which Fender and many other early tube amp builders reproduced under license].

## For me, and for a lot of players, so much of the tweed magic has to do with touch-sensitivity and dynamics and so forth.

Fender was striving to make an amp that had maximum volume and headroom. When you drive a signal into clipping, you lose a lot of information. The use of a 12AY7 in the front end, which maintains your signal integrity for the next stage, and other things, all contribute to avoiding clipping that signal too soon. For me, it all has to do with understanding that when you pick a note on a guitar, you're creating a signal voltage that can be seen at the grid of that first tube. With a typical Fender guitar, it's going to be half a volt when you've got it turned all the way up. A Gibson guitar might approach one volt, or with a harmonica microphone it might be three volts. So by varying that voltage and knowing that when you're strumming the guitar lightly you're creating less, and when you're strumming it harder you're creating a bigger one, it's the way the circuitry manipulates this that gives you the touch-sensitivity. That and all the intangible things we discussed above.

That's also why a classic tube amp like a 1960s or 1970s Fender or Marshall can be controlled so well from the guitar's volume control. So much has been said about how all you need to do is roll the volume down on your guitar to get a clean sound on a classic tweed amplifier. But what people don't understand is, all you're doing is lowering the signal voltage. Varying the signal voltage can have a profound effect on the attack and dynamics of those amps—those classic designs were meant to reproduce in a wide bandwidth, I guess. If more people knew that, maybe they wouldn't be clamoring for more powerful amplifiers all the time.

## I understand you went to great lengths to get your Victoria transformers right ...

I was just damned lucky. What happened when I was initially doing this was I'd gotten familiar with a parts distributor who was the go-to guy. Like, if you needed some bridge saddles for a 1965 Jaguar, this guy's got 'em. It might take him three days to dig through the box and find them, but he's got 'em. If you needed the knob for a '56 Deluxe, he's got the knob. I befriended him, and he gave me some advice as to sourcing out the parts and so forth.

When I was lamenting about transformers, he goes, "Oh, I know a guy who used to work at Triad. He's retired now, why don't you give him a call?" He gave me the number, and it turned out I was calling this old guy in Arizona who'd initially made the transformers for Fender—and I told him my story, that I was looking for the specs on these old Fender transformers. I'd called Fender corporate up and they had no idea what I was talking about, and so on. I'd called Schumacher, I'd called what was left of the Triad company, and nobody knew what I was talking about.

I was relating this to the old guy, whose name was Tom, and he said, "Well, the reason that none of those people have any of those specs is that when I retired I cleaned my desk out and took them with me." And he had all the original old winding data that was initialed by Leo Fender and dated 1958.

## What a find ...

Yeah. And he gave me every one of them, and I was able to take these engineers' specs to my transformer manufacturer here in Chicago and say, "Build these transformers just like this." And they said, "No problem," and that's what they did. So I'm not employing the exact same manufacturer, but I am using that manufacturer's original engineering specs.

### Is there a point with guitar amps, in general terms, where you don't want to go too far with the quality of components or make things too hi-fi?

I think so, if you're trying to recreate an old sound. Because I didn't have an electronics background and I didn't know any better, I figured that if it had a carbon-comp resistor, that's what I'd better use. If it had a solid-conductor wire rather than a stranded-conductor wire, that's what I'd better use. It just made sense to me.

Probably there is a point where you shouldn't copy the electrolytics like they did originally, because they didn't last very long. But in relation to tweed amps, I think I have copied everything as accurately as is humanly possible. I think the case can be made that a carbon-comp resistor, an old-school Allen-Bradley type, sounds different from a modern metal-film or carbon-film resistor.

Other issues that I think about, when considering the differences between these components, is that I know that these carbon resistors will work for 40 years. I've owned dozens of old amplifiers from the 1950s that have old resistors in them and they still work. The jury is out on whether the modern, 1/4-watt carbon films that are put in a Fender amp or a Rivera amp or whatnot are still going to be as reliable 40 years down the road. I guess time will tell. But as far as I was concerned, I knew that I could put a lifetime warranty on these amps, based on the fact that what I copied still operates competently 40 years down the line. And because I copied them exactly, and I had no doubt in my ability to copy them correctly, I knew it would be competent, and work.

There are a lot of companies out there that use those expensive oil and film power supply caps and whatnot, and as long as you're not trying to reproduce an old sound, go ahead and use them. They're going to sound different, the way the power supply reacts is going to be different—it's going to be faster, probably tighter—the slew rate is going to be faster, whatever the hell that is. And you could spend hours hunched over an oscilloscope analyzing it.

But to answer your original question, no. Why not let the sky be the limit, as long as you understand there is going to be a difference in sound. It might be worse to you, or it might be better, because it's very subjective.

### That's a factor throughout the guitar-amp world. It is a realm of infinite variables.

Right, and no one thing is better or worse than the other. They're just different. We all have different tastes and different needs. So one man's ceiling is another guy's floor.

### Plenty of people will talk about carbon comps being noisier and so forth ...

Yeah, I couldn't care. Sure, they are a little noisier. So what. The noise floor disappears the minute you strum the first chord. Occasionally one of them will get sputtery, but you just have to fix it. By virtue of the fact that they

are built so service-tech friendly, should you have a component that goes south—on that rare occasion where the 100k plate resistors get sputtery on you—it's a five-minute fix. I think really, at the end of the day, the most important feature of the amps I build is that they're truly meant to be professional tools. That's what the originals were meant to be. At this point, I'm kind of making modern tools as art, because it's so far removed from the way modern stuff is constructed. But back in the day, that '59 Bassman was designed to be thrown in and out of the van 300 nights a year and be reliable. And should it break, it's got to be easy to fix. I think that is the biggest benefit to owning an amp that I build, that knowledge that it is as rugged as can be, and it's easy to fix. It really is a tool.

### Certainly one of Leo Fender's greatest legacies is that he really built those things to be used on the road.

Well, he was a former repair guy and he saw the crap that came in and off of his bench, and he was determined to build something that wouldn't frustrate the next repair guy who had to look at it. I think that was very important to him.

### And they sure are a pleasure to work on, compared even to many other vintage amps—old Gibsons, or plenty of British amps.

I think the problem with those Marshalls, as far as reliability goes, is they were running the voltages kind of high, and they were using those British valves. The EL34 is a pentode. It's got more stuff in it, it's got tighter tolerances, and when you wind that thing up and demand every last watt out of it night after night, it's going to go south. And when the tube goes south, it's going to take stuff out, whether it be a power supply resistor, or a cap, or whatever. I think that's principally why Marshall gained a reputation for being less reliable, because those EL34s are just squirly tubes. Whereas with the American amps, the 6L6 is just a more rugged tube. It doesn't have the same characteristics, it doesn't drive quite as easily and it doesn't sound quite the same, but at the end of the day I think the 6L6 is the one that you're going to take on the trip to the moon.

### Are there any hidden gems out there that you can turn people on to?

You know, I don't want to comment on that until I go out and buy them all up ... No, but seriously—you want to break it down into modern and vintage? I think there are some hidden gems out there in modern amplifiers. I like the Fender Reissue Reverb units. I think it's a fine unit. I can't tell you how many times I've had people wanting me to put reverb on a tweed amp, and they just weren't designed with it and I don't like to do it. Number one, it makes the amp less reliable if you add any more components. So I think those Reissue Reverb units are a pretty good deal. Just know that when it breaks, you're going to face the decision, "Do I spend $300 to fix it, or throw it in the local landfill?"

As far as older used stuff, I think Ampegs can be considered a hidden gem. But you have to be careful with them; they sometimes use screwy tubes that are very expensive to get nowadays, and with their early printed circuit board amplifiers you have to screen them carefully. With any of those hidden gems, you're faced with the problem of, "Now I've got a 30-year-old amplifier that potentially sounds great, and I paid $250 for it, but it needs new tubes, and it needs a capacitor job—which on those amps are sometimes kind of difficult to do …" The problem with a lot of these hidden-gem amps is that the collectors market has already driven them up. Ten years ago I'd have said Supro amps, but now the price of those is going up. The old Gretsch amps are the same. Anything made by National or Valco—in Chicago, Valco made amps for everybody, whether it be Sears, National, Montgomery Ward, Gretsch, Supro—they were all made by the Valco company. Those were all pretty cool amps, but they're all going to need work at this point. And none of them were built quite as well as the Fenders, so doing the work is going to be more difficult.

***Which is probably part of why Fender's collectability has stayed so constant.***
Well, it's always been the one the others were trying to chase after. So for gems out there—silverface Fenders. They don't have to be blackface Fenders. The silverface Super Reverb might trade for $600 or so, where the blackface will trade for $2,000 or $2,500. They're excellent amplifiers, they're great for guys who want a reliable, great-sounding amp they can use professionally. There's a gazillion of them out there, and if you've got the wherewithal to "blackface" them [convert their circuits to blackface-era specs]—which it's debatable whether it's really worth doing or not—then you will get yourself a great amp. And the silverface amps are never going to garner the same status among collectors as blackface stuff, so go ahead and modify it. No one's going to be upset about it at the end of the day.

---

# Victor Mason of Mojave Ampworks

**Victor Mason founded the Plexi Palace vintage amp service center and dealership in Apple Valley, California, in 1998, along with technician Craig Tathwell. The original creations of the Mojave Ampworks company grew out of the PP shop soon after, with the first commercially available models appearing around 2001.**

### What got you started in the amp business?
The most motivating factor was that, in around 1978-79, when I was around 15, I wanted to get the Eddie Van Halen sound. I didn't know how, but I had read the first interview in *Guitar Player* magazine, so I had a big interest in how to do that. I felt, at the time, like electronics was kind of the easy way out. You had the parental requirement of achieving something with your life, then you had your own desires, which of course were a frivolous waste of time. And I kind of got the neutral ground here, you know. Electronics: it'll please the old man, plus I can do what I want to do.

### Sure. You can do the rock, and you can play around with amplifiers.
Basically that was it. And I had an interest in other sounds as well, and I think I was really lucky to grow up in that time, because the 1970s and early 1980s—and even back to the 1960s, for which I wasn't really old enough—was sort of the golden age of tone. So I had been stimulated toward getting these great tonal achievements and I hadn't been able to do it yet. I think the products in the music stores were always a cut below what you really wanted, or what you needed, depending on what store you had. So my first amp was a Music Man, then eventually I got my first Marshall and started experimenting on it—and electrocuting myself on a regular basis. I finally got the information on how to discharge the caps in the thing.

The first Marshall I had was a newer version, a 1979

Marshall. I eventually got a plexi, and I couldn't for the life of me figure out why anyone wanted that amp. It had no master volume, and it was so bloody loud.

### Which is the way people felt about them for a long time, during the master-volume craze of the mid 1970s and onward.
Yeah. And my buddy was an older guy, and he was a big Hendrix fan. He had a Marshall plexi Super Bass. He was telling me, "Really, this is the sound, Vic. You've just got to understand …" So eventually I caught on.

### They're simple amps in one sense, but it takes some understanding to really play them like a musician. And of course you have to crank them up.
I've got to say, to be honest with you, I think I was pretty lost at the beginning. And that's why I feel I can connect with the guys who call me. I know exactly what it's like to be in their shoes trying to get your sound right.

### Did you do any formal training in electronics?
I did. I started on a correspondence course, and eventually I went to community college. It seemed like I was a little more motivated than the other guys; I wanted to get something done because I wanted to get the results. All the other guys in class were always really good at the book work, and they did OK in the labs as long as they followed the directions, but I was always trying stuff that was not in the book. But I seemed to get the results, and that was the way I did it.

I'm certainly not going to make the claim that I'm a brilliant technician, because I am not. I've got a brilliant technician who works with me, and I've got guys I know who know much more than I do.

### When did you start into the amp business for yourself?
Probably in late 1998. But I have to tell you, we were actually trying to build guitar amps before that, somewhere around 1996. We had done a couple of prototypes, and we did an EF86 and four-EL84 model, with preamp overdrive and other stuff, then we ended up building a prototype 40-watt amp, a non-master volume, and then we just kind of shelved it.

### Was Plexi Palace up and running at this time?
Actually I had a small electronics company set up, doing consumer electronics repairs and professional video service. Then from my own hobby as a musician I wound up buying a lot of used music equipment, mainly overseas amps, and I was bringing them over from England. Then I just wound up piling up a whole bunch of these worn-to-hell amps, for all the money I'd spent, and I was really nervous. I had them on these roll-around carts that I had for stacking shelves, and I said, "Sooner or later, I'm going to have to repair all of these amps so I can take them to a guitar show." My tech was neck deep in Peaveys and stuff like that, so somewhere along the line we just rolled them out of the way and we both started tearing into the amps.

The good news is, it was really quite refreshing, because it was a lot nicer working on those than it is working on modern electronics. They don't build things to be easy to repair any more. It was enchanting after a while, because the history of it was amazing. Our shop was alive with an excitement because of the history of the amps. We were in it, we were hands-on. We were just one degree apart—except for the time that separated us—from being with the people that had built the amps.

I was uncovering the Marshall story on the inside, not just from talking to bands. I didn't even care who had what, all I know is I bought every kind of Marshall I could. And I bought all the different Voxes I could buy, and then I started bringing in all the different obscure British amps, so we were really getting a lesson in that stuff. We had already been elbow-deep in Fenders, so it wasn't like we didn't have an affection for them. We just had this interest in the British amps that was really motivating, and it was kind of exciting.

We were documenting stuff and trying to find out how things were going, and I still have that little quest in my head for information.

### Is that what got you moving toward your own designs?
Well, the values of these amps were high, and they were getting higher. They were costing more, and they were definitely costing us more to invest in them and buy them, because in order to get spare parts, we were buying other amplifiers as organ donors. So the cost, even if you spread it out, was so significant and was rising through the roof. It basically hit a ceiling where I couldn't do it in a profitable way.

I think the majority of amp dealers in music shops weren't doing things in the way that I was. We were by nature a service facility, and our level of quality and standards was pretty high. My tech, Craig Tathwell, is a retired Air Force engineer, and I have to give him most of the credit here in a lot of ways. The Air Force is very tight with quality control, and his affection for tube audio was really deep in the hi-fi end, and that's really precision stuff. But he's one of the best guitar technicians I have ever run into, and he knows how to do things so well. That's the level of quality that came to our shop, along with our interest in tubes and the old styles. But Craig's not a guitar player, so that's also where I come in. We're really a team between us. We're like a band: neither of us would be as much individually as we are together.

I love the old science. I love the 1940s, the 1950s, and the 1960s, and to me it all ties in. There were great minds, and these guys were great, great people. Look what they did: they brought us from caveman times and they put men on the moon, they created airplanes, and they did it on slide rules. And that's the same generation of men who created these amps. I kind of feel like there is a whole era that I am experiencing when I'm looking inside those amps.

### You might be one of the first people looking at that circuit up close since the guy soldered it together.
Yeah—and even if not, you're certainly looking at it and touching it and relating to it in the same way they did. We also have a collection of old Techtronics test equipment that was all hand-built in the 1950s and 1960s, and it's absolutely fantastic. By the way, I took a job in a TV repair shop in the late 1970s so I could get some experience, and at that time we were doing American TVs, which was kind of a neat experience. I got to see things in a different light. All those days are gone.

### What was your first Mojave amp design?
Probably the one we are the most proud of: the Coyote. I absolutely hands-down fell in love with that amp. I was working on all the variety of vintage amps and had in mind to build the Plexi 45, which is a [Marshall] JTM clone, and we actually had done one. But to be honest, the most innovative design of ours has been the Coyote.

### It's interesting that you're immersed in all of this Marshall amp history, and British tube-amp history in general, but your first real offering as a manufacturer is a very original amp.
Yeah, I think that's really cool. And I wanted to do that, and do it not just to be the "rocket-science" guy or somebody who came up with their own idea for something. But I wanted to come up with something better than I already had. I knew that I had great sounds around me, and I wanted to better them. That was the goal. I had all these seeds planted, and now I wanted to grow something from it.

The EF86 enchanted me, which is why I had worked with that in our previous design efforts. That was a beautiful tube, except that it had a lot of noise. It was fantastic for the application it was designed for, which was hi-fi and sitting on a shelf, and never being vibrated.

So that was the goal: to achieve the gain and try to get the quality of tone from the preamp, but to reduce the noise as much as possible. We basically went both directions: we went with a lower-noise device than we would have if we'd just used an off-the-shelf 12AX7-based design, and we went higher than we would have with an EF86. And our gain was a different type of gain.

### What are some of the secrets of the Coyote's design, and hence its sound?

The biggest secret is that we use the dual triode of the 12AX7s in parallel. It's an application that has been widely used in the hi-fi world, and that was what we brought to the table for guitar amps. It rejects noise better, and reduces the signal-to-noise ratio a great deal, and it increases the current output from the tube device. It behaves a little better overall.

### Something I appreciate in the Coyote, and it's appreciated by other players I talk to as well, is its simplicity.

Yeah, it's shocking almost. I have to credit that to the vintage amps. Just learning how simple a good amp can be. The credo in our company is, "Simplicity is beauty." We kind of went along with that.

### What are your thoughts on crucial aspects of quality in guitar-amp manufacturing?

Again, our servicing background taught us lessons about product quality, so it did mean a lot to us. We made choices that we thought were not only practical, but that were made for reasons of quality. Such as our choice of metal-film resistors; we chose those not only because they were low-noise, but they were also very precise and had an excellent temperature coefficient. So I killed three birds with one stone.

And on the capacitor side, I learned through the years of seeing consumer electronics, which is built on the edge of the absolute minimum standards to make it work so they can sell it—seeing how fast and how much of a failure it was to do that, it was an obvious thing not to repeat. So I went ahead and overkilled; I bought the better temperature capacitors, went the direction of making our tube sockets better because, as a service department, we knew why the phenolic and plastic tube sockets would fail—they'd arc, and so on. To prevent all the problems, I feel any good service department or manufacturer should think like that.

Our capacitors in the signal path were actually derived from our close relationship to the hi-fi world. I think having a relationship with the high-end audio world, and having a relationship with the service business, really drove us to build the products we can.

### What are those caps you're using?

Reliable Capacitor company [RelCap]. They build the capacitors themselves, and they also build the expensive MultiCap capacitors that people in the hi-fi world rave about. They're made from polypropylene.

### Touching on resistors again, the vintage craze for carbon comps and so forth doesn't bother you at all?

The intentions are good, but the results are going to vary, and I want my products to sound as good later as they do now. Also, noise is a problem. Carbon comps are hard to make precise, and they are noisy. You know, that's fine for all the guys who can handle it.

### Considering the trade-offs, I guess a manufacturer needs to factor in how much so-called extra warmth those resistors would give you.

I think the tiniest factor between resistors, in terms of the way they participate in the sound quality, is negated by the overall results achieved by your design of the amp. They contribute as a voltage-controlling device, but not too much as a signal device. The signal devices are capacitors, and those are the components that can really contribute to the sound. All resistors are really doing is controlling how much voltage is put in the circuit.

But the most significant changes in sound occur by way of tubes, and part values. Part values first, and tubes second. The values are going to determine the voicing of the amp.

### How important is output transformer selection to you?

It's pretty important. For the long haul, we want stuff to be stable and to continue to stay alive. In this application that we're all using them for, we're playing them pretty hard. I think the difference between a guitar amp output transformer and a hi-fi output transformer is pretty significant. We're creating a distortion and we don't want the cores to saturate too fast. The value of having a guitar amp transformer in place of a hi-fi transformer can change the sound significantly. There are certain attributes of a guitar amp-type transformer, versus just something off the shelf, so they do have an important factor.

The way a lot of stuff is made today, those factors often don't matter as much in the design, because they are lucky enough to just be able to carbon-copy something that exists. But a lot of these guys are building stuff now and they're not looking at the power amp for overdrive, so they're not too concerned about such attributes in an output transformer. They're generating distortion in the preamp, so the output section just becomes a slave or utility amp in that respect.

### A lot of people who are heavily into the "tone thing" will agree that a lot of it is happening at the output stage.

As long as you're not designing all those preamp circuits to shape the sound so far that it's too late to do anything with it at the output stage. Sometimes you can mask the quality of a good amp by concentrating on your preamp to the point where it's just sterilizing the sound. The preamp needs to have nothing more, really, than the right filtering, and the right kind of filtering yields a good result: bass, midrange, treble. We're getting results through the preamp, and results through the power amp. I feel that you should be looking at a combined result. Obviously the preamp needs to be concentrated on, and that's going to be determined by the "mind's ear" that the builder has, and the same goes for the power amp. I'm being influenced by the old school, and thinking obviously of the old power amp stages.

**Your amps are meticulously hand-wired. Do you think there's a broad difference between hand-wired amps and modern PCB construction?**
To produce the products at a cost level that can be competitive with the low-cost product line, there's a big change in production in order to cut the costs. That has yielded a big difference in the way products are built. I've gone over it more than once—many times—and thought about, "How is it possible for us to maintain the same level of quality but make things more affordable?" And the answer always is, we still have to hand-build the amps.

**Obviously life would be easier if you could outsource a good-quality printed board that you could just load in.**
Well, we thought about that too. And let's say we made a printed board. Now, printed boards can be made really nice, but they have to be stuffed by a machine to make it really economical, which means that the parts are going to change. And the types of parts that are available to be loaded in by a machine are not necessarily the kinds of parts you need [for a quality guitar amp]. So now you have to bend for that; you're bending a little bit already just to make your PCB, because you're going to have new issues. You're going to have stray capacitance and eddy currents, because you're sending the signal and voltage along, and they're running alongside each other. How they run across that board is going to create its own issues, so it's a different science.

Secondly, unless you hand-stuff the board, you're going to be making a second sacrifice, and that will be with component quality. It just doesn't work.

**And if you hand-load the boards, you're not saving all that much work.**
It's not much different, right. And if you have them machine-stuffed, then you're getting down to low-grade consumer electronics-type parts. That again is down to cost-cutting. The alternative is that you take your manufacturing overseas, but I can't ever see doing that. It's impossible for anyone to make an amp through a lifetime without occasionally making a mistake, but the thing is, when you make a mistake does the person have the understanding of what it is and how to solve that problem? We need to have top-quality guys.

If I had to compare our shop to something else, I'd compare us to a hotrod shop. Hands-on designers and builders, and there is an art to it. There really is a value to having the person who does the work right there on site.

**Luckily a lot of people do appreciate that today.**
Yeah, but it's getting harder to appreciate. There are two models to the business world: one of them's the WalMart model, the other is sort of an old-school model. I'm trying to bring modern benefits to the old-school model.

**It must be hard for small manufacturers like Mojave today, in an age when people are expecting consumer goods to be cheaper and cheaper. When you can buy a DVD player for $49, you expect everything else to be dirt-cheap too.**

As a consumer electronics technician for years, I would tell customers that ask me "Well, what should I do? Get it fixed, or buy a new one?" that the answer is, "You can buy a new one, but you'll be here again in a very short time with the same question." So where do you go when you're paying $100 for a piece of equipment that breaks a year later? It's difficult, but you need to figure out that you have to go out and buy something that's of a higher caliber.

**With the cost of computers, home entertainment, and everything else going down, down, down over the years, guitarists are of course expecting amps to be cheaper and cheaper too—and of course those now coming from China are. But if you look back at the price of a tweed Fender amp in the 1950s, that was a lot of money for a musician in those days. The cost of amps like yours is comparable.**
I'd like to remind everyone that if you were in the orchestra world, this stuff by comparison is a screaming bargain. Try to find a professional oboe or violin or something. Those things sell for $40,000. So we have to count our blessings.

I don't think you have to spend $25,000 to get a good guitar. In fact, we're fortunate now in that you can spend $2,500 and get a beautiful guitar. We're in a golden age of guitar building, and I think in a golden age of amp building as well.

**Can you think of any hidden gems in the used-amp world to recommend to us?**
Yeah, Traynors. They're great. I love them. In fact the little 50-watt chassis puts out about 100 watts. They have really good transformers, and they make a great little amp. I've picked them up and made them sound like a Marshall without doing too much to them.

**I remember playing in bands as a kid in high school, and there were always Traynors around, but they never got much respect. On consideration, they were always very reliable and sounded pretty good, but we all really wanted Marshalls or Mesa/Boogies, and were usually "stuck with" silverface Fenders, as it was, which were a notch above Traynor.**
Yeah, I know. Isn't it funny. Then years later you see it on your bench and say, "Wow, that stuff wasn't too bad after all." I have to give credit where credit is due, and all of the old amps we are seeing today that are still alive were obviously built well enough to survive 30 or 40 years.

**I know you put a lot of thought into your speaker selection. How do you go about trying to determine which speaker is right for a particular amp design?**
You know, that's another one of those sciences that's not widely understood. Speakers are really a very simple kind of product. But they have very unique characteristics that are very hard for a lot of people to understand on a technical level. I don't manufacture speakers, but I can go back and use my experience, with all these different amps and the kinds of speakers I've had, to gauge what the different speakers sound like, and decide which ones I want to try.

There's better science now than there was 20 or 30 years ago. They're definitely making progress. But it's sort of the same old situation. We're not building massively better speakers to accomplish the same simple task. What we're really just trying to do is build as good a speaker as we had. I think in general the ones I know of that are really good speakers are the ones I've used in the past, and were designed about 30 years ago or more. I don't have to reinvent the wheel.

**What are some of your favorites?**
I love the [Celestion] G12 Alnico Blue. It's a gift from God. And the G12H-30, the G12M-25, that's a good speaker—those are all Celestions. Also the big JBL, the D120F and the 15-inch D130F. Those are really great speakers.

**They are, and yet some people find the JBLs a little hard to handle.**
Sure, they can be, but I won't fit the wrong foot into the wrong shoe. That's the problem with amps and speakers, they're not always compatible. It kind of goes the same way with the guitar and the amp. Accomplishing the end result is what you're looking for, and if you're trying to get a really great overdrive sound with a single-coil Strat or a single-coil Tele, and you're playing it right through a Fender, you might have a real ice-pick sound.

I have good confidence in Celestion speakers right now. I know they're made in China, and they're trying to make a major attempt to keep their quality, by moving their personnel into China to work closely with them and so forth. I have to accept the fact that they're made there, and we're all going to have to accept the fact that the Chinese are in on the manufacturing process.

**That was kind of a shock when they moved production over there.**
Yeah, it was. And it wasn't just a matter of sound quality. On that level, I think your ears can be the judge. But you've got to remember, my neighbor needs a job, too, you know? Europe has done it to themselves and we're on the same path.

**That G12H has impressed me for a long time, and I was interested to see that you use them.**
I love that speaker because it has excellent bass character, and a speaker that can produce good bass character just seems to have a more robust voice to it. It has an authoritative bass, and it doesn't have a shocking, bright overdrive, so it makes for a really good speaker. The magnets are large, and that has a big, big influence on the way the speaker performs. There's a lot of flux density in the magnet, but the power rating of the speaker—at 30 watts—is conservative. They actually have a lot higher power capacity. The fact that the amps were always putting out more power than they were rated for meant that Celestion rated their speakers pretty conservatively.

**I even find some tonal similarities between the Alnico Blue and the G12H, other than the former's softer bass response.**
The fact of the matter is that what we know as the model G12 Alnico Blue is the grandfather of all the Celestion speakers. When that speaker set the tone path, they were making it for other applications. Then the manufacturers came to Celestion and said, "I want this, but cheaper." They tried with the 25-watt ceramic magnet G12 to imitate the Blue. Then with the H they did the best they could, and that's what we came away with.

**And in fact that Greenback, the G12M-25, is a good-sounding speaker, but it doesn't have the bass of the H.**
It has a good brightness to it, because the bass is different, but I think the G12H-30 was a speaker designed by Celestion, not to meet the request of a manufacturer for a cheaper speaker, but to do a job. And they did a really good job designing it. The M-25 is a compromise speaker, and that's the one they did to meet the needs of the manufacturer, on a budget.

**Have you tried Celestion's Century speaker yet, with the neodymium magnet?**
I've been told about it, and I'm just afraid that the magnet is going to be overbearing in the brightness. The problem with our ear is that we really have a narrow band that we want to hear things in, especially out of musical instruments, and it sure as hell isn't going to be over 5,000Hz. The human voice is the most soothing thing we can listen to, and a musical instrument can't go out of those spectrums so far. I don't want to give too much power to something on the high side.

That's why tubes do really well for guitar music. They will not put a man on the moon, and they will not do so well when it comes to doing modern electronic tasks, but they do really good when it comes to sound. They have their place.

**Do you feel the tube-manufacturing business is safe for now?**
It's a struggle. It's been going up and down. Svetlana just took a beating; they have been under financial stress for years. I think they were receiving a government subsidy and now no longer are. It is a difficult business to manufacture tubes. One end of it is that they're struggling to stay in business, but the other end is that there's such a good demand from a certain sector that they're coming out with new designs, and coming on line with some old tubes that haven't been built for years.

**That's encouraging to see.**
Yes it is. I think the saving grace in all of this is that there are so many guitar players in the world now, and their demand for these kinds of products is starting to keep the market alive. In fact the hi-fi world probably owes its good graces to the guitar player world. Guitar amps use many more tubes than hi-fi amps, and guitar players burn them out all the time.

**Any quick tips for players?**
Yeah. As far as guitar goes, the guitar originates in pretty much a midrange band, and electrical amplifiers can really change that. You want to try to preserve that midrange tone, and there's really a limit to how much you

want to try to add on to the bass and the brightness. If you let it breathe in the bandwidth in which it was created to work, you'll get the best sound from it.

Working on those midrange levels, those are the sounds that really come through for guitar, and are the most appealing.

# Reinhold Bogner of Bogner

Other amp designers might have dabbled in high-gain before him, but Reinhold Bogner clinched the reputation for über-gain right from the time he started modding vintage Fender and Marshall designs into fire-breathing rock monsters in LA in the late 1980s. Bogner Amplification as it exists today came into being in 1992 when Reinhold joined forces with current business partner Jorg Dorschner, the originator of the popular Fish preamp. The pair released the Ecstasy at the end of that year, and have remained a fixture in the rock scene ever since.

***Where did your interest in tube amps begin?***
It's how I grew up. I grew up in Germany, and my father was into electronics; he used to work for Telefunken and some other electronics companies. When he started in electronics it was definitely with tubes, so for some reason he started collecting tube radios. So when I grew up I was surrounded by tubes, and also the technology was still a lot of tubes. When I was like 14 or 15 I bought an electric guitar but I didn't have money to buy an amp, so I started building myself an amp with parts that my father had lying around. So it was tubes from the very start. It was very accessible to me.

***It seems like a lot of amp guys got their start that way: they acquired the guitar, but needed an amp, so they converted something, or built one ...***
Yeah, I built one from scratch. At that point it wasn't so much that I knew that the tubes were better, it was just easier for me to do.

***In some ways, maybe the different stages of a tube amp are easier to put together, and still get a good guitar sound from at least.***
Yeah.

***I understand you were getting heavily into amp modding before you moved to California.***
Yeah, initially I got schematics from a local repair shop, the reissue stuff, Orange, Marshall, Fender stuff. I based my first amp on something like that, but then I started experimenting with changing values, adding a gain stage, that kind of thing. Then slowly it evolved into ... people came to my house and played through an amp and say, "Wow, that sounds pretty good. Can you make me one?" I'd say, "Making you one is more difficult, but I can probably work with what you have." And then I started modifying people's amps from there on. And you know, there wasn't that much gain available off the shelf, so adding gain was the main thing at that point.

***You build all kinds of amps now, of course, but you are best known for the high-gain stuff.***
I guess that's what stuck with the people first, yeah. We

do make some fantastic-sounding clean amps like the Goldfinger and the Shiva, but we were first known for the gain stuff, yeah.

***Making high-gain circuits work well is not just a matter of stacking up gain stage after gain stage. What are some of the keys to making it work right?***
Like all those things, it's paying attention to detail. It affects everything, so you have to pay attention to a load of things and try to make it all work with each other instead of against each other. A lot of massaging, going back and forth, fine-tuning it so you get the best response out of it.

***Once you change one thing inside the amp everything else reacts differently.***
Right, exactly, that's why you have to go, a lot of times, back and forth, it's like a loop. If you're going to change one thing, maybe something on the end, but it affects the front end somehow. There's a lot of interaction going on inside a tube amp, so it's not something you can do on a piece of paper and compute it. Plus these things don't make a lot of sense as to *why* they impact, but a lot of times they do. Like sometimes it's the coupling in the airwaves of some capacitors being close to something because of the high-impedance circuit, or it has to do with the fluctuation of the B+ voltage while you play and things like that, spread across the whole circuit, which you don't think about that much if you just look at it on the piece of paper.

***That's a factor that a lot of people might not give much thought to—how changes in voltages will make different stages sound, or different tubes behave.***
And not only the voltage when it's idling, but it's changing while you play. Especially on a vintage amp, that changes how the whole amp reacts. Some people love it, but some people hate it. That's sometimes the magic of the vintage amp, that they have this interaction. It gives it that blooming, very organic character, you know?

***Definitely. Any keys to maintaining dynamics and***

touch sensitivity in a high-gain amp, rather than just having it come out like fully slammed brick-wall distortion?

It's a fine line between being dynamic and organic, but also having the note separation and things like that. And sometimes, you know, it's a little bit about taste; one is not necessarily better, it depends a little bit on the player, the music you play, and where you come from. There's nothing absolute, you know. It's a matter of taste. I mean, there are some things that I think are better, but overall there's a broad range of what's usable, it just depends a lot on the application.

### Which of your own designs got you the most excited?

I think the Ecstasy was definitely a milestone, in some ways. Not only did we pretty much make it 20 or 25 years ago and it's still a valuable amp, but when it came out there wasn't anything as flexible as this. So in terms of that, as a long-lasting design, I think that's a pretty good validation, because it's still good, you know? So that's one thing. But the Goldfinger's a great amp, you know? And you need different things for different applications: more flexibility or less flexibility, more transportable, whatever, so each design itself is a success.

### Some people will look at amps with a lot of features, with channel switching and so forth, and will come away with the impression—right or wrong—that you must be losing some tone somewhere along the line because the signal is going through all this stuff …

Well, there is absolutely always something true to that, that no matter what you add, whether it's just one relay or one little something else, it does affect the tone. But I think we did a very good job to make [the Ecstasy] that special. That was the great milestone of the mega-flexible amp like that. People like Eric Johnson were playing that amp in the plexi channel for a long time, and at that time he had plexis up his whatever … warehouse. And he chooses that amp with all the switching in it and it still sounds like one of his best plexis, I think that's a good accomplishment.

But I mean, there is always something. You add something, it will change it. Sometimes it's like, to some players they wouldn't even know it, you know. But it depends on how anal you are, and Eric Johnson's definitely known to be one of those guys. He hears everything. And sometimes it's the coloration, it might be good or might be bad, but more stuff usually dilutes some of the pureness, like adding a longer cable or something like that.

### Perhaps there's always a compromise, but you do the best job you can, and for many players the flexibility of such amps makes it worthwhile.

Right, exactly. Certain amps you can just play in one loud setting and then they sound great, but you can't use them in any other kind of venue where you can't play loud, or they don't sound nearly as good. That's why we make those amps fairly flexible, so they can be tailored to each situation and playing style.

### You mentioned the Shiva earlier, and while that amp has a great lead channel, I've heard one person after another talk about how much they like the clean channel on that one.

It's a great clean channel. That's what I'm saying. And most people love that. We are first of all known for the gain stuff, but we do make some fantastic clean-sounding amps. The Goldfinger's also one of those; people buy it just for that, they just use the clean channel.

### And you have dabbled in some simpler amps too …

Yeah, like the New Yorker and stuff. There's a certain appeal to just having three knobs, you know, there's a certain pureness about that too. Like we just said—less stuff, easy to operate, and it has a directness because it has less stuff in it.

### Do you have any particular process for choosing components when you're working on a new design?

As far as choosing stuff that's reliable and that … you know, every component has its flavor, and depending a little bit on what you're shooting for some are better suited than others. There's not one thing—except of course great-sounding tubes, which are harder and harder to come by—the caps and resistors and stuff do make a difference, but, depending on what sound you're going for, different brands work better than others. It's not like "this capacitor sounds great for everything."

### Have there been times when you've designed something with a certain component in mind, only to find after you put it in there that it's just fighting against you?

Yeah, exactly, because it doesn't work with the rest of the stuff somehow, and sometimes another works better. It's definitely worth going through every component many, many times and making sure it's the best one for that job.

### There's a lot of talk in the amp community about magical components, little things that make all the difference …

Yeah, there's always the search for that magic one trick you do, or the one pill you should take. Yeah, I'm trying to find that one pill, but at the end of the day it's really about paying attention to all the little details, and they will add up to be a great thing. But it's not one thing, I really doubt that. I'm trying to find it myself, ha ha! "Put this one cap in and everything will be great!" I don't know about that.

I mean, if you have a very simple design, something like a tweed Deluxe, you know, with very few components, the effect of one component will be bigger than in an amp that has five gain stages or something, because every component has a little more weight. And there are certain stages, like maybe the first stage is extra critical in a tube amp.

### Do you ever find some components are too good?

Of course, all the time. That's the thing. Better in engineering terms is not always better [sonically]. Like super low-noise resistors or super high-end caps, they're not necessarily better. That's the thing I learned early on.

Also, I went to engineering school in Germany, and you see something that looks great on paper, but you try it and it sounds horrible. So there's a big gap between what, engineering-wise, should be good, and what's good for a guitar player.

Sometimes the crappy stuff is better. A lot of times it's like that. The imperfection gives you the coloration. Because you're not making a hi-fi amp with no distortion; you *want* distortion, even in the clean sound. You don't want to be sterile. You want some extra compression and extra harmonics when it's distorting. That makes a great amp.

**Do you see much change in the amp market these days?**
Besides that there's a lot of products out these days? The digital stuff is coming in more and more. Digital for

recording, and even for live stuff. I don't have too much experience with that, but it's definitely changing. Most people are using in some shape or form some kind of digital platform, I guess. I think that's the biggest change. I don't think there's too much evolution in the tube-amp world otherwise.

**I suppose the availability of good tubes—or lack thereof—is an issue that amp makers have to deal with today.**
Well, the tube thing, it is what it is, you know? There's only that many manufacturers and the quality is definitely not getting better at this point. It is what it is, and we have to work around it. But we seem to get OK tubes— you just have to work around it and make the designs work around the tubes that are available.

# Brian Gerhard of TopHat Amplification

After repairing, modifying, and building tube amps on the side for several years, Brian Gerhard founded TopHat in California in 1994 and rapidly cultivated a reputation as a central figure on the booming "boutique" scene. After a move back to his native North Carolina in the mid '00s, Gerhard continued to produce TopHat staples, from the best-selling Club Royale to the mighty Emplexador, while introducing new Custom Shop models and continually improving each of his amp designs toward his goal of uncompromising tone.

**How did you get your start with tube amps?**
I'd been in electronics three years in high school, and had built a Dynaco amp in the 7th grade, which was not a tube amp, but I'd been into hi-fis since I was a kid, from 5th grade on. I had a three-years-older brother and we were both into it. I had some college electronics as well, never into digital electronic circuit design and that kind of stuff, but tube amps are old-timey stuff so it doesn't take the high-tech modern kind of digital understanding to know how these things work. All that, and just knowing about vintage amps and, when I had the opportunity business-wise and the time and place to do it … Even through *Vintage Guitar* magazine and others you could find these suppliers like Mojo, Magic Parts; the stuff was available to do it, where it would have seemed, somewhat earlier than then, more difficult.

I started with a tweed Deluxe, and when you hear one for the first time when you've done it yourself, you go, "Oh, that's *pretty* nice!" You know, compared to a high-gain Marshall type thing of the era, you hear this big, glorious richness of a simple design with a few parts, and it turns you on pretty quick.

**You know, I think that's the kind of thing that turned on a lot of would-be builders, and guitarists too. You hear how great the simple, older amp designs can be, and it opens up your ears.**
Yeah, you hear a spectrum—rather than this scrunched down, buzzy, little crunchy thing—you hear a guitar

sound in your hands, what your hands are doing and so forth, greatly improved.

**You got in toward the early end of what we call the boutique market these days.**
1994 officially.

**Remind us of what some of your early models were.**
The first year, going on two years probably, was mostly build-to-order custom stuff, mostly Bassman- and Marshall-based. We'd gotten up to four gain stage higher-gain stuff, and you see the limits of that when you're hand-wiring them and trying to control things in there with the wire dress and so on. It becomes quite microphonic there and stuff wants to squeal. So, we went that far, but they weren't really models yet. The first models were what we called the Club Royale and Prince Royale, a TC18 combo. That was the first. Once we'd made a big run of 100 of them, the Club Royale and Club Deluxe were the first Club amps that we started with.

**You were out in California at this time, although you're now in North Carolina, where you're originally from?**
Yeah.

**It's interesting that you were starting with custom-made Fender tweed and Marshall type amps,**

because these days you seem to be most closely associated with a more Voxy type of sound. Do you feel there's a "house sound" at TopHat?

Oh, yeah, I think that every smaller builder generally has a sound. Bogner, whoever. If it's mainly one guy's ears making the choices … and I would also include this: I'm more of a British-amp guy by nature, so that comes through in what I have a preference for. And even just the prevalence of gigantic Fender on the American market, and especially the reverb side of things, making eight thousand models, I don't need to compete there. So somewhat due to those factors, and due to what your forte is, I carry on from [my background in] vintage-based stuff—and even the Emplexador doesn't get super-modern high-gain kind of a thing, but it's fully into the wailing, sustaining master-volume Marshall with plenty of gain. But the house sound, like I say, comes from the ears and the preferred distortion characteristics.

I would also say this: I believe it's not just the ears, but when you take what I and most others would agree are the top five, eight, ten amps of all time and you play them all—the real vintage stuff, is what I'm talking about—they do converge, because they all are considered to have this great, complex, rich distortion kind of characteristic and stuff; it's usually not a straight clean thing on an old vintage amp, right? So you always have a fairly complex distortion going on.

And my supreme personal-experience example of two things that shouldn't be within miles of each other, on the one hand, was comparing one of my Club Royales, after I had refined it for a while, to a real blonde Bassman: 6L6s vs EL84s, couldn't be further apart; Class A/B vs Class A, couldn't be further apart; a lot of things. But plug in a really good guitar and play it through both, and it's not that at *any* level it happens, but in the sweet spot, on seven or wherever where tube amps are in their sweet spot, and reference them both through the same cabinet, and the similarities blew my mind. "Wow, there's so much in common, but they shouldn't be. They should be miles and miles apart." In theory, on paper if you will, most people wouldn't associate that kind of arrangement as being anywhere similar.

**As you say, if you're going for that cranked-up sound, the ideal of a really good amp, for most of us for a great general rock'n'roll sound, does converge toward something similar.**

And especially because all the early Marshall stuff comes straight from a tweed Bassman. That's why the standout oddball is the blackface, that is the other end of the world. The Bassman goes into the Marshall and the Vox, and the similarities of the preamps in the Top Boost Vox and the early Marshalls that comes from the '59 Bassman, that's why all those are tied together. And that's a lot of the greatness right there of the vintage era. Then you get to roughly the mid 60s with the blackface Fender reverb amps, and that's just a whole different sound unto itself.

**Yeah, it's funny how Fender helped to give birth to that British sound, but then changed its own sound so dramatically. Once you change that preamp's tone stack from the cathode-follower to the**

blackface tone stack sandwiched between two gain stages, it's a completely different sound.

Yeah, the EQ goes from all the way at the end of the preamp in the tweed amps to all the way at the front right off the first tube before you even get to a volume control.

**Which is why, when you hear people talk about the Super Reverb as the evolution of the tweed Bassman, with four 10" speakers and two 6L6s, it's pretty far off the mark.**

Right. And that's what I'm saying. I realized when I recognized those two things that should be far apart, that those two are common. It's not just that my ears are drawn to that, which they are. But that is the good, right stuff. You don't have to dial everything exactly into that spot, but it's all close to that. Even my Emplexador has that (even with up to three gain stages), the Club Royale has that, that's why much of what I do is going to have this fairly common thing. Class A and Class A/B again, very different feels to them, but because of the common front end mainly, other than the higher-gain mode of the Emplexador, a lot of my stuff's there.

I occasionally make an Embassador model, which is like my blackface reverb model, but I don't even put 'em up on the web site any more. That's not my focus, to compete with a gazillion different Fender reverb models out there.

**But even just looking at your Club Royale, which has long been your best-selling amp, you see how maybe on paper it looks like a slightly modified Vox Top Boost-type of amp, but with a few EQ tweaks you can get it to sound like what people think of as being really Marshally or really Fendery.**

Yeah, you can at least get a more Fendery spectrum by having the mid [control] and sucking out [the midrange], and having the bright mode, with the bass and treble up. It's not going to become a blackface 6L6 amp or something, but you can at least have that spectrum. And that's why that midrange control is so useful. There was Bruno and Dr Z, and I don't know exactly what year they started, putting the midrange onto the Top Boost tone stack; and Matchless didn't do it, he stayed pure [to the original circuit] with no midrange, and there's a teeny benefit of doing it without the mid, to do the dead-bone Vox thing; you get a slightly different interaction between the two knobs when you don't have the mid knob in there. But the variety and versatility that it has adding it is, to me, a ten-to-zero choice, just to even work with different types of guitars to match up spectrums and balance things out.

**It's funny how people refer to the Vox Top Boost circuit as being such a dramatic influence on the sound of those amps, and then you refer to what the tweed amps had, and it's all a fairly similar cathode-follower tone stack.**

The algorithm [of the Vox] is the same as the '59 Bassman with the cathode-follower, it's just with the EQ treble and slope resistor difference. And, as you know, that so-called Top Boost EQ oddball thing was actually, originally, tweed Gibson. Now, I find you can do it like when we made the Club Deluxe 6V6 only, that EQ could still work relatively well. But if you try to run that EQ on large tubes, especially 6L6s, it sucks, it doesn't work right *at all* the way the spectrum moves. It sucks dramatically, it's so odd and strange to me and doesn't work right at all. That's why we normalize the EQ on the Super Deluxe. Like, on the AC50 and AC100, I bet they didn't sell many of them. I've seen quite a few of them, and they often vary against the drawings quite a bit. But they have that EQ, ha ha, and if nothing else ruins that amp, it's the EQ. I tell you, it's a horrible EQ for those large tubes. In the treble department, the whole mid and upper end is just goofball, it doesn't work right at all.

**It just goes to show how you have to be aware of varying every stage, depending on what you've changed elsewhere. You can't just drop things in and expect they're going to work the way they worked with a different configuration in another stage.**
Yeah, but they worked right, really well, with EL84s, but not much else. You can change to 6V6s like we did on the Club Deluxe and it still works, but I don't know if it would be preferred. Once we incorporated the Club Deluxe into the Super Deluxe, and with the normal Bassman-type EQ on the Super Deluxe, now when you put the 6V6s in it I like it better—bigger and richer.

**Subtle changes.**
Yeah, the circuit in effect doesn't change, just the values within the EQ. And it's only the treble cap, the treble pot, and the slope resistor. Have you ever played an AC50 or an AC100?

**Yeah, I owned one for a while several years ago, a good vintage one, but just couldn't find much to like about it, for my own playing at least.**
Phew, I'm telling you. I've worked on them and played a few, and they're just naked and ugly, and the whole upper end past the midrange is just … harsh. you wouldn't think it could get that far from a 50-watt Marshall kind of thing, running EL34s in those, but boy, they are nothing alike. And who knows, so many Voxes, even AC30s and everything else, have been modded. So if someone's playing an AC50, did they change things? Like fix the EQ so that the thing's better. But the only guy I think I've seen in the modern world was the guy from Wolfmother in Australia, he used an AC50.

**Just brash, right?**
Yeah, it's the harshness and the naked upper end that is the problem.

**Have you had to make major adjustments to any classic circuits to make them work right in your own amps?**
Well, like on a JCM800 [the inspiration for one of the voices in the Emplexador], they use a 1-Meg master [potentiometer] in there, but if you really crank up the preamp and really crank up the master it starts getting very rash, raw and harsh. Now, if you do nothing but put, in parallel, a resistor to ground off of that master to

effectively lower it down to a 150k master, you lose almost no output, but it will control the upper end and make it much smoother, sweeter, richer, not so bright, brash, and harsh. And that's without changing the cap to try to keep it equal, but whoa it down there so that it's not pile-driving the holy crap out of the phase inverter and distorting the shit out of it and feeding that on through to the tubes. (But really the EQ already has a parallel reference to ground, so when you're using a 1-Meg master there it's really more like 250k, so you're not dropping it down as far as it seems.)

**So, you did that tweaking in the Emplexador?**
That's part of what you engage when you engage that higher-gain mode, it lowers the reference to ground at the master. Where it is a 1-Meg in the plexi mode, it is whoa'd down in the JCM800 mode.

**That's interesting. You're not just switching the gain stage, but reconfiguring the master so it works better with that gain stage.**
Right. Because even with three, let alone four or five gain stages, you're just—*waaahhhh!*—screaming bloody murder into the phase inverter, out of control. Even, like, Matchless puts a resistor reference to ground when they don't have a pre-phase-inverter master, in its place there is a resistor referenced to ground that isn't there in a Vox, that they're whoa'ing things down at the phase inverter to keep it under control. But when you're screaming, like I say, like three, four, five gain stages does, whoa'ing it down just a little bit gets some of the rash [harshness] out of there. It doesn't lower the input, but it helps to get it under control. You're still screaming right on in there.

**I know you have put a lot of thought into transformer selection recently.**
The transformers, yeah, we definitely changed, because of the Custom Shop experience. When I did the Supreme 16 and later the Vanderbilt, I did a lot of experimentation, and particularly with the transformers trying every which thing under the sun to see what does what. Because I cannot find anyone in America, or anywhere on this planet, that can give me a proper explanation of what does what [as regards transformers].

Even Heyboer, which makes great, great transformers, and other popular companies that I've talked to as well, it's a great company, but they can't tell me if I raise the primary impedance from 8k to 10k, what will that do to the sound and feel of it? Not a clue, they can't tell me anything. If you interleave it eleven times instead of five times, what will that do? Nothing. You've just got to try it, because I don't know of anyone who can tell you about it in advance.

They can talk about the plate material—which goes, in quality, from M6 to M50, higher to lower—but they can't tell you what the overall result will be. And they do breathe different, and make different overtones, especially when you're saturating them and stuff. And primary impedance certainly does a thing. I don't like to mess with the classic things too much, but certainly the plate material, somewhat how big the stacks are—that's another thing—but I just had to try a whole bunch of different stuff, and it's still subjective as to who likes what.

I have three different levels of output transformers just for the two-EL84 arrangement. One on what I would call the properly sized Club Royale and Club Deluxe, which is basically a Deluxe Reverb-size output transformer, for plate size and stack. It's 24-watt rated, which would be half of the for-sure classic 45/50-watt size on an AC30. So if you cut that in half you'd have a 22 to 25, that's the normal size. And it gets really good saturation, and keeps it in a slightly smaller realm. The other extreme was the original Vox size, when they started with the AC15 in 1957 before they made the AC30, the physical size of the output transformer relative to the tubes was the most over-sized output transformer in tube-amp history, probably by a long shot. It's the same plate size as all the Fender Vibrolux, Tremolux, Bandmaster, all the medium-sized amps, that's a 33-watt output transformer. It's that plate size, but a bigger stack, so going on a 40-ish watt size for an 18-watt amp.

### What does that do for it?

Here's the critical issue. I was going that way when I was doing my Supreme 16, to both the power supply with the choke input and that original big output transformer; and you can go from the single 12AX7 stage of the vibrato channel up to the balls and crunch and grind of a single EF86 gain stage and you're OK. When you go up to a Top Boost with two gain stages of 12AX7, which gets very aggressive crunchy grindy, and now you're breathing through that big old output transformer, you can get to where it's too nakedly exposed. You're not as gritty-crunchy-driven as with the single 12AX7 or the EF86. I believe, reasonably so, that Dick Denney was trying to make that poor little pair of tubes sound as big and fat as he could make 'em, and the way to do it was to unleash it through the output transformer, and he went humungous. No off-the-shelf stuff like Marshall did with its 18-watters. And that's what makes an old AC15 sound particularly huge for its 18 watts.

But for us, when we're putting an AC Top Boost channel and an EF86 channel in the same amp, that output transformer doesn't work so well. And this is interesting. Notice what Vox did with their reissue AC15: having the EF86 channel with a two-way switch and the Top Boost channel is kind of Vox copying the boutique guys, rather than the boutique guys copying Vox.

So anyway, that's on the big end of the original AC15 sized [output transformer]. The properly cut-in-half Deluxe Reverb size that we used for a long time is on the smaller end [of the scale], and for the Club Royale I have a "happy medium" where it is the bigger plate size of the original AC15, but not as big of a stack [the body of the transformer], and you find the sweet spot where you've kept the compression, saturation, distortion characteristics as much like the smaller one, but let the sound be as big as it can be without getting too big and naked and openly exposed.

### It's almost like you'd need switchable OTs to do it all in one amp.

Yeah, right.

### But that said, you get plenty of versatility in your amps, and most players really don't need more than a few great usable sounds, as long as they can achieve them with different guitars.

I think mine have achieved that. Certainly on the Emplexador, but even on the Super Deluxe and Club Royale. With the wide-ranging EQ, the three-way boost control, and the cut control in the output section, a master that works well, you've got as much variety as you can get out of that basic arrangement. That's what I'm trying to provide. It is still one channel, but a Tele and a Les Paul are miles apart, and you can still make those work for the gig, without adulterating the basic arrangement too much where you can't do the original thing through it.

Others, I won't mention names, but people are making Marshall-type amps especially that are big and loud, with no master volume; there's no variety switch, we've still got to jumper an overly fat and overly bright channel together to try to balance them out. Even all the stuff that's tweed-Deluxe based, some even do that with a larger power-tube arrangement, but no master volume, or a 30-watt with two EL34s running volume, volume, tone. That's radically impractical. You can hardly live with a 5-watt without a master volume in the real world, if you've got neighbors. So you've got to be as practical for the real world and add the versatility, and not just stuck in the one mode.

### Any other components that you really consider essential to the brew?

I really like the polystyrene treble caps. There's a place in Canada that has every value in them, but they were hard to find in the right voltages for a while. I like carbon comps even though they are a bit noisier. I definitely don't like metal film. Carbon film, OK for power resistors, 1-watt, 2-watt or something. To me it makes a difference. You would think things like even the cathode resistors where even the signal's not going through it—you come in the grid, and go out the plate side—and so maybe the plate resistors, that's at least touching where the signal's going before it goes over a coupling cap to the next stage. But like the cathode, it's regulating flow but the signal's not going through it itself, and even those, you do it across two, three gain stages, it's amazing [the difference made by carbon comp resistors used there].

I could tell you, and this is the most mind-blowing one that I couldn't believe you could tell: same value, the reference to ground on the phase inverter on the Bassman/Marshall type, where one side basically just goes to ground and the other side is the input side; you've got a 0.1uF/250 volt on the ground side. That one single cap, if there's one cap in the whole line of the circuit with all the couplers and everything, that should be the least significant cap—all the other ones you're breathing right through, and should be way more important—this is just grabbing the reflected side off of ground. Least important of the whole line, and just that, going from metalized polyester to polyester film-foil, changing that one single cap, same value, same medium of polyester but just whether it's metalized or not, I can hear the difference in that. You would think "no effing way."

*It all goes to show you, I guess, that tube amps are imperfect equations. It's not always the math and the precision that's always going to work best; it's often just the way certain components work together to make a tone that you like—with feeding the voltages in a certain way, as well as passing the signal along.*

Right. And can it get *too* good? Polyester is less than polypropylene or whatever, but they breathe different, they sound different, the medium definitely makes a difference in all the different caps. But too good is great for hi-fi, but not good for lo-fi vintage kinda guitar amplifiers. That's why you want the *proper good* level, not the *best* level, that sounds and acts and breathes like the good old stuff does—if you believe that the vintage breathed most wonderfully, and that's our gold reference that we're trying to achieve. If you want it to be more hi-fi, Twin Reverb grand piano, then these super high-dollar caps and components might work for you.

I'm not against—like, I do use silver-plated wire, it's copper wire but it's silver-plated rather than tinned, and Teflon coated, and then I use silver solder, because I want good connections. But I still want the caps, which are tone-creators by their medium and by their nature, they're going to affect the quality and the texture of the sound, between the socket and the cap and the cap and the pot I want it to breathe freely through nice conductors; but not crazy high-dollar like pure silver, at some ridiculous price per foot, and you can definitely go too far, too hi-fi.

To recognize a humongous point: we're not building hi-fi amplifiers, we're not trying for perfect replication of source material. We are producing a textured, complex, purposefully distorted sound. That is lo-fi by definition. Trying to twist that into hi-fi is so off base. If you want to say, "Mine's the fastest, cleanest, most hi-fi guitar amp you ever played," good on you, that's great.

### But not a lot of guys are going to enjoy playing that.

Ha ha, no, they're not. But if you're trying to do a supposedly vintage-based thing, you can definitely take things too far.

*And all of those points further confirm that the electric guitar really isn't an instrument on its own, as most players use it at least: the complete instrument is the electric guitar through a great amplifier.*

Right. Compression, saturation, distortion, at the speaker, at the transformer, at the preamp stages, at the power tubes, whether they're cleanly amplifying or being clipped all the time. It's all important stuff. And to me, some transformer builders, everything they make sounds Twin Reverb hi-fi, which is fine if it's for a new design, but if it's supposed to be a clone of a vintage transformer... that just doesn't make any sense.

### Any other contemporaries of yours building amps that you're impressed with?

Yeah, the prices make them hard to afford. But in the cleaner, roughly speaking Fender-reverb sound, those Two-Rocks, that is a glorious, rich, improved version of that sound. I've got a feeling, with the richness of the sound and how ridiculously priced they are, I have a feeling they have some really, really well-made transformers, particularly the output. I'll at least admit, that sounds like you spent some money on your amplifier, that it sounds gorgeous and rich, and there's no harsh ugliness; it's very pretty, very rich, and luscious.

And I would say amid a lot of bad stuff that Vox has done, the Night Train little baby is probably the best amp for the money on the market. And the transformers are not so dinky and undersized like even the AC15 Reissue was. Up to half way they would sound okay, but after that the compression and saturation on the output was just choking the holy shit out of it. But the Night Train, they have decent sized transformers and even a choke in there, and maybe it's not going to measure up to the boutique things, but for an intermediate player that is at least going to breathe and let him hear his hands a whole lot better than buzz-bombing cheap crap out there. For the price, *man*.

## Steven Fryette of Fryette Amplification

Steven Fryette bounced back and forth between careers as a professional guitarist and a day job repairing and modifying amps for some of the hottest players on the LA scene before founding VHT Amplifiers in the late 80s. Best known for combining gutsy power amps, scorching high-gain preamps, and cleverly wrought extra features into highly functional professional platforms, Steve moved out under his own name in the late 2000s, and continues to manufacture many classic former-VHT models under the Fryette brand, while introducing groundbreaking new products too.

### What first got you interested in tube amps?

I don't think that I was predisposed to look at any particular kind of "how it's done" amp. I just grew up with it. I started getting involved with electronics at a really, really young age, so that's just what was there. I was taking TVs and radios apart when I was eight, nine, and studying electronics books at the library. I was born in 1953. It stemmed from an interest in science fiction, and science, and monsters, Frankenstein.

### That goes great with rock'n'roll.

Yeah. Things that shoot sparks. Experiments that you could do and when you turn the experiment on, all the lights in the city would dim. All that stuff was really fascinating to me. So I always wanted, some day, to have a laboratory on the roof of my house, which would have been my parents' house, where I could go up on the roof and pull a switch and watch the lights in the town dim while I'm shooting a ray into space to communicate with aliens or whatever.

### I think tube technology continues to appeal to some people in a way that is akin to that kind of thing.

The anachronistic side of things, the fantasy of it. I'm still attracted to that—designing a new product and turning it on for the first time. Either way, it will be really exciting: if it catches fire, *that* would be exciting; if it works for the first time, *that* would be exciting. If *nothing* happens, that's a letdown. You want something to happen. So I sort of built a little fantasy world around myself. I had wires, and I had a soldering iron, and growing up there were lots of little junk stores that you could go into and get lost in. Those were the days when the St. Vincent DePaul and the Goodwill stores were just loaded with things. Other people's failed experiments, and companies' failed products. I remember seeing these medical devices that were big electrical coils with dials and things that you mounted on your head. I brought that stuff home, took it apart, and looked inside.

### Did you go on to any formal electrical training?

I started to, and then I got sidetracked by music. The minute The Beatles came out, it was all about—I wanted to be Ringo, just like Ringo.

### You were a drummer, huh?

Well, no, not until Ringo. And then it was like, "I'm

gonna be Ringo." My parents debated and debated, and on my 12th birthday a chrome Ludwig snare showed up. I don't think I looked at or thought about electronic gadgets for a good couple of years. And I have a brother who's two years older than me, and he was interested in music too. He was the guy who brought home all the new records. Once I discovered The Beatles, then after that I wanted to know about all these other bands, and my brother was the one who brought home the first Rolling Stones record, and the first Kinks record, and the first this and that, Beach Boys. And my mom was a Elvis fan, and she had picture 45s of Elvis, and my parents listened to music of all kinds, so I was constantly surrounded by all of that.

But, from a very young age, things that made noise, and mechanical things, and things that could injure you— I had an Erector set my uncle gave me, it had a motor in it with gears, and I was constantly getting my hands stuck in that. So that stuff was always around me, there was always this tug-of-war between my fascination with electrical things and gadgets, and the lure of music and the emotional reward of listening to music.

### When did you build your first guitar amp?

I didn't actually build it, I cobbled it together from things. My grandmother had this Philco radio, a floor model that didn't work, in the storage room of her house, and I messed around with it when I visited her in the summer for a couple weeks. They had all kinds of stuff around. Eastern Washington, way out in the sticks, when your car breaks down you just stick it out in the field up on blocks; when your radio breaks down, you just shove it in the closet, when your lawnmower breaks down you shove it in the barn ... That's just the way they operated, so there was all this broken stuff all over the place.

I watched my grandfather change the points on a lawnmower one day, and I went and got the broken lawnmower and copied what he did, and lo and behold the thing worked. Then I went and did that to the radio, and that worked. And so I took the radio home, and I learned about power amps and preamps, and I figured out what was the input of the power-amp stage of this little Philco radio. I had another little box that was a preamp, just one tube stage and a volume control—part of a CB radio thing—and I managed to get that to drive the radio, and that was my first guitar amp.

So I was off doing these bizarre things, and that was

the first thing I made that made original noise. Then I got a fuzz pedal and plugged that into there, and it just sort of developed from there. I started building kits—at the time kits were really big—and I made a kit home stereo system, so I was kind of indoctrinated into separate components, preamps and power amps, and their individual characteristics and how they operated.

**And you're getting a good overview of circuit stages in that way.**
Yeah, and I'd go down to the library and read Ohms Law, and I just started doing all that.

**When did you feel you could make a business out of it, and how did you get started?**
That was the culmination of probably 20 years of music and electronics. I got an amp, and when I started playing guitar in bands: I got a 50-watt Hiwatt. I fell in love with the way it looked, and I traded my drum kit for it. I played that for a while, and I was kind of in this battle with the other guitar player in the band who had a 50-watt Marshall, who sounded better, who could cut. Then I saw this 100-watt Hiwatt in a store, thinking "If 50's good, 100's twice as good," and I traded the 50-watt for the 100-watt and got it to the gig, and it was just out of control. The war with the other guy was over, it was over and done: I didn't even think about it any more, I was trying to control this thing. And that just started consuming my time. I was thinking, "Shit, I'm either going to have to go back and trade for my 50 back…" But I remembered what it was about the 50 that made me want to move on to something, and that was where I really started the quest, because there was a solution that needed to be resolved there.

I started trying to figure out what made this thing, that was only supposed to be just a little louder, a completely different animal. In terms of playing it and learning how to control it and getting a sound and battling with the sound guys, and all of that, I was immediately confronted with this problem: you either have to back up and give up, or you have to follow through on this. And all this time I'm playing music, and it wasn't until I started playing original music that I needed to have a day job; before, I was playing in cover bands and I was making decent money, actually good money sometimes, and didn't have to worry about things. But when I moved to LA, and decided I was down there to do original music, doing undemanding day jobs so I could concentrate on the music … that was a pain, because the money was crummy, so I stumbled into this gig at Valley Arts. They had been running an ad for a couple of months for a repair guy. That's where Paul Rivera was working, and he was leaving.

Valley Arts was kind of this hub; it was this highly regarded store. I figured it was going to be populated by experts; it was going to be out of my league. So I saw that ad … but in the same magazine there was an ad for another shop looking for a repair guy. I went and checked that out—it was a little store, kind of out of the way—and I thought, OK, this is an atmosphere where I can bullshit the guy that I can fix stuff. I worked there for about three or four days, and the guy would not turn on the air

conditioner in his store, and it was summer time. I could not concentrate—it was stifling in the store … So I went down to Valley Arts. They said, "What kind of experience do you have?" And I said, "I ran my own shop in Seattle but I just moved down here recently, so I can cut the gig." It was a complete lie. They hired me, and the very first thing that I did was I had to rebuild an SVT.

The thing about Valley Arts was that that's where all these guys were coming to get their gear modified. I wasn't thinking about that, I was just thinking about that I got the gig. I was like, "What the hell's modifying amps?" But then I started picking up on what Rivera had been doing and the other guy before him. And that's where I actually got into how amps work, and how you change them to make them do what you want them to do. Once I started getting into that, I started rolling that back into my "Hiwatt is out of control" project. Then I made a couple things, a preamp, and a switcher, and a rack system that I'd built, with a crazy patch bay that went into it with wires, and all this Frankenstein stuff. And I went to another repair shop, and it was there that I actually started putting all that stuff to work in an amp, because I started playing a lot and I needed an amp. I actually sold all my tools, donated my schematics to the shop, I cleared all that out, it was a distraction and I was going to play music, and I was going to find somebody who makes an amp that I want.

I went to Mike Soldano's shop and played that, and tried a bunch of other things, and Rivera had just come out with a new amp and I played that. And I just went, "Crap, you guys, I'm really disappointed. You're going to make me build my own amp, because I'm not hearing what I want." I went and bought back my equipment, and made copies of my schematics, and re-stocked that part of my life that I'd thought I was done with.

**What were you looking for in an amp that you didn't hear in those others?**
That was the point. I didn't know what I was looking for until I found it. I needed it clean, I knew that I needed it overdriven. I knew how to use the guitar's volume control to navigate that to a certain degree, but there was a level that I couldn't navigate. The other guys' stuff, they all had a little piece of what I heard in my head, but none of them had all the elements together the way I heard 'em. So, it was just a stew. I smelled it a certain way different than anybody else, and I had to keep stirring the stew until it smelled and tasted right. I didn't really know what I was shooting for. I just kinda hacked around until I went, "This is starting to feel and smell right."

**Which is a good indication of how individualistic the whole amp field is, because each of those builders you tried was doing great work.**
We all look for something, and what we're looking for is to find ourselves in our little sandbox of bits and pieces. I started making these mental associations, like, Paul Rivera, I know he's got engineering chops. He offered me a job at Fender when he was there, and he offered me a job at Rivera, he had faith in me. And he also helped me, at Valley Arts, navigate these high level studio musicians that had high expectations. And then there were other

guys that I just call "capacitor changers," because they didn't really have any engineering chops. They were fishing like I was fishing, only as far as I was concerned they were just fishing blind: "I'll just change the capacitors and see what happens." At least I had some engineering chops and some background in it.

**It seems like you got known early on for some serious rock amps, some major high-gain stuff, but also with a good clean channel involved. Once you found it for yourself, did you feel like that was a market you could help to fulfill for other players?**
Well, that's how I envisioned it, but that isn't really the way it worked out.

So I built this prototype of the Pittbull, my idea of the ultimate amp—that was from '85 to '88—and part of it was still just a hobby. I had a Harley and I was customizing that, and I knew what all the good plating shops were around town. And the first thing I did was I took the chassis down to this plating shop and had them chrome plate it. I just thought that would be cool. I didn't even think that that would be any kind of a trend, it was just all screwed up and rusty, it was an old Marshall PA chassis that had been under water for a while. I showed it to a few of my old clients, and they went, "Wow, how much?" I didn't know; I didn't even know how to price something, I'd got so much time into it. I would choke every time someone would ask me how much it would cost to do this thing, because I had no answer.

I took it around and I showed it to some people, and I took it to Andy Brauer [Studio] Rentals, because there were a lot of artists going through there, buying gear and storing gear, so they had all the guys flowing through their door on a daily basis. I showed one of the guys my amp, and showed him the effects loop. I thought I had a really good idea of how the effects loop should work, and I'd tried a lot of other amps and the effects loops never worked right. So I showed the guy, and he said "That's the best effects loop I've ever seen!" He said, "Can I stick some other stuff in just the power section of the head and see how it works?" Because they were building racks and using Mesa power amps and solid state power amps—it was all about the big rack systems and power. I'd noticed that they liked the big H&H power amps the best because they were kid of neutral, and they had enough dynamic range to make up for all the dynamic range you'd lose in a rack system going through all this junk. The guy plugged a few effects into the return of my amp, into just the power amp, and said, "This sounds really good. If you made a stereo thing of this, rack-mountable, I bet you you'd have something." I'd actually built a little stereo rack system of my own and was playing around town with it, but when he said that it kind of tied everything together for me.

I went that weekend and bought some parts ... and built [a prototype]. I brought it back and set it up on top of a rack and plugged it all in, and Andy was there and a buddy of his was there, and the guy who'd given me the idea, Lon Cohen, who still has his own cartage shop around LA. And they all go, "*Phhhh* [makes a "very impressed" sound], how soon can you make ten of these?" I'm like, "I made this one in a weekend, but I

don't think we want them to look like that." They said, "No, it's got to look like a real product." It kinda freaked me out, but they were all very, very serious. "Figure out how much it's going to cost you to make ten of them, and we'll give you 50 percent of the money up front."

I went home and my head was just spinning. I figured if I did this I was going to lose music entirely... So I got on my bike and just rode out of town, with no particular direction, to just clear my head out. And it took me two, three days of riding—I think I made it all the way through Yellowstone before I turned around—and I went back and called the guy and said, "Yeah, I think I'm ready to give this a shot."

So we made the 2150 power amp, and that was the one that got everybody's attention: Metallica, Megadeth, Steve Lukather, Steve Vai, and everybody just like by default bought one. They all had racks in progress, and wherever these guys were touring I started getting phone calls: a guy from Finland, a guy from Japan, a guy from Germany, and they all wanted 2150 power amps. That's what started it off, and that's what started our association with being this metal company. Which, I never was that; the original Pittbull was more of a classic-oriented amp. I was really trying to refine that and keep the old-school voicing to it, but everybody kept wanting more and more gain, so I was developing that on the Pittbull, and as that was developing people were making their preamps higher gain, and the 2150 power amp was bringing the clarity and articulation and tightness to the table, and from there everything that we made, from there on out, was associated with that sound.

**What did VHT stand for?**
There never was a real "what does it stand for?" That was always the question. I had been listening to a lot of avant-garde music, and I read an interview with David Byrne, where he said, "I write words on paper and cut them up and rearrange them until they sound good to say." I started trying initials, then I was thinking "SVT", nobody says "I play an Ampeg bass amp," they say "I play an SVT". It rolls off the tongue. So I just settled on VHT.

**When you describe launching VHT on the 2150 power amp, that makes total sense to me, viewed from how your line progressed after that. You have always made some other types of amps, of course, but amps like your Sig:X seem like the all-in-one head embodiment of that versatile rack mentality, in some ways: it can do a whole lot up front, through what can be a very clean and articulate power amp, with lots of switching and routing possibilities, too.**
Yeah, it really all boils down to this signal path, and I was always fascinated with power amps, right from the very beginning. Maybe because that's where the most voltage was and the most shock potential—you could start a fire, you know? So I always had this affinity for the power section of an amp, and the thing I really liked about the Hiwatt was its character and its clarity and all of that. I liked hearing what I was doing, I liked the immediacy of playing a note and having it snap under my fingers. I just loved everything about it.

That became the thing with everything that I do: I would pick up a guitar and if that quality wasn't there, it got massaged until it was there.

**A big part of that multi-channel system, or a rack system, is developing certain characteristics in the front end, then preserving it in the output stage. That is, you have to develop your distortion up front. What are you doing to preserve signal purity in big, multi-channel amps like that?**
That's a direct fallout of the 80s modification mentality. You know, "Modify the amp, make it do what I want it to do!" I learned very on that you can modify the amp and make it do *this*, and you will lose *that*. At the time, people didn't care, "I want this, I can do without that."

**In other words, you have to compromise something, because you can't do everything at the same time.**
You *always* have to compromise something. And the next thing that happened after doing modifications was *un*doing modifications. I noticed there were more and more people buying used things and wanting them returned to stock. So actually it turned all around: where I used to charge $300 or $400 to modify an amp, I was now charging $300 or $400 to put them back to stock. Out of that I realized that each amp has its own quality and its own personality, and going into developing a multi-featured amp, I started developing a recipe that would get the function to work and recognize how it has to be independent from how another thing works.

I'd noticed that amps that had been modified, or multi-feature amps that had weird characteristics, were always because the designer was trying to cut too many corners and take shortcuts to try to get as much performance out of the minimal amount of circuit paths as possible, on the logic that we want the signal path as direct as possible. But even though it's direct, it's the most challenging signal path and there are all kinds of pitfalls. It's better to split things up, and at the end of the day it doesn't really cost that much more in component number; if you do it right, it's so superior that it doesn't matter that it costs a few more bucks to do it that way.

**Sure, a few more components and a few more inches of signal path—not a major impact on anything.**
Right. The first thing people think when they see a multi-featured amp is, "The signal's going through all that stuff!" And the hardest thing to get them to understand [with a good design] is that the signal's only going through the stuff that you're using at that particular moment. When you think of it that way, the signal path isn't any more complicated than it would be in a single-channel amp like the Deliverance. It's a one-channel amp. When you play the Deliverance you can get as many sounds out of it as you can the Sig:X, but only one at a time, whereas with the Sig:X you've got three channels to manipulate.

The thing to communicate to the player is, your whole resistance to and perception of switchers is that they're somehow inferior to a one-trick pony because you understand the trick of the one-trick pony, you don't understand the trick of the multi-feature amp. And a lot of that is psychological: when you see a lot of knobs and features you're automatically intimidated, unless the panel is laid out in such a way that you can immediately begin to compartmentalize it.

What the Ultra Lead did, I noticed, was in the store, some guy would play it a while, then maybe try some odd settings that weren't great for it, and switch it off. So the next guy would come in, switch it on, play it, and walk away, thinking "This thing is god-awful."

**Because the last guy had messed it up.**
Yeah… that amp has things [to control it] that, at first glance, you aren't going to approach. Especially in one of these stores where they've got the footswitch connected, but it's fallen back behind the cabinet, you know? That first impression is just destroyed by bad presentation. And in the Sig:X, I consciously addressed that first-impression scenario: the knobs are laid out in a certain way so that this channel looks like that channel … then I set it up so that when you turn it off and turn it back on, it goes to the clean channel with the boost turned off, so that the next guy that goes and plays it is required to interact with the thing before he gets an impression.

**What are your thoughts on maintaining low signal loss—signal purity—in your switching relays?**
That goes to style, I think. In some cases a particular component that can color the sound may be an important element in the sound of that amp. Like the LDRs [light dependent resistors] that were really popular, [or] the light-dependent diodes that are LED driven, that are just light-variable resistors that turn the signal on and off. I learned very early on that, past a certain threshold, they start coloring the sound in a unique and particular way. But that was kind of the way you did it. Doing it with relays you had some pops and so forth, and I didn't really understand how that was managed and mitigated. And nobody else did either. I talked to Randall Smith at Mesa and we used to talk about it: "How do you manage that switch-pop issue? I'm still struggling with that." And he goes, "Yeah, I am too."

And then these LDR devices appeared and that just solved the problem, made the problem go away. But this was before I had built the first prototype. I had used relays in the first rough prototype because it wasn't for anyone to actually use on stage, but when I built the first production prototype I used LDRs to make it functional for the average player, and all of a sudden it had this new tone quality it never had before. I went, "That's got a very Mesa/Boogie kind of tone quality to it. That never happened before. That's weird." The only thing that was different was these LDRs, so I took them all out and replaced them with relays, and it sounded like the prototype again, so I went "Oh!"

Relays for me [are used], always, for running signal, where a relay has to perform the function of changing the tracks on the train. When the signal is going through it to another destination, it's got to be a relay. When the signal is just going to be stopped and shunted to ground, it can be anything; it can be a FET, an LDR, a relay, as long as there's no condition under which that component adds anything to the sound when it's basically not being utilized. So the Sig:X is a combination of switching technologies: relays to switch signal paths, and mostly FETs to do mute functions, to make sure that channels that aren't supposed to be operating don't bleed signal into anywhere else.

### Now, until recently, you have used printed circuit boards in most of your amps. What are your thoughts on that subject?

In every discipline there are hold-outs that have these old-wives' tales that they want to apply to whatever is going on. It's universal that when you have a comfort level with a particular thing, and then you're confronted with the new way to do that thing, there's either just full-bore, dive in, I'm all for it, or there's absolute resistance to technological development. When that resistance occurs, that's when these unsubstantiated statements about certain things get applied where they don't apply.

There is the idea that circuit boards have complications in dealing with high frequencies, so when you tell an average person "high frequencies" they're thinking "treble." But actually you're talking radio frequencies, or ultra-sonic frequencies that don't have any relevance to the application. So people sort of apply part of the rumor to whatever they can apply it to: circuit boards are unreliable because the traces crack. Well, why did the traces crack? Because the company that made that circuit board designed it the cheapest way possible, with the thinnest copper possible, so that it's susceptible to cracking. That's not because it's a circuit board, it's because there's a thing called expansion and contraction when heat and cold are applied. Circuit boards always do what the designer intends, nothing more and nothing less.

So if you've got a circuit board that's problematic, the problem was built into the design, it's not central to the quality of the material. The engineer chooses the quality of the material. The engineer chooses the application of the material or the component, and the engineer's responsibility is to understand the limitations of that. And if you breach that you're going to have a reliability problem, and then somebody is going to apply that to the whole school of thought.

### So, regardless of that, you have now applied a different technology—a hand-wired circuit—to your new Aether amp.

Talking about the Aether, people say, "Man, I really love the new direction that you've embarked upon!" And I really get a kick out of that, because, no, that's like if Dylan comes out and plays acoustic guitar for a whole set, and somebody comes up and says, "I really dig that new direction that you're embarking upon!" You know? I'm basically going back to my roots, and there was a particular reason to do that. The reason is that I always feel like I have a direction and a singular mindset about how I predict a player will interact with a guitar amp, based on their style, what instruments they are going to plug into it, the kind of music they play, all of that goes into the thought process of designing any product. What's it going to be good for? What are they going to get out of it? Etc, etc.

So the Aether really just started out of sheer boredom: "I'm so sick of hearing about point to point, I'm sick of hearing about hand-wired amps—of seeing that someone is going to pay $300 for this amp, but they'll pay $900 for the same thing just because it's hand wired." My reaction to that is, I want to blow a hole in that. I want to blow two holes. Number one is that we're a heavy metal amp, [number two is] that we're a PCB company and that that's central to the quality of our amps, which it's not. What's central to our amps are the qualities that we have designed into them with respect to how we want players to be satisfied by the result. So, let's make something that demonstrates something of how we feel about that.

The Deliverance was one outgrowth of that; the Deliverance was designed to show people that the sound of our amplifier is intrinsic to the amp, it's intrinsic to our design philosophy. That philosophy can be applied to a multi-channel switcher or to something simple like a Deliverance; here's proof. And also here's proof that flexibility and versatility are not the exclusive domain of multi-feature amps. So with the Aether project, it was thinking that there's something we can show people here, but I don't want to spend six months in CAD designing it, because I'm motivated by this thought and idea right now, and I want to get it out there quickly. In the old days when I did that, like with the first power amp, I got out a drill and some screw drivers and some spare parts and started carving, and in a few days we had something. And you know what? Nothing's stopping us from doing that right now, and this could make a really good Facebook story, just to show people a side of us that they've never seen before.

I got my people together and said we're just going to drop everything and we're going to go completely old-school, and we're going to photograph and film everything and put it up on Facebook. What's it going to be? Dunno, it'll be whatever it's going to be. I basically knew that I wanted to show people that it could be point-to-point, it could be hand-wired, and this was going to be hand-wired because this is the way we're going to build it right now. We're not going to go engineer circuit boards right now, we're just going to knock it out. And the way you knock it out is you just string components together, but with some forethought. What are we going to try to accomplish? Well, people know us for versatility, they know us for all the functions working as you expect, and there's a certain kind of clarity and detail to the sound. But there's other things that people don't know about us, about how we can manipulate woods to make the cabinet behave in a certain way, or how we can work with off-the-radar topologies and things and arrive at the same results. And that will show people that it really doesn't matter what method, what matters is that this is the result.

So we just went full-bore, and it really developed into something, and we were getting lots and lots of attention on our Facebook page about it. So obviously a lot of people are really, really interested in getting the roots of, just like an interview, where does it start, how does it develop, and how do you get to the result? When we got done, a couple of guys came over and played it and they were just aghast. And they were like, "See, it's that point-to-point! It's the pure signal path!" And so I went, "Oh, no, no …"

**Like you created the monster. Kind of disproved your own premise, in their eyes at least.**
Yeah. And when we were building these things, the method was, it was going to be all done from scratch parts, parts that we have left over around here from other things, from prototypes, sample transformers from other projects, just whatever. There's a motherload of stuff like that lying around here. The chassis that I wanted to use was not big enough, and the other chassis that we had lying around was too small. So I went, "Oh, I guess we can put the power amp in this box and the preamp in that box." And I went, "You know what's cool about this? I've just been driven back to my roots here, because I really dig power amp topologies. Something is driving this, so let's just let it *be* drive, rather than dictate."

So I built the power amp in a separate chassis, and built the preamp in the cabinet and ran an umbilical chord to it. And *that* stopped the whole, "Oh, it's because it's point-to-point. People were now, "Why have you got the power amp separate from the preamp?" It's kind of

like "what does VHT stand for?" I could say I did it for this reason, but I actually did it for that reason. In this case it was out of expediency, but it just turned out to be … you know, nobody's ever explored a topology this way, so why don't we just follow it all the way through to the conclusion.

**It's semi-random.**
Yeah, and it kicked up all these artistic possibilities, for the shape of the power amp and how … if you go back mentally to 1946 and what was going on at the time, and have some nut like me walk into a club when Wes Montgomery was playing, and I say, "Hey, I've got these things and you plug 'em in together and you might like the sound of it," he would probably just go, "Okay, let's hear it." He wouldn't go, "Why is this separate from that?" Now everybody goes, "Why is that separate from that, and what about the length of cable that the sound has to go through?" But as an engineer, and as a company that's been around for 25 years and a company that makes power amps, and as a company that's never made a product where you've ever said there's a loss of tone, or a loss of dynamics, or a loss of anything, doesn't it occur to you that maybe I've sort of *thought* about that?

## Holger Notzel of Komet

Holger Notzel met Mike Kennedy in 1993 while both were attending Louisiana State University. The pair opened Riverfront Music and founded Komet Amplification in 1998, after Notzel and his wife relocated from Germany to Baton Rouge. Soon after that they launched their first amplifier, with design input from Ken Fischer of Trainwreck Circuits. Between the Fischer-originated models and Notzel's own designs (both hand-made largely by Kennedy himself, who also owns and operates the company), Komet has become known for extremely dynamic amps intended for use by professional guitarists.

**What got you hooked on tube amps in the first place?**
I've always been into music, and I started repairing instruments when I was going to college, sort of as a side job—I'm from Germany originally—and I got into collecting vintage amps early on, when they weren't that expensive. In Germany the Marshalls and Voxes were fairly common, and you really didn't have any problems finding an old AC30 for very little money. The Fender stuff was a little harder to come by, but we had all the blackface stuff because that was imported into Germany, and I started buying some tweed amps from the States. Back then the dealers had their monthly stock lists that they would mail out to people; that was before they had *Vintage Guitar* magazine or anything like that.

So I fairly early on got into collecting vintage amps and really liked them a lot, but I was never one hundred per cent happy with any one of them. I had my favorites, but they all did something that I didn't like. A lot of them needed servicing and I had a guy that I used to bring them to that would fix them for me, and I figured at

some point it would be easier just to do it myself, because I kind of figured out what he was doing after a while. I would go to him and say, "This is too bassy," or "this is too bright," you know, and he'd change caps and resistors. So I just started fooling with this stuff myself really, and reading books and that kind of stuff and just got into it. I've never had any formal training at any of this. I just kind of figured it out as I went along, keeping up my collection and stuff. And I was gigging with these amps, so they would need servicing and biasing and all of that.

And then later on when I got here to the States I started talking to Ken [Fischer] on the phone, and that really got me fired up. I was on his Trainwreck waiting list like everybody else forever, and it became clear that I wasn't going to get an amp. Then the Soul Climax thing came out, where he had this collaboration with Gerald Weber. Ken didn't discourage me from trying to get one of those … "I might not be able to build you one." But I [wasn't entirely happy with it], so Ken started helping me tweak this and that …

*And ultimately, I guess, you decided it was easier to do it all yourself from scratch?*

Yeah, at that point I thought "Let's leave this thing alone and just *build* an amp!" So I got aluminum boxes and I got transformers, and Ken sent me circuit-board material—and I had built circuits before, and tweaked circuits—and I decided that after all these years of knowing what I liked in a vintage amp, and knowing what I don't like and what goes wrong with them, I was just going to put all that together and build an amp that didn't have the shortcomings of the vintage amps, but had the good stuff I liked about them, and had a lot of that Trainwreck stuff that I really liked.

So I just started building prototypes. I built a few of 'em, and then finally had one that really sounded great, that really did it. I had it at the shop here, this would have been 1998—and at that time we weren't an amp shop, we were a repair business, we fixed mostly guitars and amps—so that amp would be sitting out in the shop. And when I'd repair a guitar for someone they'd try the amp, and everyone said, "How can I get one of these?" I told Ken about it and how everybody liked it, and said, "You know, Ken, maybe we should just go into production with this thing." You know, I kind of expected him to shoot us down, because he was real bitter about [previous collaborations] and was never going to do anything again with anybody, but for some reason—Ken and I always got along really well—he said, "Send it to me and I'll see if I like it." So I sent it to him, and sure enough he liked it. He did a couple of tweaks to it, put a Trainwreck sticker on it and sent it back, and said, "All right, go ahead!" Ha ha! So that's that.

**This was the Komet 60?**

Yes. So that's basically the way it worked, and the amp had some input from all of us, really. The layout and all that and the construction, the design, that was my part; the circuit was stuff that I had basically lifted out of Ken's amps, and stuff that I had lifted out of old amps, and stuff that I came up with on my own. So it was sort of a collaboration between Ken and us, I guess, but the main part of the circuit was really his, honestly. And everything I knew about how to make the circuit work was his also, that's where I learned everything. And Ken had this thing where, I don't know, it sounds weird, but he had a really good ear anyway, exceptionally good, but he actually could hear stuff over the phone really well; and he was real picky about his phones, too—he had certain phones he liked because they sounded right to him, ha ha. And it was the weirdest thing; I could play an amp here on the phone, and he would tell me, you know. "Why don't you change this resistor, or do this and that …" We could do this over the *phone*, surprisingly enough, and it worked: he heard stuff. Then when we sent the amp to him he did some final tweakings, but basically it was there already.

**So that answers the questions that I had—and which a lot of people probably have—about how your association with Ken Fischer developed …**

You know, the thing about it is that Ken, to me, was a friend first, long before there was any business

association, and I wasn't going to do anything that would piss him off.

**Sure.**

If he said, "I don't want you to do this," it would have never been done. There was just no way that I was going to go ahead and do it; I had to have his OK. And it wasn't just to have the Trainwreck name on that, it was basically because it didn't feel right to rip him off or something.

**So you were really just glad to have his blessing.**

Yeah, and I wanted to keep getting along with him, because he was a real cool guy to talk to. We spoke all of the time, and most of the time not even about amps. He was into a lot of things … motorcycles, knives, guns, all sorts of stuff. But I just wanted to keep that friendship. The amp business at that point was an idea, but it wasn't in any way how I made my living, so I wasn't depending on it.

**Did you and Ken see eye to eye on component choices, and on the required qualities of things?**

One hundred per cent. Everything was with his approval. There was not a resistor in there that he didn't approve of. Ken was not easy to deal with. With him it was always all or nothing; you could not make the man happy by making a compromise—he didn't work that way. It was basically his way, or none at all. So if something happened during the first years of production where a part was discontinued and was no longer available, then we would build an amp with the new part, and first thing ship it to Ken, and he had to okay it. If he thought that it changed something in the circuit, then he would make a tweak somewhere else to compensate for it. He wanted to keep this amp sounding consistently the same.

And that happened a few times: the pots were changed a couple of times, either because the ones we had been using were no longer available or … God, there was weird stuff with Ken, too. Like when we made the Airbrake we used Ohmite resistors that were made in the United States at the time. Then Ohmite ceased production here and moved the factory to Mexico, and these resistors didn't sound the same. They looked the same, but they didn't sound the same. It was bizarre, and this was a big deal for him. And we would buy every old-stock Ohmite resistor to keep these things going, and once we couldn't get them any more he basically was no longer interested in making an Airbrake. He was like that: he was super, super picky, and if it wasn't exactly the way he wanted to hear it, it wasn't going to happen.

**From Ken's perspective, every single component was super important to assess and select. But what kinds of things have you narrowed down to being among the most important ingredients?**

Well, Ken's philosophy was that if something changed you had to compensate for it somewhere else, if you could do that. Once Mallory [filter] capacitors were no longer available and we had to switch to F&T, he would make a little change here and there because he wanted to get the response close to what it was before we changed over. That was really minor stuff, but he was always looking for that consistency. Apparently he had the sound in his head that he wanted to hear, and he would just tweak things until he got that. And when you have something like an Airbrake that's basically just one component, if that component doesn't sound the same any more, you're kind of stuck. With an amp, we tried different transformer manufacturers for a short period of time, and Ken would have them make five, six different prototypes and he would listen to every one of them, and he'd see if he could tweak the amp to where it would sound right with these different transformers.

Sometimes he wouldn't even tell us exactly what he did, he'd just call up and say, "Yeah, I've been working with this new transformer, I've been trying everything, I can't get this thing to sound right. Let's not do this …" He wouldn't say, "I changed this resistor or that capacitor," he would just basically tell us that it's not going to work.

### Are there some parts that you find people make too much fuss over, or for which the quality might be too good?
For me, I look at this like a cooking recipe: it's not so much the individual ingredients, it's more what you do with it. It's like flavors that you're mixing. Sometimes a cheaper component—for instance the treble capacitor in the tone stack—the older amps use ceramic capacitors, and then you can use silver mica, which technically have better specs, they're better capacitors, but the old ceramics introduce a little bit of a distortion that in a hi-fi circuit would be completely unwanted, but make the amp kind of sound cool when it overdrives. So you put a silver mica in the amp and it can sound great, but it sounds great in a different way. It becomes more sparkly and more crystalline on top, but it doesn't have that girth and that raunchiness any more, you know? So that's kind of where you have to balance things out. It's not always the case that a component that has better technical specs is going to sound better.

### It all comes down to knowing how to create what you want to hear, not just building somewhat randomly by the component specs.
I think these really good guys like Ken and [Alexander] Dumble, what sets them apart form everyone else is they have this incredible hearing, this is where it all starts. You really cannot build what you can't hear, just like you can't cook what you can't taste. If you don't taste the difference, you can't put it together. And when you do, then you kind of don't look at the parts the same way. If you open up a Dumble amp, there's Radio Shack stuff in there. There's Alpha pots in there, there's Peavey transformers in there, but they're the best amps ever, you know? And it's the same with a Trainwreck: there's not high-end silver wire in there, there's cheap appliance wire in there, but that wire had a certain sound that worked for that application.

### What drove you into some of your own original designs?
It was a twofold thing. First of all, boredom, basically. I

mean, you've got one amp up and running, and you want to do something else now and then. It gets boring. And Ken, for some reason—I don't know if he had hopes that he was going to get better or whatever—he didn't want us to do the Trainwreck stuff at all. He was really opposed to any reissues of Trainwrecks. We brought that up a few times, I said, "You know, maybe we ought to do a Liverpool. We've got a 60-watt amp, it would be nice to do a 30-watt amp." And sometimes he would be in a good mood and he would say, "Yeah, we'll think about it," or "Maybe we'll try a different circuit;" but then he'd say, "Nah, Trainwreck is me, and if I'm not making it it's not a Trainwreck." So it was really hard to get something out of him.

Then I would make a prototype and send it to him, that he had not seen before and I had not told him about, and he would be worried about how that would dilute the 60, and then people wouldn't want to buy the 60. It was weird, man—sometimes I didn't even understand what he was getting at. But for some reason it was incredibly hard to get another amp out of him. So I figured I'd have to do it myself. I wanted some other amps, some other models. I didn't want to change the 60. I think the whole idea with that, as with the Trainwreck amps, is you put a lot of effort into the planning and the voicing of the amp, and when it's done, it's done. If there was much to improve about it we would have done it before we brought it out. I don't see the point of taking that amp and tweaking it every year and saying, "This is the new and improved Komet 60!" You know, like Gibson does with their Historics or whatever. It's the best amp we could make from day one, so that was done. There needed to be other amps, and I like other stuff. And I love EL84s, they're my favorite tube.

### What was the next official amp? Was it the Constellation, or the Concorde?
The next official amp was the Constellation. That was completely my own design. Ken and I had heard things the same way, we liked the same stuff, for some reason. So, in that sense, a lot of what I learned from him about making an amp sound the way it should went into the Constellation, but the circuit was completely original.

### That's a great amp. I had the chance to play one at length and was very impressed.
I love the Constellation. I think it's a killer amp.

### Have you thought about re-designing that first channel to use a tube that's more readily available than the 6SN7 octal preamp tube you designed it around?
Every now and then I think about it, but it would take as much effort to get that amp in a different form as it would to just make something new. That octal's a big part of it. They're still available. If somebody has an amp they're not going to have a big problem keeping tubes in it. But as far as a production thing, where you have to get a couple hundred tubes and go through them [to sort out the bad ones], that's just become too difficult to do.

### Tell me a little bit about your relatively new Aero 33.

**What were you hoping to achieve with that amp?**

The Constellation was more or less discontinued, so we didn't have an EL84 amp in the lineup any more [*NB: discounting the 2 x EL84 K19 and the cleaner-toned 4 x EL84 Songwriter*]. And like I said, I love EL84s. My favorite vintage amp is an AC30, and I like the Trainwreck Rocket a lot too, and I always like the Liverpool more than the Express, by a good measure actually. So I wanted to make it more full-featured, because a lot of people think the number of knobs has something to do with the price of the amp. A lot of people didn't really get the Constallation [which has only three knobs]. They wanted a traditional tone stack, to be able to tweak it and all that. So I figured, let's do an EL84 amp that's not as finicky tube-wise as the Constellation was, and has the full-featured tone stack and everything, but has some of those aspects that I like about the Constellation: that almost seamless transition from clean into overdrive, and that touch response, the way the amp feels connected to your fingertips, that kind of stuff.

So that was the idea. It's almost like, I like the Concorde a lot [a 2 x EL34 amp with hot preamp stage], so it was like a baby Concorde in a way. Different, but sort of in that vein.

**I think the Aero sounds fantastic. I reviewed it for Guitar Player magazine and loved it. It has elements of that big, chunky Marshall sound and feel, but with that shimmery Voxy chime over the top.**

Yeah, that was the idea. Have you played a Komet 19? That amp is really, really cool. I think it flies a little bit under the radar.

**I haven't tried one yet, but have spoken to people who rave about them. But from what I've heard in the Aero and Constellation, you've nailed it for EL84s.**

You know, I need about 30 watts minimum for me to really be happy with an amp. I'm not into the small-amp thing myself.

**What do you find the bigger amp gives you? For example, even if you're achieving comparable volume levels with an attenuator or something on the bigger amp, what does it give you that the smaller amp, unattenuated and at the same perceived volume, doesn't give you?**

It's just a girth and a muscle there in a bigger amp. It's like motorcycles or cars: if you've got a big-block engine, you can feel that even if you go 50 miles an hour. It's just there, it's not straining, it's easy, it's just got power to spare. I like that.

**I hear you. I've been very much into cranking up smaller amps for smaller gigs, just to get them into the sweet spot without any outside help, but I have also really enjoyed playing bigger amps lately, for that depth and feel, that body, even if they have to be reined in with an attenuator or something to fit the gig.**

Yeah, definitely. I've always been a player too, and I've never used or owned channel-switching amps. I need to get everything done from the guitar, and once you get under 30 watts you're just running out of clean headroom. There's just no way around that. Without that power, if you turn it up and you get a nice distorted sound, then you wind it down at the guitar to clean it up, you're running out of steam, basically.

**Although your amps are all relatively straightforward, in the "bells and whistles" sense, I find you can fine-tune things a lot by trying different tubes. Even different makes of the same type of preamp or output tube make a big difference in the Komet 60, for example. And putting something like a 5751 in the V1 preamp position of the Aero 33 really tweaked its response, making it easier to keep it clean up to higher volumes, without sacrificing that great crunch and dynamic overdrive when you get it up to two o'clock or so.**

That's another thing that Ken always emphasized, that an amp should always sound good. It shouldn't be just a good clean-sounding amp or a good distorted-sounding amp. If an amp sounds good, the clean sound should be great and the distorted sound should be great. I really subscribe to that theory as well, because it's either good or it isn't.

**It seems like the traditional way to play a Komet is to crank it up to two or three o'clock for your lead tone, then ride the guitar's volume to clean it up when necessary. But if you really want a shimmery clean sound on the Aero and put it to ten o'clock, boy, it's a gorgeous clean amp.**

Yeah, exactly. It has to be great no matter where you set it. It's the same with these old amps that I like so much. An AC30 has a spectacular clean sound—probably the best ever, I think—and it also sounds great when Brian May plays it and overdrives the hell out of it. It should do both, in my opinion.

**What players did you listen to when you were young?**

For me it was Rory Gallagher. He used to play in Germany all the time, several times a year. I remember that combination of an AC30 and a tweed amp—it was either a low-powered '55 or '56 Twin, or a 4x10" Bassman, but it was always that combination. Later on he had other amps, he had Marshalls and all that, but the stuff that I always like was that combination of a tweed and an AC30. That's the sound I had in my head when I started working on the Constellation prototypes. I kind of wanted to get that, you know, that blend.

**Do you see the amp market changing much in the coming years?**

Yeah, I think it's going to change pretty drastically. I hate to say it, but I really think that digital stuff is going to get so good that that's really going to be a big deal. There will always be the freaks, like the guys who listen to vinyl albums, who will want the tube amps, but the general public who just want to put an amp up on stage and get a sound for their cover band or whatever, I think sooner or later they're all going to be playing digital stuff.

**You kind of see it getting a little bit more that way already. The vast majority of pros still play tube amps, but some of them are moving to digital, and the digital technology is improving all the time. Even the basic Line 6 POD HD, with their latest technology, sounds a world better than when it first came out some 15 years ago.**

Yeah. You know, I'm an analog snob and I used to always run old Fender analog reverb tanks from the 60s, and that was the only reverb I could stand, and I use a TC Electronics pedal now. It's just much easier than hauling the tank around, and it sounds so good now, you just have to face reality at some point. I think that's where it's going, and this boutique stuff will be a niche thing.

And the other thing that I think is going to make things really difficult in the future is that you just don't get anything that you need, any more, to build an amp. The tube situation is awful and getting worse, and none of that modern digital stuff uses high voltage, so the high-voltage components are going away. The Mallory capacitors we used since day one are out of business, you can't get them. Nothing needs a 500-volt capacitor any more, and nothing needs a two-watt pot any more. It's just obsolete technology. Over the last five or six years, so many of the components we use just went out of business and are just no longer available. It's not looking good, in my opinion, at all. I wouldn't want to start out today and go into the tube-amp business. I think it's not going to be around forever.

**See, you're just depressing me now.**

Yeah, I know. I get depressed about it too. But that stuff can only be manufactured in scale. You can't have a boutique capacitor maker or a boutique tube maker, that's just not possible.

**Exactly. And aside from the consumer market that used to use all this technology it was the military industrial complex that kept it going.**

Yeah, the stockpiles that they had for tubes and all that stuff, they had warehouses full of it. That's all coming to an end, and then it's going to be difficult.

Now, you're always going to be able to get some—if you want to tinker around with tube technology and you buy a few thousand dollars worth of parts and stash them away, you've got a lifetime of playing ahead of you. You don't have to worry about that. But as far as making a business out of it, I don't see that going on forever.

**I know what you're saying. And it's different for a maker like you than it is for someone like Fender or Gibson. If you're a big maker already, you've got to go with the flow, because you want to stay in business. But you got into the business out of a passion, to make an amp that was just the way you wanted it. I have a feeling you'd stop making amps rather than convert to what you can manage with poor, low-voltage components—or convert to digital modeling.**

Oh, yeah, it's not going to be worth doing. Or, it's not going to be *possible* any more. If you used to have a choice between ten or 15 different capacitor manufacturers, now you've got two or three. And once those are gone, where are you going to go? You used to be able to get everything you needed to build an amp at Radio Shack. Now all they sell are cheap cellphones and batteries.

# Mark Bartel of Tone King

Between their stylish mid-20th century looks and their high-quality PCB construction, Mark Bartel's Tone King amps of Baltimore, Maryland, have carved out their own niche in the high-end market since 1993, thanks to several models' impressive versatility and toothsome tones. Having stuck with a handful of proven original templates for the majority of the company's first two decades, Bartel has recently branched out into more British flavors and other versatile designs, as well as dabbling in some hand-wired models. He has continued to win devoted players as a result.

### What first got you interested in tube amps?

I had been an electronics tinkerer since I was a young kid, so I'd been into it way before I got into music. When I first got into it I didn't have any money, so I had to use my tinkering skills to get a guitar amp. Of course in the beginning it was pretty terrible, it was all solid-state because my father told me, "Don't pay attention to this tube stuff, 'cos those tubes are going out." Ha ha. So, I worked on a lot of tube stuff because we fixed televisions—my father was a technician, so I had basic skills from him—but I was mostly interested in having the highest gain I could out of solid-state, and making a heavy metal amp.

Then I met a guitar teacher who totally turned me around. I went from listening to Mötley Crüe in one day, and I all of a sudden discovered I had to use tube amps. So that's where that all came from, pretty early on. I went to school for the engineering stuff early on, but in the beginning developed the ability to build things.

### So you trained as an electrical engineer?

Yeah, absolutely. I went to school for engineering and worked in the industry for many years, while I was building amps. I was designing mainframe computers, worked for a semiconductor company designing chips. I think there are a bunch of us guys who came from that background. Such as Ben Fargen, who has a background that's way beyond just tube amps.

### Sure, and Mike Zaite from Dr Z was doing medical testing equipment.

Yeah, that really helps actually. Because a lot of circuit simulation work that I did at the semiconductor company I used on guitar amps, believe it or not.

### It must be helpful to be able to go to that kind of depth of engineering, especially when you're first developing new circuits. And of course then you have to test anything out to see how it really sounds ...

Yeah, yeah, definitely. Sure, there are a lot of folks out there that don't have engineering backgrounds so they use more of an experimenter approach. And there's nothing wrong with that, I respect that approach, but what works for me is using a combination of my engineering background and the experimenter stuff. You just can't be a good engineer and design a good-sounding guitar amp, because there's a lot of stuff in there that you're not going to come to naturally from an engineering perspective. You've got to have an open mind, and be willing to try things that might not make sense initially, and then figure out *why* they worked after you've experienced them.

### That's a good point. Clearly there are a lot of happy accidents in tube-amp design. And the fact that guitar amps aren't about clean reproduction—they're about this magic that distortion contributes to—makes the trial-and-error of it all the more important.

Exactly. There's an element of distortion in everything. Even what people call "clean sound," there's a lot of distortion happening there. Plug into a hi-fi amplifier, have you ever done that?

### Oh, sure...

Oh my God, it sounds terrible!

### When did you decide it would be feasible to start your own amp company?

That was one of these real lucky breaks that happened with me early on. Back in the early 90s there weren't that many boutique amplifier companies out there, and I was doing this for my own enjoyment really. I developed an amplifier, it ended up being the Imperial, but at the time I was just doing it for my own enjoyment. I decided to bring one to a guitar and amp show in New York City. I just kind of walked through it; I didn't know anyone there, I wasn't connected with the industry at all, I was just a college kid with this amplifier that looked funny—it was turquoise. And man, it was just so different in those days because there wasn't a lot of boutiquey stuff out there, so I got a lot of attention just walking this thing through. Just in one afternoon I hooked up with a couple of dealers, and I secured a review with *Guitar Player* too, which played a huge part in making Tone King successful, initially.

### Style-wise, I remember noticing you as one of the first with the really funky retro styling, which not a lot of others were catching on to yet.

Thanks. That was not so much by design as just lack of information. There wasn't an internet back then so I didn't know what an amplifier should look like, but I was into this "mid-century modern" kind of thing. So I just came up with all my own design, logo and all of that.

**That's a great way to go: set yourself a style, and it turns out a lot of people relate to that, while you stand out visually at the same time.**
Eventually it kind of got to the point where we were getting so much feedback on the look that I wanted people to concentrate on how it sounded. So when I got to the Comet model I kind of toned it back somewhat: focus on what this thing is supposed to do.

**Do you feel like there's an identifiable "house sound" at Tone King?**
Maybe not so much of a "sound," but I think there is a certain quality that is common among all the amps I've designed. It's a quality that you find in certain old vintage amps—a lively response with a three dimensional soundfield that really makes the notes pop out of the cabinet. I had done a lot of work with old Fender amps and found that some of them really have that lively quality, and that was the main thing I tried to achieve when I started designing tube amps in the beginning. Although there are certainly ways you can get closer to this quality with circuit design and component choices, I came to realize that most of this quality comes from the speaker cabinet. A lot of those old vintage cabinets have the advantage of time to change the nature of the woods and glues—crystallize any sap in the wood, and so forth, and they simply respond differently than new cabinets. My job was to get this kind of response from a new cabinet.

To me, the cabinet is at the heart of the dynamic response of an amp, and tuning the cabinet for a particular kind of response gives you a truer, more natural quality than you get from tuning the electronics to do the same thing and pumping it through a stiff, inert cabinet. I've been using this approach from the beginning, and I think it does lend a certain distinctive quality to the sound and feel of the Tone King amps.

In the beginning, I'd come up with an electronic design and plug it into a speaker in a very stiff box, and I just couldn't connect with it. It was making the right sound, but it wasn't like the experience that I got when I plugged into a 50-year-old tweed Deluxe. There was a connection there and the way that the sound filled the room, it was kind of a three-dimensional soundfield that filled the room, it wasn't just a flat plane of sound. And that's kind of been what I've been after, right from the beginning. The three-dimensional soundfield that draws you in and creates a connection with you when you're playing.

**Which leads us naturally to the fact that you put a lot of time into speaker-cab development.**
Yeah, that started out right away. I've been doing that forever. And that's one of the things where, like what we said before about electronics—where I combined my engineering background with the experimenter background—I don't have a background in acoustics, or any of the sciences that would let me design a cabinet using scientific or engineering methods, so I am *purely* an experimenter when it comes to cabinet design. I've done

the 99 percent perspiration part of it; I've built hundreds and hundreds of test cabinets over the years. You know, like the Thomas Edison of test cabinets.

I've discovered an enormous amount about how to make a cabinet sound a certain way. The two important things are, one, you have to know what you want before you start. You can't just start screwing around and say "That sounds pretty good, let's try this ..." Because that'll lead you down a wormhole and you'll never come to a design. And number two, your ears are going to play tricks on you. The only way to make progress with speakers and cabinets is to compare to a known reference. And to compare in a way that you're switching back and forth [clicks fingers] like that. Ten seconds' delay, and you're going to lose a lot of information.

So that's kind of the method, and what I'm able to achieve with it. When you think of cabinet design, you think of, "Oh, there's open-back, closed-back ..." But I'm kind of going farther than that, and there are things I can do with the cabinet with the baffle and the bracing and treatment to the surfaces that can affect the dispersion and can affect the top end independent of the mid band, etc, and really make more of a difference in the sound than going from one speaker to the next. There's a whole lot there—I'm not going to call it "a science," because I'm not an acoustic scientist—but I've developed all these little techniques and tricks that you can do with wood and cabinets over the years that you can do to tune them in a certain way.

**So through empirical knowledge you've compiled your own database of what does what.**
Yep, exactly.

**And, in the hi-fi industry there might be makers that approach it from an acoustical analysis, but there isn't a whole lot of that going on in the amp business. I bet a lot of amp makers started with trial and error, and many of them probably stopped a lot sooner than you did.**

Yeah, I don't know what other guys are doing, but I never stop. Every amplifier I do I learn something more about speaker-cabinet design. And I've gotten to the point now where I'm going further than just making it sound good *compared to another cabinet*. With the cabinets I've design lately, I try them in all different kinds of acoustical environments. I bring them home, I try them in a dead room, in a live room, I put them in a studio environment, in a stage environment, and make sure they work in all those different environments, because that's very tough to do.

**You've got some newer hand-wired series out, and have previously been a major believer in high-quality printed circuit boards through much of your Tone King work. Tell me a little about that.**
Sure, I got into that early. I had done CAD work and had the ability to run the tools and generate a decent board design, so I started way back in the beginning. Only the first dozen or so were actually hand wired. It was more, in the beginning, a matter of consistency and being able

to have a worker assemble it just the way I wanted. It's tough to train someone to wire things exactly the way you want it, but with a PC board they don't have a choice.

I've learned a lot about that as well over the years, and I think the boards I'm designing now are certainly better than the stuff in the beginning. I still am a big believer in a well-designed PC board. I think there are a lot of advantages. I can mount the components exactly where I want them, I don't have to rely on where a terminal strip is going to end up or something like that. I can position the wiring exactly where I want it to be, which I'm finding in some designs is more important than in others. For instance, in the Royalist, you know, in a plexi kind of design it's a lot more critical than in something like a tweed Deluxe. I did a lot of experimenting with that layout and with the wiring, and it does have a big effect. Certain critical components, you move it three inches away on the chassis and you're on the same electrical net but it sounds different. Again, that's another thing where my engineering side says "That's crazy," but the experimenter side says "It makes a difference, I'm hearing it."

I've been using PC boards for over 20 years, and I'm at the point where I can confidently say that the type of construction I use today, which includes PC boards, has a number of advantages over conventional hand-wired techniques. I've hand-wired plenty of amps over the years, and I'm probably one of the few who have built the same circuit (the Imperial) both hand-wired and with a PC board, using the same components, so I have some experience in comparing the two head to head. What it comes down to is that there is nothing magical about turret boards, terminal strips, or PC boards. They are all just a means to mount components. The important thing to focus on is the relative location of the components and the location and routing of the wiring. If you get this part of the design right, then the actual construction method makes very little difference.

In fact, a poorly designed hand-wired layout is just as likely to sound bad as a poorly designed PC board layout. The way I design layouts, using PC boards in combination with hand-wiring, gives me more flexibility in placement than I would have with conventional hand-wired techniques, and I think it results in a much better layout. It's a cleaner, simpler layout too, which makes it easy to work on. I have a hand-wired prototype for the last amp I designed, the Royalist, and it doesn't sound as good as the production models.

I'm kind of converging to a slightly different take on that, which involves some hand wiring in addition to the component placement on the board. I'm starting to think that's really going to be the way to go. I'm getting better results with that than with a lot of the hand-wired stuff, actually.

**And your PC board has never been for the sake of cheap components or easy mass production, it's purely for design purposes.**

Yeah, I have an open mind to using whatever it takes to get the sound I want. I know there's a lot of fetishism around creating layouts that look exactly like the layouts from the 1950s, but I'm not limiting myself to that. I want to achieve a certain feel and a certain sound from the amp, and if it has to be built different then I'll do that.

**Which makes perfect sense. The great vintage amps, with great tubes in them and turned up to a certain level, in the hands of a great player, tend to sound universally great. At the same time, if you give one to a talented player to play for a while, very often he or she will find something to modify or amend in that design, to broaden the depth or the range a little bit, or whatever.**

Yeah, and that kind of gets to my overall philosophy: I don't necessarily try to re-create an amp. With the Royalist, I didn't just want to make a plexi clone. I didn't want it to sound "just as good as a plexi." When you plug into a plexi, when I play through it, I can hear what that amp wants to be. Okay? There's a certain quality, a certain character to what it's trying to do. But I think anyone—this isn't just me—you can hear that, "Hey, it also does this thing that also kinda gets in the way of that." Maybe it farts out on the bass more than it should, or whatever, and that's not really adding to what the plexi sound wants to be. So I'm trying to get to the soul of what a certain type of amp is trying to be, and to get more of that.

**And plenty of guys are making great vintage copies of great amps, if that's what you're looking for. But a lot of the mods came about, for better or worse, because many guys could hear the potential in these vintage amps.**

Exactly.

**Do you have any firm beliefs in any particular types or quality of components?**

I really believe you need to use the *right* component for the amp, not necessarily what's objectively the highest quality component. In the early days, I actually used polystyrene 715P orange drops, because I didn't know any better. I figured, "Well, these are more expensive, they've got to be better." But I eventually learned that the cheaper polyester caps actually sounded better for the type of amp I was trying to build. So it's all about getting the component that has the right sound. You'll even see components in Dumble amps that you may scratch your head and go, "Why did he use that?" But it's all about getting the *right* component.

And that's kind of a funny thing. As an engineer you stop yourself; you're not allowing yourself to say "*This* type of cap has *this* kind of sound; *this* type of cap has *this* kind of sound," because it just doesn't make sense [from an engineering perspective]. So the way I like to think of it is, in this use, in this part of the circuit, this type of cap has *this* type of sound, where a different cap would have *this* type of sound—in this particular instance. I don't like to use global statements like "ceramic caps sound bright" or whatever.

**Funny, because I'm trying to be aware of this in my own writing lately, where I'll be conscious of phrasing something like "this contributes to this**

*type of sound…" Because you'll get the pedant who will say, "Well, caps don't have "a sound'," or "a tube doesn't have "a sound'," but using different types will contribute to different sounds, without a doubt.*

Yeah, obviously they make differences. You can clearly hear the difference between different types of caps, different types of tubes, different resistors. It's not psychoacoustic, it's really happening. I can see where an engineer would say, "Well, that's ridiculous." But you have to take it a step further and say, "That's not a pure capacitance. There's some inductance there, there's some resistance there …" You could make a more sophisticated equivalent model that would maybe explain why some of this stuff is happening, so it's a real thing and there is an engineering basis for it.

### Any particular tube-amp myths that irk you a little bit?

Oh, boy, there are so many, I don't even want to get started!

Maybe one is that a lot of people love to see a chassis layout with wires that are real straight, and then a 90-degree bend, and then straight—that look like the streets of Manhattan. We used to call that "Manhattan wiring" in the old days. I think that looks beautiful, but in two ways is not an ideal, really. From an engineering perspective it doesn't necessarily give you the best layout with the lowest parasitics; and just practically, it doesn't always result in the best sounding layout.

I got talking to Bill Krinard from Two-Rock about this a lot, where we agree that sometimes the messy layouts just sound better. Of course, you can't just make a random messy layout and expect it to sound better. The point is that wiring does have an effect on the sound, and just making it look neat on paper isn't going to give you the best sound.

### What are some of the keys in building a channel-switching amp that a purist is still going to enjoy?

That might be another myth to bust. To me, when I designed the Imperial for instance, it's got two completely separate preamps switched with a relay. So the only thing in the signal path that's extra is a switch, a relay.

### Just a connection terminal, really.

Yeah. It may be that the majority of what we think of as "channel-switching amps" do share more of the signal path or do have extra complexity or compromises in component choices that limit their potential. Whereas I just think of it as two individual preamps being switched with a switch, and I don't compromise in any way with the circuit to shoehorn it in, I just make the chassis bigger.

*And that's a good point, actually, which runs through all kinds of things in the amp world, and regarding guitars, too: we'll attribute some obvious characteristic of the breed to one part of the technology, whereas it might actually have nothing to do with that.*

Yeah, and it might also be that, when you think about it, a lot of what we think of as channel-switchers don't really do that middle-ground thing very well. They might have one channel that's super clean and another that's super distorted, whereas for me my favorite amps live between there. I might have a lead channel and a rhythm channel, but I specifically didn't call them a clean channel and an overdrive channel because I really use both for the same thing, which is between clean and dirty, maybe one a little more than the other.

### Do you see the trend of the amp market evolving much in the coming years, in any particular direction that you need to take note of?

Yeah, I think it's continued to go more toward home users, which is fine with me because *I'm* a home user, so I can sympathize with the concerns of the home user. You know, trying to get a good sound in a house, in confined quarters. But beyond that, I think there are more young people coming in, and what's surprising is that there are a lot of people who are really not familiar with the sounds of those classic amps that we talk about all the time. I just assumed that everyone had played through a vintage tweed Deluxe, blackface Deluxe, plexi, Vox, and uses those as touchpoints in evaluating any of their amps. But that's not so much the case any more. That's definitely a trend I've been seeing.

*And at some level, maybe that's not an entirely bad thing. New sounds come along, and sometimes it's not a bad thing if you can erase what's come before and simply decide whether you like the sound of something new for its own sake, not primarily because it sounds like a rendition of Fender, or Vox, or Marshall—whether you can like it regardless of what baggage we carry about it.*

True. And there's a lot of modern music that has good guitar sounds in it, like My Mourning Jacket, Wilco—man, those guys are killer.

### Can you give us any under-rated gems in vintage amps that still might be great value for the guitarist today?

Man, I love those old Gibson amps. There was one before the Les Paul one, a GA-something, couple of 6V6s and octal preamp tubes, field-coil speaker, it sounded like *nothing* I've ever heard.

# Glossary of Common Amplifier Terms

There are many terms commonly seen in literature describing guitar amplifier circuitry that can be somewhat confusing to a person with no prior background in electronics. This section will attempt to shed some light on these mysteries, and provide descriptions of common electronic terms, components, and circuitry in somewhat easy-to-understand form. Some terms, however, represent concepts that are difficult to explain in simple language, so you may have to do some additional side reading to fully comprehend them. The material is presented in an alphabetical, glossary-style form, so there is some overlap in the definitions.

**A** – the symbol for amps, or amperes, which is a unit of current flow. Common prefixes are "m", for mA ($10^{-3}$ amps), and "u", for uA ($10^{-6}$ amps).

**AC** – Alternating Current. This is electric current that periodically changes the direction in which it flows. The most common form of an alternating current supply is the sinusoidal current that comes out of a wall outlet. It has no positive or negative terminals, because AC has no polarity, other than an instantaneous polarity that changes at a rate equal to the frequency of the current. Common household AC current is supplied at a frequency of 60Hz in the United States and some other countries, and 50Hz in other places in the world, most notably, England. "Hz" stands for "Hertz," which is the name of the unit for frequency, and means "cycles per second," indicating how many cycles, or changes from positive to negative, the AC waveform goes through each second. In some older literature, you may see the term "CPS," which stands for "cycles per second," used in place of "Hz." Alternating current does not have to be sinusoidal in shape; the square wave of a distorted guitar amplifier output is also AC, because it changes polarity periodically.

**Active** – a component that needs a power source to function, as opposed to a passive component. Examples of active components are tubes, transistors, op-amps, etc. Also commonly used to refer to guitar pickups that have built-in preamps, which require batteries to operate.

**Admittance** – the reciprocal of impedance. $Y = 1/Z = G + jB$, where G = conductance, and B = susceptance. The unit of admittance is the "mho," same as conductance.

**Ali-panel** – the name given to the Marshall amplifiers that came after the "plexis" and had aluminum front panels.

**Alnico** – an alloy of aluminum, nickel, and cobalt which was commonly used in vintage speakers. It was replaced by cheaper and stronger ceramic (strontium ferrite) materials, but is making a comeback in "modern vintage" style speakers, such as the WeberVST Blue Dog and the Celestion Alnico Blue, among others.

**Amplifier** – the other half of rock'n'roll (thanks to Ritchie Fliegler for that one).

**Anode** – the "current collecting" element of an electron tube, also called the "plate." The anode usually has a large positive voltage

connected to it in order to attract the negatively-charged electrons from the cathode element of the tube. If you look at a tube, this is the large greyish metal piece that encloses most of the other elements.

**Attenuator** – (a) a network that is used to reduce the amplitude of a signal. Typically, this is accomplished with two resistors, one in series with the signal and another from the output of the first resistor to ground. This attenuates the signal by an amount dependent upon the ratio of the resistor values.
(b) a device used to reduce the volume of an amplifier. It goes between the amplifier and the speakers, allowing a non-master volume amplifier to be cranked up to full power without being overly loud, in order to get the desired overdrive tone from the amplifier.

**B** – the symbol for susceptance, also the symbol for magnetic flux density.

**B+** – the high voltage supply in a tube amplifier. The name is a holdover from the old days of battery-powered radios, which had an "A" supply for the filaments, a "B" supply for the high voltage, a "C" supply for the bias, and a "D" supply for the screen grids, if a separate supply was used. The conventions held when radios switched over to rectified AC supplies.

**Back bias** – a method of obtaining a negative bias voltage by means of a resistor or zener diode in the center tap of a full-wave rectifier circuit. The current in the center tap flows in the same direction for both half-cycles, so the voltage drop is the same for both. This full-wave-rectified negative voltage can be filtered and used as a negative bias supply. The downside is that all the plate current of the output stage flows through the back bias circuit, so it can be impractical for higher-powered amplifiers. Also, the resistive drop method should only be used for true class A amplifiers, because there can be a large difference between the idle and full-power current draw of a class AB or class B amplifier. The zener method is much more suitable, and in fact, creates a regulated bias voltage that is relatively independent of the current draw of the amplifier, provided it is above the minimum current necessary to keep the zener in the normal reverse breakdown region.

**Bias** – the amount of negative voltage applied to the grid of a tube with respect to the cathode, or the amount of idle current flowing in the tube when no AC signal is present on the grid pin.

**Biasing** – the term commonly used for the practice of setting the idle current in an output tube. Preamp tubes are biased as well, but they are biased only during the initial design of the amplifier and use what is known as "cathode biasing", and don't require rebiasing as part of general amplifier maintenance.

**Blackface** – the term given to older Fenders which had a black metal control panel. This era of Fender amps transitioned into the "silverface" amps, which had a silver metal control panel. The transition occurred at the time CBS bought the company [1965], and some "improvements" were made to the circuitry of most of the amplifiers. These "improvements" are generally regarded as

detrimental to the tone of the amplifier, which led to a practice known as "blackfacing" a Fender amp, which means converting the circuit back to the pre-CBS schematic.

**Bridge rectifier** – a set of four rectifiers arranged in a "square" or "diamond" shape (depending on how you look at it). The four diodes allow full-wave rectification without the need for a center-tap on the transformer.

**Bypass cap** – a capacitor that is connected from the power supply to ground. It "bypasses" the AC signals to ground, while passing the DC supply through. This is used to make the DC supply rail "clean," or free from AC noise. Usually bypass caps are relatively small, on the order of 0.1uF or so. Larger caps connected in the same manner are usually called "filter caps." This term is also used to refer to a capacitor connected across the cathode resistor on a tube. It bypasses the AC signal to ground without affecting the DC bias of the tube. This increases the gain of the amplifier stage. This capacitor can also be used to tailor the frequency response of the stage.

**C** – the symbol for capacitance

**Cap** – short for capacitor.

**Capacitor** – a device consisting of two parallel plates separated by an insulator, called the "dielectric." The capacitance is proportional to the area of the plates, and inversely proportional to the distance between them. Capacitors are used to block DC while passing AC. They are frequency-dependent devices, which means that their capacitive reactance, or "effective resistance" to AC increases as the frequency gets lower. This makes capacitors useful for tone controls, where different frequency bands must be passed, or for bypassing AC signals to ground while passing DC through for filtering purposes.

**Capacitance** – the "size" of a capacitor. The unit of capacitance is the Farad, but a one Farad capacitor would be quite large, indeed! The most common capacitors are sized in microFarads (uF, or mfd in very old texts): $10^{-6}$ Farads), nanoFarads (nF: $10^{-9}$ farads), and picoFarads (pF: $10^{-12}$ farads).

**Cathode** – the "current generating" element of an electron tube. The heater heats the cathode to a very high temperature, causing it to emit electrons, which are then collected by the anode, or plate, which has a high positive voltage, which attracts the negatively charged electrons from the cathode.

**Cathode biasing** – a method of biasing a tube where the bias is generated by the voltage drop across a resistor in the cathode. The grid is referred to ground through a resistor, and the current flow through the cathode resistor produces a positive cathode voltage with respect to the grid, which is effectively the same as making the grid negative with respect to the cathode.

**Chassis** – the metal box that encloses the amplifier parts. It is usually made of steel, but occasionally aluminum is used. The transformers and choke are usually mounted on top, while the passive components are usually mounted inside the chassis.

**Choke** – another term used for an inductor, most commonly an inductor used as a power supply filter.

**Class A** – an amplifier operating with the grid bias adjusted so plate current flows for the entire 360 degrees of the input waveform, by biasing the tube halfway between cutoff and saturation, in the most linear portion of the operating curves. The distortion is lowest in class A operation, but the efficiency is also very low. With the exception of single-ended amplifiers, the amplifiers most manufacturers call "class A" are actually cathode-biased class AB amplifiers.

**Class A1** – class A operation where grid current does not flow for any portion of the input cycle.

**Class A2** – class A operation where grid current flows for some portion of the input cycle.

**Class AB** – an amplifier operating with the grid bias adjusted so plate current flows for greater than 180 degrees, but less than 360 degrees of the input waveform, by biasing the tube above cutoff, but below the point required for class A operation. The distortion is higher at low signal levels than true class A, but the efficiency is higher, although not as high as class B, allowing more output power than class A for a given plate dissipation.

**Class AB1** – class AB operation where grid current does not flow for any portion of the input cycle.

**Class AB2** – class AB operation where grid current flows for some portion of the input cycle.

**Class B** – an amplifier operating with the grid bias adjusted so plate current flows for 180 degrees, by biasing the tube right at cutoff. The distortion is higher than class A or class AB, and there is usually a large amount of crossover distortion, but the efficiency is higher than class AB, allowing more output power for a given plate dissipation.

**Class B1** – class B operation where grid current does not flow for any portion of the input cycle.

**Class B2** – class B operation where grid current flows for some portion of the input cycle.

**Combo** – a guitar amplifier that has a built-in speaker.

**Common cathode** – the "standard" tube circuit where the cathode is connected to the "common" point on the circuit, usually ground, and usually through a resistor, which is often bypassed with a capacitor, placing it at "AC" ground potential.

**Common grid** – a tube stage which has the grid connected to the "common" point on the circuit, usually ground. This doesn't have to be a physical DC connection, it can be an AC ground, ie, grounded through a capacitor.

**Common plate** – a tube stage which has the plate connected to the "common" point on the circuit, usually ground This doesn't have to be a physical DC connection, it can be an AC ground, ie, grounded through a capacitor. This is the most often seen method of making a common plate stage, where the plate is connected directly to the power supply (the AC ground connection is through the power supply capacitors, which are essentially a short to ground for AC signals). This stage is commonly called a "cathode follower."

**Control grid** – a wire mesh element located between the cathode and plate of an electron tube, which controls the flow of electrons between the two elements. The control grid draws no current, and as such, presents a high impedance to the driving circuit. Voltage variations on the control grid, with respect to the cathode, cause variations in plate current, which is the basis of amplification within the tube.

**Coulomb** – a unit of electron charge.

**Coupling capacitors** – capacitors which are used between stages in a guitar amplifier. They block the DC plate voltage of the previous stage, while passing the AC guitar signal on through.

**Concertina phase splitter** – the name given to the single-tube phase inverter in which the in-phase signal is taken off the cathode and the out-of-phase signal is taken off the plate, with equal-value plate and cathode resistors. This phase splitter configuration has excellent balance, but only unity gain. Also called a "split-load" phase inverter.

**Crossover distortion** – Crossover distortion is the term given to a type of distortion that occurs in push-pull class AB or class B amplifiers. It happens during the time that one side of the output stage shuts off, and the other turns on. Depending upon the bias point, there is a small amount of time where both tubes are in very non-linear portions of their operating curves, or even cut off entirely, and this "kink" in the transfer curves results in a distortion, or notch, at the zero crossing point of the reconstructed waveform.

**Current** – The term given to electron flow. The unit of current is the "amp," or "ampere," and indicates a current flow of one coulomb per second.

**Cutoff frequency** – The "corner point" of a filter, usually the point where the response is down –3dB compared to the midband signal level.

**dB** – decibels, the standard unit of measure of volume, or "loudness."

**DC** – Direct Current. This is electric current that flows in one direction only. The most common form of a direct current supply is a battery. The battery will have positive and negative terminals. If a circuit is connected between the two terminals, a current will flow in one direction only. The actual electron flow is from negative to positive, but "conventional" current flow is indicated as a current flow from positive to negative. This has been a source of confusion since the early days of electricity, and you will see both conventional and electron flow used in literature.

**Decoupling** – the process of isolating one stage of an amplifier from another. This is usually done by adding a resistor in series with the power supply to a gain stage and a large value electrolytic capacitor from the supply to ground after the resistor.

Decoupling prevents oscillations and other noises that may occur due to unwanted feedback through the power supply connections. It also provides further filtering of the power supply to reduce ripple, producing a cleaner DC supply for the low-level preamp stages.

**Decoupling capacitor** – the large electrolytic capacitor used to filter the power supply after the decoupling resistor.

**Decoupling resistor** – the series resistor used to isolate one stage of an amplifier from another.

**Dielectric** – the insulating material used in a capacitor. Typical dielectric types used in amplifiers are: polystyrene, polypropylene, polycarbonate, polyester, and ceramic.

**Diode** – a two-element device which passes a signal in one direction only. They are used most commonly to convert AC to DC, because they pass the positive part of the wave, and block the negative part of the AC signal, or, if they are reversed, they pass only the negative part and not the positive part. This allows them to be used to generate a positive or negative DC supply. There are both solid-state and tube diodes. Since a diode will pass current in only one direction, they can also be used to "clip" the top or bottom part of a signal. Diodes are also commonly called "rectifiers" because they rectify the AC voltage, however, the term "rectifier" is usually reserved for diodes used in the power supply section of an amplifier, while "diode" is generally used in small signal, or low power applications, such as clippers.

**Direct box** – (also DI box, for "direct injection") a device that allows a guitar or amplifier to be connected directly into a mixing board without the use of a microphone. There are two basic types of direct boxes, those that go between the guitar and the amp, feeding a clean guitar signal to the board, and those that go between the amplifier output and the speakers, feeding the amp signal to the board. The latter usually contain some type of frequency compensation, or "speaker emulation" to give a sound similar to a miked speaker.

**E** – the symbol for electromotive force, or voltage

**Effects loop** – a circuit that allows insertion of external effects devices in the signal path of an amplifier. Noise performance is usually improved by using the effects loop rather than putting the effects in series with the guitar input.

**Electron tube** – (also tube for short, or valve in the UK) the device used to make guitar amplifiers sound good! Actually, this is the name given to the amplifying devices in some guitar amplifiers. They consist of a glass tube containing several elements which are brought out to pins on the base of the tube. All of the air inside the tube is evacuated at time of manufacture, which keeps the filament from rapidly burning up.

**Feedback** – a circuit that allows a portion of the signal from a later stage in an amplifier to be "fed back" to an earlier stage, or within the same stage. Feedback can be voltage or current, negative or positive. Negative voltage feedback decreases gain, and is used to reduce distortion, flatten frequency response, increase input impedance, or decrease output impedance. Negative current feedback increases output impedance, and is used in some solid-state

amplifiers to obtain a more "tubelike" response. Positive feedback will increase gain, but can make a circuit oscillate if too much is applied. Sometimes a small amount of positive feedback is used to offset the reduction in gain caused by application of negative feedback.

**Filament** – the heating element in an electron tube, also called the "heater." The filament heats the cathode to a very high temperature, which "boils off" electrons, which are then collected by the plate. The filament can be seen as the glowing element through the holes in the plate of most tubes.

**Filter** – a circuit which is used to either block or reduce a range of frequencies. There are lowpass filters, which pass frequencies below a certain point, called the "cutoff frequency," highpass filters, which pass frequencies above the cutoff frequency, bandpass filters which pass frequencies above a lower cutoff frequency and below an upper cutoff frequency, bandstop filters, which pass frequencies below a lower cutoff frequency and above an upper cutoff frequency, and allpass filters, which pass all frequencies at the same amplitude, but which have certain phase or delay characteristics.

**Filter caps** – Filter capacitors. The term used for the large capacitors used to filter out the residual AC ripple in the power supply. The rectifier converts AC to pulsating DC, since it just allows current to flow in one direction. The output of the rectifier is a series of "humps," which must be "smoothed out" to become flat, ripple-free direct current. The filter caps store up the voltage on the positive rise of the pulsating rectified AC waveform, and hold it there while the rectified waveform goes down to zero. This charge, hold, charge, hold, etc, behavior is what smooths out the ripple. In general, the larger the capacitor, the less residual ripple there will be.

**Fixed biasing** – a method of biasing a tube or output stage by using a negative DC voltage on the grid with respect to the cathode. This name is sometimes confusing, because an amplifier may have a bias adjustment pot to adjust the negative grid voltage, but it is still called "fixed" biasing to differentiate it from "cathode biasing."

**Flatness** – the peak-to-peak deviation from the nominal voltage in the passband of an amplifier. Flatness is typically measured in dB. For example, if an amplifier has a passband "ripple" of + 0.5dB, it is said to have a "flatness" of + 0.5dB.

**Frequency response** – a measure of how "wide" a set of frequencies an amplifier will pass. Typically, this is specified as the frequency span between the lower and upper points where the amplitude of the signal has fallen off –3dB, or 0.707 times the midband voltage level. Closely related is the term "flatness," which specifies the deviation from center in the passband.

**Full-wave rectifier** – a rectifier that conducts on both positive and negative halves of the incoming sinusoidal signal. It produces a "pulsating" DC composed of single-polarity "humps" at twice the incoming AC frequency. The full-wave rectifier requires less filtering than a half-wave rectifier to produce the same degree of ripple in the output DC waveform.

**Fuse** – a component designed to protect electronic circuits, usually made of a thin piece of metal mounted in a glass or ceramic tube with metal end caps, that is

designed to safely burn in two if the current passing through it exceeds the rated maximum.

**G** – the symbol for conductance.

**Global negative feedback** – negative feedback that is applied over several amplifier stages, as opposed to local negative feedback, which is applied on one stage only. An example of global negative feedback is the feedback loop in a Marshall or Fender amplifier, where there is a feedback path from the speaker output back to the phase inverter, through an attenuator composed of the "feedback resistor" and a resistor to ground on one side of the phase inverter.

**Grid** – the "control element" in a vacuum tube. The grid is normally biased negative with respect to the cathode. As the grid is made less negative with respect to the cathode, more current will flow from the cathode to the plate. As the grid is made more negative with respect to the cathode, less current will flow from the cathode to the plate. It usually only takes a relatively small grid voltage swing to control the plate current over its entire range. Since the grid element controls the current flow in the tube, it allows the tube to be used as an amplifier by taking a relatively small input signal on the grid and and generating a relatively large signal swing at the plate. The amount of signal voltage at the plate is equal to the current flowing through the tube multiplied by the resistance connected to the plate.

**Grid leak biasing** – The small amount of grid current in the tube generates a negative bias voltage across this resistor, which biases the tube to the proper operating point with respect to the cathode, which is grounded. This method of biasing is not very stable, and fell out of favor early on in the development of tube amplifiers. Most preamp stages now use cathode biasing as opposed to grid leak biasing.

**Grid leak resistor** – a very large resistor from the grid of a tube to ground, which is used to generate the bias voltage for the tube. See "grid leak biasing" for an explanation of how this works. This term is sometimes incorrectly used when referring to the grid-to-ground resistor in a cathode biased configuration, which is used to provide a DC ground reference for the grid circuit.

**Grid resistor** – the term usually given to a series resistor connected to the grid of a tube, also called a "grid stopper," but sometimes used to refer to the resistor connected from the grid of a tube to ground, which is also sometimes called a "grid leak" resistor.

**Grid stopper** – a resistor connected in series with the grid of a tube, usually right at the pin of the tube. It is used to prevent parasitic oscillations and reduce the chance of radio station interference by forming a lowpass filter in conjunction with the input capacitance of the tube.

**Ground** – The common "reference" point for the circuit. This is usually also connected to the chassis, but there can be independent circuit grounds and chassis grounds.

**H** – the symbol for magnetizing force, also the symbol for the unit of inductance, the Henry.

**Half-wave rectifier** – a rectifier that conducts on only the positive or only the negative half of the incoming sinusoidal signal. It produces a "pulsating" DC composed of single-polarity "humps" at the incoming AC frequency, with a flat "dead time" during the time the input signal goes to the opposite polarity. The half-wave rectifier requires more filtering than a full-wave rectifier to produce the same degree of ripple in the output DC waveform.

**Heater** – the heating element in an electron tube, also called the "filament."

**HT** – stands for "high-tension," meaning high voltage. Occasionally the B+ fuse on an amplifier will be labeled "HT Fuse."

**Hz** – stands for "Hertz," which is the name given to the frequency of an alternating current. The units are in cycles per second. In some older literature, you may see this represented as "CPS," which, of course, stands for "cycles per second." A prefix of "k" or "M" is used to indicated kilohertz, or kHz, and megahertz, or MHz, which indicate thousands and millions of cycles per second, respectively.

**I** – the symbol for current

**Impedance** – a complex quantity containing both a resistance and a reactance. The symbol for impedance is "Z," and the unit of impedance is the ohm. Z = R + jX, where R is the resistance, and X is the reactance of the circuit, and j is the complex, or imaginary, operator, indicating multiplication by the square root of –1. Inductive reactances have positive imaginary components, and capacitive reactances have negative imaginary components. For example, an inductor of 1mH with a resistance of 8 ohms would have an impedance of (8 + j6.3) ohms at 1000 Hz. Since an impedance is a complex number, it has both a magnitude and a phase. Typically, when discussing amplifiers or speakers, impedances are referred to as the magnitude of the complex number, instead of the rectangular form as given in the definition. The magnitude of the (8+j6.3) example is 10.2 ohms, as calculated by the square root of the sum of the squares of the real and imaginary parts (the "length" of the resulting vector). The concept of imaginary numbers can be a bit confusing to those who haven't encountered it before. If you are interested in finding out more about this, check out a textbook on introductory circuit analysis, as they usually have a good treatment of the subject.

**Inductance** – the "size" of an inductor, not the actual physical size, but the "electrical" size. The unit of inductance is the Henry, or "H." Most power supply inductors, or chokes, are measured in henries, typically 2-20H. The inductance of a transformer primary may also be several henries. Smaller inductors are measured in millihenries (mH = $10^{-3}$ henries) or microhenries (uH – $10^{-6}$ henries).

**Inductor** – a circuit element consisting of a coil of wire wound on a core material made of ferrous or non-ferrous material. An inductor resists changes in the flow of electric current through it, because it generates a magnetic field that acts to oppose the flow of current through it, which means that the current cannot change instantaneously in the inductor. This property makes inductors very useful for filtering out residual ripple in a power supply, or for use in signal shaping filters. They are frequency-dependent devices, which means that their inductive reactance, or "effective resistance" to AC decreases as the frequency gets lower, and increases as the frequency gets higher. This property makes them useful in tone controls and other filters.

**IT** – interstage transformer.

**Jack** – the input or speaker output connector on a guitar amplifier.

**Jewel** – the term commonly used to refer to the screw-on pilot light lens on Fender guitar amplifiers. These usually were red or green, but purple ones are purported to have real "mojo."

**k** – the prefix indicating "kilo" or thousands, as in a 10k resistor, which means ten thousand ohms.

**K** – the symbol for the cathode of an electron tube

**L** – the symbol for inductance.

**LDR** – light dependent resistor. Often used in referring to an optocoupler in which the active element is a photoresistor, whose resistance changes as current is passed through the lighting element, which is usually an LED or neon bulb.

**LED** – light emitting diode. These are semiconductor devices that emit light of various colors when an electric current is passed through them. They are typically used as indicators, but occasionally are used as clipping diodes because of their larger forward voltage drop when compared to a standard silicon diode.

**Local negative feedback** – feedback that is applied over one stage only, as opposed to global negative feedback, which is applied over several stages of amplification. An example of local negative feedback is a cathode follower, where the feedback signal is not so apparently derived by the current flowing through the cathode resistor, or a common-cathode stage with an unbypassed cathode resistor.

**Long tail pair** – a phase inverter topology that has a single resistor connected as a pseudo-current source from the junction of two tube cathodes, with the outputs taken off the individual tube plates, one in phase with the input signal, and the other out of phase with the input signal. The circuit gets its name from the "tail" resistor connected to the cathodes.

**M** – the prefix for mega, or millions, as in a 1M resistor, which means one million ohms.

**Mains** – the AC line voltage input (often more commonly used in British terminology). Occasionally the fuse on the AC input will be labeled "Mains Fuse."

**Master volume** – a second volume control, located at the end of the preamp section of a guitar amplifier, which allows the guitarist to turn the preamplifier up to the point of distortion, while keeping the overall volume low.

**Microphonics** – the tendency for a component to induce audible noise into the amplifier circuit when mechanically disturbed. Tubes are the most common microphonic component, and they will usually make an audible "thump" or "ring" when tapped. Occasionally, the problem is severe enough in combo amplifiers to cause uncontrollable feedback from the speaker to the tube, resulting in a "squealing" or "howling" noise when the volume is turned up loud. Although it is not commonly known, capacitors can also be quite microphonic. Different types have different levels of microphony, with ceramic types usually being the worst.

**Miller capacitance** – the effective multiplication of the plate-to-grid capacitance in a triode tube (or transistor) by the gain of the amplifying stage. Miller capacitance can decrease the frequency response of an amplifier stage by acting as a lowpass filter in conjunction with the source resistance of the preceding stage.

**Modeling amp** – a computer that is passed off as a guitar amplifier. Also see "solid-state."

**Negative feedback** – feedback in which a portion of the signal from a later amplifier stage is fed back to an earlier stage (or to the same stage) in such a manner as to subtract from the input signal.

**Ohm** – the unit of resistance or impedance.

**Ohm's law** – the fundamental relationship between voltage, current, and resistance. It is usually stated as: E = I*R, or V=I*R, where E or V = voltage (in volts: E stands for "electromotive force" which is the same thing as voltage), and I = current (in amps), and R = resistance (in ohms). The equation can be manipulated to find any one of the three if the other two are known. For instance, if you know the voltage across a resistor, and the current through it, you can calculate the resistance by rearranging the equation to solve for R as follows: R = E/I. Likewise, if you know the resistance and the voltage drop across it, you can calculate the current through the resistor as I = E/R. A related equation is used to calculate power in a circuit: P = E*I, where P = power (in watts), E = voltage (in volts), and I = current (in amps). For example, if you measure 20V RMS and 2.5A into a load, the power delivered to the load is: P = 20*2.5 = 50W. This equation can also be rearranged to solve for the other two quantities as follows: P = E*I, E = P/I, and I = P/E. You can also combine the power equation with the first Ohm's law equation to derive a set of new equations. Since E = I*R, you can substitute I*R for E in the power equation to obtain: P = (I*R)*I, or P = I2R. You can also find P if you know only E and R by substituting I=E/R into the power equation to obtain: P = E*(E/R), or P = E2/R. These two equations can also be rearranged to solve for any one of the three variables if the other two are known. For example, if you have an amplifier putting out 50W into an 8 ohm load, the voltage across the load will be: E =√(P*R) = √(50*8) = 20V RMS.

**Optocoupler** – another name for optoisolator.

**Optoisolator** – a device which contains an optical emitter, such as an LED, neon bulb, or incandescent bulb, and an optical receiving element, such as a resistor that changes resistance with variations in light intensity, or a transistor, diode, or other device that conducts differently when in the presence of light. These devices are used to isolate the control voltage from the controlled circuit. Typical optoisolators are the Vactec and photoFET devices used in channel-switching amplifiers, as well as the "trem-roach" neon bulb/photoresistor package used in the tremolo circuit in some Fender amplifiers.

**Oscillator** – a circuit that produces a sustained AC waveform with no external input signal. Oscillators can be designed to produce sine waves, square waves, or other wave shapes. They are typically used as variable speed generators in tremolo circuits in guitar amplifiers.

**OT** – short for "output transformer."

**Output transformer** – a transformer used to match the low impedance of a speaker voice coil to the high impedance of a tube output stage. Output transformers consist of at least two windings, a primary and a secondary. Some output transformers have multiple impedance taps on the secondary side, to allow matching to different speaker cabinets, typically 4, 8, and 16 ohms.

**p** – the prefix for "pico," or 1*10-12, as in a 100pF capacitor, which means 100x10-12 Farads. Originally the term "uuF" or "micro-micro Farads" was used.

**Parasitic oscillation** – an unwanted oscillation in a tube amplifier, often at supersonic, inaudible frequencies. Parasitic oscillations can cause all sorts of problems, including overheating output tubes and bad tone.

**Passive** – a component that doesn't need a power source to function. Examples of passive components are: resistors, capacitors, inductors, transformers, etc. Also used to refer to guitar pickups that don't have built-in preamps, and don't require batteries to operate.

**PCB** – short for "printed circuit board," or PC board. A piece of phenolic or glass-epoxy board with copper clad on one or both sides. The portions of copper that aren't needed are etched off, leaving "printed" circuits which connect the components.

**Pentode** – A five-element electron tube, containing a control grid, screen grid, suppressor grid, cathode, and plate as active elements, in addition to the filament.

**Phase** – the instantaneous "polarity" of an AC signal, or more correctly, the point in the rotation of the vector, measured in degrees, from 0 to 360 degrees total.

**Phase inverter (PI)** – a circuit that generates two output signals, each 180 degrees out of phase with the other. This is a bit of a misnomer, since it does more than just invert the phase of a signal, it actually generates two out-of-phase signals.

**Phase splitter** – another name for a phase inverter.

**PhotoFET** – an optoisolator in which an LED controls the turning on/off of a bilateral MOSFET device. These devices are commonly used as channel-switching devices.

**Plate** – the "current collecting" element in a vacuum tube. Also called the "anode." This is also the term used for each of the two terminals of a capacitor, which are on either side of the dielectric.

**Plate dissipation** – the amount of power dissipated in the plate element of a vacuum tube. At idle, or quiescent conditions, it is equal to the DC plate current multiplied by the DC voltage difference between the plate and cathode elements. When the tube is amplifying a signal, the average plate dissipation depends on several things, including the quiescent bias point, the amount of signal voltage between the plate and cathode, and the class of operation. Average plate dissipation can either increase, decrease, or remain the same at full power, depending on these things. In a class AB or class B amplifier, the power dissipation increases, because the signal swing above and below the quiescent point is not the same (the tube is in cutoff for a portion of the cycle) and in a true class A amplifier the plate dissipation remains the same, as the average signal change at the plate is zero, since it swings equally above and below the quiescent bias point.

**Plexi** – the name given to early Marshall amplifiers that had a gold Plexiglas control panel on the front and rear of the chassis. This was later changed in mid 1969 to gold aluminum front and rear panels, commonly referred to as an "ali-panel" Marshall.

**Positive feedback** – feedback in which a portion of the signal from a later amplifier stage is fed back to an earlier stage (or to the same stage) in such a manner as to add to the input signal.

**Pot** – short for "potentiometer."

**Potentiometer** – a variable resistor. It usually has three terminals: the two end terminals, across which the entire resistance appears, and a third terminal, the "wiper," which moves to a different spot on the resistor as the shaft is turned. In this manner, the resistance between the wiper and one end terminal gets smaller while, at the same time, the resistance between the wiper and the other end gets larger. This allows the potentiometer to be used as a variable voltage divider, for use in attenuators, such as volume controls or tone controls.

**Power** – the rate of doing work, equal to the voltage multiplied by the current in a circuit. In an amplifier, this work results in either heat or mechanical energy, such as moving the loudspeaker coil to produce sound.

**Power amp** – the high-level amplifying stage in a guitar amplifier. This is where the smaller preamp signal is converted into a high power signal necessary to drive the speakers to the desired output level.

**Power transformer** – a transformer used to convert the incoming line (or mains) voltage to a higher or lower value for use in the guitar amplifier. Typically, the power transformer will have at least one primary, but sometimes two or more, to allow use at 120V/240V/etc mains voltages. There will also usually be a 6.3V filament winding, sometimes center-tapped to allow balancing the filament string symmetrically around ground for hum reduction. There is sometimes a 5V winding for use with a tube rectifier. This winding is eliminated when using a solid-state rectifier. There is also a third winding for generating the high voltage, or B+, as it is commonly called. This winding may be center-tapped, unless a bridge rectifier is used.

**PP** – push-pull.

**PPP** – parallel push-pull.

**Preamp** – the low-level amplifying stages in a guitar amplifier. This is where the tiny signal from the guitar pickup is amplified and shaped for the desired tonality before being sent to the power amplifier, which generates the high power signal needed to drive the speakers.

**Presence** – a control on a guitar amplifier that boosts the upper frequencies above the normal treble control range for added high-end. This control is usually a shelving type of equalizer, and is normally implemented as a lowpass filter inside the global negative feedback loop. By decreasing the amount of high frequencies that are fed back, the high frequencies at the output of the amplifier are boosted.

**PSE** – parallel single ended.

**PT** – power transformer.

**PTP** – point-to-point. A method of wiring an amplifier without using a PC board or – accurately speaking – without any form of circuit card or terminal strips, etc, where points in the circuit are directly connected by the components themselves. For example, an input jack connected to a preamp tube's input by a resistor's own leads, the tube's output connected to the volume pot's tag by a coupling cap's leads, etc.
Frequently, however, the term is used to refer to construction techniques in which the components are mounted on terminal strips or tag boards, and the wiring is put in by hand to make the circuit connections. Either technique is widely regarded as "sounding better" than PCB construction because of supposedly higher bandwidth, but this is a myth, as PCBs are regularly used into the MHz region. PTP wiring is generally better than PCB for guitar amps because of ease of maintenance and durability. Many manufacturers use cheap, single-sided PC boards without plated-through holes, which tend to pull up pads when a component is desoldered. Some even go so far as to not use a soldermask or silkscreen. This type of construction should be avoided, and is a good indication of a cheaply made amplifier. In short, amps employing hand-wiring/hand-building techniques (PTP or otherwise) might be better sounding and more durable amps primarily because more care has gone into their construction and component selection.

**Push-pull** – In a push-pull amplifier, the power supply is connected to the center-tap of the transformer and a tube is connected to both the upper and lower end of the center-tapped primary. This allows the tubes to conduct on alternate cycles of the input waveform. A push-pull stage can be biased class A, where current flows in both tubes for the entire input cycle (but in opposite directions), or class AB, where current flows alternately in both halves, but less than a full cycle in each, or class B, where current flows only half the time in each tube. Most designs are biased class AB for best efficiency and power output with minimal crossover distortion (but not necessarily best "tone," although this is subjective). A push-pull stage requires at least two tubes to operate, but can have more connected in parallel with each side, resulting in an amp with four, six, or even eight output tubes for higher-power amps. This is called "parallel push-pull" operation, or PPP.

**Q** – the symbol for the "quality factor" or figure of merit for a reactive component, such as a capacitor or coil. Low reactive element Qs can affect the response of filters near the cutoff frequency. Also the symbol for "quality factor," or selectivity of a filter network, used to denote the relative "sharpness" of a filter. For instance, a high-Q bandpass filter would be one that has a very narrow width and steep slopes on the sides. It is a measure of the ratio between the center frequency and the bandwidth of a bandpass filter.

**R** – the symbol for resistance.

**RDH4** – "Radiotron Designer's Handbook, 4th edition" – the legendary "bible" of tube amplification, also known as "the big red book."

**Reactance** – the "imaginary" component of impedance, or the resistance to AC signals at a certain frequency. Capacitive reactance is equal to 1/(2*pi*f*C), and inductive reactance is equal to 2*pi*f*L. The unit of reactance is the ohm.

**Reactive load** – a load that contains inductance or capacitance, either with or without resistance as well. An example of a reactive load is a loudspeaker which has an impedance that varies with frequency, unlike a purely resistive load, whose impedance is flat for all frequencies in the range of a guitar amplifier.

**Rectifier** – this is the same thing as a diode, but the term is usually reserved for diodes used in the power supply section of an amplifier.

**Reflected impedance** – the impedance seen "looking into" the primary of a transformer when the secondary is loaded with a specific impedance. The impedance on the secondary side is transformed by the square of the turns ratio of the transformer. For example, if a 2:1 turns ratio transformer has a 10 ohm load on the secondary, the impedance measured across the primary terminals will be 40 ohms, because the secondary impedance of 10 ohms is multiplied by 2 squared, or 4.

**Relay** – an electromechanical switch, operated by passing current through a coil of wire wound around a steel core, which acts as an electromagnet, pulling the switch contact down to make or break a circuit. These are available in several types, including SPST (single-pole, single-throw), SPDT (single-pole, double throw), DPST (double-pole, single throw), and DPDT (double-pole, double-throw), and not as commonly, in multi-circuit configurations such as 3PDT or 4PDT (three and four poles, double-throw).

**Resistance** – the "size" of a resistor. The unit of resistance is the ohm. Resistors vary in size from fractions of an ohm to several million ohms. The prefix "k" is used for kilohms, or thousands of ohms, and the prefix "M" is used for megohms, or millions of ohms.

**Resistive load** – a load that contains no inductance or capacitance, just pure resistance An example of a resistive load is a dummy test load consisting of a single resistance equal to the output impedance of the amplifier under test. The resistive load has an impedance that is flat for all frequencies in the range of a guitar amplifier.

**Resistor** – a circuit element that presents a resistance to the flow of electric current. A current flowing through a resistance will create a voltage drop across that resistance in accordance with Ohm's law.

**Resonance** – a control on a guitar amplifier that boosts the lower frequencies at or below the normal bass control range for added low-end, also called "depth" or other names. This control is usually a shelving type of equalizer, and is normally implemented as a highpass filter inside the global negative feedback loop. By decreasing the amount of low frequencies that are fed back, the low frequencies at the output of the amplifier are boosted. Resonance is also the term given to an electronic circuit that contains both capacitive and inductive elements – there is a "resonant" point where the capacitive reactance equals the inductive reactance. Depending upon whether the elements are in series or parallel, this will result in a maximum voltage and maximum impedance across the elements (parallel resonance) or maximum current and minimum impedance through the elements (series resonance). If the circuit has resistance, either across the parallel resonant circuit or in series with the series resonant circuit, the maximum peak will be limited, and the bandwidth of the resonance will be broader. The relative "sharpness" of the resonant circuit is called the "Q," or "quality" factor. See the definition of "Q" for more details.

**Reverb** – a short, recirculating delay effect used on some guitar amplifiers. It is similar to echo, but instead of discrete, long delay repeats, it is a series of very short delays that add up to create a sense of spaciousness in the tone. A spring unit with a sending transducer at one end and a receiving transducer at the other end is usually used as the delay unit, although some amplifiers use an analog or digital delay line.

**RMS** – stands for "root mean square." It is a term used with AC voltages or currents to indicate the equivalent DC voltage or current. For a sine wave, the RMS value is equal to the peak-to-peak value divided by 2*√(2), or 2.282, or the peak value divided by √(2), or 1.414. You can also multiply the peak value by 0.707, which is the same as dividing by 1.414. The RMS value of the signal depends on the shape of the waveform. For instance, the RMS value of a square wave is not the peak value multiplied by 0.707, rather, it is equal to the peak value of the square wave.

**Sag** – a "drooping" of the power supply voltage in a guitar amplifier as a note or chord is played. This "drooping" causes a slight drop in volume, for an effect similar to a compressor. It adds "touch sensitivity" to the amplifier, and is one of the reasons tube guitar amplifiers sound subjectively better than solid-state guitar amplifiers.

**Scaling** – the process of shifting an electronic parameter up or down. For instance, a tone circuit that has a midrange boost/cut centered around 1kHz might be scaled to 800Hz to better suit the application. This would be an example of frequency scaling. Impedances may also be scaled up or down.

**Schmitt phase inverter** – a phase inverter configuration using two cathode-coupled tubes, with the first tube acting as a common cathode stage providing an out-of-phase signal at its plate, while the second tube operates as a common-grid stage, providing an in-phase signal at its plate. This type of inverter has moderately good balance, providing the plate resistor of the out-of-phase side is made slightly smaller than the in-phase plate resistor to compensate for differences in the amplification between the two stages. This phase inverter provides high gain.

**Screen grid** – a second grid element interposed between the control grid and the plate, to act as an electrostatic shield between them. This shielding action greatly reduces the input capacitance of the tube, which increases its frequency response, and makes the plate current virtually independent of plate voltage. There is no screen grid in a triode, only in a tetrode or pentode.

**Secondary emission** – electrons in a vacuum tube may be moving at a sufficient speed to dislodge additional electrons when they strike the plate of the tube. These electrons emitted from the plate can reduce the current flow in the tube. A third grid element, called the "suppressor grid," is used to reduce the effects of secondary emission.

**SE** – single-ended.

**Silverface** – the name given to Fender amplifiers that have a silver control panel.

The panel was changed from black to silver at the time CBS bought Fender. In addition, certain "improvements" were made to the circuitry at the same time. The general consensus is that these amplifiers don't sound as good as the blackface amplifiers, which has led to a practice known as "blackfacing" the amp, which means converting the circuitry back to match the blackface schematic.

**Silkscreen** – the name given to the "component identification" ink layer screened onto a printed circuit board. Also the name given to the lettering screened on the front and back of a guitar amp control panel. Name derives from the fine silk mesh screen template through which the ink is printed onto the component.

**Single-ended** – The term "single-ended", or SE for short, is given to an amplifier output stage configuration whose output transformer primary is not center-tapped. It has only two connections, one of which goes to the power supply, the other to the plate of the power tube. Tubes can also be paralleled for more power as in a push-pull stage, resulting in what is called "parallel single-ended" operation, or PSE. A single ended stage for guitar amplification is always biased class A. Old Fender Champs are a good example of a single-ended guitar amplifier. Higher power amplifiers are usually push-pull instead of single-ended, which allows higher efficiency and better frequency response with a smaller output transformer. Output transformers for single-ended amplifiers require an air gap to avoid saturation of the core due to the offset DC current in the transformer. This air gap greatly reduces the primary inductance, so the core must be made larger and the number of turns must be increased to obtain good low frequency response. A push-pull output transformer has no offset DC current flowing in the primary, because the DC bias current flows in opposite directions on each side of the primary, so it doesn't need an air gap, and can be made smaller. Single-ended output stages do not have the inherent even-harmonic cancellation and power supply rejection that push-pull output stages have, so the output tone is quite different, and the DC plate supply must be better filtered in order to keep the hum to a low level.

**Solid-state** – equipment using transistorized elements rather than tubes to perform their signal-processing or amplification functions.

**Solder mask** – a coating on a PC board, usually a dark green or dark blue, but occasionally a yellowish color, which is designed to insulate and protect the copper traces and keep them from shorting together during the wave soldering process. The soldermask is "masked out" at solder pads, to allow for soldering component leads.

**Speaker** – a transducer designed to reproduce audio frequencies. There are many different models of guitar speaker, each with its own particular power handling capability and tone.

**Speaker emulator** – a device composed of filters that are designed to emulate the response of a loudspeaker, commonly used for direct recording applications.

**Split-load phase inverter** – the name given to the single-tube phase inverter in which the in-phase signal is taken off the cathode and the out-of-phase signal is taken off the plate, with equal-value plate and cathode resistors. This phase splitter configuration has excellent balance, but only unity gain. Also called a "Concertina" phase splitter.

**Star ground** – a preferred amplifier circuit grounding system, where all the local grounds for each stage are connected together, and a wire is run from that point to a single ground point on the chassis, back at the power supply ground. Sometimes multiple star points are used for lower hum and noise levels in the amplifier.

**Suppressor grid** – a grid in a pentode vacuum tube that is used to minimize secondary emission from the plate, by virtue of its negative charge, which repels electrons emitted and returns them back to the plate. It eliminates the "kink" in the characteristic curves of a tetrode.

**Susceptance** – the reciprocal of reactance, measured in mhos.

**Switch** – a device that opens and closes an electric circuit.

**Taper** – the rate at which the resistance of a potentiometer changes as the shaft is rotated. There are several common tapers used in guitar amplifiers. There is linear taper, which means that the resistance changes linearly as the pot shaft is rotated, ie, the resistance at midpoint is half the total resistance from end to end. Another common taper is log taper, short for logarithmic taper, which means that the pot changes in a logarithmic fashion as the shaft is rotated, ie, the resistance at 1/10 the rotation is half the total resistance from end to end. You may hear people occasionally mistakenly call this "analog taper," but there is no such thing. There is also a reverse log taper. The taper is chosen for the application. A volume control, for instance, will be a log taper, because the ear hears sound in a logarithmic fashion, and the volume must change accordingly to be perceived as linearly changing as the pot is turned. Depending upon the type of tone circuit, the pot used may be log or linear. If all the "action" occurs at one end of the pot, chances are the wrong type of pot is being used in the circuit.

**Tetrode** – A four-element electron tube, containing a control grid, screen grid, cathode, and plate as active elements, in addition to the filament.

**Tolex** – the original DuPont trade name given to the vinyl covering used on most guitar amplifiers, such as Marshall or Fender style vinyl (hence the capital "T" if it is genuine Tolex from DuPont).

**Tone** – the characteristic sound of an amplifier.

**Tone control** – a potentiometer used for controlling the tone of an amplifier. This may be a single control or there may be multiple tone controls, commonly called a "tone stack."

**Tone stack** – The term used to describe the tone controls in a guitar amplifier. There are four main types of tone stacks used in most common guitar amplifiers. They are the Marshall style, the Fender style, the Vox style, and the lesser used Baxandall, or James style. These tone stacks vary in their construction, consisting of either a bass and treble control, or bass, mid, and treble controls. Some amplifiers have a tone stack consisting only of one control, usually a treble cut control, but sometimes it will be a single control that cuts treble at one end of the rotation, and cuts bass at the other end. These types of control are usually labeled "tone," or "cut."

**Transconductance** – the ratio of the tube's plate current to its grid voltage. The unit of transconductance is the "mho," which is measured in amps/volt, and is not surprisingly "ohm" spelled backwards, because one ohm is equal to one volt divided by one amp, so the unit of resistance, the ohm, is a volt/amp. Transconductance is one "figure of merit" for a tube. Higher transconductances mean higher gains and greater amplification from the tube.

**Transformer** – a device for changing levels of AC signals, or for changing impedances of circuits. It consists of a minimum of two coils, the primary and the secondary, wound on the same core. The core material can be ferrous (magnetic, such as iron), or non-ferrous (non-magnetic, such as an air core). Transformers used in guitar amplifiers are invariably wound on iron cores. An ideal transformer has no losses, it merely steps a voltage up or down in proportion to the turns ratio between the primary and the secondary. This is useful in converting the voltage from a wall outlet, typically 120V or 240V, into a higher voltage for the tube plate supply, typically 400V or more, and a lower voltage for the tube filament, typically 6.3V or 12.6V. The transformer will also "reflect back" to the primary the impedance which is connected to the secondary, in proportion to the square of the turns ratio. That is, if you have a 20:1 transformer with a 16 ohm impedance connected to the secondary, it will "look like" a 6.4K ohm impedance on the primary side. This is useful in matching the plate of a tube, which is very high impedance, typically on the order of several thousand ohms, to a speaker, which is very low impedance, typically on the order of 4, 8, or 16 ohms.

**Transient response** – the response of a circuit to a step waveform. An amplifier cannot perfectly reproduce an input step waveform because of the limited bandwidth and non-constant phase response of the amplifier. The transient response may indicate some "overshoot" or "undershoot" of the signal transition, or possibly some "ringing" or damped sinusoidal oscillations at the transition.

**Tremolo** – a circuit that periodically varies the amplifier output level at a rate and depth set by controls on the amplifier. The terms "vibrato" and "tremolo" are sometimes used interchangeably.

**Triode** – a three-element electron tube, containing a grid, cathode, and plate as active elements, in addition to the filament.

**Tube** – short for "electron tube."

**Tweed** – the name given to the covering on old Fender amplifiers that preceded the introduction of the Tolex vinyl covering.

**u** – (actually $\mu$, the Greek letter "mu") the prefix for "micro", meaning one millionth, as in a 1uF capacitor, which means one millionth of a Farad. A lower-case "u" is usually used nowadays.

**Ultralinear** – the term given to the amplifier configuration developed by Hafler and Keroes, which uses taps on the output transformer to provide a negative feedback signal to the screen grids of the output tubes. This gives an operating point somewhere between that of a pentode and a triode. This form of operation was given a bad name due to a particularly sterile-sounding Fender amplifier that had an ultralinear output stage and far too much global negative feedback. A few of the misinformed amp "guru" types immediately denounced all ultralinear operation as sounding bad. The stigma has endured to this day, although this is slowly changing, with the help of amp makers like Dr Z, who are willing to experiment with different output topologies to produce a better sounding amplifier. Ultralinear operation, when used without global negative feedback, can sound quite good, as the local negative feedback provided by the screen taps increases the damping factor, lowering output impedance, and "tightening up" the bass.

**V** – the symbol for voltage. Common prefixes are "m," for mV ($10^{-3}$ volts), and "u," for uV ($10^{-6}$ volts), and "k," for kV ($10^3$ volts).

**Vactec** – the common name given to the Vactrol optoisolator device used for channel switching. The name is printed on the Vactrol because the company that invented them was named Vactec, later EG&G Vactec.

**Vactrol** – an optoisolator device used for channel switching in many modern amplifiers (see Vactec above), such as Soldano and Mesa. It is a single package combining an LED and a photoresistor, which changes resistance from very high (essentially an open circuit) to very low (essentially a short circuit) as the current through the LED is turned on and off. It is used as a substitute for relays, to avoid the "clicks" and "pops" that can occur when they are used for channel switching.

**Vacuum tube** – Another name for "electron tube."

**Valve** – the British term for "tube," the full term for which is "thermionic valve."

**Variac** – the trade name for a brand of variable AC transformer. There are other brands, but this term is generically used to describe all of them. A variac allows adjustment of the incoming AC mains voltage. The better ones have meters for voltage, current, or both, and fuses for protection.

**Vibrato** – a circuit that periodically varies the pitch of a note. True pitch-shifting vibrato is not usually found on a guitar amplifier. The terms vibrato and tremolo are sometimes used interchangeably.

**Voltage** – the term for electric force. Voltage is the energy per unit charge created when positive and negative charges are separated.

**W** – the symbol for watts. Typical prefixes are "m" for thousandths, as in "mW" or "milliwatts," "k" for thousands, as in "kW" or "kilowatts," and "M" for millions, as in "MW" or "megawatts."

**Watt** – a unit of power (see W above). Contrary to popular belief, more is not always better.

**X** – the symbol for "reactance."

**Y** – the symbol for "admittance."

**Z** – the symbol for "impedance."

# Tube Types

# Preamp Tubes

**We see these mostly as the small nine-pin tubes with the all-glass bottle inserted in the first few positions of the amp, usually (but not always) to the right side of a "top-mounted" combo as viewed from the back, or to the left side of a "bottom-mounted" head such as a Marshall. In days past some larger "octal" (eight-pin) types were also used, but have rarely been seen in new designs since the 1950s. Both are mostly dual-triodes, as we encountered in our Princeton signal chain in Chapter One, but a few pentodes remain in use too.**

Preamp tubes of even the same approximate shape and pin-out are distinguished by their amplification factor, or gain, and their sonic characteristics.

**12AX7** – By far the most common preamp tube type of the past 45 years, also known by the European designation ECC83, or as a 7025 for its high-grade variant. Quality 12AX7s are clear and open-sounding, relatively uncolored when used within specifications, and offer a high target gain of 100, although many will fall below that, and a few rise above it—even from the same make and same batch. Consistency is very hard to achieve, even in the manufacturing of quality tubes, though greater inconsistencies—and failure rates—apply to the lesser brands. Through the late 1980s and much of the 1990s, 12AX7 production was in a pretty dire state. Affordable, current-manufacture tubes consisted mainly of the fairly reliable, but characterless, Russian varieties, or the more characterful but less reliable Chinese options.

Players seeking real quality in both construction and tone went in search of "new old stock" (NOS) US and European tubes made by GE, RCA, Telefunken, Mullard, Brimar and others, and supplies of these dwindled rapidly. Some of these NOS versions are still great items to get your hands on if you can find them for any reasonable price, but be aware that the small batches that turn up now and again are generally less likely to be reliable than the more plentiful stocks of a few years back. Supplies are so short now that seconds and substandard units are coming out of old reject boxes and onto the market, and some unscrupulous sellers aren't testing them in the slightest before taking your $50 for a single little glass bottle. Other good suppliers do test thoroughly and offer

guarantees too—at a price—but the little extra is worth it if you're laying out for NOS tubes in the first place. Or, if you're lucky, you can occasionally find an old radio spares supplier who has a few of these to sell at a fraction of what the big guitar amp tube suppliers are asking.

Fortunately, some great new 12AX7 types are being newly manufactured once again, and newer designs from Sovtek, JJ/Tesla, the Chinese factories, and others are offering both good-sounding and reliable tubes that can even rival some of the US and European examples of old. Large distributors like Groove Tubes and Germany's Tube Amp Doctor are even pitching in with their own designs, GT notably funding the retooling at a Chinese factory to begin reproducing an ECC83 very close in spec to one of the original Mullards—many players' idea of the best 12AX7-type preamp tube ever produced.

Whatever you put in your preamp, there certainly still are variables in sound between both the quality newer units and any NOS tubes you lay your hands on. It really pays off to invest the $7-15 each in two or three really good, tested new 12AX7s, and even to try scrounging a few NOS examples (pulled from used/junked audio gear, if necessary) and try them in the first and second positions of your favorite amp. You could fill pages on the subtle differences between Mullards, Brimars, GEs, JJs and so forth, but by the time a player absorbed all of this the NOS units referred to might have become impossible to find, and the new production units might have changed again. The point is simply that enormous variables do exist here, and that it really is worth the time and the little money required to test them for yourself.

**12AY7** – When Fender moved from old-fashioned eight-pin to newer nine-pin preamp tubes in the late-mid 1950s, this was the one that appeared in the preamps of most of their wide-panel and then narrow-panel tweed amps. The 12AY7 (also designated 6072) has a lower gain factor of 44, but is otherwise virtually a direct replacement for a 12AX7, although the tubes have different impedances and would ideally want different bias resistors to be tweaked to perfection. The 12AY7 was responsible for the smooth, crisp performance of many a tweed Bassman, Super or Pro, although as supplies gradually began to dry up, a lot of players popped in a 12AX7 instead. The more powerful 12AX7 tube yields a hotter sound in these tweed amps, and the fact that so many vintage examples have become equipped this way has probably led to some misunderstanding of the "true" tweed sound, which is rounder, more open, and offers a slightly wider frequency response than many tweed amp owners have ever experienced. A 12AX7 can sound great in these amps if you want to achieve earlier breakup for blues or rock'n'roll, but for the authentic experience (which can definitely include blues and rock'n'roll when you crank up), locate a NOS 12AY7—which are still not all that expensive—or try a 5751.

**5751** – This is another direct replacement for the 12AX7, but also with a lower gain, something close to that of a 12AY7. Dr Z uses this in the PI position in a lot of its amps to avoid distortion in that stage of the circuit. A lot of guitarists have used these for years as the "secret weapon" in position one to ease past preamp distortion and generate juicy output tube distortion; and the fact that plenty of great NOS units were available at a reasonable price made them an excellent find. Enough guitarists have apparently cottoned on, because NOS examples are becoming both more expensive and shorter in supply, but they are still worth seeking out. With a little hunting and some luck, you can probably still track down a few great GE/JAN versions of these for not a lot more than double the price of a new-manufacture 12AX7, and if it's a tested tube it should last you for years and years. If you feel any stage in your amp carrying a 12AX7 could use a little taming—in an effort to pass a somewhat truer and undistorted signal on to the next stage—try one of these. Good ones have a full, clear, clean sound that plenty of great players swear by.

**12AT7** – Found in some preamp positions, but most commonly as a phase inverter or reverb driver in blackface and silverface Fenders, this tube has a lower amplification factor of 60 and a somewhat different character than the 12AX7. It's often referred to as a lower-gain direct replacement for a 12AX7, but that is misleading. The "AT" has a considerably different impedance than the "AX," and while many circuits will work with one in place of the other, they won't work optimally—and might play other tricks besides. I recall popping a 12AT7 into the hot-modded Normal channel of a Super Reverb years ago to tame its too-quick distortion, only to find that when I plugged into the Vibrato channel there was nothing happening. The 12AT7 in the first channel was robbing the 12AX7 in the second channel of the voltage it needed to operate. Changing the AT for a 5751 instantly did the trick.

These tubes can provide an alternative to 12AX7s in many positions, but in some cases you will want an experienced tech to change the cathode-bias resistor for one of the required value. Otherwise, instead of more headroom and a cleaner sound, you might find yourself with less headroom and a flattened frequency response. The swapsies can go the other way too, and plenty of players like the sound of a 12AX7 in the phase inverter position of blackface and silverface Fenders, especially when they seek to drive the output tubes hard.

**12AU7** – Found in some vintage amps, and Ampegs in particular, this has an extremely low gain of around 18, compared to the 12AX7's amplification factor of 100. This tube is seen more in the hi-fi world, but can occasionally be useful in guitar amps where you really want to knock down a fierce overdrive stage or tame your signal in some other way.

**EF86/6267** – Here we part company with the dual triodes that are all close relatives of the popular 12AX7, and venture into the world of pentodes. A triode contains a grid, anode (plate) and cathode, along with the filament (heater) that all tubes posses, which isn't counted in its name. A pentode, on the other hand, adds two further grids that help to regulate its performance. In very simple terms, the added elements allow pentodes to develop more power, which in terms of preamp tubes means higher gain. The added goings-on inside an EF86 can mean extra handling noise (microphony) too, and these tubes have to be used carefully in preamp circuits. Some classic early Vox designs used this tube—in the AC15, AC10, and earliest models of the AC30—but it wasn't seen much in the guitar-amp world through the later 1960s, 1970s, and 1980s, until Matchless revived it for the D/C30. Dr Z, Bad Cat, and a few other lesser-known makers have employed the tube, but its tendency toward microphony has put off other potential users. Those that capture it in the right circuit find it makes for a fat, rich, full-frequencied preamp with lots of gain as required. As used by each of the makers here mentioned, the EF86 allows for a simple but powerful preamp with just one pentode gain stage, and no further gain makeup stage required before the PI. Among NOS supplies, the real prizes of EF86s are those made by GEC and Mullard, and they command extremely high prices these days.

**6SJ7** – This is the only other pentode preamp you are at all likely to encounter in a guitar amp, and not very often at that. We have moved into the world of octal preamp tubes now, which means they fit into the same eight-pin sockets that a lot of output tubes use. A 6SJ7 is found in some of the vintage Gibson BR-series amps, a couple of very early Fenders, and a few other oddballs. It's a warm and rich-sounding tube with a lot of gain—much like an EF86, but a little smoother if anything—but the scarcity of most NOS octal preamp tubes makes it an unlikely candidate for broad use in any mass-manufactured tube amps today.

**6SC7, 6SL7 & 6SN7** – These are the other octal preamp tubes you'll find most often. They're all dual triodes that were generally replaced by nine-pin 12AX7 types over the years, and appeared variously in vintage Ampeg, Fender, Valco, plus other lesser-seen amps. A few newer makers of handmade tube amps, notably Alessandro, have indulged in octal preamp designs, with some great results. Some players find that these sound smoother and more rounded than many nine-pin preamp tubes. As they required entirely different sockets and circuits, though, direct comparisons are difficult.

## Output Tubes

**The tubes that provide the output amplification in guitar amps are found either as octal tubes (6V6, 6L6, EL34, KT66, KT88, 6550, etc), or nine-pin tubes that fit the same sockets used by the majority of preamp tubes (by and large EL84/6BQ5 types). In most cases these will show up as the larger tubes in the amp, but don't be fooled by the octal preamp tubes in some older models pre-1960 (see above, for example the 6SJ7 mentioned previously). In many small single-ended amps there will just be one output tube, but the majority of amps you encounter will have at least a pair, occasionally four, and very rarely six.**

**6V6** – This is the archetypal smaller Fender tube, which powered all of the classic sub-25-watt Fenders until recent years, when EL84s were used (Pro Junior, Blues Juniors) due to a scarcity of good new 6V6s. It also appeared in countless models from other great American makers over the years. The 6V6 is often touted as the "little brother to the 6L6" and fits the same eight-pin socket, but a lot of players prefer junior "V" to the more powerful "L" tube. The "V" develops less power, so it's easier to push into distortion when volume levels are restricted in your club or studio, and it's a little smoother and "browner" sounding along with it. Good 6V6s in a well-designed amp should sound open, full-frequencied and well-defined, but often with a nice little edge of grit and a throaty roar when pushed hard. Their bottom end is by nature a little softer than that of some other, larger output tubes, but that's generally the case with smaller tubes, and their rivals the EL84s are no exception.

A 6V6 usually puts out a little more than half the power of a 6L6 in the same circuit, although they can't take the higher DC voltages that the "L" can handle. A pair will usually generate around 15 to 18 watts in push-pull, and up to around 22 or maybe 25 watts when pushed hard in a fixed-bias, class AB output stage. Most amps with 6V6s feed them between 330 and 360 DC volts, which at the higher level is just about at the maximum spec for the tube (which you'll sometimes see rated at a maximum plate voltage of only 315). A few amps push their 6V6s way beyond spec, such as the Fender Deluxe Reverb, which puts a whopping 415 volts on the plates to generate about 22 watts. Sturdy American-made 6V6s of the 1960s/70s handled this surprisingly well, but Deluxe Reverbs became good at blowing weaker Russian and Chinese 6V6s in the 1990s.

NOS 6V6s are still plentiful and not as expensive as other popular NOS output tube types, and new 6V6s are being made today that are far better than those that were available from Eastern Europe and China for many years. Good ones currently carry the Electro-Harmonic Harmonix and JJ brands. The resurgence of this tube has led a number of amp-makers to design around it once again.

**6L6** – Here is your big Fender output tube, the bottle that powered everything from the tweed Bassman to the Twin Reverb to the Showman, and all the 25-watt-plus models in-between. It has full lows, generally even-sounding mids, and pronounced, shimmering highs. This tube was also frequently seen as the upgraded 5881 variant in the 1950s and 1960s, but newly manufactured tubes labeled 5881 are generally just 6L6s in all but number. The 6L6 is often described as "bright, crisp" even "a little harsh," but in the right circuit they can be very smooth, with a great, aggressive bark and roar when pushed. The fact that they've been seen most in fixed-bias, class AB designs has probably helped determine their overall sonic image, but I have a pair in a very nice cathode-biased amp with no negative feedback that generates around 30 watts, and at some settings you'd mistake the sound for a sweet, sparkling, juicy AC30. A great tube, when you get a good one, and fortunately there's a pretty broad range of decent newly manufactured 6L6s available today, and good, tested NOS pairs can still be found too.

A pair of 6L6s in class AB, fixed-bias, usually puts out a maximum of around 50 watts, although many amp manufacturers using them will claim 60 watts. These tubes can vary quite a lot with make and model, so if you have an amp you like that uses them, it behooves you to try pairs from a number of different sources to discover what you like best. A little taste-testing of 6L6s can yield tubes that offer either more or less compression and breakup, a tighter or looser sound, recessed or more pronounced mids, and so on. Go on, enjoy yourself.

**EL34** – This is the British colleague to the American 6L6; its story and sonic character is pretty thoroughly defined in Marshall's move from the 6L6/5881/KT66 in the JTM45 to the EL34 in the plexi models of the late 1960s. This tube is a little crunchier and crispier-sounding than the 6L6 when pushed, sometimes with more breakup in the lows, but fat, ballsy bass response nonetheless, especially when roaring through the big 4x12" cabs that frequently accompany them. Good EL34s were also in short supply in the 1980s and 1990s, after the majority of stocks of excellent Mullards and other British and European makes started drying up. Eastern European makes of the time often couldn't handle the high voltages applied to these tubes in many amps. A good EL34 should be capable of handling a fair bit more than a 6L6, and of putting out more wattage along with it—60 watts is no stretch at all for a pair, with up to 70 watts possible when handled right. As with 6V6s, the tables have turned recently— luckily for all the Marshall players out there—and some of the Eastern European factories are turning out great EL34s again.

**EL84** – This tall, slender, nine-pin bottle has been one of the most popular output tubes for smaller and medium-sized amps of the past couple of decades. Many makers turned to EL84s (known as the 6BQ5 by US codes) when the quality of new 6V6s began to suffer, and the tube has won a lot of fans among players just for its sound, too. It is a bright, harmonically rich tube at lower volumes, with a juicy crunch, raunchy mids, and shimmering, even glassy highs when cranked up. The archetypal EL84 amps are obviously the early Vox classics such as the AC15 and AC30, but Marshall used them in its 18-watt and 20-watt heads and combos, they frequently appeared in Gibson amps, and they have been a favorite of the boutique-amp revolution.

A pair of EL84s in cathode-bias usually puts out around 15 watts, or up to 20 watts in class AB fixed-bias. True class A performance should keep them down around 12 watts or so. Most amps run these at between 320 and 350 DC volts on the plates, although the Matchless Lightning pushes them to about 365 volts, and some versions of Traynor's Guitar Mate had these little tubes seeing as much as 390 volts on the plates. Voltages like this require sturdy, reliable tubes; fortunately some very good newer makes are available once again, and matched pairs of NOS examples can often still be found. If you have a good EL84-based amp and can get your hands on a tested pair of Mullards, you are in for a treat. I have also had US-made Philips and GE EL84/6BQ5s that sounded out of this world.

**KT66** – This big, Coke-bottle-shaped European tube is a direct replacement for the 6L6 in guitar amp circuits, but has a beefy, succulent sound all its own. It is best known for its appearance in Marshall JTM45 heads and "Bluesbreaker" combos after the US-made 5881s that these designs started out with became scarce. These KT66s themselves were extremely hard to come by for many years, but a couple of newer makes are again proving to be great-sounding and reliable tubes. If you have a reissue Marshall JTM-type amp, pop in a good set of KT66s and feel the amp come alive. The all-time classic of this tube was the version manufactured in Britain by GEC, and NOS examples of these fetch extremely high money these days. A few newer amp-makers have latched onto the KT66, notably the Mojave Plexi 45 and the Dr Z Route 66, and THD recommends them as a good tube to swap into its Univalve and Flexi 50 amps, which can handle a wide range of output tube types. The single-ended Mercury from boutique maker Carr uses a single KT88 to generate a very tasty 8 watts.

**6550** – Here's the sound of late 1970s/80s US-distributed Marshalls, which had big, sturdy 6550 output tubes retrofitted to them in place of the British EL34s, which were failing at unusually high rates at that time. This tube is related to the 6L6, but will handle more voltage, put out more wattage, and offer a bolder, firmer sound along with it. The 6550 has usually been the choice of amp-makers seeking a big, loud, clean amp. Ampeg put six of them in the revolutionary SVT bass amp to generate around 300 watts, which really put the stadium bass rig on the map. The rugged, American-made Sunn amps were big into these tubes too. A few makers have put this firm, loud tube to sweeter use, most notably George Alessandro, who uses them in his larger amps such as the Bloodhound, Greyhound, and Redbone. A number of usable makes from Eastern European factories have become available in recent years.

**KT88** – Here's a seriously powerful tube for you, and an impressively large bottle. It fits the standard eight-pin socket, although you might not think so at first glance. Marshall used four of these to generate 200 watts in the massive Major amp, and two of them to put out around 75 watts in the Park 75. This is a tube that had all but vanished in anything other than extremely expensive and rare NOS examples, but decent new versions are now coming from both China and Slovakia.

# Rectifier Tubes

**With rectifier tubes, it's mostly a matter of whether they function correctly or not—although a few years ago, with some Soviet and Chinese tubes it was all too often "not." The task here is to fit the correct rectifier tube to the job, and that match will be determined by how much high-voltage AC your power transformer's secondary puts out, and how much DC the amp design needs to convert that into. Different rectifier tubes have different warm-up characteristics too—how many seconds they take to reach full operating power as their heaters warm up. This has some bearing on choice, but their AC-to-DC conversion capabilities are of primary consideration.**

For the most part, replace your tube rectifier with the best you can afford of the type specified in your amp's manual/tube chart. In some cases, a step up or down to a more or less powerful rectifier might be desirable. Try to find out from the distributor how well any given new make follows the specs of the original tube type—such as how much DC it converts, and how fast its warm-up is. For example, many 5Y3GTs supplied from Soviet/Russian factories in the 1980s/90s were really just weak 5AR4 types, and provided higher DC levels than many amps carrying proper 5Y3GTs would prefer to operate on. And many 5AR4/GZ34 types were a little underpowered and reached full power too quickly. If a quick warm-up sounds like a good thing, it's not—at least not in an amp without a standby switch, one that's relying on that rectifier tube's inherent delay to let the signal tubes warm up slowly.

If your amp is a newer model that was designed around and supplied with a particular newer Chinese or Eastern European rectifier, the same should do just fine as a replacement. If it's a vintage amp, you may want to shop more carefully. A new make might do the job just fine, but you'll want to source a good one that performs to the specifications of the type. Otherwise, try to find a good NOS example; US-made 5Y3GTs in particular can still be had for little more than twice the price of a new make, sometimes less if you shop around.

# Index

# Bibliography of Tube Amp Books

*Amped: The Illustrated History Of The World's Greatest Amplifiers* by Dave Hunter, Voyageur Press, 2012; ISBN-10: 0760339724)

*Ampeg: The Story Behind The Sound* by Gregg Hopkins & Bill Moore (Hal Leonard Publishing, 1999; ISBN 0-7935-7951-1)

*Amps! The Other Half Of Rock'N'Roll* by Ritchie Fliegler (Hal Leonard, 1993; ISBN 0-7935-2411-3)

*The Complete Guide To Guitar And Amp Maintenance* by Ritchie Fliegler (Hal Leonard, 1994; ISBN 0-7935-3490-9)

*Dave Funk's Tube Amp Workbook* by Dave Funk (Thunderfunk Labs Inc, 1996; ISBN 0-9650841-0-8)

*A Desktop Reference Of Hip Vintage Guitar Amps* by Gerald Weber (Kendrick Books, 1994; ISBN 0-9641060-0-0)

*Electric Guitar Amplifier Handbook, 2nd Edition* by Jack Darr (Howard W. Sams & Co Inc, Indianapolis, Indiana, 1968; Library Of Congress Catalog Card Number: 68-59059)

*The Fender Amp Book* by John Morrish (Balafon Books, 1995; ISBN 0-87930-345-X)

*Fender Amps: The First 50 Years* by John Teagle & John Sprung (Hal Leonard Corporation, 1995; soft cover ISBN 0-7935-3733-9, hard cover limited edition ISBN 0-7935-4408-4)

*Gibson Amplifiers 1933-2008: 75 Years Of The Gold Tone* by Wallace Marx Jr. (Alfred Music, 2009; ISBN-10: 1886768900)

*Guitar Amps & Effects For Dummies* by Dave Hunter (Wiley, 2014; ISBN-13: 978-1118899991)

*The History Of Marshall* by Michael Doyle (Hal Leonard, 1993; ISBN 0-7935-2509-8)

*Principles Of Power* Kevin O'Connor (Power Press Publishing, London, Ontario, Canada; ISBN 0-9698-6081-1)

*The Soul Of Tone: 60 Years Of Fender Amps* by Tom Wheeler (Hal Leonard, 2007; ISBN-13: 9780634056130)

*The Tube Amp Book, Deluxe Revised Edition* by Aspen Pittman (Backbeat Books, 2003; ISBN 0-87930-767-6)

*The Ultimate Tone* by Kevin O'Connor (Power Press Publishing, London, Ontario, Canada; ISBN 0-9698-6080-3)

*Vox Amplifiers: The JMI Years* by Jim Elyea (History For Hire Press, 2012; ISBN-10: 142431769X)

*The Vox Story* by David Petersen & Dick Denney (The Bold Strummer Ltd, 1993; ISBN 0-933224-70-2)

*Valve Amplifiers* by Morgan Jones (Newnes/Butterworth-Heinemann Ltd, 1995; ISBN 0-7506-2337-3)

*Vox Amplifiers: The JMI Years* by Jim Elyea (History For Hire Press, 2012; ISBN-10: 142431769X)

# Acknowledgments

The author wishes to acknowledge the following for their help with this book, for general assistance through the course of the project, or for past or recent contributions to his personal knowledge-pool of all things related to guitar amps: David Petersen and Brinsley Schwarz of Chandler Guitars; Denis Cornell; Bruce Collins of Mission Amps; Dan Dykema of Tubegarden; Dave Harris; Victor Mason of Mojave Ampworks; Aspen Pittman and Myles Rose of Groove Tubes; Jim Elyea; Don Butler; R.G. Keen; Ted and T.A. Weber of Weber VST; Marc Lesser at CE Distribution; and John Harrison and Charlie of Tone Tubby. I would also like to thank all of the interview participants, and especially Michael Zaite of Dr Z Amps, whose generosity and willingness to share his knowledge has been overwhelming.

A special thanks to Brian Fischer of Ear Craft Music in Dover, New Hampshire, and to Gary Traversy and Paul Tibbetts of Gary's Guitars in Portsmouth, New Hampshire, for opening the doors to their gear cupboards (tweed Fender Champ, Fender Bassman, and Marshall JMP50—Brian; Fender Super Reverb, Traynor Bass Master, and Peavey Prowler—Gary). Also to Nigel Osborne, Tony Bacon, and all at Backbeat Books for their hard work and constant support; to Paul Quinn and John Morrish for their conscientious editing; and to designer Paul Cooper for the look of the book. Further thanks for amp and photo contributions to Matt Hertel and Todd Duane, Val Rothwell, Steve Olson, and Dave Matchette of Elderly Instruments, and Jerry McKinsey. Thanks, too, to my editors Art Thompson, Michael Molenda, and Kevin Owens at *Guitar Player*; Ward Meeker at *Vintage Guitar*; and Andrew Vaughan at Gibson.

And thanks most of all to Jess, Freddie, and Flo, for keeping me grounded.

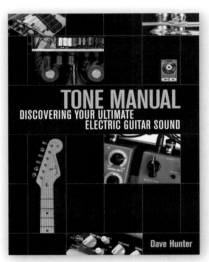
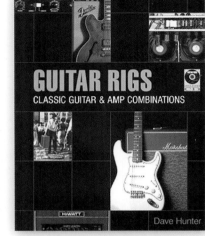
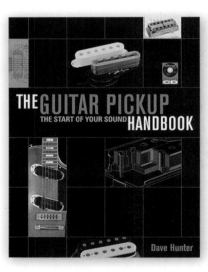

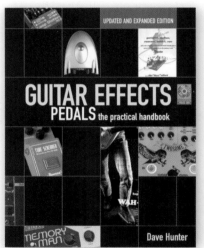